4-10 rr

04-14-5c

2/17 JK

D0216433

PROJECTING POLITICS

PROJECTING POLITICS

POLITICAL MESSAGES
IN AMERICAN FILMS

TERRY CHRISTENSEN AND PETER J. HAAS

M.E.Sharpe
Armonk, New York
London, England

Library of Congress Cataloging-in-Publication Data

Christensen, Terry.
 Projecting politics : political messages in American films / Terry
Christensen and Peter J. Haas.
     p. cm.
 Updated ed. of: Reel politics. 1987.
 Includes index.
 ISBN 0-7656-1443-X (hardcover : alk. paper)
 1. Motion pictures—Political aspects—United States. 2. Politics in
motion pictures. 3. United States—Politics and government—20th century.
I. Haas, Peter J. II. Christensen, Terry. Reel politics. III. Title.

PN1995.9.P6C47 2005
791.43'658—dc22   2004027997

Printed in the United States of America

The paper used in this publication meets the minimum requirements of
American National Standard for Information Sciences
Permanence of Paper for Printed Library Materials,
ANSI Z 39.48-1984.

♾

BM (c) 10   9   8   7   6   5   4   3   2   1

Contents

Appendixes

Preface

This book contains elements of both a remake and a sequel. First published in 1987 as *Reel Politics* and authored by Terry Christensen, that version was intended for a general audience interested in movies and politics as well as for students of political films, but in some ways it satisfied neither. Nevertheless, its initial release sold out long ago and continues to merit many requests for photocopied excerpts for use in the classroom. Since its publication, both coauthors of the present edition have taught courses on film and politics and have noted the lack of a textbook meant explicitly for use in such courses. With *Projecting Politics,* we have therefore both updated and significantly supplemented *Reel Politics* to make it more useful in the classroom (although we hope some readers will find it interesting enough to read independently).

Interest in the relationship between politics and film appears to be on the rise. Explicitly political films like *Fahrenheit 9/11* are filling theaters. Academically, a casual search of the World Wide Web reveals that courses on the subject are being offered at campuses across the country. Perhaps this interest is the result of the political spectacle of the war in Iraq, global terrorism, and the 2004 election, or perhaps it coincides with the increasing popularity of movies generally.

We have taught politics and film several times during the past decade, and although there is no paucity of books on the general subject, few if any are geared toward a comprehensive survey of the subject tailored to the needs of students and instructors in the discipline of political science. Some books explore political themes in movies in much the same way as scholars of English literature pursue themes in novels, while others examine the politics of filmmakers and Hollywood. In this book, we attempt to do both as well as explore topics that we think many instructors find important when teaching film and politics courses. A brief review of the types of movies assigned for such courses and the content of the many books dedicated to the subject reveals disagreement, if not confusion about what exactly constitutes a political film and why. Students conducting research in this area will encounter a bewildering array of critical and analytic approaches. We hope that this book provides a coherent overview of the subject that will prove both useful and interesting to instructors and students exploring the topic.

We believe that the most important and overarching aspect of the study of politics and film is the political messages that movies may transmit. We therefore believe that such messages have potentially tremendous political significance that transcends mere critical analysis. But a major obstacle to the task of analyzing film from this perspective is the general lack of reliable data and research that demonstrate (a) that movies indeed send messages and (b) that these messages have verifiable and measurable effects on the political behavior of individuals and institutions. Although we present some research and reasoning that support these assumptions, it is not within the scope of our intentions for this text to prove that they are wholly valid.

Our interest here is exclusively with (more or less) American films. Certainly foreign films present an intriguing canon of politically interesting releases, but in addition to limiting our study to a manageable scope, we believe that American movies are the most likely both to be seen by our students and to influence American politics. Thus readers with an interest in comparative studies will want to supplement this text with other materials. On a related note, we devote most of our attention to popular movies. Certainly other volumes could be devoted to films that few people actually see, but we think that popular movies are the ones that are most likely to be politically salient—they are also the most accessible, both in terms of audience comprehension and ready availability.

Projecting Politics is divided into three parts. In Part I, we provide a conceptual overview of the relationship between politics and film. The first chapter explores the notion of exactly what constitutes a political film. Although the political significance of many films may be intuitively obvious to some students, other students seem to struggle with the task of identifying and analyzing films from a political perspective. That is not entirely surprising, given the apparent disagreement among film scholars, critics, and perhaps political scientists as to the appropriate focus or foci for the political analysis of film.

Chapter 1 of this book explores the meaning of the term "political film" in a systematic way, so as to assist those who study politics and film. The goal is to identify a practical approach for thinking about and classifying *all* films with respect to their political significance. Such an approach should be useful for students and others seeking to analyze the movies they view in and out of the classroom. This framework is therefore intended primarily for use in a classroom context, although it may be of some general theoretical utility as well.

Chapter 2 explores how the various techniques involved in the production of movies help to create political messages. This chapter is also intended to provide a basic introduction to film techniques for political science students who may have no background in film study. We examine the elements of film production briefly and nearly exclusively from a political standpoint. Many other texts and scholarly works can provide students with more in-depth analysis. Even our cursory survey of film techniques reveals, however, that each element can be used to shape political messages in various ways.

Although most of this text emphasizes the potential impact of movies on politics, Chapter 3 examines the reciprocal aspect of that relationship. In other words, how does the "real world" affect the "reel world" of Hollywood and filmmaking? Although this chapter provides only a brief and relatively superficial look at this question, we find that, historically, political forces have had a profound impact on the making of films. We also argue that the worlds of film and politics are increasingly intertwined and even interdependent, as recent events like the release of *Fahrenheit 9/11* and the election of a Hollywood action hero as governor of California have demonstrated.

In Part II, we provide a historical overview of American films of political significance. Each chapter covers the films of a decade. We recognize that categorizing films in this way is somewhat arbitrary. Both historical trends and trends in filmmaking overlap decades—and we take this overlap into account. But at the same time, referring to decades provides a ready historical context for the movies we discuss and helps readers comprehend change and development in political filmmaking by providing a rough chronological order. Although we try to look at the tenor of *all* films in each decade, we generally focus most intently on films with overt political themes and content (i.e., "pure" political films per our typology in Chapter 1). Despite our contention that every movie has a political meaning, we focus on the movies that seem to have the most overt political messages as well as the most political content. We believe that most instructors want to discuss such films in their courses and that such films arguably are most likely to create political impact. Nevertheless, we also discuss a significant number of less overtly political, "reflective" films that seem to mirror their social and/or political environment. However, our choice of films is not intended to be in any way exhaustive, and some instructors may want to explore other films.

Our discussion of each decade of movies is not intended to be entirely systematic from a critical-analytic perspective. In some instances, we seek to explore the political messages of films; in others, we examine the impact or potential impact a film had. We are also interested in why some films of political significance are more popular with critics and the public than others, as we believe that the reasons films are successful have implications for the relationship between film and politics. But we do not mean to imply that financially unsuccessful movies are categorically without merit or significance.

We sometimes refer to the opinions of movie critics to help explain why and how movies are particularly successful (or unsuccessful) at evoking political messages. To these we sometimes add our own opinions, and discerning readers may notice a certain bias in these viewpoints: we tend to like movies that are both entertaining *and* politically meaningful. We realize that there is a place for movies that are seemingly without any political referents and movies that are devoid of entertainment value, but we strongly believe that movies that can both entertain and challenge the mind are the most likely to create political resonance.

Part III of this text compiles three topical approaches to film and politics. Because many instructors prefer to explore movies from a topical or issue orientation, we hope that the three visited here (documentaries, race, and gender) are of interest to many. *Reel Politics*, the first edition of this book, excluded political documentaries, mostly because covering fictional films seemed ambitious enough, but also because few documentaries reached mass audiences. Michael Moore and a small cadre of other documentary makers have changed all that, and documentary films seem to be reaching a new level of popularity with audiences that merit more consideration in this new volume.

Our discussion of minority films is limited to movies about blacks and racial politics, primarily as a means of limiting its scope to manageable proportions. However, we feel that most other minorities have received similar treatment from the film industry, although volumes could have been written on the specifics for each group.

The final chapter in Part III explores the roles of women in American film, with particular emphasis on the most recent decade. Elizabeth Ann Haas (sister of a coauthor of this text) is the sole author of this chapter. Her background as a scholar of film and particularly women in film (including a doctoral dissertation on the films of Barbara Stanwyck) makes her especially well-suited to contribute on this subject.

We hope that instructors and students alike will benefit from the material we have placed in various appendixes (the "extras") to this volume. The first appendix is intended to help students analyze and write about movies. Realizing that different instructors will have different goals for written assignments and that many approaches are feasible, we present a flexible approach that is meant to prod readers toward various analytic perspectives as much as direct their studies. The second appendix contains a brief guide to researching movies on the Web—it is really just the tip of the Internet iceberg, of course, but it should be a good place to begin an initial foray. The third appendix is a political filmography that compiles the more blatantly political films in this book, plus others that space and time did not permit us to address. The fourth and final appendix contains lists of each decade's top-grossing movies, along with box office data for documentaries and political films of the 1990s. (We had intended to compare box office data for political films for each decade, but the available data are far too incomplete for such a study.)

We hope that both instructors and students will enjoy *Projecting Politics* and find in these pages a springboard for meaningful discussions and future explorations of political films.

Acknowledgments

———*Dedicated to our friends who like movies with messages.*———

Both authors wish to thank Niels Aaboe and the *outstanding* editorial staff at M.E. Sharpe as well as the anonymous reviewers.

Terry Christensen wishes to thank Ray Allen and many friends who watched a lot of movies out of loyalty rather than preference. Fanny Rinn, Jim Zuur, and Phillip Bergson were all essential to the making of the original *Reel Politics.* Peter Tessier provided timely and conscientious technical and research assistance for this sequel. Students from the 1970s to 2005 inspired both the original book and this one. Both books were improved by their comments as a preview audience.

Peter Haas wishes to thank the following individuals and groups for their assistance with research: Deborah Crawford (proprietor of Movie Madness in Washington, DC), Cobie Harris (Department of Political Science, San José State University), Steven Brown (Department of Political Science, Kent State University), Michael Haas (CEO of the Political Film Society), Stuart Shulman (Graduate School of Public and International Affairs, University of Pittsburgh), Roy Christman, and various members of the Costello Café listserv, including Mario Artecuna, Jean Filkins, John Harrison, Vern Morrison, Steve Horan, and Craig Wood. Christina Rockwell provided financial data and Web site information. Mary Buuck provided invaluable editorial assistance and Elizabeth Ann Haas added considerable substance beyond the chapter she wrote. Peter also wants to express special thanks to Kevin Armold for his influential moviegoing camaraderie and James Combs (professor emeritus, Department of Political Science, Valparaiso University) for his inspirational instruction and pathbreaking research in the fields of media and politics and film and politics.

Studying Political Films

1

Setting the Scene

A Theory of Film and Politics

Wag the Dog (1997)

The study of movies does not fit neatly into the discipline of political science or the other social sciences. Although film is a mass medium, political scientists have devoted decidedly less attention to it than to mass news media such as television and newspapers. For one thing, data about movies are difficult to quantify in meaningful ways.

From one perspective, movies are independent variables, cultural stimuli that potentially address and modify the political attitudes and behaviors of audiences and society. However, many films—particularly the most financially successful ones—seem themselves to be "caused" by external social and political conditions. Furthermore, certain films seem to assume a life of their own and interact with the political environment. Well-publicized and sometimes controversial and politically charged movies such as *Wag the Dog* (1997) and *Primary Colors* (1998) can even become part of the political landscape and vocabulary.

However, thinking of movies as independent variables does not seem likely to shed light upon the more nuanced aspects of the relationship between film and politics, especially for films that are—on the surface, at least—not very political. And the relationship may be far more complex and nuanced than the typical social science model of clearly identified independent and dependent variables. As political scientist Phillip Gianos notes, "politics and movies inform each other . . . . Both tell about the society from which they come."[1] Thus, political analysis of film has commonly taken a qualitative or even literary approach, although some intriguing research has explored the direct behavioral impact of specific films.[2] One major obstacle to the systematic study of films is the lack of a clear definition of what constitutes a political film. In this chapter, we offer a plausible framework for classifying films that may be used as a tool for in-depth analyses.

Political Content

Perhaps the most commonly used approach for distinguishing political films is political content. In this approach, political films are presumed to be those that depict various aspects of the political system, especially (but not necessarily) political institutions, political actors, and/or the political system. Whereas nearly every movie that focuses on political content of this type would probably qualify as sufficiently political, many other films, some entirely devoid of explicit political references, are excluded using this approach. But in a sense, *every* film has political significance and meaning. Students of political science and others with an interest in the impact of movies must be prepared to sift through any movie as a potential vessel of political meaning.

For better or worse, however, there is little critical unanimity about precisely which form and content would unarguably indicate a political film; American political films have not widely or uniformly received recognition as a specific genre. There are perhaps enough films that are overtly political to most viewers to constitute a genre, yet they are not commonly acknowledged as such. In film criticism, a genre is usually defined as a category or group of films about the same subject or marked by the same style—musicals, for example, or western, gangster, war, science fiction, or horror movies. Films in the same genre tend to look alike and observe certain conventions, although there are exceptions to both rules. Critics often group movies into genres for the purpose of comparison and discussion; audiences, sometimes unknowingly, do the same thing. But political films do not seem to fit the bill of a unique and recognizable genre. For example, is an obviously political movie like *The Candidate* (1972) political in the same sense as a satire like *Election* (1999)? Both movies deal with the political process in the largest sense, but they share little in terms of content, structure, or message to the viewing audience.

We can suggest at least four reasons for the lack of a clearly defined genre of political films:

1. Supposedly political films lack the internal consistency of other film genres—the forms that political movies take vary widely (e.g., *The Candidate* and *Election*).
2. Political films do not share as many conventions of plot and character as do other genres.
3. Overtly political films often allow for variation within the genre by combining descriptions, as in "political comedy" or "political thriller," thus vitiating their status.
4. Some filmmakers and perhaps critics fear the label of political film as box office anathema, meaning that filmmakers may consciously avoid making political films or attempt to depoliticize the ones they do.

Even if there were a widely recognized and readily recognizable genre of political films, it would probably not help to identify the kinds of political messages that can appear in many less explicitly political films. It would thus tend to divert attention from the frequently interesting political aspects of otherwise seemingly apolitical films.

Sending Political Messages

A second common approach to identifying political films places emphasis on the political and/or ideological messages they impart. Samuel Goldwyn's famous bromide ("Messages are for Western Union!") notwithstanding, movies frequently do convey political messages.[3] Rather explicit ideological messages may be present in films entirely devoid of explicit political referents; however, many of the political messages sent by movies are not the result of conscious planning by filmmakers.[4] The depiction of gender roles in movies of the 1930s and 1940s has been interpreted as speaking volumes about the gender politics of that era, although in many cases this effect was surely not the intent of the filmmakers. Indeed, it is probably safe to say that most contemporary American movies are not intended to send any particular political or ideological message; most are probably meant only to entertain and, more importantly, to make money.

Regarding the perhaps unintentional political statements offered by many movies, political scientist James Combs offers a useful analogy of the movie as a political participant: "A film participates in a political time not in how it was intended, but how it was utilized by those who saw it."[5] This outlook raises the question of whether the intentions of filmmakers are a legitimate and significant focus for the political analysis of films. For among many film scholars and critics, discussing the filmmakers' intent implies a problematic methodological and conceptual conundrum. First, many if not most Hollywood films are the result of a group filmmaking process, so to talk about the political intentions of the filmmaker may be truly inaccurate. Second, many scholars and critics of the literary tradition regard cinematic output as a text that must speak for itself. According to this approach, the political motives of the creators of films are ultimately irrelevant to the meaning and the effects a film has upon its audience.

However, when the task at hand is political analysis, the intentions of filmmakers are arguably much more germane. As Beverly Kelley notes, "movies reflect political choices."[6] In this respect, to create film is to participate politically. And like all political participation, some filmmaking is more rational, effective, and ultimately more politically noteworthy than the rest. Therefore, the political motivations and intentions of films and filmmakers should be of great interest to students of political films, which is one reason why this book tends to focus on films that seem to have been made to impart a political message.

Political Film as Political Theories

Another way of looking at the relationship between film and politics is to regard films as potential vehicles of political theory. After all, the almost magical capacity of films to create or alter reality can be seen as analogous to the machinations of political theorists. Most movies seek either to mimic and/or re-create reality or to bend and twist reality in creative ways. Some movies may even do both, or attempt to. The two predominant dimensions of political films—content and intent—seem to parallel the two major strands of political theory—empirical and normative.

Political content, which frequently entails more or less accurately depicting some aspect of political reality, resembles empirical (or descriptive) political theory. Thus, films that emphasize describing political institutions, processes, and actors—rare as they may be—may help audiences to better understand political phenomena. Conversely, if such films do a poor job of representing political reality or if they contradict the assumptions and perceptions of their audience, they may incite objections or even ridicule. Regardless of its accuracy, this kind of political content almost always makes movies seem more political. Like empirical political theory, political content usually helps to describe and explain how politics works. Of course, many movies only marginally invoke this kind of political content. For example, legal thrillers such as *A Civil Action* (1998) almost invariably provide some insight into the judicial system, but such content is usually not part of the film's focus.

Political intent generally resembles normative (or judgmental) political theory in that it seeks to judge, prescribe, and/or persuade. Films that are loaded with intentional political messages explicitly challenge the values of the audience and may even incite it to political action. On the other hand, the political messages of many movies may be lost on the audience amid a sea of competing cinematic themes—usually more personal than political. Like normative political theory, however, movies rife with ideological messages may fail to reach unreceptive audiences who reject their exhortations. Or, as often seems the case, political messages may be squarely aimed at the choir of true believers who are likely to agree with a film's message without having seen it.

A Basic Typology of Political Films

The two dimensions of political content and intent identified earlier may be combined to create a rudimentary means of classifying films according to their political significance. Figure 1.1 illustrates the matrix created by the two dimensions. Most films probably fall well within the extremes described by this matrix, but these extremes suggest pure types that may be useful as tools for analyzing movies. At the positive extremes of both political content and intent, in the upper right corner of the diagram, arguably lie the most obviously political of all films, consistent with the label of pure political films. Such films are set in a recognizably political environment and depict political actors and institutions, thus providing cues to their audiences and presumably describing the filmmaker's view of political reality.

Figure 1.1 **Types of Political Films Suggested by Dimensions of Content and Intent**

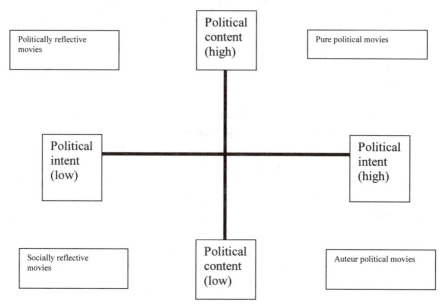

Note that the "pure" designation does not necessarily mean that such films are more or less political than others; however, it does suggest that the political nature of such films will be fairly evident to most audiences. In fact, pure political films may suffer in a sense from their very transparency. Audiences may understandably recoil from movies that combine heavy doses of both political context and ideological cant. Combs and Combs find that such efforts are prone to evoking the "politics of the obvious."[7]

Most movies, we will argue, send political or protopolitical messages that audiences may not even notice, but these overtly political films are political in a way that all of us readily perceive: they focus on politicians, elections, government, and the political process (Table 1.1). These are the explicitly political films, the message movies that Goldwyn warned against. The tradition of the political film, narrowly defined, began even before *The Birth of a Nation* (1915) and lives on to the present day. Some political movies are comedies, others are thrillers, many are melodramas, and a few are biographies. Many (e.g., *All Quiet on the Western Front*, 1930; *Platoon*, 1986) deal with the issues of war and peace, while others (e.g., *Gentleman's Agreement*, 1947; *I Am a Fugitive from a Chain Gang*, 1932; *Brubaker*, 1980) confront social problems such as discrimination, the need for prison reform, and the moral responsibility of the press in a free society. More contentious issue

8

Table 1.1

Examples of Film Types

Politically reflective films	Pure (overt) political films
Independence Day	*Mr. Smith Goes to Washington*
Invasion of the Body Snatchers	*The Candidate*
Many legal, western, and gangster films	Most social problem and documentary films
	Propaganda films
Socially reflective films	Auteur political films
Pretty Woman	*The Godfather*
Gone With the Wind	*Natural Born Killers*
Many other genre films	

movies such as *Norma Rae* (1979) and *The China Syndrome* (1979) are even more obviously political. Most of these films criticize specific aspects of the political process, but a few go even further by offering a broad critique of the entire political and social system. All of these movies have as their core a political message that any viewer can perceive; their themes are not hidden beneath a coating of special effects or couched in, for example, the lifestyle of a hooker with a heart of gold (à la *Pretty Woman,* 1990).

In the lower right corner of the diagram, where extremely high political intent meets diminished political content, lie films that may be described as "auteur" political movies. The "auteur" designation does not necessarily confer the traditional meaning of a director with firm artistic control (discussed in Chapter 2); rather, it suggests films in which political meaning is imparted—perhaps artistically—without overt reference to obvious political imagery. Such films may typically invoke symbolism and other artistic devices to transmit their politically charged messages.

The upper left corner of the diagram depicts films with obvious political content that are more or less devoid of intentional political messages. Films in this area are designated "politically reflective" because they often mirror popular ideas about political phenomena. This label covers films from other genres (romantic comedies, thrillers, etc.) that use political institutions as convenient backdrops to other sorts of themes. For example, the 1990s witnessed the release of a spate of films featuring the American presidency. These films do, of course, address political issues, but they generally use the institution as a convenient ploy to evoke other themes; the intentional political agendas of films such as *Independence Day* (1996), which features a president as a kind of action hero, seem marginal at best.

9

Such films may be of particular significance with respect to providing symbolic referents to political phenomena. Dan Nimmo and James Combs provide a compelling description of how such films can unintentionally create political meanings for audiences.[8] Nimmo and Combs work from Murray Edelman's postulate that the mass public does not experience politics through direct involvement; instead, its perceptions are founded upon and filtered by symbolic representations, such as those provided by the film medium.[9] So movies set in political or quasi-political contexts are likely sources of the symbolic content that informs mass understanding of the political system.

Films that avoid both overt political messages and reference to explicitly political events are located in the lower left corner of the diagram and are labeled "socially reflective" films. Most Hollywood movies probably fall near this designation, if not squarely in it. The majority of movies neither have blatantly political contexts nor evokes intentional political messages to audiences; however, that is not to say that most movies are not at all political.

Despite the benign intentions of their creators, both the socially reflective and politically reflective types of film are frequently pregnant with political meaning. Nimmo and Combs further contend that *all* social reality is "mediated" by means of communication—much of it the mass communication exemplified by film. Film, moreover, is a "democratic art," whose success as an enterprise is dependent upon the favor of mass audiences.[10] Successful movies, therefore, tend to be the ones that show the public what it wants to see— just as successful political candidates typically tell the public what it wants to hear. Thus, a very popular movie can tell us something about the audience.

Analyzing the Unpolitical Political Film

Most students can recognize overtly political films; however, many students find it difficult to recognize films that fall roughly into the lower left quadrant of Figure 1.1—socially reflective movies—as examples of political filmmaking. A casual observer can interpret and understand the obvious political films, and some can navigate the subtle ideological nuances of auteur political efforts. Archetypical political classics such as *Mr. Smith Goes to Washington* (1939) and *The Candidate* are generally well received by contemporary student audiences despite their dated qualities. More difficult for many is the leap toward understanding how otherwise ostensibly benign films such as *Close Encounters of the Third Kind* (1977) or even political thrillers such as *Blow Out* can imply messages—both from the filmmaker and about the audience as well as society itself. With this text, we hope to provide students with the examples and analytic tools they need to make these interpretations more readily.

How do otherwise mostly apolitical movies evoke political themes? First and foremost, movies intended for mass audiences are invariable money-making propositions. Gianos notes that "biases follow from films' most basic role as vehicles for profit making . . . these biases, of course, are the point."[11] Nimmo and Combs state that "those movies that sell and those few that endure do so because they have treated selected cultural themes that were on the minds, or in the back of the minds, of large numbers of people."[12] Popular movies, in other words, invoke popular ideas about politics. Such films may individually be more or less innocuous, yet collectively influential: "The power of any single movie to influence one's viewpoint is limited, but obviously repetition has its effect."[13]

A potential problem for scientific observers (and students) of political films is recognizing within themselves the proclivity to respond to such themes. A useful analytic question to pose when viewing such films is this: To which mass, politically relevant beliefs, hopes, or fears does this film appeal? This is not a straightforward question to answer, because as Nimmo and Combs observe, "people sort themselves on the basis of the cultural [film] fantasies that they want to believe."[14] As moviegoers, we must examine not only our own values and beliefs but also those of others and of society at large. The following section explores various avenues of analysis by which students of film and politics may arrive at insights into the political aspects of inexplicitly political films. Whereas these patterns may be found in all types of film, they are perhaps most likely to appear in socially or politically reflective films.

Sublimated Politics in the Movies

Fantastic Displacement

Nimmo and Combs draw particular attention to movies that involve what they call "fantastic displacement . . . the process of placing fantasies of an age in a melodramatic setting and story that covertly mediates the political fantasy for a mass audience to make their fantasies palatable and entertaining."[15] As an example of this process, Nimmo and Combs cite the science fiction films of the 1950s, which seemed to substitute fears of alien invasions and the like for anxiety about the spread of the ostensible Communist threat. (The spate of eco-catastrophe films of the late 1990s and the beginning of the new century might be analyzed in terms of substituting fantastic threats like asteroids and volcanoes for anxiety about the fragile ecosystem of earth.) Although many students are readily able to identify these patterns in older films, such as *Invasion of the Body Snatchers* (1956), they tend to miss—or even emotionally reject—similar patterns in movies of their own era.

Portrayals of Race and Gender

Perhaps one of the most common means by which political messages seep through Hollywood films is through portrayal of sex, race, and gender roles. Students are typically able to identify and analyze the significance of dated portrayals of race and gender in old films (e.g., the black porters and the deferential female roles in *Mr. Smith Goes to Washington*), but are often at a loss to identify equally dubious portrayals in more contemporary films. One problem with identifying politically significant portrayals of race and gender is the wide variety of ways they may reflect political concerns. Among the many possibilities: some films invoke offensive or dated stereotypes; others use plot devices to punish certain types of characters, such as independent women or minority figures.[16]

Genre

Gianos states that the conventions of many film genres—through repetition and development—become well known to filmmakers and audiences alike.[17] The content of this repetition is replete with clues about the political and social values of both. Audiences expect certain outcomes (e.g., the good guys should win). Once again, contemporary students tend to be much more comfortable identifying such patterns in older genre efforts (e.g., westerns) than they are with contemporary releases (e.g., slasher films).

Types of Political Messages

Americans in general do not trust politicians. In fact, politics as a respected profession ranks well below medicine, law, engineering, teaching, dentistry, and the ministry. A Gallup poll found that almost two-thirds of those surveyed regarded politics as a corrupt rat race. Clergymen, pharmacists, doctors, dentists, and professors rated at the top for honesty and ethics. Politicians were close to the bottom with realtors and union leaders. Only advertising people and car salesmen ranked lower.

People get their ideas about politicians from experience, the news media, and the process of political socialization. Movies play a part in this process by creating or reflecting attitudes about politicians, and as we will see, the cinematic portrait of politics and politicians is almost invariably negative. Politicians are often the villains in movies. They are frequently corrupt, greedy, self-serving, and ruthlessly ambitious. Conversely, real politicians of the past, such as Abraham Lincoln and Franklin D. Roosevelt, are treated with such reverence in movies that they become boring and unbelievable. Neither depiction is accurate, of course, but both reinforce the popular view of politicians as either murderous crooks or heroic saviors.

Condemning the cardboard clichés of corrupt politics and conniving politicians, senators William S. Cohen and Gary Hart have charged that film and television producers are naive about how Washington really works and are dangerously misleading their viewers.[18] Television commentator Andy Rooney responded that the public "understands that the crooked politician is a standard dramatic cliché that is no more typical of the average politician than the winding marble staircase in a home shown on television is typical of a staircase in an American home."[19] Cohen and Hart suggest that movies and TV shape our view of politicians, whereas Rooney insists that we know the difference between fact and fiction. Like others who feel maligned by the media, the senators may be laying too much blame on the movies, but Rooney is probably letting filmmakers off the hook too easily. Movies really do shape, reflect, and reinforce our opinions, even though we often dismiss them as silly—"It's only a movie."

Movies, as we noted earlier, also tell us about the political system and how it works, or whether it works—that is, whether it can solve our problems. Usually, they tell us that bad people can mess up the system and good ones can set it right. On the whole, these movies reinforce the status quo, telling us that all is well in America and that any little problems can be worked out, usually with the help of a heroic leader. They seldom point out fundamental defects in the system, and they rarely suggest that social problems can be solved by collective or communal action. They simplify the complex problems of a complex society, solving them quickly and easily so we can have a happy ending. Some critics see a conspiracy in this pattern, but most agree that it is unconscious and, to some extent, executed in collusion with audiences more willing to have their opinions reinforced than challenged. Selective perception enables us to ignore even movies that question our biases. Hollywood's ubiquitous happy endings further mute such challenges by suggesting that problems can be easily solved. The results are what film scholars call "dramas of reassurance," movies that support commonly held ideas and tell us that everything is fine.

Political movies send messages about other important aspects of public life, too. Their images of politics, politicians, and the political system influence participation in politics, for example. If politics is corrupt or if heroes and heroines always come to the rescue, perhaps there is no need to fight city hall. If the movie version of politics makes those of us who are not stars irrelevant, perhaps we need not participate. Power is another frequent subject of movies, almost always treated negatively, usually by falling back on the old maxim that power corrupts. Only a handful of totally selfless, godlike leaders such as Hollywood's favorite president, Abraham Lincoln, manage to exercise power and still come across as virtuous.

13

Most American movies avoid, ignore, oversimplify, or denigrate political ideology, yet ideology is essential if we are to understand politics. Ideologies help us make sense of the world around us. They help us decide whether we are satisfied with the status quo or willing to change it. All of us have some sort of ideology, but many Americans pretend they have none, and so do most of our movies. No wonder the political motives of most film characters are personal ambition and greed. The rare ideologues in American political movies are one-dimensional and often silly, thus caricaturing ideology itself. As a consequence, American movies, lacking a rich variety of perspectives on society, tend to see conflict as a struggle between good and evil or right and wrong. Political scientists have noted that Americans, as a people, are pragmatic rather than ideological. They adapt to conditions rather than reacting to them from a fixed point of view. Such ideology is vague and largely unarticulated. Alternatives are seldom expressed, and we have been taught, partly by political movies, that ideology is foolish, impractical, or evil. Indeed, American ideology as exhibited both in political film and in the larger society might be said to be essentially anti-ideological because of its emphasis on pragmatism and consensus. We like to make things work, and we do not like conflict. Both of these orientations lead us to mute ideology. But we also place a high value on individualism, competition, and social equality, all of which are traditional components of an ideology—and all of which are themes that recur in American political films.

Political movies thus send many different messages. They describe us, shape us, and sometimes move us. Although some themes recur, the messages and our reactions to them tend to vary over time, reflecting the historical and political context. This survey therefore treats American political movies chronologically, although we will return to their common themes and focus on some specific issues. Subsequent chapters of this text will explore how the films of various eras and genres evoke the various kinds of political significance we have discussed.

The Impact of Political Films

The study of political films interests us as political scientists primarily because we theorize that such films might have some kind of impact on the political system; however, the specific forms of such an impact remain largely unexplored by our discipline. A priori, we can hypothesize several non-mutually exclusive ways that movies affect politics:

1. Movies contribute to general social and political learning, including affective patterns. Movies are part of a larger political socialization

process. Just as we learn about our political system in school and other social institutions, we learn by going to movies. This socialization process may include learning affective patterns, such as support for or opposition to the role of government. For example, if one attends enough movies like *Independence Day* (1996) as an impressionable youth, one might be disposed to expect extraordinary achievements by U.S. presidents.

2. Movies provide information about and/or orientation to specific issues or events. Not all learning at the movies needs to occur by means of slow, subtle processes of socialization. Attending a specific movie can provide viewers with information and possibly change their attitudes concerning specific issues. For example, viewing *The Insider* (1999) might both inform a viewer and instill a negative perception about the tobacco industry.

3. Movies affect specific political behavior, such as voting in elections. A movie whose message contains a specific political target—for example, *Fahrenheit 9/11* (2004)—might convince a voter to vote against President George W. Bush. The documentary film *The Thin Blue Line* (1988) resulted in the exoneration of a man who had been imprisoned for murdering a police officer.

4. Movies affect the knowledge and behavior of specific groups, especially political elites. Some elected officials, for example, cite John Wayne movies as influencing their political careers; in Chapter 3, for example, we discuss a theory that President Ronald Reagan in effect reenacted some of the movie parts he played while in office.

5. Movies spark public debate and/or media interest in specific issues. Even films that are not seen in great numbers by the general public, such as *Wag the Dog* (1997), may have a tertiary impact on the political system because the mass media or other elites discuss and use its imagery in public discourse, which may eventually filter down to other groups, including the general public.

This is only a partial list of possible means of impact by movies, but it suggests that the collective effect of movies may be profound indeed. Several mediating influences on the power of movies to affect politics ought to be borne in mind, however.

First, decades of political research teach us that, as a rule, individuals possess considerable capacity to screen their own beliefs from outside stimuli such as those presented by political messages in movies.[20] A person with a firmly established partisan identity, for example, is unlikely to be swayed by the heavy-handed ideological message of a *Bulworth* (1998). It also bears mentioning that many movies (particularly small, independent ones) are not even accessible to many would-be viewers. Film studios put many movies in limited release, meaning that they are seen only in major urban centers or perhaps only in New York and/or Los Angeles.

Moreover, a person with a strongly conservative worldview is probably unlikely to go see a movie like *Bulworth*. Thus, attending movies is a self-selected political stimulus. Except perhaps as children, we generally choose the movies we want to see and exclude ourselves from many others. Therefore, many movies with strident political messages may wind up only preaching to the choir of its predetermined supporters. Little research exists to document this quality of movies and particularly its ability to mediate the movies' effect on political perceptions, beliefs, and actions.

A recent analysis by the *New York Times* found that the audiences for the liberal documentary *Fahrenheit 9/11* and those of the traditional or conservative *The Passion of the Christ* (2004) were markedly different geographically and demographically. The theaters where *Passion* audiences were the largest tended to be in suburban settings and dispersed across the country, whereas the biggest *9/11* audiences were located in New York, Los Angeles, San Francisco, and a few other urban centers.[21] The studios and their distribution networks contribute to this pattern by placing movies in areas where they think the audience will be the largest.

Finally, audiences are not monolithic. What little empirical data we have suggest that people experience movies politically in fundamentally different ways. Recent research by Young suggests that moviegoers have different motivations for seeing movies; for example, some just want to kill time while others are trying to keep up with current trends.[22] Stephenson's groundbreaking research identified remarkably variable reactions to a short film from the American Cancer Society, reactions that seemed to depend on the viewers' own experience with cancer.[23] We can therefore expect that different kinds of political movies will have varying effects on different kinds of audiences. Whereas that may seem like a self-evident conclusion, remarkably little is known about which sorts of films are most efficacious (and why), which types of audiences are most susceptible to which types of film, and so on. For now, we must take it as an article of faith that movies are an important "participant" in our political system in a variety of ways.

Summary and Implications for the Systematic Study of Film and Politics

With the goal of helping students to approach the study of film and politics systematically, this chapter has suggested a typology of political films. The typology is based largely on two important dimensions of such films: (1) political content—the extent to which a film reflects a political context or setting, and (2) political intention—the extent to which filmmakers actively seek to impart political or ideological messages. Whereas movies that exhibit a great deal of either dimension tend to be readily identifiable as political films, those with understated—or even totally sublimated—political content or expression pose relatively greater challenges to contemporary students. Several critical approaches to identifying political meaning in less obvious political films were briefly discussed. Finally, the means by which political films may theoretically affect the political system were briefly explored, along with a series of potentially mediating factors.

This framework can be tested in the classroom and the cinema as a practical means of orienting students to the task of analyzing political films. Additionally, it may be possible to integrate other dimensions of political films, such as genre, propaganda, and satire, into this framework, at least on a probabilistic basis. In other words, as suggested by Table 1.1, certain kinds of movies may be more likely than others to fall within one of the four quadrants discussed earlier.

Finally, much of the study of political film rests on largely untested assumptions about the effects of cultural symbols on the political attitudes and actions of mass audiences. The rather nascent research linking exposure to movies and other media to mass behavior needs to be linked to these often tenuous assumptions.

2

The Making of a Message
Film Production and Techniques and Political Messages

Citizen Kane (1941)

Movies can send political messages in many ways, from the most explicit political preaching to far more subtle means involving techniques of filmmaking that most viewers may take for granted. This chapter analyzes how each step in the filmmaking process—from conception of the idea for a film to its release (and even thereafter)—can achieve the effect of political messaging to an audience. Political messages may be present in films as the result of either intention by the film's creator or largely unintended reflections of political and social realities, or perhaps both. In this discussion, we focus primarily on intentional messages, as they are generally easier to identify.

The Filmmaking Process

Creating a popular motion picture in the current era is an expensive, time-consuming process that can involve (literally) a cast of thousands. In this section, we analyze the film production process into a series of steps and isolate the possible contribution each step can make to the political impact of a film. The steps we identify are "ideal" ones that in fact may occur in combination with one another and/or in different sequences. For example, the conception of a movie—the very idea of creating it—may likely coincide with (or even precede if the film is an adaptation) the creation of the basic story that the movie will tell. And although promotion is relegated to one of the final steps in the process, it is frequently created and implemented long before a film is completed, which is evident when a movie trailer (promotional short that precedes a movie) is shown months or even more than a year before a film is seen in the theater. But breaking the process into its constituent parts enables us to see how individual production decisions can create or affect political messages in films. It also provides an opportunity to explore the technical aspects of filmmaking (and the accompanying terminology) that are of the greatest relevance to the study of politics and film.

Conception

"Conception" refers to the idea of making a film. In current American cinema, the ideas for movies can originate in a number of ways. Some films are the creation of an individual whose vision (and access to the necessary resources) enables him or her to fashion a very personal or individualized statement. Many other films are created by means of a complicated process involving large studios and teams of writers and other production personnel. All things being equal, smaller (i.e., less expensive) films that originate in an individual artistic vision are more likely to contain overt and/or intentional political messages than are big-budget, major-studio projects. Most popular films fall into the latter category, and we will focus on these films in analyzing the filmmaking process.

Production

Movie production is an extremely important, yet often unclear, aspect of moviemaking. There is no specific list of tasks, responsibilities, or roles that is *necessarily* undertaken by a movie producer. However, a film producer is generally the first person (beyond a screenwriter or other story source) professionally involved with a film project. Among the activities generally associated with film producers are the following:

- Identifying and hiring the major creative talents who will work on the film (including the director, screenwriter, cinematographer, costumer, art director, casting director, editor, major stars, and so forth.)
- Maintaining a presence during the shooting of a movie to help with the practical challenges involved in completion of a film project. (This role may or may not create conflicts with the movie director.)
- Serving as the individual regarded by the studio or production company as the ultimate authority on the project who has ultimate responsibility for its successful completion. (Again, such a role may lead to confusion or conflict with that of the film's director.)

However, the major and overarching role of a movie's producer is to ensure its financial viability. "He or she supervises the budgeting process, approves major expenses, and answers to the studio or production company when there are problems."[1] The focus of film production can thus be said to be the commercial aspects of a project rather than the artistic—which tend be the province of film *direction*. Movies are produced to make money, and their content is strongly influenced by economics. U.S. filmmakers receive no government subsidies, so movies are business ventures and expensive ones at that. The cost of a feature film averaged just $400,000 in 1941; by 1985, it was more than $12 million. The cost of marketing alone for an average Hollywood blockbuster was recently reported to be more than $60 million![2] That means high finance. The big studios used to provide this money and often still do, but banks, insurance companies, and individual investors are now more prominent. These institutions and people tend to be conservative, both politically and economically. They invest accordingly.

Nevertheless, depending upon the context of their involvement, movie producers can help to shape political content. As Gianos reminds us, "films are produced to make money . . . it is essential to understand that films are a commodity intended to make money to understanding their relationship to politics and of politics' relationship to film."[3] This profit-making motive—in an endeavor whose production costs may reach hundreds of millions of dollars—tends to push producers in certain ways. Perhaps most important, the profit motive tends to lead producers to err on the side of caution when making movies. Political controversy, although not inevitably anathema for a movie's bottom line, is one risk that many producers may seek to avoid. Hiring a director with a known political agenda, for example, might be typically eschewed in favor of a safer choice. Scripts may be toned down or flat-out rejected for their potential political sensitivity. Actors with safe images may be favored over those with outspoken political beliefs or images.

The conservative orientation of investors is thus widely believed to have increased since the 1960s as the corporate moneymen took over and the power of the studios declined, but in fact, the collapse of the studio system made it easier for independent filmmakers to develop political projects. They still need lots of money, which means finding investors. Some artists solve this problem by starting their own production companies and investing themselves. Small investors also have become more important, and cable television and videocassettes have provided new outlets and new investors. Independent filmmakers still need the studios at least to some extent for both investment and distribution, but even the studios have changed. Would any of the old studios except perhaps Warner Brothers have laid out $52 million for *Reds* (1981)? Paramount did—under the corporate ownership of Gulf and Western. The conglomerate thought the film would make money so it was willing to invest, even if it did not endorse the film's politics, just as other studios invested in *Missing* (1982) and *The Killing Fields* (1984). "Hollywood has nothing against message films as long as they make money," said director John Frankenheimer in 1984. "You could get *The Manchurian Candidate* made today—provided you had Jack Nicholson in the Sinatra role and Rob Lowe playing Raymond Shaw."[4] Frankenheimer proved remarkably prescient: in 2004 Paramount produced a remake of the noted political thriller—vastly inferior to the original—with bankable stars Denzel Washington and Meryl Streep!

Whereas this discussion might lead us to assume that movie production is somehow biased toward films espousing a conservative, patriotic, and even nationalistic viewpoint, there is by no means agreement on that point among observers of the film industry. Conservative critics, like Michael Medved, in fact claim the opposite: that Hollywood producers favor films that denigrate so-called traditional American values. Medved wrote in *Hollywood vs. America:* "Americans are passionately patriotic, and consider themselves enormously lucky to live here; but Hollywood conveys a view of the nation's history, future, and major institutions that is dark, cynical, and often night-marish." Medved's book goes on to assert that movies frequently attack main-stream religion, promote promiscuity, malign the institution of marriage, encourage foul language and violence, and generally "bash America." [5]

Most critics and scholars would agree that most movies are indeed produced on the basis of their ability to make their investors money. Whether that motive drives them toward a particular ideological message in their films is debatable. Clearly, however, films can be vehicles for all kinds of political messages, and in many cases the content of that message will be in the eyes of beholder.

The film industry appears as a whole to be at best ambivalent about investing in political films. Directors from D.W. Griffith and King Vidor in the early days to Sidney Lumet and Oliver Stone today, along with some studios, producers, writers, and stars, have defied the Goldwyn rule frequently and flagrantly. At least a few movies with political messages are made every year, and some periods, such as the 1930s and the late 1970s, have seen higher rates of production. Such movies generally get more than their fair share of recognition: witness the success of *Platoon* in 1986. Hollywood likes to congratulate itself by giving an occasional Academy Award nomination, and sometimes even the Oscar itself, to a film that at least pretends to have a message. Critics may give political films a rough ride, but they pay attention to them and regard them as "important works." And contrary to conventional wisdom, audiences do not ignore political films. Although message movies hardly ever rank as blockbusters, many have actually turned a handsome profit. So producers clearly do not reject political films out of hand.

All political films are not necessarily discriminated against. Film critic Stephen Holden recently observed that Hollywood is reluctant to make films with *any* kind of serious, adult-oriented content.[6] The number of vacuous big-budget movies aimed at what is often seen as a key demographic group—teenagers—seems to far outnumber serious movies of any kind.

Screenplay and Story

Probably the most obvious way films send political messages is via the screenplay, which prescribes the basic content of a movie: its subject matter, characters, and plotting. As we have noted, American movies are noteworthy for their general tendency to avoid overtly political subject matter. As Gianos notes succinctly, "the conventional wisdom of the industry is that political subjects are to be avoided." According to Gianos, therefore, a primary message transmitted by the film industry as a whole is that "politics is neither interesting nor important."[7] Of course, some movies with overt political content and themes are made, but on the whole, more movies with other kinds of political messages are seen by the general public.

The words or dialogue may be even more important in political films than in other movies. Politics itself is a medium of words, so more is spoken in these films and what is said is given greater weight. If too much is said, however, the movies become static and boring or, worse, obvious, broadcasting the message heavy-handedly and thereby subverting it. On the other hand, if a movie is too subtle, the message might be missed altogether. Movies are probably most effective when they let us reach our own conclusions or at least let us think we have.

Subject Matter/Genre

"Genre" refers to a class of films with conventional settings, characters, and plots. Among the most commonly recognized film genres are horror movies, romantic comedies, and science fiction. We have observed earlier that political films do not seem to constitute a genre or "type" of movie unto themselves. But other genres do tend to be associated with certain kinds of political messages.

Perhaps the oldest and most commonly invoked genre is the American western. The central plot of the classic western film is the struggle to maintain law and order on the frontier in a fast-paced action story. Good and evil are generally represented in stark contrast, and as a rule, the good guys wearing the white hats emerge victorious. Many early westerns affirm the basic goodness of early America while depicting Native Americans as savages whose defeat was just and appropriate. Countless variations on the basic western have been produced, making it a quintessential American genre that tends to reflect "American values" widely construed.

But genres are subject to mutation over time. In the case of the western, for example, recent efforts tend to downplay the essential goodness of American settlers and cowboys and instead explore the tragic plight of Native Americans. *Dances with Wolves* (1990) was a hugely popular movie that won director and star Kevin Costner an Academy Award and featured a sympathetic perspective on Native Americans. Yet the more things in movies change, the more they stay the same: *Dances with Wolves* also featured a white protagonist who was able to master the nobly portrayed native culture. One could argue that the movie co-opts Native Americans into the white man's world. Thus the film does not really undermine the traditional values of the western genre. A variation on the same theme is present in the more recent *The Last Samurai* (2003), wherein an American soldier from the fron-

24

tier era is sent to Japan, masters the art and culture of the samurai, and succeeds to preserve it on behalf of the Japanese. Once again, the message is not so much that the foreign culture is venerable, but that an American can master it against the forces of evil.

Movie Conventions

Movies of any genre tend to follow time-proven conventions to which audiences have grown accustomed. With respect to movies with overtly political content, Gianos identifies four such conventions, each of which serves to minimize the political conflict of storylines that might otherwise arouse controversy[8]:

- Personalization: Movies with political subject matter frequently focus on the individual drama of politically active roles, which tends to make them more palatable to mass audiences. The Vietnam War classic *The Deer Hunter* (1978) involves the viewer in the drama of a group of friends enmeshed in the war, thus tending to avoid overt commentary about the war itself.
- Sugarcoating: Another frequent approach to political content is to cover potentially strong political content with other genres. Gianos notes that *Reds* (1981), which concerns an American journalist who is a Communist sympathizer, is presented largely as a love story. More recently, *Conspiracy Theory* (1997) and *Enemy of the State* (1998) redirect content dealing with concerns about Orwellian government into more conventional thrillers.
- "The Unlabeled Bottle": By this, Gianos is referring to the tendency for political themes to use extremely generic terms to defuse possible political controversy. He notes that in *Mr. Smith Goes to Washington* (1939), no party (or ideological) labels are provided, allowing the audience to read its own interpretation into the story. Indeed, very few movies with politicians in key roles—particularly fictional movies about presidents, such as *The American President* (1995), *Independence Day* (1996), and *Dave* (1993)—provide party labels.
- Ambivalence: Many films present both sides of a political conflict with an even hand, thus deflating criticism of favoritism toward a particular side or cause and possible bad publicity. Gianos notes that director Spike Lee's *Do the Right Thing* (1989) presents a case for both violence and nonviolence in racial conflict; more recently, *Citizen Ruth* (1996) lampoons both extremities of the abortion debate in a way that favors neither side.

Additionally, the requirement to entertain, the focus on individuals, and the need to solve problems by the end of the movie can result in oversimplification, which is why American political films almost invariably deal with only one problem at a time. Even a single issue may be simplified so much that the outcome is obvious. In *Guess Who's Coming to Dinner* (1967), for example, the solution is so readily apparent that our own racist attitudes are not really challenged: of course our daughters could marry nice black doctors like Sidney Poitier. *Red Dawn* (1984) and *Rambo* (1985) leave us no options either. The villains of such movies—whether they are racists, Communists, bureaucrats, or businessmen—are so broadly caricatured that we have no choice but to reject them, and we certainly cannot identify with them.

Direction

A movie's director is generally considered the single most important contributor to a movie's final artistic impact and the one with the most control over the final product. The actual duties of the director vary from film to film (and perhaps overlap with those of the producer, as discussed earlier). Film directors are usually responsible for not only "directing" the actors (à la a stage director) but also determining the many visual and aural aspects of a movie, including the choice of shots, camera angles, lighting, light filters, composition, and editing. Directors also usually make major costume and set-design decisions.[9]

In Hollywood's classic era, moviemaking was purportedly a group endeavor, but since then film has increasingly become the artistic province of the director. One reason for this evolving role of the director was the influence of French film theorists of the 1950s, whose "auteur" theory prescribed the director as the true "author" of a film. The French theorists proposed that

> the greatest movies are dominated by the personal vision of the director. A filmmaker's signature can be perceived through an examination of his or her total output, which is characterized by a unity of theme and style. The [screen] writer's contribution is less important than the director's, because subject matter is artistically neutral. The director dominates the treatment, provided he or she is a strong director or *auteur*.[10]

Certainly the best-known explicitly political American films are almost always the handiwork of a specific director. Directors such as John Sayles, Oliver Stone, and Spike Lee bring a well-known political agenda to their work that is frequently evident in their films; however, even directors with a less obvious interest in political themes, such as Steven Spielberg and Brian De Palma, have created films with interesting political implications. Critics of auteur theory point out that many movies with "no-name" directors are nevertheless excellent films. Michael Curtiz, who directed the World War II classic *Casablanca* (1942), had no distinctive style or personal vision, yet he created many excellent movies.[11] However, the average big-studio director, even though he or she may create films with a distinctive style, seems more likely to reflect political reality than to comment on it intentionally.

Peter Biskind notes that the same director can send different kinds of messages over the course of a career, and liberal directors can work with conservative writers and producers, and vice versa: "Particular directors are often able to put their stamp on their work, intentionally insert messages into their movies. But these are exceptions, and it often happens that the films of an individual director, even one with a strong directorial personality, convey different ideologies."[12]

Regardless of political messages, films tend to fall between the extremes represented by two major approaches to direction: realism and formalism. Realism is a filmmaking style that seeks to imitate or duplicate reality. This is typically achieved by means of an emphasis on authentic locations and a minimal amount of film editing. Formalism, by contrast, emphasizes aesthetic forms and symbols rather than objective reality. Formalist films tend to distort reality in a variety of ways—often by means of unusual set designs, lighting techniques, and aggressive film editing.

Neither realism nor formalism necessarily connotes a political emphasis in filmmaking, and either approach could conceivably be used to create a film with a particular sort of political message. Moreover, many Hollywood films combine the two approaches to create a smooth, almost transparent style of direction that may be difficult to discern at all. But when directors emphasize a realistic or formalistic approach or technique, it provides viewers with clues as to the kind of political message, if any, that the film seeks to convey. For example, in *Apocalypse Now* (1979), director Francis Ford Coppola used a variety of formalistic techniques, including light filters and music, to dramatize the horror of war in Vietnam. Other directors, such as Oliver Stone in *Platoon* (1986) and Steven Spielberg in *Saving Private Ryan* (1998), used a more realistic approach to achieve a similar message.

The nature of movies as an art form also may moderate their politics as much as the directors. The auteur notion of the all-powerful director is vigorously disputed by writers and other collaborators in filmmaking. "It sure as shit isn't true in Hollywood," declares screenwriter William Goldman. "Movies," he insists, "are a group endeavor."[21] Directors may be central figures, but many creative people, including writers, producers, cinematographers, editors, designers, and actors, contribute to the final shape of a film. The politics of these individuals may differ, and their perceptions of what audiences want to see, need to be told, or will accept also may vary. Out of the conflict of these differing biases and perceptions comes the movie.

The following elements and subelements of film direction also play a role in sending political messages; each also may be used in a way that is realistic or formalistic.

Titles

Movie titles can be used to prepare the audience for a political message. A frequent device is the use of "typewriter" fonts that suggest a newspaper exposé of a given topic, such as those used in *Missing* (1982), which exposes CIA involvement in foreign affairs. More fanciful titles may cue the audience to suspend any political critique of the proceedings, although some directors choose credits that provide an ironic contrast to the serious political nature of their film. *Far From Heaven* (2002) is about racism and homophobia in 1950s Connecticut, but opens with a drifting title sequence suggesting a standard melodrama about lost romance.

Sound and Dialogue

Like direction generally, sound in films can emphasize a realistic or formalistic approach. Several directors have emphasized realistic sound to help define their filmmaking style and political emphases. Robert Altman, for example, is known for films such as *Nashville* (1975), wherein a clutter of voices is allowed to express the political anarchy that the film dramatizes. In Francis Ford Coppola's *The Conversation* (1974), a multilayered soundtrack of voices helps convey an atmosphere of paranoia and suspicion in the work of an eavesdropping spy. (The bugging and tape recording eerily anticipated the Watergate scandal that exploded soon after the film's release.)

Music

Two kinds of music are usually used in movies: original music scored and played expressly for a particular film, and soundtrack music, which is drawn from existing music. Either form of music can be played in the foreground or the background of a particular scene, and either can transmit political messages. Beginning with the opening credits, serious (frequently classical) music can cue the audience to prepare for a serious political message, whereas breezy or jazzy music connotes lighter fare.

The soundtrack tells us who the good guys and bad guys are. Patriotic tunes arouse our emotions, and martial music sets the adrenaline flowing, building excitement. When the campaign catches on in *The Candidate* (1972), so does the music. We know something is happening and we are caught up in it. Music can communicate dread, too. Along with lighting effects, camera angles, and editing, chilling music gives *All the President's Men* (1976) some of the qualities of a thriller.

Increasingly, directors of popular movies are using soundtracks composed of popular music to enhance the mood they seek to create in a particular scene. Coppola's *Apocalypse Now* (1979) brilliantly juxtaposes a scene of American soldiers waterskiing with the Rolling Stones' "(I Can't Get No) Satisfaction" to dramatize the decadence of the Vietnam War. Altman's *Nashville,* which climaxes with a political assassination, ends with a crowd singing along to "It Don't Worry Me," a hymn to apathy and alienation that reinforces the film's theme.[13]

Editing/Montage

Editing (also known as "montage") is the joining of one uninterrupted sequence of film (or "shot") to another. For many film theorists, editing is the foundation of film art. As mentioned in the earlier discussion of approaches to directing, extensive use of editing is usually associated with formalism. That is because editing is a means of manipulating time and space in a movie that, although inherently unrealistic, can effectively convey complicated narratives . . . as well as political messages. Editing can be relatively simple, such as moving from a close-up of two actors to a more distant perspective (or "long shot"), or it may involve an extremely complicated series of rapid shots strung together ("jump cutting") or any mixture of shots of varying lengths.

Editing techniques can be used to transmit political messages in any number of ways. A famous sequence at the end of *The Godfather* (1972) splices scenes from a Catholic wedding with a series of vicious mob hits, suggesting the new godfather's corruption of even the church as he consolidates his power in the world of organized crime. Generally speaking, extensive use of film editing tends to draw attention to the director and, presumably, to his or her message. Longer, unedited camera shots tend to focus greater attention on the subject matter. Either approach can enhance the transmission of a particular message.

Composition/Mise-en-scène

Composition (also known as mise-en-scène in Europe) is the construction of movie scenes—the placement of people and objects in the frame of the camera lens. Different kinds of composition help directors propel their narratives and also help transmit political messages. Among the elements of a typical composition within an individual movie scene are (1) the dominant object or objects, (2) the camera angles, (3) the distance of the camera from the scene, (4) the colors and lighting, (5) possible distortion by use of lenses, (6) density or complexity of the image, (7) character placement, and (8) framing of the images.[14] Manipulating these and other elements in a given scene helps the director say different things even before any action is filmed. Audiences do not normally consciously think about composition, but its use is a powerful tool for manipulating audience reaction to characters and events within a film. The final shot of *Bulworth* (1998) shows a dead, splayed Bulworth (Warren Beatty) cradled by Halle Berry's character, reminiscent of famous shots of Bobby Kennedy's assassination at the Embassy Hotel in Los Angeles. The shot also features witnesses pointing in the direction of the gunman, reminiscent of Martin Luther King's assassination.

Photography/Cinematography

Photography in movies (frequently referred to as cinematography) entails a number of techniques, including the use of lighting and color, camera angles and placement, and the selection and/or creation of movie sets, props, and special effects. A brief discussion of each aspect of photography follows.

Lighting and Color

Directors and their cinematographers use a variety of devices that affect the lighting and perception of color in a film. They may choose to rely on natural lighting and use lamps to create additional light or shadows. Filters may be used in conjunction with various sorts of lenses that distort the natural colors in a scene. All these effects can enhance the potential political impact of a scene. In *All the President's Men* (1976), for example, the lighting juxtaposes the well-lit pressroom of the *Washington Post* with a dark, seedy parking garage where the truth is divulged by a secret source nicknamed Deep Throat. The contrast highlights the journalistic truth (and pure motives of the journalists) compared to the dirty political reality.[15] *Traffic* (2000) contrasts different settings through dominant color tones. The scenes in Mexico are saturated with a yellow ochre color, whereas the U.S. scenes involving Michael Douglas as a judge who discovers that his own daughter is a junkie are filmed in a dominant blue tone. The deep coloring of both worlds suggests a parallel between them: the open corruption of the Mexican police is not so far removed from the politicization of the antidrug movement in the United States.

Camera Angles and Placement

The position of the camera and the angle of the scene being photographed are tools that directors can use to insert messages about the subject matter of their films. Here, too, filmmakers make crucial choices. Generally speaking, extreme camera angles emphasize the meaning of the projected image. A high-angled shot suggests a different interpretation from that of a low-angled shot. Much of Orson Welles's masterpiece *Citizen Kane* (1941) is shot from a low angle, giving the characters a larger-than-life quality and thus emphasizing the politician Kane's mythical quality.[16] A close-up of Jane Fonda's face in *The China Syndrome* instead of a long shot of the nuclear reactor room subtly influences the moviegoer's perception of the situation. The use of close-ups serves a number of purposes, political and otherwise, in a film. Among them is the crucial function of drawing the audience deeply into the action. "We are held to films by the human face," Leo Braudy writes. "Faces hold us more than plot, direction, photography."[17] Close-ups are artistically and emotionally satisfying, but by focusing our attention on one person at a time, they may cause us to lose sight of the shared experiences of the characters or the historical and political context of events. All is reduced to the one person we see; everything is individualized. Movies do not have to do this, however, and directors from Griffith to Frank Capra, Robert Altman, Martin Ritt, Sidney Lumet, and Alan Pakula have found ways to let us see their central characters in larger contexts.

Sets, Props, and Special Effects

In many movies, settings are an important contributor to the theme and storytelling. Unlike stage sets, which are limited to a small physical area, movie sets can evoke anything from a small room to the vastness of outer space, thanks to the ever-evolving artistry of special effects. "In the best movies . . . settings are not merely backdrops for the action, but symbolic extensions of the theme," observes Giannetti.[18] The approaches of realism and formalism suggest greater use of location and studio sets, respectively, but realism can be forged on a Hollywood set as readily as formalism can be expressed using location shooting. Oliver Stone uses both approaches in his extremely formalistic *Natural Born Killers* (1994). This phrenetic film moves from cartoonlike set action to gritty outdoor scenes, allowing Stone to achieve a "combination of technical virtuosity and dark commentary on the modern American landscape."[19]

All the filmmaking techniques discussed earlier can help shape the audience's perceptions of a film's setting. Imagine, for example, the variety of messages extended by scenes ostensibly shot in the White House in movies ranging from romantic comedies (*The American President,* 1995) and political thrillers (*Absolute Power,* 1997) to powerful political biographies (*Nixon,* 1995). The same basic location can be manipulated to inform an endless variety of moods and messages.

Product Placement

A controversial aspect of film sets is the increasing intentional use of recognizable brand names in movies. Such placements are the results of negotiated contracts between product sponsors and film producers. In addition to the commercial information they extend to audiences, product placements tend to reinforce corporatism in American political culture. In *E.T.* (1982), a blockbuster directed by Steven Spielberg, an endearing alien is enticed to come out of hiding with Reese's Pieces candy. In the wake of the movie, sales of Reese's Pieces soared, and the result was the birth of modern product placement. Some directors, however, use products as an additional nod toward realism. In *The Last Detail* (1973), for example, stars Jack Nicholson, Otis Young, and Randy Quaid down endless cans of Schlitz beer in a variety of seedy bars and flophouses. In this case, the product's lowly status seems to reinforce the film's message of working-class antiauthoritarianism. Mark Miller, noting that many famous American auteurs have directed commercials (including, e.g., Robert Altman and Martin Scorsese), argues that movies and commercials are becoming increasingly similar in both form and content.[20] The political implications of product placement are unclear; extensive use of placements, however, seems to tell audiences that corporate America generally has the endorsement of the actors, the director, and the filmmaking industry.

Actors and Acting

Casting

The decision of which actors and actresses to cast in a movie can create and send political messages. Looking at the history of film, James Monaco argues that the fact that movie celebrities even exist is "evidence that film has radically altered traditional values": "Previously, heroic models for society were either purely fictional creations or real people of accomplishment (whom we knew at only one remove). Film fused the two types: real people became fictional characters. The concept of the 'star' developed—

and stars are quite different from 'actors.'"[22] According to Monaco, early film producers—apparently wary of the potential phenomenon of movie stardom—insisted that actors work anonymously; however, fan magazines soon appeared that identified stars such as Mary Pickford and Charlie Chaplin, and these early stars were soon vying for the first million-dollar movie contracts.[23]

Movie stars soon, if not immediately, begin to project messages based on the images their films have helped create for them. "Stars [are] the creation of the public: political and psychological models who demonstrate some quality that we admire."[24] Thus, the casting of an actor known for patriotic roles—Harrison Ford, for example—reassures an audience that the movie they are seeing supports national (American) values. John Wayne, of course, is perhaps the ultimate cinematic symbol of American political (and military) will. Tom Hanks's association with NASA in *Apollo 13* (1995) and the miniseries he produced, *From the Earth to the Moon* (1998), as well as his role in the World War II movie *Saving Private Ryan* and the television miniseries he produced, *Band of Brothers* (2001), cast him in an eternal American hero glow. Hanks is in many ways a modern-day Jimmy Stewart, a star whose presence in a film almost always signifies the goodness of America.

The images that stars take on can resonate in any number of political ways, including racial and sexual stereotypes. Denzel Washington won an Oscar for his portrayal of a corrupt, drug-dealing cop in *Training Day* (2001), an African-American stereotype that his previous film roles had eschewed but one that Hollywood audiences themselves were quick to recognize. By way of compensation for the lack of black actors in central roles, a different stereotypical role for blacks emerged in the late 1970s: the black judge whose on-screen time is minimal but who nonetheless seems important by virtue of wearing judicial robes.

Sometimes decisions are made to cast actors "against type," meaning in a role or situation that notably contrasts with their normal character type. This may be done in an attempt to highlight a particular message, as audiences will usually sense the contrast between a star's image and a particular role that diverges from it. When Hanks played a hit man in *Road to Perdition* (2002), it cut against the grain of his good-guy status.

Giannetti explains that stars generally can be divided into two categories: personality stars, who tend to play roles that "fit a preconceived public image," and actor stars, "who can play roles of greater range and variety." According to Giannetti, the so-called star system frequently cues the audience to the political values transmitted by a movie.[25] Personality stars such as Kevin Costner—because they project a more or less predictable image—are more likely to convey ideological messages than are actor stars such as Robert De Niro.

The politics–film nexus is further manifested when politicians to try (or least, seem to try) to emulate movie-star icons. Ronald Reagan's presidency was marked by frequent invocations of the American western movie hero. In California, meanwhile, actor Arnold Schwarzenegger used lines made famous by his own movies to promote his successful campaign for the office of governor. (We will further explore this reversal of the film–politics relationship in the next chapter.)

Characters

Certain types of characters—some frequently associated with certain film genres—tend to transmit political messages. Gianos notes that characters representing political figures frequently tend to be "male, white, at least middle-aged, overweight, self-important, not terribly bright, not terribly well-informed, and with a cigar."[26] Such stereotyping reinforces already negative views about politics and politicians that many filmgoers hold.

On the other hand, stereotypical underdog characters, frequently from minority groups or female, are often used to emphasize the struggle against "the system" or "the political establishment." Two successful films about political underdogs featured women: Sally Field (*Norma Rae,* 1979) and Julia Roberts (*Erin Brockovich,* 2000). Both played feisty, attractive, working-class women who prevail against the (predominantly male) establishment. The fact that these protagonists were female may have made the movies seem less threatening than similar films with male leads.

More generally, of course, stereotyped characters merely reflect dominant social conventions, values, and attitudes. Prostitutes, for example, are frequently portrayed as "hookers with hearts of gold," reflecting the tolerance (or familiarity, at least) that most audiences have for the commercialization of sex. Minority roles tend to be stereotyped in the sense that unless a script specifically calls for, say, a black policeman, most characters in a film are likely to be white. When a member of a racial or ethnic minority (particularly a nonstar) appears in a film, audiences are cued to expect something that reinforces stereotypes from that character.

Names

According to Gianos, even the names of movie characters are sometimes used to project a political message. The practice of using names to signify political and other themes carried over from literature into film. "Jefferson

Smith" of the film classic *Mr. Smith Goes to Washington* suggests both a common man and a representative of America's patriotic past. The title role of *Bulworth* suggests that a politician is worth (or full of) bull. Frequently, the significance of character names is lost on the audience and only noticed by film critics and buffs in hindsight. The letters of the evil computer's name "HAL" in *2001: A Space Odyssey* (1968) are one letter removed from "IBM."[27]

Distribution and Promotion

As we noted in Chapter 1, a movie is unlikely to have great political impact if nobody sees it. The extent to which a movie is distributed and promoted is critical. The film industry has become increasingly dominated by a few conglomerate companies, in part because of the astronomical cost of producing blockbuster attractions. Although hundreds of cheaper, "smaller" independent films are produced each year, they are unlikely to be seen outside of a few film festivals and (in some cases) large American cities. Gomery links this centralization of the film industry to the content of movies: "To those who champion film as an art form, the coming of media conglomerates has meant that corporate chieftains prefer safe, formulaic films to even the most elementary experimentation. To those who look to film to help with ideological struggle, media conglomerates have effectively strangled the marketplace and kept alternative means of expression marginalized."[28]

Viewing

The culmination of the filmmaking process is, of course, an audience seeing a completed film in the theater. To this point, we have explained how various aspects of the movie production process can foster the transmission of political messages. This perspective, however, assumes that audiences can receive messages and that the received messages are somehow effective in altering the perceptions, attitudes, and ultimately the actions of movie audiences. What is there about the moviegoing experience that might lead us to believe in the power of movies as "independent variables" that may affect the minds and ultimately the behavior of audiences?

In contrast to a vast literature that dissects the political meaning of hundreds of movies, very little empirical research has been devoted to testing their actual impact on their audiences. Few would debate that movies (and other vehicles of popular culture) have *no* impact, but the extent to which films—individually and collectively—change political behavior is largely unknown; however, using reason and observation, it is possible to buttress the case for the efficaciousness of films on American politics.

As Gianos notes, going to the movies is both a special and a social event. Compared to, for example, watching television, going to a movie requires initiative on the part of the audience. Although the audience usually consists of strangers, there is nevertheless a communal aspect of experiencing a film. At a movie theater, the screen and sound command our attention as television generally cannot, so we are perhaps more susceptible to, or at least more accessible to, whatever messages a movie may transmit.[29]

A significant development in recent years has been the advent of home theater systems that enable at least a portion of the moviegoing experience to be re-created in the homes of many Americans. The DVD movie format enhances the at-home experience with higher sound and picture quality, with greater accessibility afforded by ubiquitous video-rental shops. Although such equipment cannot quite match the grandeur of a large movie theater, its impressive visual and sound quality does make it even more likely that more films will have the opportunity to affect the minds of the American public.

Movies are always more than mere entertainment. They can illuminate our society and political system. They can increase our understanding of government and politics. Some also can help shape the way we think and feel about politics and political participation. Some films try very hard to persuade, advocating policy positions on current issues. A few political films, such as *The Birth of a Nation* (1915) and *The China Syndrome* (1979), appear to have had a direct impact on politics. Did *The Day After Tomorrow* (2004) impact the debate over global warming?

Every film that deals even peripherally with politics contributes to our political socialization—that is, our familiarity with the political system and our understanding of the part we play in it. Through this process, we are taught our society's political ideas and values as well as its accepted political behavior, such as voting and deference to elected officials. The most important agents of political socialization are the family, peer groups, friends, and schools, but in a mobile, atomized, fragmented society like the United States, where families break down and friends and peer groups change, political scientists believe that the media gain power as socializing agents.

All mass media contribute to this political socialization, but movies are the least studied, except perhaps in terms of sexism and racism. The other political messages of films may have received less attention because their impact is difficult to measure or because political films are seldom blockbusters. But political socialization is a cumulative process, to which many forces contribute, and movies are part of that process—teaching, reinforcing, and sometimes even challenging. Film heroes and heroines become our role models. They teach us that we cannot fight city hall, or that we can, and under what conditions.

Movies may be a particularly powerful medium of political socialization because of the way we see them. We go voluntarily, often for social reasons, with a positive, receptive attitude. We expect to be entertained, so our guard is down. We do not go to learn, yet any teacher will tell you that the first problem in teaching is getting the student's attention, and that is what movies are designed to do. The social aspects of moviegoing also enhance their influence. Most of us go to the movies with someone else, and afterward we talk about the film. Perhaps this talk is mostly about acting and action, but sometimes content is mentioned. "Well, maybe nuclear power isn't such a hot idea after all," we say, or "I don't think all politicians are really *that* bad." Any talk at all extends the socializing power of movies, strengthening their message or hardening people's rejection of it.

The communal nature of moviegoing also intensifies the experience. When a film holds an audience in rapt attention, when they laugh or cry or boo or applaud, we know something is happening, and the movie's effect is more powerful. The process begins even before we go to the movie because the larger audience helps us choose which film to see. Ads, critics, conversations, friends, the particular people whose opinions about movies we respect—all encourage us to see a film and alert us to its significance. *Gandhi* (1982), for example, was an improbable success. Americans got the idea that this biography of a foreign pacifist was a "significant" film, a "must see." And they did, often applauding at the end.

Movies also are one of the few things to which we give our exclusive attention. Turn around and look at the rest of the audience sometime. They sit in the dark, eyes riveted to the screen and totally attentive to the unfolding story, letting waves of sound and image pour over them. The power of movies is further enhanced by their appeal to emotion rather than intellect through nonverbal elements such as close-ups and music. This emotional manipulation makes movies more effective socializers, giving them a power beyond words. Over half of today's filmgoers are under age twenty-one, and the power of movies may be even greater for them because they are probably more impressionable than older filmgoers. That should make us at the least apprehensive about the crude political messages of some popular films of the 1980s, like *Rambo* (1985) and *Invasion U.S.A.* (1985).

Other media, especially television, may be more pervasive—and invasive—but movies are a formidable force for the gentle inculcation of ideas and for persuasion. They remain the most talked about and most reviewed medium. Their power is even greater because we regard them as mere entertainment and are sometimes unconscious of their influence on us. Only when political films cross the line from entertainment into direct persuasion and propaganda do we begin to resist, and even then we may be unconsciously influenced.

Political films also can help us understand the forces we fear, putting them in perspective and thereby affecting how we cope with them. Movies that deal with war, corruption, racism, assassination, or the danger of a nuclear accident provide either catharsis or reassurance. "Entertainment is not a full-scale flight from our problems," Michael Wood writes, "not a means of forgetting them, but rather a rearrangement of our problems into shapes which tame them."[30] Movies also are historical artifacts that help us understand the past and how people then thought about politics. And films may even give voice to a society's subconscious fears and desires. German film theorist Siegfried Kracauer asserts that "the films of a nation reflect its mentality in a more direct way than other artistic media [because they] address themselves and appeal to the anonymous multitude [and] satisfy . . . mass desires."[31]

Some theorists, known as structuralists because they search for the underlying structures of societies in their myths and stories, see movies as our modern myths, symbolically expressing our deep subconscious. Structuralists tend to focus on horror movies and the like, but explicitly political films also express the wishes, needs, and fears of a nation, reflecting the longing for a strong leader or concern about a war or a new group of immigrants. In so doing, they may arouse us or set our minds at rest.

Movies influence our taste in fashions, hairstyles, music, dance, and cars. A single appearance by Clark Gable without an undershirt in *It Happened One Night* (1934) is said to have devastated the men's underwear business. More than forty years later, Diane Keaton's ragamuffin look in *Annie Hall* (1977) set a trend in women's fashions. In the same way, political movies can shape the way we think and talk about politics, helping to define, clarify, and entrench issues or attitudes. President Reagan, for example, often relied on catchphrases from movies in order to make his point. He quoted Knute Rockne ("Win one for the Gipper."), Dirty Harry ("Go ahead—make my day."), Obe Wan Kanobe ("The force is with us."), and Rambo ("We get to win this time.") along with other movie characters. If movies can affect our behavior in these matters, is it difficult to believe that they can alter our political behavior, both individually and collectively?

Besides contributing to the way we think and talk about politics, political moviemakers sometimes make a conscious attempt to influence political issues and even to provoke action. *Country* (1984), *The River* (1984), and *Places in the Heart* (1984), for example, tried to build sympathy for the plight of farmers. Similarly, *The China Syndrome* (1979) and *Silkwood* (1983) were explicit warnings about the dangers of nuclear energy. Throughout the 1980s, political filmmakers debated American involvement in Central America and Vietnam. Films like these consciously seek to persuade. Others do so unintentionally. Twenty-eight people are alleged to have died playing Russian roulette after seeing *The Deer Hunter*, and John Hinckley Jr. is supposed to have gotten the idea of shooting President Reagan from *Taxi Driver* (1976).

Filmmakers, however, argue that the influence works both ways. "Mass entertainment," one analyst insists, "cannot depart too far from the tastes and beliefs of the masses."[32] Moviemakers bear their audiences in mind as they create their products. They are constantly aware that audiences seek entertainment, not offense, so it is safer to make movies that reinforce people's biases rather than try to change them. The content of a film may thus be, at least to some extent, a reflection of what its audience already believes. "Our condition," observes the fictitious movie producer in F. Scott Fitzgerald's novel, *The Last Tycoon,* "is that we have to take people's own favorite folklore and dress it up and give it back to them."[33]

Political films, then, may reflect rather than shape the nation's politics because that is the safest way to draw an audience. When political movies attempt to convert us, they risk being rejected as propaganda if they come on too strong or not making their point at all if they are subtle.

Even the most tendentious American political movies usually opt to persuade gently, however, perhaps by introducing us to issues about which the filmmakers think we are uninformed, like nuclear energy in 1979. Or they try to communicate to us how it feels to be discriminated against, or they evoke our sympathy by using stars in sensitive roles. Sidney Poitier probably did more than we know to increase white tolerance of blacks in the 1960s, while Jack Lemmon gave credibility to middle America's doubts about nuclear power and about U.S. involvement in the Chilean counterrevolution (in *The China Syndrome* and *Missing,* respectively). Costa-Gavras, one of the most consistently ambitious and successful makers of overtly political films, says that films do not make big changes, "but they can make people feel a little, discuss a little."[34]

The effect of movies on audiences is not a one-way street, for audiences— or filmmakers' perceptions of audiences—also influence politics in the movies not only because decades of boycotts and protests have made filmmakers cautious about political subjects but also because the box office has become the ultimate measure of a movie's success. To sell tickets, filmmakers try to please us. We in turn expect to be entertained, perhaps because movies have trained us to. Collectively, we seem to prefer to be terrified by slasher movies rather than forced to think by social or political commentary. Many filmmakers therefore refrain from making us think by muting their films' political content or rejecting politics altogether. The political message of a movie may be played down to avoid offending any major segment of the diverse American audience or it may be moderated so that as many people as possible will agree with it and buy tickets.

Unfortunately, audiences have been changing in ways that can only increase the difficulties political filmmakers face in reaching them. "The audience today is dumber than it was," says Sidney Lumet. "They're morons. They don't know how to behave in theaters—they can't even be quiet. . . . They're totally corrupted by the television experience. And they expect the same television emotional results: sentimentality instead of emotion, tactile sensation and shock instead of thrill."[35] Accustomed to TV, we grow impatient with wordy movies or slow, subtle films that take time to build characters and approach their points. Our impatience impels filmmakers to oversimplify, goose up their movies with action, or avoid talk. Films today must grab us and take us for a fast ride not only because of our TV orientation but also and significantly because movie audiences are young; a majority is under twenty-four years of age, and this is the only segment of the audience that is growing. The bigger this part of the audience gets, the more moviemakers go after it and the less articulate their movies become.

Some scholars of politics and popular culture, however, argue that the impact of film upon political life is far more potent than that implied by the experience itself. According to political scientist James Combs, movies have a direct and profound impact on our entire political system:

> In the twentieth century, the movies have been a central aspect of the American popular experience. They have expanded and enriched the popular imagination while deriving much of what they depicted from that imagination. The relationship between the movies and us is truly transactional, an interplay of the influence between moviemakers and movie audiences (as well as the larger population and power structure) that takes subtle twists and turns in the relationship as time goes by. The imagination of moviemakers extends popular experience, and the experience of moviewatching extends the popular imagination. Although we shall never know for sure, it seems reasonable to conclude that the movie experiences have made a difference in the shaping of our national imagination, in other words, that we would not be whom we are, nor do what we do, without the movies.[36]

Perhaps identifying and verifying the true impact of movies on American politics is indeed impossible. Intuitively, however, Combs's argument is a strong one, and students of politics ignore the world of movies and their political messages at their peril.

3

Causes and Special Effects
The Political Environment of Film

Film star and California governor, Arnold Schwarzenegger

This book focuses mostly on the content of movies themselves and how it may create political messages and therefore potentially affect the political system. However, as we noted in Chapter 1, the relationship between politics and film is scarcely a one-way street: the political system interacts directly with the world of film in a variety of ways. In fact, in many instances it is difficult to ascertain which is affecting which. For example, a study of American movie plots from 1920 to 1960 found a sharp rise in the number that portrayed "foreign elements as a danger to the hero/heroine" from 1940 to 1944.[1] Presumably, filmmakers were responding to the threat of World War II as they created movies with foreign villains. At the same time, however, these movies portraying "foreign" danger were intended to shore up popular support for American war efforts and might be viewed as propaganda. So these films reflected the political reality of the times, but also were intended to affect it.

On a much more individual scale, some observers noted that when President George W. Bush celebrated the putative end of hostilities in the Iraqi war in 2003 by landing on an aircraft carrier in a jet fighter, the resulting image strongly resembled the movie *Independence Day* (1996), in which a president flies a fighter plane to battle alien invaders. Did this movie somehow inspire President Bush or his staff to re-create the scene and somehow profit politically from the resemblance? Or did the movie merely seek to reinforce the common stereotype of the president as superhero-savior?

When filmmaker Michael Moore accepted an Oscar in March 2003, his brief speech included the following broadside: "We live in a time where fictitious election results give us a fictitious president. We are now fighting a war for fictitious reasons. Whether it's the fiction of duct tape or the fictitious 'Orange Alerts,' we are against this war, Mr. Bush. Shame on you, Mr. Bush, shame on you."[2] Moore's comments brought film-based political controversy about the war into American living rooms and made him a bête noire among conservative commentators. How do Moore and other entertainment industry figures participate in the political process, and with what impact?

The complicated relationships between the world of movies and the real world of politics are frequently difficult to distinguish. In this chapter, we focus on aspects of movies and moviemaking that are generally *external* to the movies themselves. We explore the various ways in which the world of politics (and economics) seems to affect the movies and the movie industry, generally recognizing that the relationship is usually bilateral.

The Red Scare and McCarthyism: HUAC and Hollywood

The most obvious and perhaps most noteworthy impingement of politics into the world of film was the Red Scare of the late 1940s. Led by Senator Joseph

McCarthy, the House Un-American Activities Committee (HUAC) of the U.S. Congress presided over a ruthless interrogation of film and television industry figures. Claiming that Hollywood had been subverted by foreign Communists, McCarthy and his allies used HUAC hearings to publicly expose supposed agents of the Soviet Union. But the greater impact of the HUAC hearings was the response by Hollywood, which was essentially to blacklist (refuse to hire) individuals who refused to cooperate with the committee by providing it with names of their associates who might have been involved with the Communist Party.

The House Un-American Activities Committee discovered Hollywood in 1939 when it held its first hearing on subversion in the film industry. The committee returned in 1947 to begin investigations that resulted in a cause célèbre, the Hollywood Ten—a group of moviemakers who were jailed on a charge of contempt of Congress for refusing to talk about their political activities. The Hollywood Ten included Edward Dmytryk, Dalton Trumbo, and John Howard Lawson—all of whom had directed or written political films. Hollywood at first rallied to their defense, then cravenly backed off and introduced the infamous blacklist, systematically refusing to employ men and women who had allegedly supported leftist causes. The investigation continued until well into the 1950s, destroying many careers and helping others, and influencing the kinds of movies that were or were not made.

The film industry was not the only major American institution that was investigated by the anti-Communist crusaders, but it was a special attraction because of the massive press coverage it produced and because of the presumed power of the movies. Besides, Hollywood really was a center of liberal and even Communist political activity. The Communist Party had made the industry a special organizing target in 1936, a move that reflected Lenin's belief in the power of cinema. Proclaiming that movies are "the weapon of mass culture," the party organizers urged their recruits to at least "keep anti-Soviet agitprop" out of the movies they worked on.[3] The Communist Party had some recruiting success during the Great Depression, the New Deal years, and the Spanish Civil War, but news of Stalin's purges and the Nazi-Soviet nonaggression pact stopped its advances. In the 1950s, HUAC finished it off.

Communist infiltration of Hollywood was never very successful, however, and the investigators probably knew it. They found a lot of film people who leaned to the left, but HUAC never came up with evidence of undue party influence on the movies. The investigators kept looking, however, because they were less interested in reality than in publicity, and glamorous Hollywood provided plenty of that. Besides, the investigations gave ambitious, conservative congressmen like Richard Nixon a chance to attack people they did not like much anyway—for many of Hollywood's elite were rich, Jewish, liberal, Democratic, and intellectually arrogant.

The HUAC investigations provided an opportunity for politicians to bring mighty Hollywood to its knees, and they did. Dozens of film workers were jailed, usually for contempt of Congress as defined by their refusal to testify against their friends. Others were forced to inform on friends and coworkers to save their own careers.

Even the unions joined the purge, after initially resisting. "Do they [HUAC] expect us to constitute ourselves as a little FBI of our own and determine just who is a commie and who isn't?" Ronald Reagan reasonably demanded as president of the Screen Actors Guild (SAG), but soon he, too, was testifying that there were cliques in SAG that "follow the Communist party line."[4] Liberals also joined the purge, and some Hollywood Jews became particularly vigorous anti-Communists because they were afraid the attacks would turn anti-Semitic.[5] Once the united front was broken, every member of the film industry was on his or her own. Some, like director Elia Kazan and a young Ronald Reagan, cooperated fully with the committee. Others, like writer Dalton Trumbo, resisted and went to jail. Still others, like playwright Lillian Hellman, talked about their own activities but refused to name anyone else.

Ironically, the investigators found little evidence of subversion in the testimony of those who were willing to talk. Walt Disney alleged that the Cartoonists Guild had tried to "subvert" Mickey Mouse. Ginger Rogers's mother testified that her daughter had been given the line "Share and share alike—that's democracy" in *Tender Comrade* (see Chapter 4), a film written by Dalton Trumbo and directed by Edward Dmytryk, both members of the Hollywood Ten. Conservative novelist Ayn Rand cited "a suspicious number of smiling children" in *Song of Russia* and also pointed out certain suspicious elements in *Mission to Moscow* and *The North Star*.[6] All three movies were transparently pro-Russian, however, because they had been made with government encouragement to strengthen the U.S.–Soviet alliance during World War II. They were not hits, and they were poor evidence of a Communist conspiracy.

For all its efforts, HUAC never came up with much evidence of Communist propaganda in American movies, much less a massive conspiracy. Most of those accused had worked on patriotic war movies as well as projects that reflected a liberal ideology. In fact, Hollywood's radicals never got much beyond defending President Theodore Roosevelt and attacking fascism. Dorothy Jones's detailed analysis of 300 films on which Hollywood "Reds" worked reveals that some were "vaguely liberal," but none contained actual Communist propaganda. Furthermore, "none of the 159 films credited over a period of years to the Hollywood Ten contained communist propaganda" or were cited by the conservative Motion Picture Association of America (MPAA) for such content. Jones argues that the collegial method of making films fragmented responsibility and muted any propaganda, while "the habitual caution of moviemakers with respect to film content" and the "self-regulating practices of the motion picture industry as carried on by the Motion Picture Association" were further preventives.[7]

HUAC, however, did not require evidence to act. The impact of the hearings and the blacklisting on Hollywood was immense. But as the HUAC hearings proceeded, it became virtually impossible to bankroll a film with a leftist message. Instead, between 1947 and 1954 almost forty "explicitly propagandistic anti-Communist films" were made in Hollywood,[8] including such formidable viewing fare as *The Red Menace* (1949), *I Married a Communist* (1950), and *I Was a Communist for the FBI* (1951) (see Chapter 7). Although nearly all of these movies lost money, the studios continued to put the products out, hoping to avoid further controversy. (We discuss the creation of propaganda per se later in this chapter.)

Many progressive film workers were driven out of the industry after the 1947 hearings, and many more followed after another round of hearings that began in 1951. A few committed suicide, some were imprisoned, others went into exile, and many merely went underground. Those who continued working avoided political subjects or social issues. Professor Jones discovered that while fully 28 percent of Hollywood productions in 1947 dealt with "social and psychological themes," only 9.2 percent fit into this category by 1954. She concludes that the HUAC attack was based less on real concern with the Communist threat than on a "fear . . . of movies getting serious about social and political problems."[9] Besides digging through Hollywood's past, the investigations intended to influence its future, and they did.

The blacklist was eventually broken, and eventually many of those who had been demonized by the Red Scare were recognized as heroes by the Hollywood community. Several movies (*The Front,* 1976, and *Guilty by Suspicion,* 1991) have dealt with the period in a way that depicts the blacklisted individuals as victims and/or heroes, and their accusers as evil incarnate. In fact, a sort of backlash has occurred as some individuals who were known to have cooperated with HUAC became themselves the object of scorn and isolation from the Hollywood mainstream.

The chief impact of this period in film history is to clearly illustrate the potentially awesome influence of the government on free and creative expression. "When the question was raised, the moguls of Hollywood and Madison Avenue came to heel at the behest of a congressional committee without formal authority over them as meekly as the most obedient member of the Soviet cultural committees under Stalin and Khrushchev," writes one scholar.[10] Contemporary advocates of free expression frequently invoke the misdeeds of the era when defending the industry against its critics. Some contend that the entire episode marked a watershed for American films, transforming them from frequently progressive and artistically challenging vehicles to vacuous and politically toothless husks.[11]

Censorship and Regulation

Another important way that politics affects movies is by means of the government's authority (or potential authority) to regulate and censor the film industry. Although various local governments enacted censorship statutes during the early days of the cinema, the most notable era of film censorship in the United States occurred when the Motion Picture Producers and Distributors of America (MPPDA) adopted the so-called Hays Code. Named after its author, Postmaster General Will Hays, the notorious code went far beyond simply prohibiting nudity and swearing in films. It included provisions that regulated the conduct of actors and actresses off the set as well.

By the end of World War I, pioneer moviemaker D.W. Griffith and others had made the movies a widely accepted art form with an expanding middle- and upper-class audience. Recognizing the potential influence of films, the nation's economic and intellectual elite became concerned that this influence might be subversive. The fact that the film industry was dominated by immigrants and Jews made the Yankee elite even more nervous, and they soon advocated government inspection of movies. Film scholar Robert Sklar argues that "the struggle over movies was an aspect of the struggle between classes," with the proponents of censorship demanding the suppression of "any idea or image harmful to the moral, social or political health of the state."[12]

By the early 1920s, eight states and ninety cities had established censors, and in 1922 the public outcry over a widely reported Hollywood sex scandal produced demands for national censorship. Filmmakers reacted defensively by forming the MPPDA with Will H. Hays, a political crony of President Warren G. Harding, as its executive. The Hays Office was hyped as a self-policing effort by a concerned industry, but it was really a symbolic action intended to ward off government censorship, and it worked, at least for a time.

Initially subservient to its studio masters, the Hays Office attempted to keep a lid on the private immoralities of the stars. But soon Hays grew bolder, producing a list of two hundred "morally dangerous" people who were banned from movies. He also published an "index" of books and plays deemed unsuitable for the cinema for moral or political reasons. In 1927, Hays issued a list of "don'ts" and "be carefuls," warning the industry to keep away from certain subjects, including drug addiction, sexual deviance, miscegenation, and nudity. Any violations of the Ten Commandments, or the Hays amendments to them, were permissible only if the perpetrators ended unhappily. Hollywood could titillate its audience, but the final message had to be that sinners were punished.

Though rarely specifically directed at political films, this censorship must have discouraged those who considered producing such movies. Some observers argue that the limits on expression created by the Hays Code were a primary reason for the near disappearance of social and political criticism from a once-progressive mainstream film industry. Or perhaps the cautious motion pictures of the 1920s reflected a decade of prosperity, isolationism, and dull, conservative presidents. The emergence of the big studios also must have contributed to the caution and conservatism among political filmmakers. Like factories, these studios churned out movies feverishly for an ever-expanding audience. Their near-monopolistic control of the industry, extending to distribution and exhibition, discouraged independent-minded filmmakers and led to reliance on traditional plots and genres, with only slight variations. Nevertheless, the sheer volume of films being produced let some political and even less-than-conservative movies slip through.

The enactment of the Hays Code was the result of pressure by religious and political leaders after a series of Hollywood scandals in the 1920s that involved sex and drugs. Although it did not constitute government censorship, per se—because members of the motion picture association complied voluntarily—the code represented de facto censorship, making it difficult if not impossible for films to deal with sensitive social issues. If the studios occasionally skirted and toyed with its provisions, the code was nevertheless, on the whole, a highly effective means of limiting creative expression, and one that did not require political debate. In the 1960s, however, broad societal change (along with the collapse of the rigid Hollywood studio system) made the code obsolete. A reconfigured industry group, the Motion Picture Association of America (MPAA), moved to create a new means of regulating film content. Jack Valenti, a former fighter pilot with ties to the Kennedy and Johnson administrations, was appointed president of the MPAA and charged with the challenge of creating a new, more workable system of regulating cinematic content.

Of this task, Valenti said:

> From the very first day of my own succession to the MPAA President's office, I had sniffed the Production Code constructed by the Hays Office. There was about this stern, forbidding catalogue of "Dos and Don'ts" the odious smell of censorship. I determined to junk it at the first opportune moment. I knew that the mix of new social currents, the irresistible force of creators determined to make "their" films and the possible intrusion of government into the movie arena demanded my immediate action.[13]

Working as quickly as his words would imply, Valenti created the ratings system which is still in effect (with a few changes over the years).

As was the case with the Hays Code, the MPAA ratings system does not represent overt censorship, since compliance is voluntary and the government is not formally involved in its machinations. Instead, a panel of from eight to thirteen individuals, whose views are supposed to reflect those of the average American parent, constitutes the Classification and Ratings Administration (CARA) or film-rating board. CARA panelists—all of whom must be parents or former parents—view films months before they are released and pronounce their ratings, using the now familiar G, PC, PC-13, R, and NC-17 rating scale.

Whereas the film rating system has undoubtedly freed movie creators to delve into more controversial (and politically charged) subject matter than during the days of the Hays Code, it is not without potential for censorship-like impacts on movies. The rating system places enormous pressure on filmmakers to change their work to suit the tastes of the CARA panel, as box office receipts are highly sensitive to the film ratings. Relatively few cinemas will show NC-17 movies, and even fewer will show unrated movies.

What frequently occurs, therefore, is proactive editing by moviemakers in an effort to remove the NC-17 stigma. This reportedly occurred in the case of 662 films in 1998 alone. (Similar machinations also occur with respect to R-rated movies seeking higher ratings, although sometimes producers actually prefer an R-rating to a PC-13 or PC rating.) Furthermore, an unknown number of films are either never made or are significantly modified to satisfy the ratings system.

Says Chris Roth, "this scenario is unsettling because legal, adult-to-adult communication was eliminated."[14] Roth quotes a representative of the American Civil Liberties Union (ACLU) as saying, "The 'look and feel' of the film can be changed when a sequence is cut or shortened. It is very difficult to put limits and bounds on things and pretend that the film is not being significantly altered."[15] Additionally, the ratings system is frequently criticized for consistently allowing much more violence than sexual or other controversial content.

From time to time, the content of movies inspires political debate. In the election of 2000, Democratic vice presidential candidate Joe Lieberman made a series of high-profile attacks on Hollywood and other entertainment outlets. Lieberman accused the film industry specifically of corrupting America's culture and its children. Oddly, one of his attacks occurred shortly before the Democratic Party convention in Los Angeles as President Clinton was being feted by Hollywood stars at a fund-raising party. Lieberman warned that Washington might impose legal restrictions if Hollywood refused to "draw some lines themselves."[16]

Although the content of American movies is a continuing source of public debate (and Lieberman had some history of criticizing the film industry), the issue was scarcely begging for comment. Instead, it appeared that the attacks were part of a conscious effort by Lieberman and presidential candidate Al Gore to give themselves a "hard moral edge" and distance themselves from the publicly perceived moral lapses of President Clinton. In fact, such attacks are rarely part of a serious policy agenda, and both parties use the film industry as a whipping boy to impress that part of the electorate that responds to this sort of moral indignation. Both parties accepted millions in campaign contributions from the entertainment industry, and serious government intervention into filmmaking seems unlikely in the near term.

Political Involvement by Hollywood Celebrities and the Film Industry

An obvious and apparently growing phenomenon that further blurs the line between film and politics is the enlistment of various members of the moviemaking industry into political campaigns and causes. Such involvement can run the gamut of what political scientists consider "political participation," ranging from making donations to campaigns and political organizations to actually running for (and holding) political office. (We discuss the latter case in a separate subsection.)

For many years, the actor who perhaps most exemplified a political image to many Americans was John Wayne. Most of his preeminence as a political icon stems from his films, many of which he chose and altered to promulgate his political views. But Wayne was also an activist. In 1948 (amidst the hoopla of the HUAC hearings on Hollywood), Wayne became president of the Motion Picture Alliance for the Preservation of American Ideals, a group that had helped create the Red Scare by inviting HUAC to investigate Hollywood. In the 1960s, Wayne joined the infamous right-wing John Birch Society, a group that claimed that the U.S. government was secretly run by Communists. He publicly endorsed a number of conservative Republican candidates and over time became a symbol of that aspect of American political life.[17] Wayne's status as a political symbol is inextricable from his activities as a political participant.

Another star who engaged in political activism, albeit one with a larger reputation as a popular singer, was Frank Sinatra. To perhaps a greater degree than John Wayne, Sinatra paved the way for entertainers to become high-profile political figures. Generally, Hollywood figures had avoided overt partisan political activity lest their public images become controversial and drive away their audience. Originally an outspoken Democrat (who was accused of Communist sympathies by HUAC), Sinatra sang for Democratic presidential nominee Adlai Stevenson at a large election-eve rally and was a close friend and ardent supporter of John F. Kennedy.

Due to a snub from Kennedy that was perceived, if not real, Sinatra eventually converted to the Republican Party in the 1970s. He supported California gubernatorial candidate Ronald Reagan. He was a heavy contributor to Richard Nixon's 1972 reelection campaign and an even more visible supporter of Vice President Spiro Agnew, loaning him $200,000 after his scandalous resignation from office. He raised $250,000 for the Reagan presidential campaign. Although Sinatra was occasionally an embarrassment to those he supported, his advocacy of candidates and causes proved to the rest of the entertainment world that such involvement was not anathema to commercial success.[18]

Flashing forward to the contemporary scene, Hollywood celebrities have gradually become de rigueur fixtures on the American political scene. Film industry personnel have become visible and vocal participants in all types of political causes and campaigns. Bill Clinton's campaigns fueled the practice and gained notoriety for including the financial and in-kind support of such Hollywood figures as Steven Spielberg, Barbra Streisand, Alec Baldwin, and a host of others.

Both parties culled a host of Hollywood celebrities to their causes in the bitterly fought 2000 presidential election. Democratic candidate Al Gore received support from such moviemaking mainstays as Oliver Stone, Rob Reiner, and Kevin Costner, whereas Republicans were swift to counter with their own bevy of tinsel, including contributions from Chuck Norris, Jack Valenti, and Bruce Willis. Both parties received contributions in the millions of dollars from the film and entertainment industries. (Not to be outdone, Green Party candidate Ralph Nader boasted support from Warren Beatty and Susan Sarandon.) However, the Democratic Party has received significantly more donations from the film industry specifically. In eight national elections between 1990 and 2004, Democratic candidates received 87 percent of the more than $46 million in total contributions from the "movie production" industry.[19] According to another account, before the 2004 election cycle had begun, "Hollywood had given the Democratic Party contributions roughly equivalent to what Republicans received from their friends in the oil and gas industries."[20]

Of course, other political causes boasted their stars and benefactors, such as the National Rifle Association (actor Charlton Heston became its president), the National Abortion Rights Action League (actress Cybil Shepherd is a frequent spokesperson), and so on. The 2004 campaign looked to reprise the star-studded 2000 campaign, although election-law changes lowered the amount of money individuals could contribute.

The overall impact of this phenomenon and whether it is of lasting political import are difficult to ascertain. It certainly further frays the line between Hollywood imagination and political reality. The motives of Hollywood celebrities are probably the same as those of other elites—they can use their status to pursue their political goals much more easily than average citizens. They also may be attracted to particular candidates and perhaps aspire to be regarded as serious public figures. Politicians and political organizations presumably value celebrities for the fund-raising cachet they bring to campaigns and, perhaps, the glamour. Political scientist Michael Nelson sees an additional reason to suspect that the affinity will continue:

> Entertainers and politicians face similar challenges. Whether on screen or on the hustings, they must woo the public and adjust to changes in style and taste. Since the 1980s, the distinction [between the public and private lives of politicians] no longer has prevailed in media coverage of politics. In almost all aspects of their careers, therefore, celebrities and politicians can not only help each other, but can also empathize with each other in a way that few outsiders can.[21]

Actors as Politicians, Politicians as Actors

Although much of interest in the subject of film and politics concerns how actors *portray* politicians, the logical conclusion of the trend of celebrity involvement in politics is actors actually *becoming* politicians. Before Ronald Reagan's improbable rise from actor to governor of California to president, this scenario seemed unlikely. But the electability of actors (and other celebrities, such as professional wrestler and Minnesota governor Jesse Ventura) is no longer at question nor even novel. Nevertheless, the 2004 election of action-film actor Arnold Schwarzenegger to the governership of California seemed to transfix the nation anew.

As we have seen, the distinction between the roles of actors and politicians has diminished in recent decades. Hastened by the overwhelming importance of the mass media—and particularly television—politicians increasingly seem to need to be able to demonstrate their acting ability in order to succeed. That professional actors would thrive at this challenge is hardly surprising.

When George H.W. Bush said to Congress, "Read my lips," he was consciously invoking the tough-guy image of Clint Eastwood's Dirty Harry. His son, George W. Bush, made similar use of cinematic tough-guy talk when he declared that the sponsors of terrorism against the United States were "wanted dead or alive," and we have referred to his cinematic landing on an aircraft carrier. "Bring 'em on," Bush declared, when asked about guerrilla attacks on U.S. troops in Iraq in 2003. But these incidents seem, on the whole, to be isolated and staged. Neither Bush is particularly convincing as an actor, it would seem, although the extent to which politicians' worldviews are derived from the world of movies is open to question. Such free appeal to movie lines and imagery may reflect the increasing dominance of pop culture in the United States, according to English professor Allen Metcalf: "We're all so used to pop culture" that when Bush talks like a movie hero, "we get the message that he's serious, he's being tough."[22] It seems likely that political use of cinematic words and imagery will only increase in the coming decades.

What is perhaps even more significant is the prospect of politicians behaving like actors, in the sense of emulating movie roles and concepts drawn from cinematic fiction. Former House Speaker Newt Gingrich, when asked by a reporter whether he had gone too far when the federal government closed down over a 1995 budget dispute, replied, "I learned from Sgt. Striker [the hero of the John Wayne film *Sands of Iwo Jima,* 1949] that you have to be tough on your own for their own good. That was the formative movie in my life."[23] This type of cinematic "learning" is largely unexplored by political scientists, but clearly represents an important aspect of the politics–film nexus.

Similarly, Michael Rogin argues that Ronald Reagan's entire presidency was a kind of reenactment of his movie roles.[24] Analyzing Reagan's ascent from actor to the presidency, Rogin identifies a number of instances when Reagan drew from Hollywood movies for key phrases as well as conceptual foundation for his policies:

- During a 1980 Republican presidential debate, Reagan uttered, "I am paying for this microphone, Mr. Green." The line was spoken by Spencer Tracy as a fictional presidential candidate in the film *State of the Union* (1948).
- In 1983, Reagan remembered the pilot of a World War II bomber plane who was posthumously honored with the Congressional Medal for choosing to die aboard his crippled plane rather than abandon a wounded crew member. It was soon discovered that the hero in question was drawn from the 1944 war movie *A Wing and a Prayer.*
- Reagan's Strategic Defense Initiative system (commonly known as "Star Wars," but not inspired by that film) closely resembled the "inertia projector," a defense system that "stops and destroys anything that moves" in *Murder in the Air* (1940), which features a secret agent played by Reagan.

In Rogin's view, Reagan's entire worldview was etched by simplistic Hollywood movies that—among other things—presented an evil foe and an always virtuous America. The validity of his specific connections between movies and Reagan's words and actions as president is sometimes questionable, but Rogin's central argument about the power of film to transfix political elites must be taken seriously. It is consistent with the view of political scientists James Combs and Sara Combs that "the motion picture must be accorded a central role in the expansion of popular learning." [25] If even only marginally valid, Rogin's thesis casts the significance of understanding the political content of film to an even higher level.

Reagan is not the only president to be linked to Hollywood. Ian Scott's analysis of the Clinton presidency suggests similar patterns of the blur between the silver screen and the White House. In Scott's view, Clinton's reputed obsession with spin control stemmed directly from his "dangerous obsession with movie culture." [26] Scott interprets Clinton's facility and fascination with Hollywood personalities as a direct contributor to his actions as president.

Action hero Schwarzenegger was not loath to borrow from his movie roles on the campaign trail. He shouted "Hasta la vista, car tax!" (paraphrasing a line from *Terminator 2: Judgment Day,* 1991) as a crane dropped a weight onto a car to illustrate his promise to cut the unpopular tax. After his election in 2003, his campaign to pass a pair of citizen initiatives was to resemble "a Hollywood production, a neat blending of show business and politics." Schwarzenegger believes that acting and political leadership overlap significantly: "In acting what is important is that it's organic . . . and that you connecct to the people so they can look at the scene and buy in. But it's the same here [in government]. You have to connect with the people, and the more organic you are . . . that's what then makes people buy in." [27]

Propaganda and the Military Uses of Film

Another way that politics and film interact is through the creation of propaganda. The dictionary defines propaganda as "material disseminated by the advocates or opponents of a doctrine or cause." As media of all kinds are routinely used to persuade the public, propaganda is a "dominant form of communication," according to Combs and Combs. [28] We routinely sift through all kinds of propaganda every day, much of it in the form of advertising. Movies are particularly valuable as vehicles for propaganda because "much of the movie experience is play . . . more fun than work," thereby making movie audiences vulnerable to subtle forms of persuasion embedded in films. [29]

However, as Combs and Combs observe, "In some broad sense, *all* films have propaganda value, the potential to be used, or taken, as a message that should be propagated." [30] This statement is similar to our earlier contention that all movies must be considered in some way political, so we need to have a means of differentiating films that represent propaganda in its purest form from everyday, run-of-the-mill entertainment. For the purposes of this discussion, we will confine our focus to *government-created, -sponsored, or -enabled films* that seek to persuade the public in favor of governmental causes, specifically support for war-making efforts.

Combs and Combs trace the earliest propaganda to the Spanish–American War of 1898, when the War Department helped filmmakers film battle action at Fort Meade, Maryland, that glorified the American cause. Before America's entry into World War I, J. Stuart Blackton produced a film paradoxically titled *The Battle Cry of Peace* (1915), which advocated military preparedness and featured the "nefarious traits" that would characterize Germans throughout the century. Theodore Roosevelt promoted the movie, and 2,500 actual marines were allocated to the set. A competing, propacificist film, *Civilization* (1916), which was openly promoted by President Woodrow Wilson, quickly followed.

Once America entered the war, the Committee on Public Information (CPI) was formed with the mission of selling the war to the American public. The CPI and its director, George Creel, found that the movie industry was a willing ally in this effort; it produced trailers to sell war bonds, created "documentary" newsreels, and let its major stars tour the country in support of the war. Combs and Combs note that "the movies had proven to be powerful stuff, and now that power was available to anyonewho wanted to propagate a social or political message."[31]

World War II created the need for another movie to sell the American public on the need for war. The Office of War Information and various other government entities forged an alliance with the film industry's War Activities Committee. Combs and Combs write that "Washington did not merely want Hollywood to confirm, it also wanted the creative genius of the producers, writers, technicians, and directors."[32] Most prominently, director Frank Capra produced a series of motivational films for soldiers titled *Why We Fight* for the War Department. The films, directed by Capra and other Hollywood stalwarts such as John Huston and John Ford, were so successful that President Franklin D. Roosevelt ordered them to be shown to civilian groups, and millions of Americans viewed them.

The cold war opened up new avenues of government-sponsored propagandistic filmmaking. Combs and Combs note that "studios making war films could count on the assistance and cooperation of the military if they had a measure of script approval that would propagate a positive image."[33] Filmmakers who met this assurance were allowed access to military bases and other forms of what amounted to subsidization of propaganda films by the U.S. military. Such films included movies about the need for "preparedness" in the face of the Communistic threat, such as *Strategic Air Command* (1955) and *Take the High Ground* (1953).

The cozy relationship between filmmakers and the military fizzled somewhat with the onset of the Vietnam War, setting the stage for the generally more confrontational tone of the Vietnam (and Gulf) War movies that are discussed in later chapters. But the propaganda role served by movies in the form of military assistance to filmmakers continues, as films like *Top Gun* (1986) served as virtual reruitment films. At the same time, some films face a form of censorship when the military refuses to provide them with such assistance. Said director Oliver Stone, who was refused military assistance for his Vietnam War-era films, "They make prostitutes of us all because they want us to sell out to their point of view."[34]

An internal military memo concerning production of the popular spy film *Clear and Present Danger* (1994) expresses the situation even more explicitly:

> Perhaps the biggest hurdle the public service affairs officers had to overcome was the filmmakers' sense of our meddling in their product and our sense that they weren't taking us seriously. There was a tension, almost until the day filming began, which manifested itself in our comments which went unanswered in subsequent drafts of the script. When the filmmakers realized that unless the services were satisfied with the script, approval [from the military] would not be granted, the changes were finally made.[35]

More recently, the Marine Corps sucessfully "convinced" the producer of the Nicholas Cage film *Windtalkers* (2002) to delete a historically accurate scene in which a Marine pries gold teeth from the mouth of a dead Japanese soldier.[36]

Thus, the distinction between censorship and propaganda is sometimes blurred. It is difficult to imagine cooperation between government and filmmakers without some compromise of the purposes and products of the latter. Such a pattern seems most likely to occur in the context of war/military/espionage films, but can certainly spill over into films about crime, terrorism, and other politically sensitive issues.

Centralization of the Film Industry

A final way that the external world may affect movies is the organization of how they are produced, distributed, and shown. The salient pattern in this respect is the growing centralization and corporatization of film production, distribution, and exhibition. Except for MGM, the seven major movie studios in Hollywood are presently owned by global media conglomerates: Disney,

AOL/Time Warner, Viacom, News Corporation, General Electric, and Sony. The trend toward fewer firms controlling an increasingly greater proportion of the film industry is mirrored in the American mass media generally, as these same corporations also have vast holdings in other media, such as cable television, television stations, and the Internet. For example, by one estimate, whereas approximately fifty firms dominated the mass media in 1983, by 2001 that number had decreased to nine companies including those that own the Hollywood studios.[37]

The corporate control of the movie industry goes far beyond mere ownership of the studios. The same conglomerates also own significant interests in film distribution, video and DVD sales and rentals, theater ownership, ticket sales, and related merchandise. Among many other media-related outlets, Viacom, for example, owns Paramount Pictures and Blockbuster Video and co-owns United Cinemas with another conglomerate. Similarly, Vivendi Universal owns Universal Studios and several other studios, Universal Studios Distributing, Ticketmaster, and TicketWeb and co-owns Paramount Home Entertainment, as well as Universal Video & Music Distribution, Universal Studios Home Video, and MCA/Universal Merchandising.[38]

The impact of corporate ownership of film production and distribution companies (along with other mass media) is debatable and perhaps too recent to judge definitively; however, potential politically sensitive outcomes are readily identifiable. Perhaps the most frequently stated consequence is the belief that corporate owners, ever mindful of the bottom line, may further skew film production toward politically safe themes and content. This would effectively constitute corporate censorship of the entertainment industry.

For many observers, this effect is a fait accompli. *Variety* editor in chief Peter Bart believes that corporate ownership of the film industry has changed it "only about 150 percent." Bart explains that

> it's only in relatively recent years that Hollywood became the playground of multi-national corporations, which regard movies and TV shows as a minor irritant to their overall activity. So, it's become a corporate town. It was not a corporate town 10, 15 years ago. [I]t affects the decision-making process on movies, because, for example, what big corporations want most is risk-averse pictures.[39]

Furthermore, although the studios directly control relatively few cinemas in comparison to the golden age of the studio system, ownership of theaters and theater chains also is becoming increasingly centralized. One firm, the Anschutz Corporation, now owns close to 20 percent of the screens in the

United States, and corporate control of distribution and exhibition is on the rapid increase.[40] According to industry observer Jon Alon Walz, Anschutz and others who are acquiring theaters hope to cash in on the potential of digital projection technology to increase the profitability of owning large numbers of theaters. "Digital cinema" includes the production, delivery, and projection of full-length motion pictures in theaters using digital technology. Utilized to date in just thirty-four contemporary American theaters, the digital system distributes motion pictures that have been digitized, compressed, encrypted, and delivered to theaters using either physical media distribution (e.g., DVD-ROMs, tape, or hard-disk drive) or other electronic transmission methods (e.g., satellite or other broadband services). "With digital delivery to theatres, economies of scale at the 6,000-screen level and above might finally be possible. Freight and projector maintenance costs are eliminated, as is the job of film splicer and, for all practical purposes, projectionist."[41]

Such centralized ownership of cinemas could result in limitations on the viewing of politically controversial films. Anschutz Corporation owner Philip Anschutz, for example, is a financial patron of conservative causes such as Colorado's highly publicized Amendment 2, which would have overturned laws protecting gay rights. Politically motivated theater owners on the magnitude of Anschutz could conceivably limit the exposure of a film whose political messages they disliked.

Of course, not all movies are produced and distributed by the major studios and their corporate owners. Independent films (i.e., those not produced by the major Hollywood studios) are ostensibly the product of a more artistically liberated creative process. Such productions have come to be increasingly important in the film industry, particularly since the 1980s, when independent films like *Desperately Seeking Susan* (1985) and *El Norte* (1983) demonstrated that small, non-Hollywood movies could turn a profit. Every year hundreds of these small films are produced and released in hopes of re-creating the success of previous independent breakout successes like *Pulp Fiction* (1994) or *The Usual Suspects* (1995).

However, the trend among such films—at least the commercially successful ones—is increasingly toward cooptation by the larger film industry. First, the major studios have begun to see small films as potentially worthwhile investments, thereby providing competition in the turf of the independent films—small, independent, art house cinemas. Concomitantly, independent producers have been increasing the size of their budgets to become potentially more profitable. "[Independent filmmakers] are now no longer content with a modest profit, but instead want the next *Full Monty* or *The English Patient*. Ironically, earning studio-level gross profits has become a near necessity in the new economics of independent films, which now requires a significant infrastructure to accommodate increased demand."[42] In any event, without national distribution of their films, independent filmmakers cannot achieve much success at the box office.

The prospect for truly independent films to represent a significant counterbalance of political messages is small. Since the 1960s, the major film studios have accounted for approximately 95 percent of the domestic film marketplace. The remaining 5 percent goes to foreign films and to independent films that are bought by major studios.[43] So the number of people who are actually attending non-Hollywood films is quite small, although this group may prove to be unusually influential.

Nevertheless, independent cinema represents the potential for a true "cinema of outsiders," not tightly constrained by massive profit seeking or other corporate agendas. Truly small-scale and independent productions may thrive on the basis of the emergent digital filming and projection technology described earlier.

Conclusion

In this chapter, we have sketched the contours of forces external to the movies that have affected the creation of movies in the United States. It is an incomplete and somewhat arbitrary list, but it demonstrates that movies are not created in a political vacuum—they can be directly and profoundly impacted by the social, political, and economic environment of their times. Although several of the factors discussed in this chapter would seem to inveigh against the creation of overtly political if not controversial films, the fact is that such films continue to be made and viewed.

Most recently, the stunning commercial success of independent filmmaker Michael Moore's documentary *Fahrenheit 9/11* (2004, discussed in greater detail in Chapter 12) demonstrates that overt political content is not necessarily box office anathema. Moore's film exemplifies many of the concepts explored here, such as the use of film as propaganda (albeit antigovernment propaganda), the role of corporate distribution, the emergence of independent filmmaking, and actors as politicians as well as film as the object of political campaign debate. Whether over the longer term *Fahrenheit 9/11* proves to be merely an exception that proves the rule remains to be seen.

II

Political Films by Decade

4

Politics in the
Silent Movies

The Birth of a Nation (1915)

Although many movies reflected the social reality of the times, the overtly political films of the first period of American films—the Silent Age—were dominated by the work of one filmmaker, D.W. Griffith. In this chapter, we explore the political significance of silent motion pictures, paying special attention to the epic masterworks of this most influential director. As we shall see, Griffith exemplifies much of what critics admire and detest in mainstream films even in the contemporary era.

Because the medium was so new, the moving images of the first films must have powerfully affected viewers. Their impact was heightened by the excitement of live music, usually a piano banging away or, in classy establishments, an organ or sometimes even an orchestra. The power of these silent films is hard for us to imagine now, but thanks to the efforts of film historians, more of these movies can be seen today as they were originally seen—with music, appropriate technical equipment, and good prints—and more of us can experience the early cinema. Even so, the audience for these revivals is limited because today's moviegoers expect sound and because the melodramatic acting style that was necessary in a medium that used few words seems ludicrous now. But even if audiences were more accepting, access to the films of the silent era is limited. Many old movies are in museums or in private collections, and more have been lost as a result of neglect. But even a cursory study of these early movies reveals a variety of subjects, styles, and perspectives perhaps richer than that of later eras. This diversity was increased by foreign films, which were then fully accessible to audiences because language was not a barrier.

One- and Two-Reelers

Movies were telling stories, albeit short ones, right from the beginning. Limited to the amount of film that would fit on one reel of a projector, most early films, like Edwin S. Porter's *The Great Train Robbery* (1903), were less than fifteen minutes long. Predominantly comedies and melodramas, enough of the films of this era survive to give us an idea of what the founders of the American film industry thought about politics.

The birth of the medium at the turn of the century coincided with the Progressive movement, which dominated American politics into the 1920s. It was a time when crusading reformers and muckraking journalists attacked political machines and big economic interests. And filmmakers joined the attack. According to British film historian I.C. Jarvie, these early days of filmmaking rank with 1930–1934 and 1966–1976 as periods when films were most critical of American society.[1]

Films like *The Ex-Convict* (1905), for example, treated crime as a social problem, showing how poverty could drive a decent family man outside the law. Others, such as *The Eviction* (1907), condemned avaricious landlords. Bankers and factory owners were also targets of criticism. Workers, however, enjoyed a rare moment of favor in the film industry. This sympathy— perhaps a predictable bias in an era of reform—was evident in the treatment of labor–management conflict in films like D.W. Griffith's *The Iconoclast* (1910). Comics such as Charlie Chaplin and Mack Sennett also touched on politics when their films made fun of bureaucracy and authority.

In the 1920s, sympathetic movie portraits of workers and unions became rare. The Russian Revolution made Americans paranoid about Communism, but as filmmaking in Hollywood became an industry, producers were running into labor union problems of their own. Although a few filmmakers, such as Charlie Chaplin, remained sympathetic to workers, immigrants, and the downtrodden in general, heroic workers became rare at the movies, and union organizers were more often portrayed as thugs than as saviors.

Attitudes about race and ethnicity were more consistent in the silent era, a time when America's white Anglo-Saxon Protestant majority felt threatened by mass immigration. Movies reflected this fear with ethnic and racial minority characters that were lazy, evil, and lustful. This was especially true of African-American or Asian characters. Northern European immigrants were treated more sympathetically, but white ethnic immigrants from elsewhere often were not, and the depiction of Jews in early films was almost always negative. The treatment of immigrants and Jews was ironic given that most early film producers and investors were immigrants and many were Jewish. But instead of showing sympathy for those of their own background, the early filmmakers seem to have been pandering to their audiences and denying their roots.

One aspect of their experience as immigrants did shine through, however. For the early filmmakers, the American dream had come true. Hard work and good fortune had made them rich and famous. Naturally, they believed in the dream, and their faith showed up in their movies. But their flag-waving served a political purpose, too. By proving how American they had become, they diverted the kind of criticism that might have led to government control of the film industry, a threat they were nervous about while the anti-immigrant attitudes were a political force. Their nervousness was not entirely justified, however, because America's political and intellectual elite in those days ignored movies as an art form and as a medium for ideas, condescendingly assuming that motion pictures were just entertainment for the masses.

Films that portrayed racial minorities and immigrants—and probably most films of the silent era—were socially reflective movies according to our typology, low in both political content and intent. Others, including some of the comedies of Chaplin and Sennett as well as the films about workers, landlords, bankers, and criminals mentioned earlier, had clear political content, but were probably not intended to impart a political message. According to our typology, they would be politically reflective movies, relatively high in political content but low in intent. Mostly they restated or reinforced popular stereotypes and prejudices.

A few movies of the silent era were more explicitly political. For example, *The Politicians* (1915) is a relatively pure political movie high on political content and surely intentionally so. A clear reflection of Progressive attitudes about politics, *The Politicians* condemned corrupt machines and bosses. This film and others of its time nourished the popular stereotype of the corrupt politician that would be reiterated throughout the history of American political film. But the explicitly political film of the silent era that had the greatest impact was undoubtedly D.W. Griffith's *The Birth of a Nation* (1915), which contained clear political messages and persuaded America's intellectual elite that films were more than entertainment for the masses.

History in Lightning

The Birth of a Nation was almost certainly the most important film of the silent era, both artistically and politically. Griffith made many movies before his epic, but like most others at the time, his earlier films were short, and only a few of them—including *The Politician's Love Story* (1909), *The Iconoclast* (1910), and *The Reformers, or the Lost Art of Minding One's Own Business* (1913)—touched on politics. At over three hours, *The Birth of a Nation* was the longest film ever made in America up to that time and the most technically dazzling, with its creative camera movement and angles, close-ups, long shots, panning and tracking, crosscutting to simultaneously occurring events, montage editing, iris shots, split screen, fade-ins and fade-outs, and thoughtful framing and composition. These techniques had been used before, but never to such great effect and never in such a way as to involve the audience so deeply. Film historian Kevin Brownlow observes that *The Birth of a Nation* was the "first feature to be made in the same fluid way as pictures are made today. It was the most widely seen production of the time and it had the strongest influence."[2] *The Birth of a Nation* was ambitious in more than length and technique. Its content also gave it impact, a content so substantial and so controversial that the film, among the first to make people take movies seriously, helped to give birth to film criticism. So many people saw *The Birth of a Nation* that the film is credited with widening the film audience beyond the working class to include the middle class and intellectuals. Even President Woodrow Wilson saw it—at the first screening of a movie at the White House—and was said to have declared that it was "like history written in lightning."[3]

Griffith developed his script from *The Clansman* by Thomas Dixon Jr. From this popular play and novel of the Civil War and Reconstruction, Griffith shaped a film with a distinct point of view on the events, politics, and politicians of its period. The story centers on two families: the Southern Camerons and the Northern Stonemans. Their friendship as the film begins symbolizes a united country, but Griffith's politics soon become apparent: the "first seeds of disunion," one of the titles explains, were planted by the "bringing of the African to this country." Griffith blames the Civil War and its aftermath on blacks and politicians—with the exception of Abraham Lincoln, who is treated reverentially. In a carefully composed scene replicating the signing of the proclamation calling up the first troops, Lincoln is seated apart from the other politicians to make the point that he is different, that his only motive is to do good. When the signing is completed, the camera lingers on Lincoln, alone and looking miserable about what he has just done. Later, as the war comes to an end, he argues against those in his cabinet who would be vindictive toward the South. And when he is assassinated in another meticulously reconstructed sequence, the title announces that "our best friend is gone."

Griffith's once-happy families illustrate the consequences of these events when they are divided by a war that the movie labels "futile and abhorrent." The large and lavish battle sequences, still hauntingly beautiful, must have moved audiences enormously. In these scenes, masses of men move through the smoke of firing cannons, falling and dying. The younger sons of the Northern and Southern families die in each other's arms, reiterating Griffith's point that a hateful war has divided a loving people. Later, the director suggests the devastating effect of Sherman's march through the South with a single, eloquent close-up of a trembling, fatherless family, from which the camera pans to marching troops in the valley below.

As the fighting ends and Reconstruction begins, *The Birth of a Nation* follows Dixon's story more closely, and its view of history grows more and more distorted. The elder Cameron brother returns to his impoverished, grieving family, which becomes the focus of the film. He is soon followed by Senator Stoneman, a representative of the evil, vindictive forces of Reconstruction, who hopes to build a presidential career by reorganizing the South with carpetbaggers, black voters, and black politicians. His only motive is personal ambition, and his evil, racially embittered mulatto house servant and mistress encourages him. In a state legislature, we see Stoneman's black puppets in power—slovenly, barefoot politicians slouching in their chambers and lustfully eyeing the white women in the galleries. Senator Stoneman's immediate goal is to put his protégé, the mulatto Silas Lynch, in charge of the state, making him "the peer of any white man living." This ambition sours in the end, however, when Lynch, taking Stoneman's promise seriously and acting as the white man's peer, pursues Stoneman's daughter Elsie, played with doll-like sweetness by Lillian Gish.

Meanwhile, another doll-like daughter precipitates a crisis. Flora Cameron (Mae Marsh), youngest member of the Southern family, skips into the woods to fetch water—an indication of how low the family has fallen since the war. Diverted by the antics of a squirrel, she wanders too far and is spotted by Gus, an evil black man. His eyes bulge with lust as he follows her through the woods; hers bulge with fear when she spots him. She runs, he follows, and she throws herself off a precipice rather than submit to the advances she assumes he is about to make. Needless to say, this upsets her family. Ben, her eldest brother, scratches his chin as he takes a solitary walk, wondering what can be done. The carpetbaggers are running the town, and the Old South is falling apart. Then he sees some white children garbed in white sheets frightening black kids, and an idea is born. He forms a fraternity of white men who wreak vengeance as they ride through the night in white costumes "made by women," according to the titles, and the Ku Klux Klan is born.

The climax comes when angry blacks besiege a little band of whites in an isolated cabin and the Ku Klux Klan rides to the rescue, just as Silas Lynch is about to have his way with Elsie Stoneman. In one of the greatest chase sequences in American movies, Griffith cuts from the galloping Klansmen to Silas and Elsie and then to the cabin. This exciting and emotional sequence ends happily: the Klan arrives in time, everybody is rescued, and Senator Stoneman is chastised for having betrayed not only his people but also his own daughter through his alliance with blacks. In Dixon's view, somewhat obscured in the film, this scene marks the birth of a white nation unified by the pain of war.

The Birth of a Nation was a vivid, dramatic rewriting of history that suited a lot of people at a time when blacks were migrating to the North in great numbers and racism was increasing there. Intentionally or not, Griffith's film promoted the revival of the Ku Klux Klan outside the South. The son of a Confederate officer, he was telling the story as Southerners saw it. But it was a distorted and exaggerated version. Blacks held majorities briefly in only two state legislatures and never had much genuine power; the real problem for the South was the white carpetbaggers. But Griffith's version of history— a romantic view of an Old South where everything was fine until the North got meddlesome—endured for a long time. Griffith's message was regarded so seriously at the time that schoolchildren throughout the country were taken to his movie to learn history. Subsequent movies on the subject followed the same line, although with less offensive racism.

Appalling as its message seems now, *The Birth of a Nation* was the blockbuster of its day. Grossing a preinflationary $18 million, it was the second-biggest box office success of the silent era. Immediately perceived as a classic, it was rereleased in 1921, 1922, and 1930. Some 200 million people saw it before 1946.

This movie was politically significant not only because of its content and popularity but also because of the contemporary reaction to it. Latter-day viewers see it as over-the-top racism, often dismissing it too readily for that reason and perhaps assuming that audiences at the time of its original release were oblivious to its bias or approved of it. But objections to *The Birth of a Nation* in 1915 were intense. Many reviewers condemned its racism, including a *New York Times* critic who called it "inflammatory" and "controversial" even as he praised it as an "impressive new illustration of the scope of the motion picture camera."[4] The National Association for the Advancement of Colored People (NAACP) organized a precedent-setting national boycott of the film, probably the first such effort and one of the most successful. There was a mass demonstration when the film was shown in Boston, and it was banned in three states and several cities.

Griffith, claiming to be shocked by these objections, denied that he was racist, although he warned that the NAACP favored interracial marriage. Nevertheless, the widespread criticism of Griffith's black characters—all of whom are either evil or stupid and, perhaps even more offensively, most of whom were played by white actors in blackface—forced him to delete some scenes of blacks molesting white women as well as the final scene in which blacks are deported to Africa. He had already softened the racism of the novel by adding the "good souls," the Camerons' happy and loyal house servants. But these concessions did not silence the protesters, and their continued objections made other filmmakers skittish about including blacks in their movies. Race, racism, and especially intermarriage were forbidden subjects after *The Birth of a Nation,* and except for a few happy servants like the "good souls," blacks disappeared from mainstream movies until the 1940s.

The Birth of a Nation also portrayed women in a manner that now seems objectionable. Griffith's female characters were doll-like possessions of men; they were treated with reverence, but they were objects. Purity was all-important; death was preferable to defilement. The constructive task for Griffith's women was making the Klan costumes. The one exception was the lascivious Lydia, Stoneman's mulatto housekeeper and mistress, who used sex to manipulate her man. At a time when women were fighting for the vote, Griffith's attitude was far from progressive, but he probably was no more sexually conservative than most of his audience.

Griffith's portrait of politics and politicians made use of stereotypes and conventions that later became entrenched in the movies. He used, for example, the contrasting stereotypes of the saintly leader (Lincoln) and the evil politician (Stoneman and Lynch). He also provided the kind of populist, collective solution that is seen in later political films: instead of seeking a leader to help them or working through the regular political process, Griffith's oppressed white Southerners banded together, forming a vigilante group, and took the law into their own hands.

Griffith's main concern, however, was rewriting the history of the South and the Civil War, and he was well aware of the power of his medium. He saw film as an educational tool, and he set out to use it as such—an intention that was in itself political. *The Birth of a Nation* was the first important American political film not only because it reshaped the image of the South but also because it influenced the way Americans thought about politics—in addition to its encouragement of racism and the revival of the Ku Klux Klan.

Intolerance (1916), Griffith's next major project, consists of four interwoven stories, set in different historical periods, on the theme of intolerance. In the modern story, an evil industrialist pursues a typical Griffith heroine whose sweetheart is involved with a sleazy political machine. When the lustful capitalist falsely accuses the boy to get him out of the way, the girl saves him by appealing to the governor. A good politician and laws that protect the innocent bring to this story a happy ending that stands in contrast to the suffering of persecuted innocents, including Christ on the cross, in the three other tales. Made partly to refute the charges of racism provoked by *The Birth of a Nation, Intolerance* condemned persecution and criticized the excesses of capitalism—only to be labeled "Communist" itself.[5] But in *Orphans of the Storm* (1921), a movie about the French Revolution, Griffith made it clear that the rule of the masses was not acceptable either. "The tyranny of kings and nobles is hard to bear," read one of the titles, "but the tyranny of the mob under blood-lusting rulers is intolerable."

Griffith went on to make *America* (1924), a Revolutionary War epic, and later returned to his favorite president with a sound movie, *Abraham Lincoln* (1930). His later political films were less successful than *The Birth of a Nation,* although some film scholars regard *Intolerance* as his masterpiece. All of Griffith's movies with political themes—from the one-reelers to *The Birth of a Nation, Intolerance,* and beyond—portrayed politics and politicians in much the same way, however. Most politicians were evil and corrupt, motivated by base self-interest.

The Twenties: Corruption and Redemption

Most of the 10,000 or so films that were produced during the 1920s were domestic melodramas, westerns, comedies, love stories, costume dramas, or crime movies, but a few straightforward films about politics were made despite the ominous presence of the Hays Office (discussed in Chapter 3). The American Film Institute (AFI) index for this period lists fewer than two hundred feature films with political themes, although this may be a conservative estimate because the index's definition of politics is narrow.[6] At any rate, the film industry's lack of interest in politics—or fear of political subjects—appears to have been well established by this time.

One safe political topic showed up early in the decade in a group of films reflecting paranoia about the revolution in Russia and unionization at home. Put those two fears together and you have the Bolshevik labor organizers who are the villains in more than a dozen movies of the time. In *Dangerous Hours* (1920), for example, Russian agitators infiltrate American industry, but their efforts to foment a strike are foiled by a good American hero.

Another favorite villain is the political boss. Scheming politicians who indulge in seduction, graft, and blackmail show up in *Manslaughter* (1922), *By Divine Right* (1924), *The Blind Goddess* (1926), *A Boy in the Streets* (1927), *Broken Barriers* (1928), and *Apache Raiders* (1928). In *Wild Honey* (1922), a political boss scorned by the heroine schemes to flood a river valley, but is foiled when she saves her true love as well as the settlers and the valley. In *Contraband* (1925), the town's leading politician is exposed as a gangster leader, and in *The Vanishing American* (1926), decent Indians are cheated by corrupt government agents. However, the politics of these melodramas was usually so peripheral that audiences probably did not notice it. Those who did contemplate the political messages of these films could only have concluded that politics was directly related to sin and corruption and that politicians were very bad men indeed.

At least, most of them were men. *Her Honor the Governor* (1926) features a female politician as its central character. Although this film's heroine is the governor, a political boss holds the real power in her state. After she blocks a water project that is dear to his heart, he frames her son for murder. The governor's son is convicted, but she cannot pardon him because she herself is impeached. Finally, the truth comes out and all is well, but the governor caves in, retires from politics, and remarries. The feminism of the movie is undercut completely by this ultimate retreat from politics, but it had already been weakened by scenes that show the governor dusting her own office and sewing buttons on her son's clothes. *Her Honor the Governor* is not only an object lesson for women, however. The ultimate message is that politics itself is evil, corrupt, and best avoided by honest people.

Other films of the 1920s, however, see politics as redemptive. *What Every Woman Knows* (1921) and *The Battling Mason* (1924) feature formerly sinful men who run for office to prove to the women they love that they have reformed. In other movies, heroes and heroines redeem themselves by exposing crooked political bosses and civic corruption. In *One Glorious Day* (1924), for instance, a meek professor defeats a gang of political scoundrels after he is nominated for mayor. In *That Old Gang of Mine* (1925), a nasty political situation is cleaned up when the opponents reminisce about their common roots, unite, and overcome a still nastier enemy. In *Law and Order* (1928), a boss is transformed into a reformer as a result of the love of a good woman. All of these movies focus more on politics than those in which the politician is clearly the villain, and all are relatively positive about the potential value of political activity. Some even suggest that we can fight city hall and win, a message that must have been encouraging to the reformers of the time.

The historical films of the era are even more positive about politics, although today some of these starry-eyed hagiographies of national leaders seem ludicrous. Filmmakers and audiences in the 1920s, perhaps inspired by *The Birth of a Nation* and Griffith's other historical epics, were fascinated by the re-creation of history. American biopics such as The *Dramatic Life of Abraham Lincoln* (1924) and *George Washington* (1924) were popular, though they lacked real insight or lasting interest.

Social Criticism

A few movies of the 1920s clearly offered social criticism without focusing specifically on politicians and government. Perhaps the most renowned of these is Erich von Stroheim's *Greed* (1923), based on the novel *McTeague* by Frank Norris. Von Stroheim's original version took ten hours to tell the grim story of California immigrants and their destruction by the capitalist system and their own avarice. Producer Irving Thalberg cut it to three hours, and some film scholars say he ruined the movie. Audiences nevertheless rejected *Greed.* "Spectators laughed and laughed heartily at the audacity of the director," reported the *New York Times.*[7]

King Vidor, one of Hollywood's most prolific directors and one whose perspective was solidly from the left, made more successful social commentaries. His antiwar film, *The Big Parade* (1925), was the biggest box office hit of the silent era, topping even the success of *The Birth of a Nation.* It tells the story of a trio of young men who succumb to social pressure and enlist in the army during World War I. They soon learn that war is horrible, and their romantic illusions dissipate. *The Big Parade*'s remarkable battle scenes are reminiscent of those in *The Birth of a Nation,* but they must have been even more striking to those moviegoers who were veterans of World War I. When the survivor of the trio goes home, he discovers that he has lost his girl to his brother, who stayed behind to manage the family business. Disillusionment with the war is compounded by disillusionment with the attitudes of the people at home, but in the end the young man is happily reunited with a girl he met in France.

The Big Parade was a resolute, but not heavy-handed, antiwar film. Audiences loved it, partly because it dealt with a war that was still vivid in their memories. The critics also approved. Calling it "a romance with war as the villain," the *New York Times* rated it one of the ten best films of 1925 (the newspaper's annual ratings were just starting).[8] It might seem surprising today that an antiwar movie would have been so popular in the 1920s, but *The Big Parade* was not radical for its time nor was it the only antiwar film of the era. Disillusionment with World War I was common, and isolationism was the key concept of America's foreign policy.

Vidor followed *The Big Parade* with *The Crowd* in 1928, the story of a young couple struggling for success to differentiate themselves from "the crowd." A softer version of *Greed,* this film is a tough commentary on urban alienation and isolation—at least until the couple strike it rich in a happy ending that was added over Vidor's objections. This imposed ending, like the drastic cutting of *Greed,* illustrates the conservatism and the power of the studios in the 1920s.

Sound and the Depression Mark the End of an Era

The silent movies of this early era provided a healthy variety of political images, although the conservatism of a country presided over by Coolidge, Harding, and Hoover probably muted that variety. The lack of political boldness no doubt also reflected the filmmakers' fear of censorship, and the Hays Office institutionalized that caution.

Change came swiftly at the end of the decade, however, as sound came to the movies and the Great Depression descended on the nation. In 1929, nine "audible" films ranked among the *New York Times*'s top ten movies, yet even in 1930 sound was still enough of a novelty for critics to marvel at the battle noise in *All Quiet on the Western Front.*

Sound had a special impact on political movies because it gave words greater power in relation to images and thus facilitated the expression of more complex stories and ideas, allowing political films to escape from the realm of pure melodrama. Directors who were grounded in the silents and whose work was highly visual often stuck with images to communicate political concepts, but for others, words were liberating. Words made it easier to express political ideas, but in a way sound was a mixed blessing for political films. The Big Speech, pounding in the message with a sledgehammer,

71

often spoils political movies. Film is still a visual medium, and wordiness weakens its message.

While filmmakers were learning to put words and images together, the prosperous 1920s came to a precipitous end with the stock market crash of 1929 and the Great Depression. Political change was in the wind, and Hollywood soon reflected that change. What followed was one of the most political periods in the history of American movies. Yet the films of the silent era and the early talkies are worthwhile avenues of exploration for students with an interest in the political evolution of film.

5

The 1930s

Political Movies and
the Great Depression

Mr. Smith Goes to Washington (1939)

The Great Depression and the advent of sound marked the beginning of an extraordinary period for American movies. By 1930, 23,000 movie theaters—the most ever in the United States—were screening films for 90 million people a week. Attendance slipped during the Depression and did not fully recover until the late 1940s. In the early 1930s, however, Hollywood was churning out over 500 films a year, an output made possible by the factorylike production methods of the ever-growing studios, which also owned most of the theaters they were servicing. The huge volume of films produced during the 1930s resulted in a diversity of subject matter rarely matched in the history of American movies. The demand for a large number of movies accounts in part for the abundance of political films made in those years. Producers in search of stories may have been more willing to take a chance on message movies.

This was also an intensely political era, with the Great Depression driving the nation to desperation and Franklin Delano Roosevelt riding to the rescue with his New Deal. This turmoil affected the movies. The Depression caused a widespread questioning of traditional values, faith in the rewards for hard work, and the fairness of the American system. This questioning was most apparent in the social issue films of the early 1930s. At first, the movies were cynical and despairing, offering no hope of salvation, but soon they grew optimistic, offering simple solutions that usually involved reliance on a strong leader. Some flirted with fascism, but others promoted Roosevelt's New Deal. Once the New Deal was well established, however, the output of social criticism and political films almost ceased.

A coherent political left emerged in Hollywood in the 1930s as a result of the Depression, the popularity of Roosevelt, and the organization of unions. Although its presence influenced some movies, conservative forces within the film industry were more powerful. Film production had become more rigidly organized and more dependent on bankers and other investors, often from conservative eastern institutions. These investors were more conservative both aesthetically and politically than the Hollywood producers. To avoid government censorship, the film industry also increased self-censorship, including discouraging some forms of political content.

At the end of the decade, a new form of government pressure emerged when the Justice Department brought an antitrust suit against the eight studios that, together, made nine-tenths of all American films. The government charged that the studios' control of production, distribution, and exhibition (ownership of theaters) constituted a monopoly. Hollywood sweated, but the suit was dropped in 1940 when five studios agreed to allow more flexible booking in the theaters they owned. Meanwhile, the House Un-American Activities Committee (HUAC) began showing interest in Hollywood in 1939, which eventually led to the blacklisting discussed in Chapter 3.

Through all this turmoil, Hollywood made some of its most explicit political films, high on political content as well as intent. Other films were less overtly political, but raised serious social issues. Still others indirectly addressed the sociopsychological concerns of the era as popular genre films, including horror movies, musicals, westerns, costume dramas, and films about gangsters, G-men, prisons, and liberated women.

Social Cynicism

One of the first big hits of the era was a political movie intended by its producer to be "a great work for peace," bringing "home the wastefulness of war."[1] More than a hundred million people have seen *All Quiet on the Western Front* (1930) by now. The movie was, and still is, a success with audiences and critics alike. The film industry must have liked it, too, because it won Academy Awards for best picture and best direction, marking the beginning of a long tradition of Oscars for message movies.

Taken from Erich Maria Remarque's antiwar novel, the film tells the story of a German soldier in World War I. In a way, it resembled the great box office successes of the silent era, *The Big Parade* and *The Birth of a Nation*. *All Quiet on the Western Front,* however, focuses not on an American victim of the war, but on a highly sympathetic German soldier (Lew Ayres), whose ghastly experiences are quite similar to those of the central character in *The Big Parade. All Quiet* pushed the antiwar message a little further than the earlier film with the soldiers' speculation about the causes of war, a passage more easily achieved with the dialogue of a sound film than with the images and titles of a silent. One young soldier blames national leaders for the war; another says its causes are rooted in pride; a third blames those who profit from war; a fourth says that things just get out of hand.

In contrast to the high-minded message of *All Quiet on the Western Front,* other films of the time concerned themselves primarily with lowlife. Gangster movies, for example, were a popular genre of the period. Crime and violence dominated the action in movies like *Little Caesar* (1930) and *Public Enemy* (1931), but these films also deal with class and ethnic conflict, reflecting the emerging doubts and questions about how well the American system was working. "Could this system save itself from the Depression?" the movies ask. Could ethnic minorities and the working class count on the system to save them? The answers provided by the gangster movies were not very optimistic. About the best you can do, they seem to say, is to stand up and die honorably, with guns blazing. Although the gangsters are punished in the end, they are usually treated with some sympathy and even admiration, and the movies frequently suggest that society has made them what they are.

While the gangster films criticized society somewhat indirectly, comics like W.C. Fields, Mae West, and the Marx Brothers made fun of it. All were in their primes in the 1930s, and all of them challenged traditional values, from morality to authority. The Marx Brothers' *Duck Soup* (1933) is their most direct assault on politics, with Groucho as the tin-pot dictator of Fredonia leading his nation into a farcical war. At the other end of the spectrum, horror movies such as *Frankenstein* (1931) and *Dracula* (1931) subliminally addressed the Depression-era audience's deepest fears, like slasher movies today.

Like the gunfire of the gangster movies and the fast talk of the comedies, the songs and thudding tap dances of the musicals of the early 1930s celebrated sound. Musicals presented an upbeat outlook on life and on the future, but they did not always skirt the problems of the times. *Gold Diggers of 1933,* for example, opens with Ginger Rogers singing "We're in the Money," but her ironic song is interrupted by workers arriving to repossess the sets and costumes for the show she is rehearsing. Despite their eviction, however, the kids of the cast get a show together. Their big number is "Remember My Forgotten Man," a Depression dirge about veterans who fought in World War I and farmed the land but are forgotten in their hour of need.

The *Gold Diggers* movies (1933 and 1935), *Footlight Parade* (1933), *42nd Street* (1933), and other musicals portrayed groups pulling together to overcome adversity, although at least one critic has suggested that directors like the one played by James Cagney in *Footlight Parade* signified dependence on a strong leader like Roosevelt.[2] While the gangster films reflect the despair of the Depression, the musicals incorporate the optimism of the New Deal. Instead of giving up and going out with a blast, like Little Caesar, chorus boys and girls could work hard and become stars. The system would function, dancers could surmount the barriers of class—provided they submitted to the robotic choreography that was so fashionable at that time.

Many of the gangster films and musicals came from Warner Bros., which has been called "the workingman's studio," not only because of the audience it aimed for but also because its films contained more social comment than most other examples of the two popular genres. But Warner Bros. went beyond genre to produce some of the most powerful message movies of the 1930s. *I Am a Fugitive from a Chain Gang* (1932), directed by Mervyn LeRoy (who also directed *Little Caesar*), is a pessimistic study of the victimization of an innocent man by the American legal system. Paul Muni plays the fugitive, driven further and further outside society and unable, despite his efforts, to overcome the forces against him. Unlike most films of the era, *Chain Gang* makes no attempt at a happy ending. A modest success with audiences and critics, the movie won Academy Award nominations for best film and best actor (Muni), demonstrating again the willingness of the film industry to honor serious movies. More upbeat endings reflecting the nation's longing for what film scholar Andrew Bergman labels "benevolent authorities"[3] were provided by other Warner productions, however. In *Wild Boys of the Road* (1933), a judge saves the juvenile victims of the Depression, while in *Massacre* (1934), the federal government, symbol of the New Deal, steps in to save the good Indians from their exploiters, just as it would save the nation.

Shysters and Saviors

Explicitly political films about government and elected officials nearly became a genre in and of themselves during the early 1930s, as a nation dissatisfied with the way it had been governed by Hoover's complacent Republicans searched for new solutions and a new leader. Nevertheless, the political films of the early 1930s were cynical about the possibility of improvement. They projected the nation's disillusionment and held out little hope of change for the better. Most presented politicians as crooks and shysters; only later did a few saviors appear.

Several of these movies were comedies, among them *Politics* (1931), in which the formidable Marie Dressler, then Hollywood's top box office draw, plays a housekeeper who becomes mayor when the women of the town go on strike in her support. The film's mildly feminist politics and upbeat ending were unusual for the early 1930s—more like films of the musical genre than other political films of the time.

The Phantom President (1932) combined the musical and comedy genres in a tale about mistaken identity involving a presidential candidate and an entertainer, both played by George M. Cohan. In the film's prologue, portraits of Washington, Jefferson, Lincoln, and Theodore Roosevelt come to life to sing "The Country Needs a Man" to lead it out of the Depression. A gang of political bosses is running Theodore K. Blair, a banker, for president, but Blair has "no flair" and, as a woman senator keeps mentioning, "no sex appeal." By chance the bosses come across Varney, a look-alike medicine man and minstrel. "Every time the Congress goes in session," Varney sings, "they achieve a gain in the Depression. Maybe someone ought to wave the flag!" The politicians know that the country needs "a sober man," but the public wants someone with "ginger and pizzazz" who can deliver "a musical comedy presidential campaign," so the bosses persuade the minstrel to substitute for the candidate temporarily. "I do the act and he takes the bows," Varney says. Blair grows envious and tries to get rid of Varney, but the plot is revealed and Varney is elected president in his own name. A lightweight comedy, *The Phantom President* reiterates popular clichés about politicians. A close-up of a horse's rump fades to a close-up of an orating politician's face. The country is run by bosses and buffoons, and the people are fools, easily seduced by "a musical comedy presidential campaign." But lest the message seem too cynical, *The Phantom President* opts for what was becoming the movie-cliché solution to all problems: a good man.

The Dark Horse (1932), yet another comedy, was a greater popular and critical success with more to say about politics. A naive nobody is nominated for governor and ruthlessly packaged by his managers. The candidate is coached always to give the same answer to the press: "Yes—and again, no." The film still rings true to some extent, possibly because today we are even more aware of the packaging of candidates. But while the message was funny, it was also cynical: politics was all pretense and manipulation, an unlikely means of salvation.

Like these comedies, melodramas of the 1930s also conveyed a cynical view of politics. In *Washington Masquerade* (1932), a young senator fights "the Interests" behind a corrupt water project. Although seduced and diverted by an evil woman they set on him, he redeems himself by testifying against "the Interests" before he dies. *Washington Merry-Go-Round* (1932) tells a similar story. A young man is elected to Congress with the help of bosses, but when he attempts to rally reformers in Washington he is shocked to discover that the politicians are all there to get something for themselves. The political machine unseats him, but he has already discovered "an invisible government" led by a sinister boss. "I have plans," says the boss. "Italy has her Mussolini, Russia her Stalin. Such a man will come along in America!" After a message-laden moment of meditation in the Lincoln Memorial, our reformer rallies the unemployed to take the law into their own hands and force the evil boss to commit suicide. Like the comedies, these Washington melodramas saw politics as corrupt, but they had a solution: a good man. Despite corruption, these films said, one good man could make the system work.

Gabriel over the White House (1933) had a different vision, however, moving from whimsical fantasy to the implication that a fascist leader could solve the nation's problems. Publisher William Randolph Hearst was a major influence on the film, even contributing to the script, although the major auteur of *Gabriel* was producer Walter Wanger. A member of President Wilson's staff at the Paris Peace Conference, Wanger was a friend of President Roosevelt and one of Hollywood's most political producers *(The Washington Merry-Go-Round, The President Vanishes, Blockade)*.

Gabriel is the story of Jud Hammond (Walter Huston), a political hack who becomes president by making the right deals, who plans to stay in office by paying off the right people with jobs and contracts, and who shows little interest in dealing with the Depression and crime—mere "local problems," he scoffs. Hammond has an accident while taking a joyride in the country (symbolic of an economy out of control, say some film scholars),[4] and at this point the angel Gabriel intervenes. The hack is transformed into a benevolent leader, committed to solving the nation's problems by the most efficient means possible. Using radio as his communication medium (a technique Franklin Roosevelt was just beginning to exploit), he inspires the nation, gets the powers he wants from Congress, which he then suspends, and proceeds to feed the hungry, eradicate unemployment, and end crime by declaring martial law and sending out the army to destroy the gangsters (the only cause of crime) by putting them before firing squads without benefit of trial. He then eliminates war, too, by bullying the rest of the world into joining the United States in a disarmament agreement. With the problems of the nation and the world solved, the angel Gabriel disposes of the president, presumably to protect us from dictatorship.

When MGM boss Louis B. Mayer and Will Hays of the Motion Picture Producers and Distributors Association (MPPDA) saw an early screening of *Gabriel,* they were appalled, not because of the film's fascist implications, but because it seemed pro-Roosevelt and they were staunch Republicans. Mayer took the film in hand, reshooting some scenes and toning others down.

The film premiered just before President Roosevelt took office. An instant hit, it was one of the big box office draws of 1933 and also won critical approval. "For its uncannily prophetic foreshadowing of the spirit of President Roosevelt's first month in office . . . for putting into film what scores of millions think our government should do," gushed *Photoplay,* "this will unquestionably be one of this year's most talked-of pictures."[5] Some members of Congress complained, but President Roosevelt enjoyed the film and saw it several times.

Film scholars view *Gabriel* as an expression of longing for strong leadership bordering on fascism. Their case is strengthened by the fact that William Randolph Hearst, widely considered a fascist sympathizer, was a principal backer of the film. Certainly the movie proposed a dictatorship, albeit a benevolent one, and the police in the movie behave in a fascist manner. But this view probably exaggerates the intentions of the filmmakers, who more likely merely wanted to encourage strong leadership and amuse the audience. In most ways, *Gabriel* was like other American political films: it saw politics as dirty, dominated by shysters, and redeemable only by a miracle, in this case the intervention of an angel. *Gabriel* was different from other films, however, in that it willingly, if fantastically, accepted the overthrow of democracy.

Producer Wanger followed *Gabriel* with *The President Vanishes* (1934), a more benign and less successful film with a more distinct leftist bias. The threat in *The President Vanishes* comes from a right-wing coalition of big businessmen, corrupt politicians, and fascist Gray Shirts plotting to drag the United States into a war in Europe in order to make profits for the arms industry. They are foiled when the president fakes his own kidnapping and disappears on the very day Congress is set to declare war. Public sympathy turns to the president, and when he returns, the country is mobilized for peace. While *The President Vanishes* is an overtly antifascist film, it, too, reflects pessimism about democracy. In it, the public is manipulated first one way, then the other. As in so many American political films, one man saves the day.

Other Visions

While some films put their faith in a strong leader, *Viva Villa* (1934) offered a revolutionary alternative. Its location shots, filmed in Mexico, are still impressive, but Wallace Beery's folksy Pancho Villa comes off as a horny buffoon. The evil rich drive young Pancho to banditry until Francisco Madero, reverentially portrayed as a Mexican Abe Lincoln, asks him to join the Revolution of 1910. When Madero is killed by a cabal of evil army officers, Villa reluctantly takes his place as leader. But he is a fighter, not a politician, and he is soon bewildered by the responsibilities of government. Once he gets the land reform that Madero had promised, Villa retires to the country. Unfortunately, his boisterous ways land him in exile, and in the end a man whose sister he's dishonored assassinates him. The messages of this film were mixed, to say the least. *Viva Villa* seemed to say that revolution was sometimes justifiable, but it was fraught with difficulties.

The best alternative vision and the most radical film of the 1930s, *Our Daily Bread* (1934), came from King Vidor, the maker of *The Big Parade* and *The Crowd*. Improbably inspired by a *Reader's Digest* article on collective farms, this film is the story of the itinerant unemployed of the Depression. Tom and Mary, an all-American couple, flee the hopeless life of unemployment in the city to take over a bankrupt farm. They are joined by other itinerants, each of whom has a useful skill to offer. A thriving cooperative community is soon established. This utopia is nearly subverted by a blond temptress from the city who lures Tom away from the collective endeavor. His conscience soon brings him back, however, and the farm is saved when its irrigation problems are solved by a cooperative ditch-building effort. The opening of the ditch—presented in a dramatic montage sequence—is the film's climax.

The collective politics of *Our Daily Bread* put it well out of the American mainstream, yet in other ways it was consistent with the other films of the era. It was antiurban in its suggestion of a return to the land and to rural values, although this was an unrealistic solution in the dust bowl days of the Depression. Furthermore, threats to Tom and Mary's rural enterprise came from city forces: a banker and the blond seductress. More significantly, despite its collective rhetoric, *Our Daily Bread* insisted on the need for a strong leader. The members of the co-op decide they need "a strong boss," settling by acclamation (not election) on Tom, the film's Roosevelt-figure, according to Andrew Bergman.[6]

Our Daily Bread is an impressive and unusual film. Remarkably, it was a modest success at the box office and even won some critical approval. Although the Hearst papers denounced it as "pinko" and the *Los Angeles Times* refused to accept advertising for it, the *New York Times* declared it "a brilliant declaration of faith in the importance of cinema as a social instrument . . . a social document of amazing vitality and emotional impact," concluding that "it is impossible to overestimate [its] significance."[7] Other critics agreed on its worthiness, although some correctly pointed out that the acting and writing were turgid at best. Banks and the studios had refused to finance the film, and its budget limitations are apparent in its production qualities. Today it is the spirit of the film that holds up, especially in the dazzling ditch-building sequence. Although some judged it radical at the time, in retrospect the political message of *Our Daily Bread*—pulling together in hard times—does not seem much more radical than the message of some Depression musicals.

While *Our Daily Bread* expressed faith in collective action, other films of the decade portrayed "the people" as a dangerous mob. In *Fury* (1936) and *They Won't Forget* (1937), angry mobs resort to lynching. These films were part of a national campaign against lynching, which had reached a sickeningly high rate in the early 1930s. It seems odd in retrospect that the victims in the films were both white while most real-life lynching victims were black, but Hollywood in the 1930s avoided racial issues and aimed its movies at a white audience. Two other films of the era, *Black Fury* (1935) and *Black Legion* (1936), centered on American workingmen who were led into misadventure by crooks. In *Black Fury,* a miner (Paul Muni) is duped into leading a strike by agents of a company that stands to make a profit by breaking up the strike. And in *Black Legion,* Humphrey Bogart joins a Ku Klux Klan–like, antiforeigner group that turns out to be a profit-making venture for its organizer. Both films played on the foolishness of the people and the ease with which they could be misled.

These movies and others of the era expressed a theme that runs through American films: a mistrust of the people and collective action. Despite America's revolutionary and democratic heritage and all the "we the people" rhetoric, American filmmakers have not manifested great faith in the people who make up their audiences. Except for occasional nonmainstream movies like *Our Daily Bread,* group endeavor is rarely depicted in a positive manner. More often, the group turns into a lynch mob or passively follows venal leaders. These movie themes may have reflected the American establishment's genuine fear of revolution in the 1930s. The Depression had put the masses on the move. Union activism and left-wing political movements reached a high point. Roosevelt's New Deal was, in some ways, a concession to these forces and, in others, a way of buying them off, thus preventing revolution. And the movies played their part in this process by discouraging collective movements that challenged the nation's basic political and economic structures.

Politics in Movieland

As the messages of these films suggest, filmmakers were becoming more interested and active in politics. In national politics, some movie moguls, such as the Warners and W.R. Hearst, owner of Cosmopolitan Pictures, were enthusiastically pro-Roosevelt; others, like Louis B. Mayer at MGM, remained militantly Republican. They were unified, however, in 1934, when they intervened in politics more blatantly than ever before or perhaps since.

Upton Sinclair, the socialist novelist, had won the Democratic Party nomination for governor of California and might have been elected had it not been for a combined film and print media smear, the biggest up to that time. Apparently terrified by the popularity of socialist Sinclair, the state's leading newspapers, with the Hearst press in the forefront, accused Sinclair of being a Communist, a homosexual, and an atheist. Meanwhile, the film studios produced anti-Sinclair trailers that looked like newsreels and screened them in their theaters all over the state.

Other political divisions followed. Film workers wanted to form unions, but the producers resisted; no wonder their films showed a mistrust of mobs and rarely dealt with labor relations. The Communist Party reached the peak of its popularity in the 1930s, too. In Hollywood, Communist organizers pushed hard for the formation of unions, and many Depression-radicalized liberals joined the party. When the Spanish Civil War began in 1936, the antifascist cause became a rallying point for the Hollywood left.

These leftist leanings, however, rarely showed up on the screen, possibly because Hollywood's self-censors would have quashed them anyway. Over the years, Will Hays's MPPDA had become more than a mere symbol of self-regulation. As discussed in Chapter 3, the establishment worried about sexual mores in the movies and about gangster movies, which allegedly encouraged the lower classes to rebel.[8]

But even as the advisory code was toughened up, Mae West, the Marx

Brothers, and the makers of gangster films challenged it. Mae West's *She Done Him Wrong* (1933) and Walter Wanger's *Gabriel over the White House* especially alarmed Will Hays, who warned moviemakers away from films about sex, violence, and any political stance that might give offense.

Hollywood found a way to get around the Hays Code and keep violent action in movies by shifting its focus from gangsters to lawmen, but few political films were made in the mid-1930s. Perhaps filmmakers and audiences lost interest in politics because they now had a president they trusted to lead them out of the Depression. But the code was also a factor in discouraging political films, as was establishment concern about political unrest. Besides the antilynching movies *(Fury, They Won't Forget)* and the movies about duped workingmen *(Black Legion, Black Fury)*, the mid-1930s produced only Cecil B. DeMille's nation-building epics *(The Plainsman* and *Union Pacific)* and a few comedies such as *First Lady* (1937), which played on the Hillary-esque idea of a president's wife as the power behind the scenes. There was nothing to match *Gabriel, Our Daily Bread,* or the other serious political films of the beginning of the decade. At the very end of the decade, however, political films made a comeback.

The Politics of Dorothy and Scarlett

Two of America's classic films, *The Wizard of Oz* and *Gone with the Wind,* were released in 1939. Both were directed by Victor Fleming and both became *Variety* "Box Office Champions." Both were also filmed in color, which may have helped them hold favor with later audiences.

The Wizard of Oz had no overt politics or political intentions, but some latter-day critics managed to discern political messages. The Scarecrow and the Tin Man, for example, were supposed to represent a longing for a populist alliance between farmers and workers, a dream that may have occurred to the author of the *Oz* books, but one that had faded by the time the film was made. The fake leadership of the wizard, all promise without delivery, was a more apparent political theme, reflecting a common view of politicians. *The Wizard of Oz* concluded with the message of most Hollywood musicals: have faith in your own ability to solve your problems. Like earlier Depression musicals, however, it also suggested that group support helped.

Most people do not think of *Gone with the Wind* as being any more political than *The Wizard of Oz,* but the film that swept the Oscars and led in box office receipts for 1939 has its political themes. After all, it is about the Civil War and is even more resolutely pro-Southern than *The Birth of a Nation.* The sacrifice and suffering of the South are made much of, while the depiction of Reconstruction features crude, greedy carpetbaggers swarming over the vanquished South. Like the Southern gentlemen in the earlier movie, Ashley (Leslie Howard) and Frank (Scarlett's second husband) go off to a "political meeting," apparently a KKK raid, during which Frank is killed. Unlike *The Birth of a Nation*, however, the Klan is not presented as the savior of the South. Instead, Scarlett (Vivian Leigh) eschews collective action and offers her determined individualism and faith in the land as the answer. Her individualism is mitigated somewhat by the film's condemnation of her selfishness and by her willingness to save her plantation not only for herself but also for her family and its faithful retainers. Nevertheless, *Gone with the Wind*, like *The Birth of a Nation*, romanticized the Old South and helped entrench American racism, a bias that probably had more political impact than its other messages. Critics pointed out the racism of *Gone with the Wind*, just as they had done with the earlier film, but there was less general outrage, perhaps because none of the black characters in *Gone with the Wind* were evil and because Scarlett's mammy (Hattie McDaniel, who won an Oscar for the role) served as the sympathetic moral arbiter of the film.

Mr. Smith

Although *Gone with the Wind* and *The Wizard of Oz* were not primarily about politics, the other great hit of 1939 was. *Mr. Smith Goes to Washington* was one of the most popular political films ever made, coming in second only to *Gone with the Wind* in 1939 box office receipts and Academy Award nominations.

Frank Capra, one of Hollywood's most prolific, popular, and political directors, made *Mr. Smith* when he was at the height of his career. He had already directed a string of hits that included *It Happened One Night* (1934) and *Lost Horizon* (1937). He had shown an interest in politics with two of his earlier efforts: *Forbidden* (1932), a melodrama about a corrupt politician and a crusading reporter, and *Mr. Deeds Goes to Town* (1936), a movie about a small-town poet (Gary Cooper) who inherits a fortune and tries to spread it around during the Depression. Capra's films were characterized by an all-American hokiness that the director himself called "Capracorn." Others have called it populism, by which they seem to mean faith in the people. Although written by Sidney Buchman, who later admitted membership in the Communist Party and was blacklisted, no such ideological proclivities were visible in *Mr. Smith*, which was distinctively Capra's movie.

The story is set in motion by the death of a U.S. senator from a western state. Political boss Jim Taylor (Edward Arnold in one of his many boss roles) meets with his flunky, the governor (Guy Kibbee in one of his many flunky roles). Standing in shadow, the boss gives orders to his resistant, dejected flunky, who sits in the light. Later, during a chaotic family dinner, the gover-

84

nor complains that he is unwilling because of "howling citizens" to appoint Boss Taylor's man to the vacant Senate seat, and his children suggest that he appoint Jefferson Smith (James Stewart), the leader of the Boy Rangers. The governor likes the idea because the appointment would be popular and the inexperienced Smith could be managed by the state's senior senator, Joseph Paine (Claude Rains), who happens to be Smith's hero and, unbeknownst to Smith, a secret ally of Boss Jim Taylor.

Flattered, Smith accepts the appointment, and his arrival in Washington is a classic of American political cinema. A bunch of political hacks, all familiar faces from other movies, wait to hustle him into seclusion, but he slips away for a tour of the capital, seen in a stirring montage featuring the Jefferson Memorial, the Washington Monument, the White House, and the Capitol, accompanied by a medley of American patriotic songs. The tour concludes in the Lincoln Memorial as Smith listens to a child reading the Gettysburg Address to an old man.

The cynical Washington press corps soon shatters his idealism, however, making a fool of him at his first press conference. When he complains, the reporters explain that it was their duty to expose him: "You're not a senator, you're a stooge!" Depressed, Smith determines to try to accomplish just one worthwhile goal during the short time he has in office—a boys' ranch for his home state. Clarissa Saunders (Jean Arthur), the aide of the dead senator, agrees to help him. The land Smith wants for his boys turns out to be part of a corrupt water project included in a bill being carried by Senator Paine for Boss Taylor. When Taylor finds out, he threatens and then slanders Smith, who retreats, devastated, to the Lincoln Memorial. Saunders, who by now is in love with him, finds him there and inspires him to fight back. Later, as she coaches from the gallery, he embarks on a filibuster, blocking Senate action for as long as he can speak in the hope that public opinion back home can be rallied to his cause before the bill comes up for a vote. As the filibuster gets under way, H.V. Kaltenborn, a real-life contemporary radio newscaster, explains the process to the audience and notes that "the diplomatic gallery includes envoys of two dictator powers, here to see what they can't see at home: democracy in action!"

The camera stares down at the filibustering hero, dwarfed in the immaculately reproduced Senate chamber. Capra's message—that this is a little guy struggling against large forces—cannot be missed. Smith's call for support from the folks back home is suppressed by the boss, who controls the press and uses it to smear Smith. But the reporters and young Senate aides cheer Smith on in Washington while back home his Boy Rangers print a leaflet in an attempt to get the truth out. All this is done in a fast-paced montage that culminates with an anti-Smith rally at home and the dumping of sacks of mail opposing him in the Senate chamber. Dejected, Smith is prepared to admit defeat when Senator Paine, who is ashamed of what he has done to further his presidential ambitions, rushes out of the Senate chamber to attempt suicide. When his effort is foiled, he blurts out the truth, and the film ends as the Senate erupts into chaos and we assume, according to cinema convention, that Smith has triumphed.

Capra's message in *Mr. Smith,* as in his other movies, is simplistic: a problem caused by bad men—not the faults of the system or its institutions—can be fixed by good men with the support of the people. Even some of the apparently bad guys, like Rains's senator, do the right thing when they get a chance. Although the country was still in the Depression, Capra's faith in the system was unshaken, perhaps because of his own Horatio Alger–like rise from poor Sicilian immigrant to Oscar-winning Hollywood filmmaker. *Mr. Smith* has been labeled "populist" because it seems to show faith in "the people," but its message is more complicated, perhaps darker, than that. It shows faith in one man—Smith, as Everyman—but it is hard to see how the film shows faith in a public that is so easily manipulated. Even the faith in one good man does not stand up to scrutiny. Smith is saved from losing only by Senator Paine, who gives up everything when he tries to shoot himself, the action that brings out the truth. Smith and the people are saved by Paine's crisis of conscience and bad aim.

Capra's movie presents a prototypical American view of politics, with messages and a style that recur in other movies about politics, but it also accurately observes some aspects of the workings of politics, including the process of appointing a senator, the Senate's institutional clubbiness, the filibuster as a parliamentary device, and the job of presiding over the Senate. The film recognizes the power of the press as well as the importance of public opinion in both Smith's appointment and his legislative battle.

If *Mr. Smith* seems somewhat conservative now, moviegoers in 1939 did not see it that way. Written by a confirmed leftist (Buchman), *Mr. Smith* won the applause of the left, presumably because it showed the enemy as an evil boss with economic interests and placed its faith in the common man. Washington, however, hated *Mr. Smith.* When it premiered in the capital, journalists complained that the movie portrayed them as cynical hacks, a movie stereotype of the time—although in *Mr. Smith* they were allowed to redeem themselves by rallying around the hero in the end. The politicians were even more upset. One senator called it "grotesque distortion," while another denounced it as "exactly the kind of picture the dictators of totalitarian governments would like their subjects to see." Joseph Kennedy, father of the future president and then ambassador to Britain, tried to prevent the film from being shown in Europe because he thought it reinforced Nazi propaganda about the corruption of democracy and would demoralize the Allies. Efforts were made to buy up the film and suppress it, but they failed.[9]

Such strong reactions to so moderate a movie show just how narrow the limits on political films were. Only the fact that *Mr. Smith Goes to Washington* was a box office success can have encouraged Hollywood to make other political films.

Ford and Fonda

While Frank Capra was establishing James Stewart as one of America's most enduring images of the good man, John Ford was doing the same for Henry Fonda. These two directors repeatedly took up political themes, with Ford generally perceived as conservative and Capra as liberal. The two reassuring actors were also frequently cast in political roles, and eventually Stewart became associated with conservatism and Fonda with liberalism. All four names crop up repeatedly in the history of American political films.

Ford first worked with Fonda in 1939 on *Drums Along the Mohawk* and *Young Mr. Lincoln.* In the latter, Fonda plays the future president as a lawyer defending some nice young men who have killed a bully in self-defense, but whom a mob wants to lynch. Lincoln wins their freedom and we are instructed in respect for the law. The film illustrates two of Hollywood's favorite political themes, condemning lynch mobs and providing a hero to show the people the way. *Young Mr. Lincoln* is reverential toward its subject, relying on our knowledge of what he would become to give the movie its portentous tone. By contrast, John Cromwell's *Abe Lincoln in Illinois* (1940) presented a complex and sometimes stormy portrait of the great man's personal life that was almost embarrassing, given the respectful treatment Hollywood's favorite president got in other films.

Ford and Fonda had a greater success in 1940, however, with *The Grapes of Wrath,* an adaptation of John Steinbeck's moving novel about dust bowl migrants in the Depression and a good example of filmmaking as a collaborative art. The project was initiated by its producer, Darryl F. Zanuck, who acquired the rights to the book and assigned Ford to direct it. Zanuck was also deeply involved in shaping the script, which muted Steinbeck's radical and pessimistic social criticism. Part of a new generation of producers who pursued profit in a more calculated way than their hit-or-miss predecessors, Zanuck hoped to avoid offending the Production Code Administration (PCA) or HUAC while pandering to the traditional values of audiences; Ford was the perfect director.

John Ford began working in films in 1914. He played a Klansman in *The*

Birth of a Nation and had started directing by 1917. Eventually he became one of Hollywood's most prolific craftsmen, with 200 films to his credit by the time of his death in 1973. His style was distinctive enough to earn him the title of auteur, one who leaves a personal imprint on a film even while working within the confines of the studio system. Visual style is the most obvious signature of the auteur, but philosophical themes also emerge, like Capra's corny populism. In Ford's films, a conservative faith in the common man and nostalgia for a simpler, agrarian past are apparent.

In their work on *The Grapes of Wrath,* three other superb film artists aided Zanuck and Ford. Nunnally Johnson wrote the tight script, and Alfred Newman composed a score based on a folksy version of "Red River Valley," which suited Ford's sentimental style perfectly. Cinematographer Gregg Toland, best known for his work on *Citizen Kane* (1941), made an even greater contribution, using his photography to communicate what could not be made clear through dialogue. Long shots of the horizon give a sense of space and the dreariness of the dust bowl. At times Toland's mobile camera pans to make visual connections and at other times it puts the viewer right in the action. The film as a whole retains a documentary quality that is radically different from the style of other films but perfectly suited to *The Grapes of Wrath.*

The movie starts with a long shot of the plains, followed by a shot of a lone man, Tom Joad (Henry Fonda). He is coming home from prison just as his family prepares to give up their farm and migrate to California. Tenant farmers, they are being driven off their land, a process described by a neighbor in a touching flashback in which the landowner's agent denies responsibility for the eviction by blaming "orders from the East." "Then who do we shoot?" the neighbor's son demands. The film avoids fixing the blame, an example of its muted politics, but also a realistic point, since a whole system rather than any individual produces the eviction. The flashback sequence is done in eloquent montage, highly effective as a summary of the farmers' plight.

The people's despair is turned to hope by a flyer announcing "plenty of work in California: 800 pickers wanted." The Joads pack up and take off in their old jalopy. They face hard times on the road. Elders die, the family runs out of food and money, and they are harassed by state border patrols. Ma Joad (Jane Darwell in an Oscar-winning performance) struggles to keep the family "whole and clear," but she is working against the odds. The Joads are aided, however, by waitresses, truckers, and other migrants, working folk who have learned to stick together.

Two key moments come as the family arrives in transient camps. Both scenes unfold through a subjective camera, so we see the camps as the Joads see them from their rickety old car. Starving children stare at them from grim huts as they enter the first camp, a hellish place run by growers. They soon learn that California is not the paradise they had hoped for. There are too few jobs for the thousands of people who have been lured there by growers' propaganda intended to ensure a surplus of cheap labor. Despondent, the Joads move on, eventually arriving at a second camp, which turns out to be an oasis. As they enter, the camera zooms in on the sign above the gate: "Department of Agriculture." A benign attendant clad in white welcomes them in a mellow voice, explaining that the camp is a cooperative run by the federal government. The Joads are shocked by their good treatment, the absence of cops, and the idea of residents running the camp. The camp is an obvious symbol of the New Deal, complete with Roosevelt-like manager.

But the pull of "the people" is too strong for Tom Joad to rest content with this oasis. He has been thinking, and he suspects that unions could help. At the first camp, Tom saw his friend Casey killed by the growers' thugs for doing union work. Drawn into the scuffle, Tom inadvertently killed one of the thugs, another reason for his restlessness. Earlier, he had wondered, "What is these reds, anyway?" Now he thinks that "these reds" might not be so bad if they help people. He finally leaves the family, apparently to become a union organizer. He reassures Ma Joad that he will always be around, though, because "we're all part of the one big soul that belongs to everybody." She gets the film's closing monologue: "Rich fellas come up and they die, an' their kids ain't no good, and they die out, but we keep acomin'. We're the people that live. Can't wipe us out. Can't lick us. We'll go on forever, Pa, 'cause we're the people."

The message in *The Grapes of Wrath* was faith in the family, the land, and the working people, a message of longing for the past and despair for the present. The Joads slowly figure out that they are victims of the system, but they do not know what to do about it. Only the federal government, as represented by the clean, happy co-op camp, offers salvation.

Ford's movie considerably toned down John Steinbeck's sensational novel. The film replaces Steinbeck's emphasis on class with the family and "the people." To conform with the cinematic tradition of happy endings, the film reversed the order of arrival in the camps: the happy camp comes first in the book, second in the film. The ordering of these events in the movie also suggested greater faith in the federal government as the people's savior and stressed Tom's situation as a fugitive. Steinbeck made it clear that Tom goes off to become a union organizer, but running from the law seems to be his main motive in the film. The novel's assertion that unions might be the answer to the migrants' problems was also weakened in the film. As the book ends, the strike has been broken, Casey has been killed, Tom has been beaten, and in the final scene, one of the young Joad women breast-feeds a starving man. It is a desperate, despairing ending, one Hollywood could not accept, so the film ends in the government camp with Ma Joad's "we're the people" speech implying that all will be well. Survival, not change, is the theme.

The Grapes of Wrath seems moderate today, but in 1940 it was controversial and, some said, radical. Unlike *Mr. Smith,* Ford's film dealt with a real-life problem. The issue of migrant workers was hot when the film was made. California growers were shifting over to native white workers like the Joads for cheap labor. Japanese immigration had been halted, and Mexicans were being repatriated. Union activity was growing. The Hearst press denounced *The Grapes of Wrath* as Communist propaganda, and even before it was completed, the filmmakers were under pressure from growers and banks. They were so nervous that they kept their shooting locations a secret and, as we have seen, considerably muted the book's message. American critics and audiences liked the movie, though. It was a box office hit, and it won two Academy Awards.

But while Capra and Ford focused on domestic politics, other moviemakers were turning their attention to international politics, priming for war.

6

The 1940s

Hollywood Goes to War

All the King's Men (1949)

The 1940s was a turbulent decade for the world, the United States, and Hollywood. When isolationist America was dragged into World War II, Hollywood enthusiastically signed up. Many movies manifested high political intent—rallying the nation to war—but few articulated complex political ideas or confronted social issues. After the war, however, Hollywood made some of its strongest social issue films as well as some powerful movies about the political process, but the regulators of the Production Code Administration (PCA), the breakup of the big studios, and paranoia about Communism soon discouraged the making of such films.

Hollywood and the nation concentrated on domestic politics through the 1930s, but toward the end of the decade, international troubles intruded. The Spanish Civil War caught the imagination of some moviemakers, dividing and politicizing Hollywood from its beginning in 1936. The Spanish conflict was romantic for some, but others saw it as part of the wider rise of fascism. Hollywood debated whether or not to oppose fascism in the movies, but some antifascist films were made and many more movies alluded to the need for national involvement, a position that ran counter to the isolationism that had dominated U.S. public opinion since World War I.

When the United States finally entered World War II, Hollywood was enthusiastic. Before Pearl Harbor, Warner Bros. had been the most political and most pro-Roosevelt studio, and the political left had been the chief advocates of intervention. Once war was declared, all the studios and filmmakers across the political spectrum rallied around the flag, turning out entertainment films that supported the cause, making training films, and joining the campaign to sell war bonds. At this point, domestic politics and social issues all but disappeared from American films except as background in such movies as *The Glass Key* (1942), a murder mystery complicated by machine politics. Throughout the war years, filmmakers stuck with optimistic stories of heroism, patriotism, and antifascism. Thanks to the rapid production methods of the studio system, these movies were hitting the screens within months of America's declaration of war.

After the war, Hollywood's audience reached a high point and then started a long decline. From 1946 to 1948, an average of 90 million people went to the movies every week, but by 1950 weekly attendance had plummeted to 50 million. As it moved from fat times to lean times, from security to insecurity, the film industry experienced great changes. Hollywood and America started the postwar years cheerfully. The United States had won the war and was the most powerful nation in the world. The economy was booming. A baby boom started and the suburbs burgeoned. People spent their wartime savings on cars, refrigerators, washers, and television sets. But the good times were not perfect. Inflation, labor unrest, and a recession resulting from reduced military spending caused economic jitters for a nation that had not forgotten the Depression. Veterans had problems coming home; women had problems staying home after being pushed out of the workforce when the men returned from the war. Racial tension increased as blacks, more assertive after their wartime experience, moved out of the South and grew impatient for equality. The Soviet Union expanded into Eastern Europe and China went Communist. Then in 1949, Russia exploded an atom bomb and America began to worry about Soviet spies. Postwar political films reflected these changes, starting with optimistic crusading, then growing cynical and avoiding political topics.

Internationalism and Antifascism

Hollywood launched the theme of internationalism in the 1930s with a number of pictures focused on Latin America. The studios perceived a vast audience there, but other factors were at work as well. The Rockefeller family had acquired RKO studios and immediately set out to promote Latin America, where it had major economic interests. Nelson Rockefeller formed a committee to improve relations with Latin America, persuaded Twentieth Century-Fox to alter scenes that were less than flattering to Latin America in Carmen Miranda's debut film, *Down Argentine Way* (1940), and encouraged Walt Disney to make the pro-Latino *Saludos Amigos* (1943) and *Three Caballeros* (1945).

Juarez (1939) was more distinctly political as well as internationalist, however. Directed by William Dieterle, who had cautiously raised the issue of anti-Semitism in *The Life of Emile Zola* (1937), *Juarez* centers on the attempt of Napoleon III (Claude Rains) to impose monarchy on Mexico by installing Maximilian (Brian Aherne) and Carlotta (Bette Davis) as its rulers. Juarez (Paul Muni) and Porfirio Diaz (improbably played by John Garfield) lead the resistance, countering the hubris and decadence of the Europeans with native democracy. They win, but the film gives them the Lincoln treatment, presenting them with such deference and dignity that they seem stiff and boring. Audience sympathy and interest shift to Maximilian and Carlotta, who agonize as the people they wish to help reject their good intentions. Napoleon III, with his imperial ambitions, is the villain, while the savior is the United States. French intervention is bad, but ours is good because we support Juarez and "the people"—and because Abraham Lincoln is invoked, even though he was dead by the time the United States took action in Mexico. Despite its transparent politics, *Juarez* was a critical and box office success. The *New York Times* declared it "a stirring restatement of faith in the democratic process . . . ideologically flawless . . . socially valuable," but admitted that the dialogue was a little stiff.[1] Congressman Martin Dies of the House Un-American Activities Committee (HUAC), however, denounced *Juarez* as propaganda.

Another group of films, from *The Charge of the Light Brigade* (1936) to *The Sea Hawk* (1940), *That Hamilton Woman* (1941), and ultimately *Mrs. Miniver* (1942), were directly or indirectly internationalist and unabashedly pro-British, reflecting Hollywood's substantial British contingent.

While these films emphasized internationalism, others were explicitly antifascist. One of the first antifascist movies was *Blockade* (1938), a tale of espionage in Civil War Spain, produced by Walter Wanger, directed by William Dieterle (*Juarez*), and written by John Howard Lawson, a Communist, union activist, and later one of the Hollywood Ten (see Chapter 3). Set in Spain in 1936, *Blockade* follows the adventures of Marco (Henry Fonda), a peasant who rallies his neighbors to resist an invading force referred to only as "the enemy." He is soon assigned to root out saboteurs who are preventing food from getting past the enemy blockade to the starving people. *Blockade* never specifies which side is which, although its populist orientation and the military might and brutality of "the enemy" are obvious clues. The movie's main point is a warning to America: "As I sit here," a journalist writes, "I see nightmare visions of air raids sweeping over great cities . . . London, New York . . . San Francisco." Later, Marco sounds like Tom Joad: "We're part of something, something greater than we are." Turning to the camera in the film's final scene, he passionately cries, "Peace? Where can you find it? Our country's been turned into a battlefield. There's no safety for old people and children. . . . It's not war. War's between soldiers! It's murder, murder of innocent people. There's no sense to it. The world can stop it. Where's the conscience of the world?" But despite its apparent good intentions, the movie's sympathy for Republican Spain drew criticism from right-wing and Catholic groups, critics panned it, and the public ignored it.

Confessions of a Nazi Spy (1939), also from Warner Bros., features Edward G. Robinson as an FBI agent who infiltrates the Nazi underground. Unabashedly antifascist, the film is said to have been inspired by the studio's fury when its representative in Germany, a Jew, was beaten to death. *Confessions* was a popular and critical failure, although some reviewers praised the filmmakers for their daring. They had faced hostility while they were making this movie, and they came in for even greater hostility, especially among German-Americans, when it was released. Nazi sympathizers burned down the theater where it was shown in Milwaukee.

The most overtly anti-Nazi film of this era was Charlie Chaplin's still-popular *The Great Dictator* (1940). His earlier films consistently championed the struggle of the little guy against repression by bullies or institutions, but this movie is more specifically political. It is a gentle comedy in which

Chaplin plays both a Jewish barber and his look-alike, the dictator of Tomania, Adenoid Hynkel, known as "the Phooey." Hynkel is a burlesque character, but his political motives—including lust for power, hatred of Jews, and competition with his neighbors—are clear. The film ends with the little barber taking the Phooey's place at a big rally and addressing a resoundingly antiisolationist, antifascist speech directly to the movie audience. The war in Europe was well under way when *The Great Dictator* was released, but the movie was controversial nonetheless. Efforts had been made to stop its production, and there was hostility to its message. Liberal critics dismissed it as belated, pointing out that Hitler was not funny anymore, and complained that it was too obvious, especially its concluding speech. Audiences loved it, however, and made it a box office hit in both 1940 and 1941. Franklin Roosevelt liked *Dictator* so much that Chaplin was asked to reprise the little barber's big speech at the president's birthday celebration.

As unexceptionable as this and other antifascist films now appear, they were controversial in a prewar America still committed to isolationism. And of course German-Americans and Nazi sympathizers objected to them. HUAC's Congressman Dies charged that all these films were propaganda, attacked Chaplin for his left-wing sympathies, and even alleged that Shirley Temple was a Communist dupe. The Senate set up a subcommittee in 1941 to investigate "any propaganda disseminated by motion pictures . . . to influence public sentiment in the direction of participation by the United States in the European war."[2]

Citizen Welles

Often proclaimed the best film of all time, *Citizen Kane* (1941) was not primarily antifascist or, some would say, even political. But while the political content of *Citizen Kane* may have been low, its political intent was surely high. Orson Welles, the twenty-five-year-old auteur of *Citizen Kane,* was its star, director, and coauthor. Basing his film on the life of newspaper magnate William Randolph Hearst, Welles tells us that power corrupts and money cannot buy happiness. This is an old Hollywood message, but it was not so much the message that made *Citizen Kane* great as the way that message was conveyed.

Kane's life is told in a series of flashbacks by a variety of witnesses, all filmed using dramatic composition and extreme camera angles to emphasize power and impotence, an expressionistic style brilliantly executed by cinematographer Gregg Toland *(The Grapes of Wrath)*. The witnesses tell their tales to an unseen newspaper reporter who seeks to unravel the character of the late Charles Foster Kane by learning the meaning of his dying word,

"Rosebud." But even though *Citizen Kane* is primarily a study of the private life of a public figure, it is political in its obsession with power and in its depiction of Kane's election campaign.

Although the young Charles Foster Kane begins his media career frivolously, because he thinks "it would be fun to run a newspaper," he is idealistic when he writes the "declaration of principles" for his first issue: "(1) I will provide the people of this city with a daily newspaper that will tell them all the news honestly, (2) I will also provide them with a fighting and tireless champion of their rights as citizens and human beings." He stands in the dark, however, as he reads his declaration, a portent of things to come.

"If I don't look after the interests of the underprivileged," the young crusader declares, "maybe somebody else will, maybe somebody without money or property." His politics are liberal, but elitist, a sort of noblesse oblige. In fact, he holds the people in contempt and manipulates public opinion with increasing cynicism. He stirs up a crisis in Cuba to boost newspaper sales. When his correspondent wires that there is no war, Kane responds, "You provide the prose poems, I'll provide the war!" Before long, he is openly announcing that "the people will think . . . what I tell them to think!" Kane's friend, Jed Leland (Joseph Cotten), sums up the publisher's shallow, elitist liberalism when he observes that the American worker is "turning to something called organized labor, and you're not going to like that one bit when you find out that it means he thinks he's entitled to something as his right and not your gift."

Kane runs for governor on a sort of populist-progressive platform, attacking "the machine," which is represented by Boss Jim Geddes (Ray Collins). The campaign culminates in a big rally. A massive portrait of Kane hangs over a crowded auditorium—a scene modeled after the fascist rallies of the time. The crowd is a painted backdrop, dots rather than faces. The looming visage of Kane and the blurred crowd are an apt comment on Kane's politics and the politics of personality as well. But the dark figure of Boss Jim Geddes gazes down on the rally from the back of the auditorium. Just as Kane is within reach of victory, Geddes demands that he drop out of the race. If he refuses, Geddes will tell the press that Kane has been keeping a mistress, a revelation that would cost him both the election and his family. Kane stubbornly refuses to quit. The story of his "love nest" is published and Kane loses both his wife and the election. Welles concludes this segment of *Kane* with his most succinct and cynical comment on politics and the media as Kane's newspaper prepares alternative headlines for the day after the election: "Kane Elected" and "Fraud at Polls." Kane retreats to exercise his formidable power in private life, much as Hearst did, pushing the career of his mistress and building his palace, Xanadu, which closely resembles Hearst's famous estate, San Simeon. His politics, referred to only indirectly in the latter part of the film, move to the right and are ultimately discredited when he poses with Hitler in Germany and returns to the United States to announce that there will be no war.

These scenes hint at antifascism, but *Citizen Kane* is more clearly an antielitist, antiauthoritarian reiteration of the axiom that power corrupts. *Kane* is more cynical than earlier films, because it offers no salvation. The good characters in the movie cannot stand up to Kane, the reporters cannot figure him out, and the people continue to buy his newspapers without protest, rejecting him politically for the wrong reasons—because of his mistress, not his egotistical elitism. Other American movies had dealt with political corruption, from the nearly contemporary *Mr. Smith* back to *The Birth of a Nation* and beyond. But *Kane* was different because Welles refused to offer simple solutions. Another distinction is *Kane*'s focus on the corrupt man himself. Instead of a Jefferson Smith or Tom Joad, we get Charles Foster Kane, a nasty man whom we do not like but for whom we feel some sympathy because of his lost childhood and his youthful exuberance and good intentions. Although "Rosebud" provides a simplistic explanation of Kane's character, the film's closing shot focuses on a No Trespassing sign outside Kane's lavish estate, suggesting that we cannot really know what makes people tick anyway.

Citizen Kane was not a great box office success, despite positive, if qualified, reviews. Writing for *McCall's,* Pare Lorentz praised the technique, but felt that Welles's acting was not strong enough to carry a film about so unsympathetic a character.[3] Other critics called *Kane* "a magnificent sleighride" and "a curious adventure in narration."[4] The *New York Times* acclaimed the film, saying it was "as realistic as a slap in the face," but expressing reservations about the "undefined character" of the "eminent publisher."[5]

Despite its criticism of the press, *Citizen Kane* was applauded at its New York City press showing, but the Hearst newspapers assaulted the film vigorously. They had begun doing so while it was being made, with Hearst gossip columnist Louella Parsons campaigning to get RKO to "junk the project."[6] Once it was released, the attacks escalated, focusing especially on the film's cowriter, Herman Mankiewicz, who had been friendly with Hearst and his movie-star mistress, Marion Davies. Even before the film was released, the PCA objected to scenes in a brothel, resulting in the deletion of a character called Madam Georgie and the toning down of a scene with dancing girls so they are not so obviously whores. Louis B. Mayer and others tried unsuccessfully to buy up all the negatives of the film, and theater chains, including Warner Bros., refused to screen it until RKO, Welles's studio, threatened legal action.

Citizen Kane had made a stylistic and political splash. Besides its gleeful attack on one of America's most powerful men, *Kane* almost offhandedly condemned Hitler and ridiculed the foolishness of people like Kane who thought that war could be avoided. This was perhaps a cheap shot by 1941, but still made for controversy. Beyond that, *Citizen Kane* marked an advance for political films because of the complexity of Kane's character and because of its broad, if pessimistic, attack on power and capitalism.

Frank Capra's *Meet John Doe* (1941) expressed similar pessimism, as corrupt political bosses and media moguls nearly succeed in getting their dupe, a bum played by Gary Cooper, elected president. They are foiled not by "the people," who love the phony candidate, but by John Doe himself. Perhaps alarmed by the rise of Hitler and Mussolini, both Capra and Welles expressed a fear of demagoguery. Neither of these filmmakers, however, seemed optimistic about whether America could resist it. But by 1941, after years of isolationism, America was finally shifting its attention from domestic to international politics.

From Casablanca to the Rhine

Among the first American films to address the growing concern with the international situation was *Casablanca* (1942), a Warner Bros. movie directed by Michael Curtiz and written by Howard Koch, a team that had already expressed itself on isolationism and preparedness in *The Sea Hawk* (1940). *Casablanca* made a more urgent case for involvement, though, with the cynical American expatriate Rick (Humphrey Bogart) reluctantly joining the Free French and giving up Ilsa (Ingrid Bergman), his true love, to another freedom fighter (Paul Henreid). "If it's December 1941 in Casablanca, what time is it in New York?" Rick asks. "I bet they're asleep in New York. I bet they're asleep all over America." Waking up was clearly the right thing to do, in case anybody still doubted it in 1942. Gracefully presented in a seductively romantic story laced with humor and adventure, *Casablanca*'s political message went down well, and the movie was a box office and critical hit, winning Oscars for best picture, director, and script.

Encouraged by the success of *Casablanca* and the active urging of President Roosevelt, Warner Bros. churned out war movies for the next couple of years. James Cagney took the lead in the patriotic but otherwise relatively apolitical *Yankee Doodle Dandy* (1942), also directed by Michael Curtiz. Bogart was back in *All Through the Night* (1942), fighting saboteurs and spies on the home front. Errol Flynn joined the war effort in a string of straightforward adventure stories: *Desperate Journey* (1942), *Northern Pursuit* (1943), *Edge of Darkness* (1943), and *Objective Burma* (1944). In 1943,

Action in the North Atlantic, Air Force, and Destination Tokyo came from Warner Bros. at the request of President Roosevelt. These films were straightforward, inspirational calls for support of the war effort. Some of them condoned collective action and egalitarianism, but these normally left-wing themes had suddenly become widely acceptable because of the war. In the early 1940s, oppression and military necessity justified both collectivism (we had to stick together) and egalitarianism (we needed everybody, regardless of class or race). Anyway, there was usually a WASP leader to guide the cross section of society that made up the little bands of warriors.

Although Warner Bros. took the lead, other studios joined the cause. At United Artists, Ernst Lubitsch directed and produced *To Be or Not to Be* (1942), a black comedy about a troupe of actors caught up in anti-Nazi espionage. Paramount produced *For Whom the Bell Tolls* (1943), based on Hemingway's novel about the Spanish Civil War, although even in 1943 the studio shied away from politics and emphasized the love story. Less shy were three propagandistic anti-Nazi movies: RKO's *Hitler's Children* (1943), Paramount's *The Hitler Gang* (1944), and MGM's *Hitler's Madman* (1943). MGM also produced *Mrs. Miniver* (1942) and *Thirty Seconds over* Tokyo (1944). Only a few of these films, including these two MGM productions and *Casablanca,* were hits with audiences and critics.

One of the most memorable was *Watch on the Rhine,* a Warner Bros. production adapted by Dashiell Hammett from the play by Lillian Hellman. Kurt Muller, a German freedom fighter superbly played by Paul Lukas, takes his wife, Sarah (Bette Davis), and their children home to her family in pre-war America. "I am an antifascist," he explains to his in-laws when they ask about his profession and his failure to settle down in one place. But even in America, the Mullers are not safe. A Romanian houseguest learns that Kurt plans to return to Germany with money for the resistance. The Romanian threatens to betray Kurt to his Nazi friends at the German embassy. When Sarah's family learns of the Romanian's plot, they try to buy him off. "The new world has left the room," the Romanian says when he finds himself alone with Kurt and Sarah. "[They] are Americans," Kurt responds. "They do not understand our world, and if they are fortunate, they never will." But the Americans aid the freedom fighter. "We've been shaken out of the magnolias," the matriarch declares.

Meanwhile, Ginger Rogers and her housemates, a cross section of American womanhood, await the return of their men in *Tender Comrade* (1943). Edward Dmytryk and Dalton Trumbo, both later members of the Hollywood Ten, directed and wrote this story of a group of war wives who work in an aircraft factory and live together in a co-op. The film focuses on their home life, complete with refugee German housekeeper, and teaches lessons about the need for sacrifice, the dangers of hoarding, the reasons for rationing, the importance of keeping mum about troop movements, and the tragedy of the "murder" of German democracy. Ginger Rogers says, "Share and share alike, that's the meaning of democracy"—a line that would later be offered as testimony of "Communist content"—as the women solve individual problems while working together toward a common goal.

Even Alfred Hitchcock joined the antifascist struggle with *Lifeboat* (1944), written by John Steinbeck and Jo Swerling. Like many movies of the era, *Lifeboat* features a microcosm of humanity—a group of survivors set adrift in a small craft after their ship is sunk by a German submarine. Tallulah Bankhead plays a glamorous but self-absorbed journalist who eventually helps the group effort by giving her furs to a freezing mother and offering her jewels for use as a fishing lure. An industrialist automatically assumes leadership of the survivors, but a working-class sailor whose socialist sympathies prompt Bankhead to accuse him of being "a fellow traveler" soon displaces him. Growing dispirited as the lifeboat drifts, the survivors eventually begin to depend on the strong and confident leadership of the German U-boat captain (Walter Slezak), whom they have rescued. When it finally dawns on them that they have drifted into fascism and been misled by this strong leader, they kill him (lynching was okay for Nazis), concluding *Lifeboat*'s tidy, if somewhat belated, morality tale.

And On to Moscow

As the war went on, a few movies crossed the line into more overt propaganda. President Roosevelt urged them on, pressing first for films about the Asian front, then for movies about the European Allies, especially Russia. *Mission to Moscow* (1943) was made, Jack Warner said, at the specific request of Roosevelt, who wanted to "flatter" Stalin and "keep [him] fighting" as well as to educate the American public.[7] Directed by Michael Curtiz and written by Howard Koch, the team that had made *Casablanca,* the pro-Russian movie was as bad as their earlier film was good.

Mission to Moscow starred Walter Huston as Joseph E. Davies, the real-life American ambassador to the Soviet Union from 1936 to 1941. Davies himself introduces the movie with praise for the Warner brothers, "those great American patriots." Then we see Huston as Davies, happily fishing before President Roosevelt calls him out of retirement to take on an urgent assignment. On his way to Moscow, Davies passes through Germany and is appalled at the regimentation and authoritarianism that held sway there. He watches grimly as Jews wearing identification tags are marched by. The cruel totalitarianism of the enemy is thrown into sharp relief when the ambassador reaches the Russian border, where cheerful soldiers and happy women engineers welcome their American friends with food and laughter. The film goes on to present a portrait of Russia that is strictly party-line propaganda. The purges of the 1930s are presented as unimportant exercises carried out only for purposes of internal security. The Hitler–Stalin nonaggression pact of 1939 is blamed on American isolationism and European appeasement. Russia's occupation of Finland is explained away as a strategic necessity for which the Soviets had asked—and received—Finland's permission.

Bogged down with narration and stagy explanations of American policy and Soviet politics, *Mission to Moscow* may have been high in political content and intent but it is a pretty bad movie. The film industry press nevertheless gave it grovelingly good reviews and pointed out the significance of movies "flexing their muscles in human crisis."[8] The *New York Times* proclaimed it "the most important picture on a political subject any American studio has ever made," but criticized its glowing portrait of the USSR and its sloppy history.[9] Others were less kind, calling it a "mishmash" and "a lot of rot" and denouncing its "cuddly, reverential treatment" of Franklin Roosevelt.[10] The Hearst press and Republican presidential candidate Thomas E. Dewey condemned its pro-Communism while liberals objected to its Stalinist portrait of Trotsky.[11] Audiences avoided the movie. Hollywood's most serious attempt at sending a message—approved and encouraged by the president of the United States—bombed.

Other World War II message movies did not do much better. *The North Star* (1943), directed by Lewis Milestone and written by Lillian Hellman, is set in a happy and charming Russian village (populated by Dana Andrews, Walter Huston, and Walter Brennan) that is overwhelmed by Nazis (led by Erich von Stroheim). Producer Samuel Goldwyn said it was about "people who think and act as do Americans,"[12] and the clear intent was to make the American people more enthusiastic about their Soviet allies. MGM and RKO responded to Roosevelt's urgings with *Song of Russia* (1943) and *Days of Glory* (1944), both hyping our Russian allies. Like *Mission to Moscow* and *The North Star,* both movies flopped, probably not so much because of what they said as because they were bad movies. When American filmmakers tried hardest to make political points, they failed most dismally, perhaps because they were trying too hard to please Washington and not hard enough to please their audiences.

Winding Down the War

As the fighting on the European front drew to a close, Hollywood shifted its attention to the war in the Pacific. In *The Fighting Seabees* (1944) and Edward Dmytryk's *Back to Bataan* (1945), both starring John Wayne, the racist portrayal of the enemy was even more extreme than the depiction of the villainous Nazis of the antifascist films.

But by 1944 Hollywood was also looking forward to peacetime with films like *Hail the Conquering Hero.* Preston Sturges wrote and directed this comedy about a hero's son (Eddie Bracken) who is discharged from the marines because he has hay fever. Unable to face the folks back home, he sets out to drown his sorrows, but he is saved by a group of sympathetic marines who decorate him with borrowed medals and send him home. Welcomed as a hero, he is drafted as a candidate for mayor. He confesses, but the townspeople are so unaccustomed to hearing the truth from politicians that they continue to believe he is a hero and elect him anyway.

Like Sturges's earlier films, this one was cynical (albeit funny) about politics. Sturges's *The Great McGinty* (1940) had been about a bum who gained favor with a political boss but ruined his career when true love turned him honest. In *Sullivan's Travels* (1941), Sturges made fun of Hollywood's social concerns. In *Hail the Conquering Hero,* the innocent triumphs for no apparent reason except that he is good, in contrast to the incumbent mayor, who is inept, pretentious, and hypocritical. The well-meaning man who usually runs against the mayor denounces his own dullness and steps aside in favor of the young hero. Room must be made for the returning warriors, the movie tells us. More disturbingly, it also informs us that politics is like love: "You don't need reason." The sophisticated Sturges may have been working with his tongue in his cheek, but audiences loved his film nonetheless.

Wilson (1944) was a loftier, if more ponderous, contemplation of the aftermath of world war. The big biopic of the year was produced for Twentieth Century-Fox by Darryl Zanuck, written by Lamar Trotti, and directed by Henry King. Zanuck, who was determined to make an epic, spent $5 million (a great deal of money in 1944) and employed a cast of 13,000, headed by Alexander Knox as President Woodrow Wilson. "Sometimes the life of a man mirrors the life of a nation," the film's prologue announces, but *Wilson* was not so much about the man as about the peace ending World War I and the need for international cooperation. Zanuck's epic argued that the League of Nations and collective security could have prevented World War II.

Wilson deserves credit for taking politics seriously, but while the movie's intentions were good, it was long and dull. Personalities, issues, and political processes were radically oversimplified, and Wilson himself got the Lincoln treatment: he is wise and good while Europeans are greedy and vindictive and the Americans who oppose the League of Nations are fools. The movie was successful despite its lecturing, winning both audience and critical favor. The *New York Times* called the film's politics "authentic," singling out the exciting scenes at the party convention where Wilson first wins the presidential nomination, although the reviewer conceded that the movie was chauvinistic in its exclusively American viewpoint and gave no credit to European leaders or perspectives.[13]

Not everyone agreed with this assessment, however. *Wilson* caused almost as much of a furor in 1944 as *Mission to Moscow* had the year before. Republicans and isolationists denounced it as propaganda for Roosevelt's 1944 reelection campaign. Darryl Zanuck, its producer, denied the charge, pointing out that he was himself a Republican. The film, he said, was his "personal crusade for world peace."[14] Although a million people went to see *Wilson* within five weeks of its release and it earned over $3 million in two years, the film did not recoup its $5 million cost. The loss, combined with the controversy, may have discouraged Twentieth Century-Fox from making other movies with similar themes.

With few exceptions, the propagandistic wartime movies were flops, and even the exceptions were controversial. As a consequence, Hollywood grew increasingly cautious about sending political messages, for even when quality and profits were highest, the movies came under attack from politicians who did not share the filmmakers' point of view. Both the House of Representatives and the Senate accused Hollywood of encouraging war, promoting Roosevelt, or leaning to the left (never the right). The Production Code Administration also kept the pressure on, although a few filmmakers challenged its rules. As early as 1943, Howard Hughes let immoral people have a happy ending in *The Outlaw,* starring Jane Russell.

The close scrutiny of the censors and the intense attacks of the politicians indicated how influential they thought the movies were. And if the tremendous size of the audience was a measure of the influence of films, they were right. But even as their audience was at its largest, filmmakers retreated from political topics. This retreat may have reflected the mood of the country after long years of depression and war. The sheer size of audiences may have led filmmakers to seek maximum profits by avoiding controversial topics. Most likely, producers and studios refused to support political projects because of their wartime disasters and their nervousness about interference from Washington.

Socially Reflective Movies versus Social Problem Movies in the Postwar Era

The increasing cautiousness of filmmakers reflected the mood of the nation, as the optimism that immediately followed the war mixed with fear of the future precipitated by the cold war abroad and difficulties in adjusting to peacetime at home. The musicals of the late 1940s expressed the optimistic viewpoint while the style that came to be known as film noir expressed the fear.

From *Meet Me in St. Louis* (1944) through *Easter Parade* (1948), and *On the Town* (1949), Hollywood sang and danced its way through the postwar era, led by Judy Garland, Gene Kelly, and Fred Astaire. MGM virtually specialized in the genre. Less political than the musicals of the early 1930s, these movies presented an almost perfect world in which problems could be solved simply by making an effort.

Film noir was just the reverse, as dark in its mood as in its lighting. In movies like *The Strange Love of Martha Ivers* (1946), *The Postman Always Rings Twice* (1946), and *The Lady from Shanghai* (1948), dangerous women (Barbara Stanwyck, Lana Turner, Rita Hayworth) lured weak men (Van Heflin, John Garfield, Orson Welles) to their fate, often aided and abetted by charming villains. Although not overtly political, these movies reflected the postwar sense of social breakdown and dislocation and commented on class structure through their use of rich villains and poor victims. There was nothing reformist about these films, however. They portrayed a big, bad world where sinners—especially grasping women—were punished. Among these motion pictures, only Abraham Polonsky's *Force of Evil* (1948) stands out as a forthright condemnation of the corrupting qualities of capitalism.

Another little group of postwar movies combined the optimism and pessimism of the times in their treatment of social issues. Their look and point of view often resembled film noir, but their resolution was almost always optimistic as good people overcame adversity through love, understanding, or individual effort. One of the first and most important of these social problem films was *The Best Years of Our Lives* (1946), a melodrama about three soldiers adjusting to civilian life. This sad and moving film criticized the treatment of returning veterans by callous civilians bent on business as usual, but it offered no solution other than the assurance that the love of a good woman and the passage of time would heal all wounds. *Pride of the Marines* (1945) and *Till the End of Time* (1946) tackled the same subject, but *The Best Years of Our Lives*, produced by Samuel Goldwyn, was the most successful of these films, becoming the top box office attraction of 1947, winning the approbation of the critics, and sweeping the Academy Awards.

Director Edward Dmytryk combined the problems of veterans with racial bigotry in *Crossfire* (1947), the story of a demented ex-soldier who murders a Jew. Anti-Semitism was also the theme of Elia Kazan's *Gentleman's Agreement* (1947), in which Gregory Peck plays a writer who pretends to be Jewish for eight weeks. He confronts crass prejudice in hotels and eventually condemns even those who claim to disapprove of anti-Semitism but who say nothing and thereby condone it. In *Pinky* (1949), Kazan dealt with the problems of a young black woman trying to pass as white. Prejudice against blacks was also the subject of *Home of the Brave* (1949) and *Intruder in the Dust* (1949). *Home of the Brave* dealt with the discrimination suffered by a black GI, while *Intruder* reiterated the antilynching theme of the 1930s but faced up to the fact that most of the victims were black.

Most of these movies seem transparently naïve and didactic today. They rarely got beneath the surface of the problems they tackled, and their solutions were invariably based on the assumption that we are all alike anyway. Veterans, Jews, African-Americans, Native Americans, Latinos, and juvenile delinquents were all portrayed as human beings in need of understanding. Prejudice was bad, according to these films, but the solution was simple because the problem went no deeper than ignorance. Racism was not institutional but personal; delinquency was not social but individual. These movies seem mild now, but they were testing the limits then, and at least one study found that films like *Crossfire, Gentleman's Agreement,* and *Pinky* had a slightly positive effect on viewers' tolerance of the minority groups that were their subjects. The oversimplification of these problem films is put into historical context by Leonard Quart and Albert Auster, who argue that they are "yet another sign of the overwhelming optimism of the era; an optimism which refused to see any problem as insoluble."[15]

These films were taken seriously in their time, however, and some of them were big hits. *The Best Years of Our Lives, Crossfire, Gentleman's Agreement,* and *Pinky* all did well with the public and the critics and won Academy Award nominations. Both *Best Years* and *Gentleman's Agreement* won the Oscar as best picture. But these movies were also controversial. *Gentleman's Agreement, Force of Evil, Home of the Brave,* and *Pinky* were condemned as Communist propaganda because they presented a negative picture of the United States. A Texas theater owner was jailed for screening *Pinky.* Clearly, the "overwhelming optimism of the era" had its limits.

Political Films Reject Politics

With the Justice Department antitrust suit in progress and congressional investigations beginning in 1947, Hollywood tended to steer clear of politics and limit its messages to tolerance and understanding. Filmmakers rarely exercised their power to fight back. It must have seemed easier just to keep quiet for a while and wait for the politicians to go away. Hollywood therefore avoided political films, except for a few comedies and stories about bosses or martyrs, all fairly safe bets. Some, like *The Senator Was Indiscreet* (1947), were throwbacks to the 1930s. William Powell plays a senator who seeks his party's presidential nomination but loses out when he misplaces his little black book, which is full of dark secrets about the party—a standard portrait of dirty politics.

Billy Wilder directed and cowrote a more timely and sophisticated political film in *A Foreign Affair* (1948). In this acute satire, Jean Arthur is a member of a congressional delegation investigating the morale of American troops in postwar Berlin. She gets involved with an army captain (John Lund) whose German mistress (Marlene Dietrich) provides a sharp contrast between American naiveté and European world-weariness.

Meanwhile, Frank Capra was pushing the movie view of domestic politics into the postwar era with his prescient *State of the Union* (1948). Like his earlier film, *It's a Wonderful Life* (1946), this movie lacked the frothy Capracorn that had marked his work during the 1930s. The postwar world seemed more dangerous to Capra, and his solutions were neither simple nor happy.

In State of the Union, Grant Matthews (Spencer Tracy) is a rich airplane manufacturer and all-round good guy who is drawn into politics by his mistress, Kay Thorndyke (Angela Lansbury), a powerful Republican publishing heiress with a lust for power. Matthews, a populist and an idealist, is eager to bring his good works to government. When he becomes a candidate for president, Matthews needs his estranged wife (Katharine Hepburn) by his side, and she voluntarily complies. Not a normal politician, Matthews says just what he thinks, but this only increases his popularity. He advocates world government and condemns interest groups for caring only about themselves and not the greater good. Thorndyke, his publisher-mentor, puts him under the guidance of a cynical, corrupt political hack (Adolphe Menjou), who introduces Matthews to some harsh political realities: "The only difference between Democrats and Republicans is that they're in and we're out." When the candidate is impressed by public admiration, the hack is incredulous. "Those letters are just from *people*," he sneers, "not state chairmen!" He soon has his candidate stumping for support from labor, farmers, business, ethnics, southerners, and professional politicians. Pushed by the publisher and the hack, Matthews begins to want the nomination enough to make any deal to get it.

He is kept loyal to his own principles by his wife and her ally, a wise-cracking, good-hearted journalist (Van Johnson). These two, but especially Hepburn as the wife, function as Capra's voice in *State of the Union,* encouraging the candidate to say what he thinks and put his faith in "the common man." Capra also makes his points though the voices of waiters and maids who express faith in Matthews. But the candidate is seduced and ready to sell out until he sees his wife sell out herself by making a televised speech about him that she does not believe. In the end, he recoils with disgust and announces that he will dog the politicians to make them tell the truth, but he will not be a candidate himself. Husband and wife are reunited; publisher and hack move on to their next victim.

State of the Union stirred up almost as much controversy as Capra's *Mr. Smith,* partly because, unlike other fictional political films up to that time, it named real people and real parties. Some saw it as favoring then-President Truman because it seemed to attack the old, Harding-style Republican machine. Capra may have felt sympathy for Truman as the closest the nation has come to putting one of his idealized common men in the White House, but Truman was hardly free of the taint of machine politics. Neither the controversy nor good reviews earned much of an audience for *State of the Union.*

This movie deserved better, however, because its treatment of politics was so much more sophisticated than that in earlier political films. Capra's portrait of interest group politics and his hint at the future importance of television put the film ahead of its time, but he had also moved away from his earlier faith in the common man and his depictions of good-hearted citizens triumphing over corrupt politicians. Here he presented a political world ruled by a power elite represented by the publisher, the party boss, and a gaggle of character actors who spoke for various vested interests. In the 1930s, Mr. Smith had stood, fought, and won; in the late 1940s, Grant Matthews saves his integrity by walking away. The people support him, but they are not strong enough to defeat the organizational elite. This cynical view of politics was all the more powerful coming from Frank Capra.

The populism familiar from Capra's earlier films had a darker tone in this one and grew even darker in *All the King's Men* (1949), which warned against the public tolerance for corruption and propensity to fascism. Broderick Crawford plays Willie Stark in this fictionalized version of the career of Huey Long, the populist demagogue who dominated Louisiana politics for a generation. Robert Rossen, one of Hollywood's most progressive filmmakers, wrote and directed the movie based on Robert Penn Warren's novel.

Willie Stark begins as an idealistic man of the people. He runs for office but loses to the corrupt local organization, so he adapts and comes to terms with the machine: "I'd make a deal with the devil if it'll help me carry out my program." When he becomes governor, he fulfills his promises, building roads and hospitals for the rural folk who elected him. The ends seem to justify the means, and we are on his side, but Willie soon becomes cynical and corrupt, a demagogue who misleads and manipulates his people, misusing and wasting their tax money on useless projects. He crudely compromises the old elite, represented by an affluent, educated, liberal family, when he takes their daughter (Joanne Dru) as his mistress and their son (John Ireland) as his aide. The adoring masses are symbolized by another of Stark's aides (Mercedes McCambridge), who is blindly in love with him and resolutely loyal. These three are sympathetic characters, but it is apparent that their own weakness has betrayed them. Willie Stark is assassinated in the end, punished for his transgressions, as was Huey Long.

Aside from the Academy Award–winning performances of Broderick Crawford and Mercedes McCambridge, Rossen's preachy film has not held up well over time. Some critics noted its preachiness in 1949, but others admired the film. The *New York Times* thought it was "raw, racy . . . pictorial journalism," a "rip-roaring film."[16] Power corrupts, this movie tells us—not a new theme in American political films, but one that was frequently reiterated after the war. *All the King's Men* also warned against putting too much faith in leaders. The film was careful, however, to make it clear that the fault was not only in the leaders but also in the corrupt and decadent society that accepted them. Fascism could arise in America, in other words, if the masses put their faith in the wrong leaders.

In *State of the Union,* Grant Matthews must walk away from power to retain his integrity, a conclusion that condemned not only power but politics as well—good men could not get involved. In *All the King's Men,* Willie Stark takes the other path and is destroyed when he goes too far. Perhaps it is reassuring that such an evil leader is doomed, but the alternatives presented by these two films of the late 1940s represent an alarmingly discouraging view of politics and a shift in the messages of political films. Although earlier movies had criticized the corruption of politics and politicians, they always provided a solution, usually in the form of a heroic leader or "the people." The movies of the late 1940s and early 1950s were more profoundly cynical. Great leaders like Roosevelt, good programs like the New Deal, even faith in the people, were no longer enough. Postwar optimism had already turned to pessimism, even cynicism, especially about politics. This bleak view would dominate political films for three decades.

7

The 1950s

Anti-Communism and Conformity

The Last Hurrah (1958)

The antipolitical films of the late 1940s and early 1950s played to an apolitical nation, a nation that chose a nonpolitician, the moderately conservative Dwight Eisenhower, to serve as its president from 1952 to 1960. This was a prosperous time for America, a time for big cars, television sets, suburban houses, and large families. Joan Mellen, author of *Big Bad Wolves,* suggests that the films of the 1950s reflected this prosperity in their "glorification and reinforcement of individual success and crass material gain."[1] But Americans in the early 1950s also had to come to terms with an increasingly urban and corporate nation. The old emphasis on individualism had to be tempered to suit the new organizational context, which demanded conformity and consensus, and this change, too, showed up in the movies. America in the 1950s was also adjusting to being a world power. The cold war grew hot in Korea in 1950 and cold again when that "limited war" ended in stalemate in 1953. At home, the threat of Communism produced fear that bordered on paranoia, and that fear reinforced consensus and conformity and gave birth to a fervid anti-Communism that culminated in the career of Senator Joseph McCarthy.

The forces of conformity and consensus were so strong in the 1950s that they dominate our memories and images of the decade. Postwar optimism and faith in the future had been strengthened by prosperity and widespread support for the moderate conservatism of President Eisenhower. But the nation was not as placid as it seemed. International politics was dominated by the cold war, and the sense of American hegemony was fading. In 1956, America stood by as the Soviet Union invaded Hungary. The following year Russia launched its *Sputnik* satellite, and America felt technologically inferior for the first time in decades. When Fidel Castro signed a trade agreement with the Soviet Union in 1959, Communism seemed to have arrived at America's doorstep. And the threat of nuclear war loomed over all the events of the decade.

Even as the world became a more dangerous place, the paranoia of the House Un-American Activities Committee (HUAC) and Senator Joseph McCarthy fell into discredit, and domestic politics became more complex as liberals grew braver and new social movements emerged. The civil rights movement gained momentum and by 1957 was in the forefront of American politics, where it would stay for two decades. Rock and roll and the Beat movement drove a significant wedge between generations, and journalists pounded the wedge in deeper by mocking the bland conformity of suburbia and the organization men in their gray flannel suits.

All these changes were mirrored and sometimes predicted by the movies. Political films were still made, though they were fewer and different. Social issue films peaked in the late 1940s, but kept appearing right through the 1950s. Among them were an increasing number of movies about rebellious teenagers, like *The Wild One* (1953) and *Rebel Without a Cause* (1955). But this was also

110

a time when new genres emerged and old ones changed as the power of the studios and the Production Code Administration (PCA) broke down.

As the nation and world changed, the film industry itself was restructured by the studios' divestiture of their theater chains. In 1949, the Justice Department had given them five years to implement divestiture, which, when completed, denied them their captive exhibitors and thus their captive audiences. By the 1950s, theater owners could compete for films by bidding and could refuse to show studio productions that they perceived as inferior or controversial. This development may have discouraged the studios from taking risks on political subjects, for few political films were produced after divestiture was implemented in 1954, but it also gave independent producers access to audiences. As a result, independents were the major source of political films by the late 1950s.

Even more than divestiture, the studios worried about television. Weekly movie attendance dropped from 90 million a week in 1948 to 40 million in 1958. TV broke the habit of regular moviegoing. A worried Hollywood tried to lure audiences back with extravagant historical epics and technical innovations that TV could not match, like VistaVision and 3-D. "Movies are better than ever," a desperate advertising campaign declared.

The result of these elaborate efforts and declining box office receipts was fewer, more costly films designed to draw huge audiences. Annual production fell from 383 films in 1950 to 154 in 1960. And the more spectacular Hollywood films became, the less political they were, at least in terms of overt, contemporary politics. Independent filmmakers like Stanley Kramer made a few political films during the 1950s, and the lack of studio controls may have let the independents express their ideas more freely, but their political output remained modest, because the caution of investors and distributors made it hard to raise the necessary money. However, the studio-produced epics, westerns, and science fiction movies of the era sometimes had political content. Michael Wood points out that persecution of minorities is the theme of several epics, including *Quo Vadis* (1951), *The Robe* (1953) and *Ben Hur* (1959), while Stanley Kubrick's *Spartacus* (1960) delivers a lesson about revolution.[2] Other film historians have noted the allegorical politics of westerns like *High Noon* (1952) and sci-fi movies like *The Thing* (1951) and *Invasion of the Body Snatchers* (1956).

As it turned out, however, Hollywood had another reason to avoid political films in the form of the HUAC and the Red Scare (see Chapter 3).

Hollywood Joins the Anti-Communist Crusade

Hollywood made at least thirty-three anti-Communist films between 1947 and 1954,[3] although many more scored antired points allegorically or featured

Communist villains. These productions, peaking in number just after the 1947 and 1951 hearings, suggest that the film industry got the hint when HUAC asked director Leo McCarey, a cooperative witness, if he thought Hollywood made enough anti-Communist films.

The first among those that did get made was *The Iron Curtain* (1948), a box office failure produced by Darryl Zanuck and directed by William Wellman. This was a traditional espionage story in which the Communist characters were so villainous that outraged leftists picketed it when it opened. The following year saw the release of three box office flops: *The Red Menace, The Red Danube,* and *I Married a Communist*, a Howard Hughes production starring Robert Ryan, which *Time* magazine referred to as "a celluloid bullet aimed at the USSR."[4] This movie also attacked the West Coast dockworkers union, which then had Communist leaders, and it was allegedly used to test the politics of various directors, thirteen of whom refused to work on it.[5] When the film failed, Hughes withdrew it, edited it so as to deemphasize its politics, and then released it as *The Woman on Pier 13,* but it was no more successful. Despite their failure, these movies entrenched the "dirty Commie" stereotype. Sleazy, immoral, often fat and effeminate, these characters left no doubt that they were bad guys, and audiences saw them over and over in the 1950s, just as they had seen the same stereotypes as Nazis a decade earlier.

A somewhat less overtly anti-Communist film, *The Fountainhead,* was also released in 1949. Surprisingly, King Vidor, the progressive maker of *The Big Parade* and *Our Daily Bread*, directed this one. The principal source of the conservatism in *The Fountainhead,* however, was not Vidor but the reactionary author of the story, Ayn Rand. She was a leader of the archconservative, anti-Communist Motion Picture Alliance for the Preservation of American Ideals and the formulator of the "Screen Guide for Americans." Published to coincide with the 1947 HUAC hearings as a supplement to the Motion Picture Producers and Distributors of America's production code, Rand's guide advised filmmakers not to "smear the free-enterprise system . . . success" or "industrialists," not to "deify the 'common man,'" and not to "glorify the collective."[6]

The Fountainhead reflects these directives in its story of Howard Roark (Gary Cooper), an avant-garde architect who is nearly hounded out of his profession by traditionalists and conformists. He gets a few jobs and becomes a modest success, but when his design for a public housing project is altered, he blows up the building. At the trial that follows, he makes an impassioned plea for artistic integrity and individual rights. The jurors swallow the dynamiter's line and let him off.

The Fountainhead clearly expressed Rand's right-wing libertarianism. The enemy is the public, whipped up by cynical media manipulators. The declared intent of one of them, improbably an architecture critic, is to raise the collective and destroy the individual. But despite the movie's condemnation of the masses and public opinion, in the end Roark demands public approval for his act of destruction and gets it from the jury and a courtroom audience. Thanks to its often ludicrous sexuality, *The Fountainhead* has become a camp classic, but contemporary critics did not think it was funny. "The most asinine and inept movie that has come from Hollywood for years," sneered the *New Yorker*; "long-winded, complicated preachment . . . pretentious . . . turgid . . . twaddle," agreed the *New York Times*.[7] Apparently critics did not feel compelled to please HUAC by praising a right-wing film.

The Fountainhead was unusually indirect, however, in its attack on Communism. Far more typical was *Big Jim McLain* (1952), which starred John Wayne as a HUAC agent purging Communists from Hawaii. Production of these anti-Communist films peaked with thirteen in 1952 alone, just a year after HUAC renewed its investigation. Among these was *My Son John,* Leo McCarey's response to HUAC.

McCarey's movie is about the all-American Jefferson family, played by familiar actors in familiar parts. Dean Jagger is the American Legionnaire father, Helen Hayes the devoutly Catholic mother, and Robert Walker their misled son John. When the intellectual, college-educated John comes home for a visit and makes sarcastic remarks about the American Legion, his father questions John's Americanism. Then a visit from the FBI worries Mom, who is reassured when John swears his loyalty on her Bible. "John stands for everything I stand for," she explains. "He's just a liberal. Saint Paul was a liberal." Dad is not so sure, though. "How's your supper coming?" he asks his wife, sending her scurrying away so he can have a man-to-man talk with his son. They argue, John makes some anti-American remarks, and Dad hits him with a Bible. When John returns to Washington, his mother follows him to return a key he has left behind. Learning from the FBI that the key is for the apartment of a female spy, Mom uses the key and confronts her son. He confesses to having an affair, but denies that he is a spy. The unbelieving mother turns him in to the FBI, then with rosary in hand, tearfully begs him to confess. "Take him away," she says when he refuses. "You have to be punished, John." The FBI agent urges him to "Use whatever free will you have. Give up. Name names." John escapes, then remorsefully phones the FBI and agrees to turn himself in and become an informer. On his way, the Communists shoot up his taxi, which crashes ostentatiously on the steps of the Lincoln Memorial. Fortunately, he has left a tape-recorded confession, which is melodramatically played for the graduating class at his alma mater.

Like other films of this cycle, *My Son John* casts suspicion on intellectuals and liberals, who are perceived as easy dupes for Communists. The film disapproves of John for rushing off to see his egghead professor when he first comes home instead of staying with his parents, who represent the traditional American values of patriotism, religion, and family. John is advised to emulate the simple-minded patriotism of his father and "think with your heart, not your head," as his mother puts it. Nobody in this film does much thinking, however. Fortunately, the FBI is there to take care of things, although one agent admits that "those with something to hide" often criticize its methods.

My Son John was better than most of the anti-Communist movies, although its thinking was muddled and its plot was jumbled, possibly because lead actor Robert Walker died before the film was completed. The critics noted both flaws. The *New York Times* called it "cultural vigilantism," endorsing a "stool pigeon" mother and a father's "stubborn bigotry" as well as taking "a snide attitude toward intellectuals."[8] Although the critics did not like *My Son John,* Hollywood signaled its approval by nominating McCarey's original story for an Academy Award, perhaps for HUAC's benefit. McCarey himself argued that the film had a happy ending, saying, "I've never yet ended a film on a note of futility."[9] John is dead and his family is broken, but McCarey saw John's tape-recorded speech as a kind of redemption. Better dead than red!

My Son John was one of the last of the crusading anti-Communist films. By 1954, Senator McCarthy had brought about his own downfall through his investigation of the army and his attacks on the president. HUAC also faded away. The cold war went on and so did the blacklist, but few anti-Communist movies were made after 1953, partly because the pressure was off and also because audiences had not flocked to the earlier films.

The Quiet American (1957), a film that was both behind and ahead of its time, was perhaps a vestige of this cycle. Writer-director Joseph Mankiewicz puts a distinctively American twist in his adaptation of a novel by British author Graham Greene. The scene is Vietnam in the early 1950s, with the French fighting a Communist-nationalist revolution. Thomas Fowler (Michael Redgrave) is a British journalist cynically observing the decline of European imperialism and the rise of American power and the Third World. He tells the story of an American, played by Audie Murphy. Caught between the two men and the worlds they represent is Phuong (Giorgia Moll), a Vietnamese girl who spurns her European lover when she falls for the American.

The film follows Greene's novel closely at first. The American arrives in Saigon spouting his professor's theory about the need for "a third force" that is neither imperialist nor Communist. Fowler, the journalist, presumes that the American is an undercover agent for his government. In the book, this is true and the American is destroyed when his plot goes awry, but Mankiewicz balked at this anti-American message. "I have no politics," says the journalist, but a nasty Communist agent persuades him that the American is aiding terrorist murderers and insists, "Sooner or later, one has to take sides." Fowler gives in, losing his professional objectivity and aiding the Communists, not only to prevent terrorism but also to destroy his rival. The American turns out to be innocent, merely a do-gooder who imports food, not bombs. A French policeman explains that "the idea had to be murdered," apparently meaning that aid was as threatening to Communists as military intervention.

Although better than earlier anti-Communist movies, *The Quiet American* also flopped with critics and audiences. These films may have failed less because of their message than because of their sledgehammer delivery—their political intent was too obvious for their own good. In the end, they may have hurt the anti-Communist cause more than they helped it. A 2002 version of *The Quiet American* starring Michael Caine as the anguished Brit and Brendan Fraser as the American stuck closer to Graham Greene's novel and made its political points with more subtlety.

In Other Words

But Hollywood did not enlist en masse in HUAC's holy war. Dissenters survived and even dared to speak out against the cold war and HUAC's witch hunt, although they often did so indirectly or allegorically.

High Noon (1952) was a western, but according to Carl Foreman, who wrote it, "What *High Noon* was about at the time, was Hollywood and no other place but Hollywood."[10] Producer Stanley Kramer, a leading Hollywood liberal, and Foreman, who was soon to be blacklisted, were commenting on the filmmakers' abandonment of their colleagues who were under attack by HUAC. This film is about a sheriff (Gary Cooper) who gets no help from the townspeople when a vengeful gang of killers comes after him. No cavalry arrives representing the federal government, nor do the people rally around their sheriff, as in the populist movies of the 1930s. *High Noon* is a bleak story of one man's courage in a cowardly society. Its left-leaning politics were smoothly folded into a movie that became a hit with audiences and critics and picked up Oscars for Cooper's performance and Dmitri Tiompkin's music.

Meanwhile, those who had cooperated with HUAC defended themselves in works like *On the Waterfront* (1954), written by Budd Schulberg, featuring Lee J. Cobb and Leif Erickson, and directed by Elia Kazan, all of whom had named names for HUAC. Kazan had joined the crusade against Communism with *Viva Zapata!* (1952) and *Man on a Tightrope* (1953), in which a Czechoslovakian circus owner tries to escape from Communism, but *On the Waterfront* was not so much an anti-Communist movie as a vindication of informers.

Making an informer into a hero, however, was no mean feat. Stool pigeons had always been disdained in American folklore and movies.

Terry Malloy (Marlon Brando) is the informer in *On the Waterfront.* His girl friend (Eva Marie Saint) and a priest (Karl Malden) urge him to tell a government investigator (Leif Erickson) the truth about the corrupt activities of a union boss (Lee J. Cobb). Terry must choose between his loyalty to friends and coworkers and a higher order represented by the girl, the priest, and the investigator. His choice is simplified when the mob rubs out not only Terry's brother (Rod Steiger), but his pet pigeons as well.

"The message is clear," Victor Navasky writes. "The injunction against informing is all right as a guideline for an adolescent gang, but it won't do for adults who are obliged to look at each situation in its own moral context. (What's ratting for them is telling the truth for you.) Squealing is relative."[11] Besides, Terry really has no choice, and the audience has no option but to sympathize with him. Not only must he avenge the murder of his brother and loss of his pigeons, but he must also fight the corrupt union, win the girl, and please the priest and the investigator.

Beyond its justification of informing, *On the Waterfront* is politically orthodox. Like other movies about politics, it praises individual action and a benign government. It never occurs to Terry, for example, to rally the troops and reform the union from within; collective action simply is not an option. Instead, like a good corporate liberal, he puts himself in the hands of the federal agents. Still, Kazan managed to make *On the Waterfront* and his other socially conscious films complex enough for their messages to be palatable. The public and the critics liked *On the Waterfront,* and it swept the Oscars.

An even grittier movie about the working class was made the same year, however. Funded by a mine workers union, *Salt of the Earth* was a collaborative effort by blacklisted filmmakers, including its director, Herbert Biberman. Except for Rosaura Revueltas, a Mexican movie star, and a few American character actors like Will Geer (who later played Grandpa Walton on television), the cast was made up of miners and their families.

In *Salt of the Earth,* the Mexican-American zinc miners go on strike because Anglo workers in their company's other mines have better pay and working conditions. The company says it "can't afford equality," however, and it uses cheap Mexican labor to keep the Anglos in line. While the men strike over salaries and working conditions, the women meet and independently decide to strike over housing and sanitation in the company town. The men shrug these demands off, saying they are not as important as working conditions, but when a court order prohibits them from picketing and the women replace them, the men take over the housework and soon agree to include the women's demands in the bargaining. The vote to put the women on the picket line is the turning point that solidifies the community. The miners are aided by their international union and others, but the film makes it clear that they are essentially on their own and treats them with great reverence. Only the company men and the sheriff (Will Geer) come off badly; they are caricatured in a turnabout of Hollywood tradition.

Salt of the Earth was remarkable for being feminist when no movies, liberal or conservative, recognized women's issues, but what was truly remarkable was that a leftist film was made at all at the height of McCarthyism. Not surprisingly, the production process was often disrupted. The filmmakers were harassed by gun-carrying townspeople on location, and the Mexican actress who played the lead was deported three times during the shooting of the film. After it was completed, distributors boycotted it and the projectionists' union refused to screen it. In the end, *Salt of the Earth* was screened in only eleven theaters, most of them in New York and Los Angeles, and then it was not seen again for a decade. Even now, the film is shown mainly in union halls and at leftist conferences, and it is not listed in most film reference books.

Salt of the Earth was attacked out of all proportion to the size of its audiences. The American Legion condemned it, and the cinemas showing it were picketed. Film historian Andrew Dowdy remembers being "warned to park [his car] blocks away . . . because FBI men were taking down license plate numbers at the theater."[12] *Variety* screamed that the Russians had to be prevented from getting prints or they would use the movie as anti-American propaganda,[13] but other reviews were more balanced. *Time* conceded that "within the propagandistic limits it sets," it was "a vigorous work of art" from which "social anger hisses."[14] Whatever its flaws, *Salt of the Earth* provided an alternative vision of workers and unions and was particularly notable for its feminism. Many Americans shared its political perspective, a perspective that they rarely saw on film. Nor did most of them see *Salt of the Earth*. And Hollywood, of course, took note of its fate.

A more direct rebuttal of HUAC came in Daniel Taradash's *Storm Center* (1956), "a sure loser as the only attack on HUAC ever made in a Hollywood studio," according to Andrew Dowdy.[15] In this movie, Bette Davis plays a librarian who refuses to remove from her library a book called *The Communist Dream*. She is accused of belonging to Communist front groups and fired, but a boy gets carried away and burns the library down. *Storm Center* attacked the inquisitorial, guilt-by-association techniques of HUAC, but the message of free speech was so oversimplified that even the Daughters of the American Revolution endorsed it, and the movie was an unqualified flop. *Storm Center* was not Hollywood's last word on the deep trauma of the investigations, the pain of which is still not forgotten. But even in the early 1950s and certainly later in that decade, other issues were arising in the nation and in the movies.

117

Other Takes on Politics in the Early 1950s

While the Red Scare dominated Hollywood and shaped the themes of most of the political films of the early 1950s, more traditional films about politics and social issues were also produced, though they were fewer and more cautious.

Hollywood expressed its liberalism in a number of films that featured minorities. The image of Indians, for example, was rehabilitated in *Broken Arrow* (1950), with Jeff Chandler playing Cochise and James Stewart as the government agent who understands him. In *Apache* (1954), Indians, portrayed as pretty much like the rest of us, settle down on farms. Latinos received less attention, but Joseph Losey, later a target of the HUAC witch-hunters, directed *The Lawless* (1950), an update of *The Grapes of Wrath* centering on Mexican-American migrants, and Elia Kazan cast Marlon Brando as the lead in *Viva Zapata!* (1952). Later, *Giant* (1956), a precursor of TV's *Dallas* and *Dynasty,* starring Rock Hudson, Elizabeth Taylor, and James Dean, preached a mild sermon about equality for women and Latinos. Sidney Poitier made his debut in *No Way Out* (1950), while conservatives Ginger Rogers and Ronald Reagan did their bit in the anti-KKK *Storm Warning* (1950). Poitier was back in *The Defiant Ones* (1958), and racism was also a theme in *Imitation of Life* (1959). A different social problem, juvenile delinquency, hit the screens in 1955 in *The Blackboard Jungle* and *Rebel Without a Cause.* Both were controversial, but *The Blackboard Jungle* was condemned as Communist propaganda because it presented a negative picture of the United States.

Meanwhile, three films of the early 1950s took on politics in a more direct and traditional way. One was a comedy, one a biopic, and one a drama, but all three were high on both political content and intent.

The most successful of the three was *Born Yesterday* (1950), a comedy directed by George Cukor. After a shot of the Capitol that tells us where we are, we meet Harry (Broderick Crawford), a junk man who has become a big time "dealer in scrap metals" in Washington and who has attempted to further his own interests by bribing some congressmen. With him is Billie (Judy Holliday), his crass mistress. Harry persuades Paul (William Holden), a reporter, to coach Billie and make her more presentable; Paul agrees in order to spy on Harry. "Harry's a menace," Paul instructs Billie. "The whole history of the world is the story of the struggle between the selfish and the unselfish. . . . All that's bad around us is bred by selfishness. Sometimes selfishness is a cause, an organized force, even a government, and then it's called fascism." Paul, on the other hand, represents intellect, enlightenment, altruism, even democracy—plus he is cute. He wins Billie's affection, and she helps him expose Harry. Good triumphs over evil, and *Born Yesterday* makes it clear that Harry is out of date when even his cynical attorney tells him that despite

118

"a few bad apples," congressmen are basically honest. Cukor's film was well received by both the public and the critics and is still a favorite, thanks largely to Judy Holliday's performance, for which she won an Oscar. Melanie Griffith played the part in a less successful remake in 1993.

Viva Zapata! (1952), a biopic about the Mexican peasant revolutionary Emiliano Zapata, was written by John Steinbeck and directed, perhaps surprisingly, by Elia Kazan, who had named names as a witness before HUAC. Zapata, played by Marlon Brando, is motivated to lead a revolution not out of any profound political beliefs, but to win land for his people. The revolution succeeds, but its leaders bicker and more fighting ensues until Zapata reluctantly accepts the presidency. He is encouraged by Fernando (Joseph Wiseman), a bizarre-looking political manipulator who is dressed in black and apparently intended as a stereotypical Marxist revolutionary. Zapata soon feels he is being corrupted by power, like other leaders before him, so he resigns and returns to his people where, eventually, he must again lead a guerrilla revolution. The new rulers know how to end this one, however. "Cut off the head of the snake, and the body will die," Fernando advises. "Kill Zapata, and your problem's solved." Zapata, however, has trained his people not to need him. "You've always looked for leaders," he instructs them, "strong men without faults. There aren't any. They're only men like yourselves. They change. They desert. They die. There are no leaders but yourselves. A strong people is the only lasting strength." Zapata goes Christlike to his death, apparently knowing that he has been betrayed but that his spirit will be an inspiration to his people. "Sometimes," an army officer observes, "a dead man can be a terrible enemy."

Viva Zapata! was a modest box office success, perhaps surprising for a movie about a Mexican revolutionary released at the height of McCarthyism in the conservative 1950s, but its message was more romantic than revolutionary. The movie never addressed the root causes of the Mexican Revolution in class conflict, focusing instead on straightforward corruption. Evil men subvert the revolution, presumably in their own interests, and Kazan later claimed that these characters made the movie anti-Communist.

A Lion Is in the Streets (1953) was a more traditional political drama that reiterated the condemnation of demagoguery sounded in *All the King's Men*. *Lion* stars James Cagney as an ambitious man of the people who betrays his own supporters to win the favor of the machine. When even this fails, he leads an armed mob on the state capitol to demand that the legislature resolve a tie vote for the governorship in his favor. Like Willie Stark in *All the King's Men*, he is ultimately assassinated by someone he has wronged. Although the movie's warning about the dangers of strong leaders and mobs was timely in the era of McCarthyism, the movie was pretty much ignored.

With reactions like this plus divestiture, HUAC, and other worries about censorship, no wonder Hollywood backed away from political and social issue films. For all their worries, however, filmmakers continued to challenge the production code and some even became more daring in the conservative, conformist 1950s. Otto Preminger managed to get his sex comedy, *The Moon Is Blue* (1953), screened without code approval despite dialogue that seemed scandalous in those days. He then took on the forbidden subject of drug abuse in *The Man with the Golden Arm* (1955) and got away with that, too. In 1956, the PCA bowing to pressure from the film industry, amended the code to permit the subjects of drugs, abortion, prostitution, kidnapping, and miscegenation. The remaining rules quickly crumbled. Films about homosexuals began to appear, for example, including *Tea and Sympathy* (1958) and *Suddenly Last Summer* (1960). Gradually, fewer and fewer "sinners" were punished.

Most of the code-shattering filmmakers were liberals, but their defiance of the old rules probably had more to do with finding an audience than with the Bill of Rights. Television had taken over middle-of-the-road family entertainment, and moviemakers had to be more daring to sell tickets. They made epics and introduced new techniques (3-D, CinemaScope, VistaVision), but they also made more adult movies, sometimes challenging the intellect, though more often merely titillating with controversial subjects, especially sex.

Changing Genres

While some filmmakers of the 1950s challenged the production code, others remolded old movie genres to suit the changing times. War movies, for example, underwent a transformation after World War II. Peter Biskind points out that World War II films were written mostly by liberals like Lillian Hellman, Dalton Trumbo, and John Howard Lawson. These writers "were preoccupied with articulating war aims—democracy, freedom, brotherhood—and went out of their way to explain why we fought." Films about the Korean War, however, were apolitical adventures, because the moviemakers "didn't know why we fought, and what's more, they didn't care."[16] Biskind goes on to describe three different political perspectives in the war movies of the 1950s. *Attack* (1956) and *Paths of Glory* (1957) were leftist films criticizing war and the military, while *The Court-Martial of Billy Mitchell* (1955) was a conservative condemnation of bureaucracy. The mainstream political ideology of the decade, however, was expressed in the centrist *Strategic Air Command* (1955).

In this film, Dutch (James Stewart) is a baseball player and U.S. Air Force reservist who is recalled to temporary duty. Over the objections of his wife

(June Allyson), he signs up permanently. She would not object, he tells her, if there was a war on, and he explains that "there is a kind of war. We've got to stay ready to fight without fighting. That's even tougher." A bad arm excuses Dutch from service, but not before the film demands public support for the men of the air force and their dependents. Dutch, his wife, and the air force all win, providing a centrist solution, but only after the husband and wife express their willingness to sacrifice their selfish preferences to the greater cause. The film educated audiences on the military policy of the day and, as in the other war films of the decade, shifted the focus from the groups of enlisted men featured in movies about World War II to the officer elite, in whom the nation was to place its trust.

While war movies changed, another genre grew in prominence in the 1950s. The popularity of science fiction movies fed on the new interest in outer space and the anxiety about atomic power. Mostly low in both political content and intent, these films are best understood as socially reflective movies featuring fantastic displacement in which the nation's fears were played out in the fantasy of the movies. Some, however, were more clearly political. In an era when direct political commentary was dangerous, science fiction offered a rich source of allegory. Whether the aliens in these movies were mutants affected by radiation or invaders from another planet, they could represent any threat, from technology gone mad to Communist infiltration.

As with war movies, Peter Biskind sees the political right, left, and center in sci-fi. While the centrist movies reassured us that we were in good hands, the left and right used sci-fi to deliver utopian and antiutopian messages and to warn us not only about invaders but also about the ineptitude of our rulers. Proponents of all three perspectives seemed to agree on the need for vigilance. Right-wing sci-fi was paranoid about infiltration (*The Thing*, 1951; *Them!* 1954) and about people hopelessly searching for utopias (*Forbidden Planet,* 1956) and getting into things they should have kept out of. Science and government often saved the day, as in *Them!* and *Forbidden Planet,* but sometimes they were inept and average guys became heroes, as in *The Thing.* Left-wing sci-fi, on the other hand, had benign aliens offering utopia only to be rejected by dumb humans (*The Day the Earth Stood Still,* 1951). Biskind quotes Jack Arnold, the director of *It Came from Outer Space* (1953), who declared he "wanted to have some meaning to it all. I think science fiction films are a marvelous medium for telling a story, creating a mood, and delivering whatever kind of social message should be delivered. . . . If ten per cent of the audience grasped it, then I was very successful."[17] In centrist sci-fi, danger usually came when nature went berserk (*The Black Scorpion,* 1957; *The Creature from the Black Lagoon,* 1954). Radiation, a new worry in the 1950s, was often at fault, but these movies trusted good scientists or the government to come to the rescue. Alien pods turn normal people into un-feeling automatons in Don Siegel's *Invasion of the Body Snatchers* (1956). Now seen by some film scholars as a leftist condemnation of the conformity of the 1950s, few doubted when it was first released, that it was a rightist denunciation of Communist mind control. The ending, to which Siegel pur-portedly objected, was centrist, however, with the federal government step-ping in to save the day. The invasions and disasters of sci-fi were a perfect medium for centrist messages because they "dramatized the necessity of con-sensus, of pulling together," according to Biskind.[18] Happy endings, pro-vided by government, science, or the military, reassured us that we were in good hands.

Political Films in the Late 1950s: Angry Men, Bosses, and Demagogues

According to Biskind, however, the ultimate centrist political movie of the 1950s was the drama *Twelve Angry Men* (1957), directed by Sidney Lumet. The men of the title are members of a jury, a convenient cross section of American males. They vote 11 to 1 to convict the defendant, but the lone dissenter, a liberal architect played by Henry Fonda, gradually turns them around. The court system works in this film, but only because of the pres-ence of one good man. Although the lone liberal dissenter prevails, it is also important that all the others agree with him in the end, providing a centrist solution typical of the conformist 1950s.

The Last Hurrah (1958) was less distinctly contemporary than *Twelve Angry Men,* but although it reminisced about the good old days of machine politics, it also had something to say about politics in the coming decade. Based on Edwin O'Connor's novel about an aging boss, *The Last Hurrah* was directed by John Ford, whose treatment oozes with nostalgia for a sim-pler past. Although the movie's portrayal of the machine was sympathetic, Boston's mayor James Michael Curley thought its fictional city was suffi-ciently like his own to attempt to have the film suppressed.

Ford's casting of the always-benign Spencer Tracy as boss Frank Skeffington immediately suggests that the machine cannot be all bad. Sev-eral touching scenes in which Skeffington helps his people solve their prob-lems reinforce this impression. The machine is shown to be corrupt only on a small scale, and the point is repeatedly made that politics is a means of social mobility for Irish immigrants like Skeffington. When the town's lead-ing banker, a Yankee aristocrat (Basil Rathbone), refuses to lend the city money for a project Skeffington needs to ensure his reelection, saying "the banks don't consider the city a good risk under the current administration,"

Skeffington responds, "The city is no longer yours, it's ours. That's what really bothers you."

But he is wrong. The power of the machine is crumbling, partly from sheer age, a point made both visually and verbally. The old Yankee aristocracy plots to run a slick but vacuous media candidate against Skeffington to attract the emerging urban middle class, the children of Skeffington's supporters. "Politics is the best spectator sport in the country," Skeffington says as he tries to make the most of his rallies and speeches. But he knows that his old-fashioned campaign style is "on the way out. It'll all be TV," he explains. His bland opponent puts his family on TV in a scene reminiscent of Richard Nixon's famous Checkers speech, complete with dog, and wins the election as Skeffington dies.

The critics found *The Last Hurrah* sentimental, old-fashioned, and oversimplified, although a few thought it gave a good sense of how politics worked. Slow and one-sided as it was, Ford's film is a rich portrait of machine politics that could have been improved by a less saintly Skeffington and a less callow opponent. The younger candidate is so ludicrous that his victory looks like a condemnation of the voters' gullibility—and of TV, which may have reflected the filmmakers' attitude toward the competing medium and its audience. Still, *The Last Hurrah* showed how the machine helped immigrants assimilate and how it cared for people, humanizing and personalizing their government. Sociologists were writing about these functions of the political machines in the 1950s; *The Last Hurrah* illustrated them.

Despite its sentimentality, the movie respected politics, treating politicians as caring and distinctly human people. The younger generation of politicians came off less well, however, as did the old aristocracy. The portrait of this Anglo elite plotting against the upstart Irish gave *The Last Hurrah* added depth by making the class basis of political conflict clear, something few other American political films have accomplished. Condemnation of the elite was not balanced by faith in the masses, however. No respect was shown for the voters in *The Last Hurrah,* no Capra-like trust in the people. Rather, they seem to get what they deserve when the media candidate wins the election.

Such pessimism about the power of television and the gullibility of the people became the theme of several American movies in the 1950s. Elia Kazan took it up in *A Face in the Crowd* (1957), written by his *On the Waterfront* collaborator Budd Schulberg. In this movie, Lonesome Rhodes (Andy Griffith) is a bum who is discovered by a local radio station and catapulted into stardom as a singer and populist philosopher. He ends up grooming a dull conservative candidate for president in return for the promise of becoming secretary for national morale if the candidate wins. Rhodes is cynical, using his talent and the television medium only to gain sex, wealth, and power.

The politicians are equally cynical, using Rhodes and his methods to sell themselves rather than their programs to the voters. Rhodes is done in when a spurned lover leaves a microphone on after he thinks he is off the air. The demagogue's insulting remarks turn his audience against him, and his fame and power dissipate over night.

Kazan was commenting more on the superficial power of television than on politics, but *A Face in the Crowd* made it clear that politicians would use that power and that the public would be duped unless good people told the truth—and there were not many of them around. Like Ford, Kazan seemed pessimistic about the people.

On Toward Camelot

Political movies had changed during the 1950s. They had begun to deal with discrimination, they had confronted the cold war, and they had learned to look at the Communist threat and the anti-Communist crusade from a new perspective. The result was a substantial body of political films from an era that is commonly perceived as dull and apolitical. Films like *State of the Union, The Last Hurrah,* and *A Face in the Crowd* had new and different things to say. Generally more cynical, they were also more complex, sophisticated, and realistic. Unlike the redemptive politics of some 1920s movies or the longing for strong leaders of the 1930s or even the uplifting triumphs of the people and their innocent leaders best captured by Frank Capra, the political films of this era saw good men destroyed. The message of the 1950s was more a warning than a rallying cry, however, urging conformity over either individualism or collective action.

And while the film rolled, America went from Truman to Eisenhower to Kennedy, from postwar optimism to 1950s paranoia and conformity and, finally, to Camelot. Political films had grown more sophisticated by the Kennedy years, but the liberalism that Kennedy inspired did not catch up with either the nation or its filmmakers until after his assassination in 1963.

8

The 1960s
From Mainstream to Counterculture

Dr. Strangelove or: How I Learned to Stop Worrying and Love the Bomb (1964)

America's youngest president took office in January 1961, ushering in a new political era. John F. Kennedy's tragic death less than three years later has perhaps caused us to exaggerate his stature as a leader, but even so, his presidency signaled a change. The roots of that change were not so much in his politics as in his image.

Kennedy, a moderate Democrat more interested in foreign than domestic policy, identified a "missile gap" between the United States and the Soviet Union and promised to get America moving again. He did, increasing military spending and launching the space program. He also introduced a boldly active cold war interventionism that included the disastrous invasion of Cuba at the Bay of Pigs, a nuclear confrontation with the Soviet Union over missiles based in Cuba, and the beginnings of U.S. involvement in Vietnam.

Kennedy was not so active or interested, however, in such issues as civil rights, urban decay, and poverty. These were issues for which the 1960s would be remembered, but they emerged during and after Kennedy's term in office. He awoke to them as the nation did, but his close election and an uncooperative Congress made domestic politics treacherous for him and he moved slowly on these issues. It was left to his successor, Lyndon B. Johnson, to develop and implement the programs that distinguished the era, assisted by the political momentum of the spirit Kennedy had awakened and by his martyrdom.

While the Kennedy spirit helped liberalize the nation, the civil rights movement provided political momentum, driving both Kennedy and Johnson to the left. Martin Luther King Jr. led the great march on Washington in 1963. The following year saw riots in several urban ghettos to which Johnson responded with his Great Society program. Meanwhile, a wave of student activism started in 1964, evolved into the radical New Left, then into the antiwar movement, and eventually into a youthful counterculture.

Where were the movies? In 1962, *Advise and Consent* caught some of Kennedy's joy in politics, although its conclusion was as consensus-oriented as that of any 1950s movie and as confident that the system worked as *Mr. Smith Goes to Washington*. That same year, *The Manchurian Candidate* expressed some of the wit of the era by putting down McCarthyism, but it managed to do so safely by portraying the Red-baiters as the real Reds. In 1963, *P.T. 109,* an action movie about the World War II exploits of John Kennedy (Cliff Robertson), simultaneously contributed to and cashed in on the young president's popularity. For the most part, however, Hollywood lagged behind the nation, perhaps because it was a bad time for the film industry.

By 1960, average weekly attendance had dropped to 40 million, half what it had been in the 1940s, and by 1970 it had fallen to only 20 million. The number of movie theaters declined, and so did the number of films made, bottoming out with 154 in 1960. Some major studios, like MGM, quit making movies. Multinational corporations absorbed others, including United Artists and Paramount. Moviemakers grew more cautious and profit-conscious, producing fewer films as they concentrated, without great success, on blockbusters.

The movies launched a surprising revival later in the 1960s, however, even as television replaced the motion picture as America's primary entertainment medium. Television took over the middle of the road, freeing movies to search for more selective audiences and thus to take more chances, even on politics. This risk-taking was limited, though, by the studios' corporate conservatism and profit orientation, which now forced them to take lucrative TV sales into consideration when making movies. The continued dominance of a few major distributors was also a constraint, but independent producers like Stanley Kramer could win wide distribution by first proving their films during art house runs in New York and Los Angeles. The number of independent producers grew as distribution opportunities appeared, and liberal filmmakers began to take advantage of the nation's new political mood. Stanley Kramer, Sidney Lumet, Stanley Kubrick, and Martin Ritt became more active, and others, like Dalton Trumbo and Abraham Polonsky, returned to work after having been blacklisted. They were joined by a new generation of politically oriented filmmakers, including Robert Altman, John Frankenheimer, Alan Pakula, Mike Nichols, and Arthur Penn.

There were new audiences, too. Some filmmakers began to exploit the large numbers of young ticket buyers, a move that resulted not only in beach-blanket movies but also in such classics as *Bonnie and Clyde* (1967) and *The Graduate* (1967). Others aimed at the growing and increasingly sophisticated art film audience in big cities and university towns, an audience capable of making "small" movies profitable. The beach-blanket and art house audiences even merged to make big hits of a few independent productions with counterculture themes, like *Easy Rider* (1969).

In the liberal 1960s, the production code finally succumbed to defiant filmmakers, civil libertarians, court decisions, changing politics, and the need for movies to attract audiences by giving them what they could not get on TV. By 1966, the code was advisory rather than mandatory, but it still recommended rewarding virtue, condemning vice, and dealing cautiously with sex. For the first time, it also suggested limits on violence. In 1968, the code was replaced by the more liberal rating system, which limited film audiences to specified age groups, mainly to protect the young from sex, violence, and obscene language. Filmmakers were undoubtedly happy to be free of the code's restrictions, but investors and the public still served as censors, rejecting subjects that offended or angered large groups of people.

Although Hollywood was slow to pick up the politics of the decade, a number of political films of the 1960s mark the beginning of a period during which American filmmakers more willingly criticized the dominant values of their society. Ironically, the decade that is often perceived as America's most political produced fewer political films than the consensus-oriented 1950s or even the 1920s. The American Film Institute subject index of films of the 1960s lists more than seventy movies that touch on political themes—only half as many as are listed for the 1920s.[1]

On the Beach and the Political Films of the Early 1960s

On the Beach, one of the first movies to catch the spirit of the 1960s, was actually made in 1959. Its director, Stanley Kramer, was one of Hollywood's most consistent liberals, generally seeing the people as victims rather than the dupes portrayed in *The Last Hurrah* or *A Face in the Crowd.* Kramer started as producer of *Home of the Brave* (1949), a film about the racism experienced by a black war veteran. He went on to produce *High Noon* (1952), *The Wild One* (1954), and *The Defiant Ones* (1958), which he also directed. All these films as well as Kramer's films in the 1960s were unabashedly political in intent and content, although none dealt explicitly with the political process.

Based on Nevil Shute's best-selling novel, *On the Beach* was an early disaster movie in which the last survivors of a nuclear holocaust, a cross section of humanity played by an all-star cast, await the radioactive clouds of death, mostly with dignity. *On the Beach* opened portentously with "a global premiere" in seventeen cities, including Moscow. It was treated as a profound statement on the need to face the possibility of an atomic future, a theme that had been touched on by sci-fi films but never by a big-budget movie with stars like Gregory Peck, Ava Gardner, and Fred Astaire. It became the film people talked about and felt they had to see. Critics liked it, too, although a few pointed out that it left audiences feeling helpless because it gave no clue as to what could be done to prevent the atomic holocaust. They also observed that the end of the world was more bland than horrifying in *On the Beach.* *Time* noted "what really is horrible about the end of the world: boy does not get girl."[2]

Kramer followed *On the Beach* with *Inherit the Wind* (1960), the story of the Scopes trial, which involved the teaching of Darwin's theory of evolution in Tennessee schools. An impassioned plea for free speech, praising the good citizens who stand up for the persecuted teacher at the risk of angering the mob, the film said as much about the 1950s as it did about the trial. Kramer next turned to persecution and prosecution on a grander scale with *Judgment at Nuremberg* (1961), which tells the story of the Holocaust through the trial of German war criminals. He dealt with anti-Semitism again in *Ship of Fools* (1965), and he took on race relations with *Guess Who's Coming to Dinner* (1967).

Some reviewers considered Kramer's films overly sentimental and simplistic, and they certainly seem so now, but they were popular hits, often garnering Academy Awards and nominations, and they were almost always treated respectfully as must-see movies. Remarkably, Kramer managed to elicit this response despite his consistently liberal perspective. His use of all-star casts helped, and the softness of his liberalism made his messages easy to swallow. He never demanded much more than tolerance, and he rarely called on people to do much more than stand up for the rights of others, although this may have seemed like a lot in the post-McCarthy 1950s and early 1960s. Kramer's movies surely contributed to the development of the social consciousness of the decade's activists, a generation of Americans who were teenagers when Kramer was most prolific.

As the 1960s began, other filmmakers were also showing an interest in politics. *Sunrise at Campobello* (1960) told the story of the beginning of Franklin Delano Roosevelt's career and his battle with polio. One of the last of the big biopics, *Sunrise* was also one of the increasingly rare movies that presented politics as a worthwhile pursuit with a politician as hero. Other political films of the early 1960s took up more contemporary topics. *Exodus* (1960), directed by Otto Preminger and written by Dalton Trumbo, was a popular epic of the founding of modern Israel. Elia Kazan's less successful *Wild River* (1960) dealt with the eradication of traditional rural life by progress in the form of federal dam-builders. *The Ugly American* (1962), a movie about Communism and nationalism, also flopped, despite the star power of Marlon Brando and its prescient focus on southeast Asia. Director Billy Wilder, on the other hand, had a hit with *One, Two, Three* (1961), a daring satire of the cold war starring James Cagney.

Mainstream Politics in the 1960s: The Best Men?

While all these films were clearly political, a few movies of the 1960s dealt more explicitly with the political process, high in both political content and intent. Two of these pure political films are classics whose messages about politics hold up today.

Melodrama combined with realism in *Advise and Consent* (1962), a political movie in the Hollywood tradition but with a skillful evocation of the Washington scene and a more probable plot than most such films. Based on the novel by Washington journalist Allen Drury, *Advise and Consent* was directed by Otto Preminger, who toned down the novel's conservatism.

In this film, Robert Leffingwell (Henry Fonda) is the presidential nominee for secretary of state, awaiting approval by the Senate, which must advise and consent. Right-wingers label him soft on Communism and denounce his "egg-headed arrogance." We are on Leffingwell's side from the outset, not only because he is played by Henry Fonda, but also because his chief opponent is the reactionary old southerner, Seab Cooley, portrayed with great relish by Charles Laughton. Pushing from the left is the ruthless, dogmatic Senator Fred Van Ackerman (George Grizzard), who is willing to violate all the rules to make Leffingwell secretary of state. Leader of a national prodisarmament group, Van Ackerman is always surrounded by zombielike aides (Communist automatons?). Caught between them all is the senate majority leader (Walter Pidgeon), an honorable man who only wishes to get his president the ratification he wants, even though he knows it will not be easy.

Van Ackerman wants to chair the subcommittee that will hold the hearing on Leffingwell's nomination, but although he is the logical choice, he is rejected because his ambition has led him to violate the Senate's unwritten rules of conduct. ("He doesn't belong here," the Senate leaders say. "No tact.") They choose young Brig Anderson (Don Murray) to chair the hearings because "he knows how to be a senator." Anderson seems perfect—he is clean-cut and polite, a mature and sophisticated version of Mr. Smith; he has a nice family, plays by the rules, and honors his elders, but he turns out to be a bit rigid. Senator Cooley dredges up evidence that Leffingwell was once a member of a Communist cell. When Leffingwell denies the association, Anderson, learning he has lied, turns against him despite pressure from the president and the majority leader, who understand that "we all make mistakes" in youth and that "everything isn't black and white." But Anderson, the pure young idealist, plans to denounce Leffingwell until a mysterious caller threatens to expose Brig's past homosexual affair unless he supports the confirmation. Unable to cope with the truth about himself and unwilling to compromise his position on Leffingwell, Brig commits suicide. The Senate deliberations proceed, but as the vice president (Lew Ayres) prepares to cast the tie-breaking vote, the president dies and the issue is moot. It turns out that the evil Van Ackerman was behind the blackmail, and he is scorned by his fellow senators. "Fortunately this country is able to survive patriots like you," the majority leader tells him. "We can tolerate about anything, but you've dishonored us." Senator Cooley, however, is still in the club because he played by the rules.

Although it was made in 1962, *Advise and Consent* carries a 1950s message of consensus—characters that do not fit or will not play by the rules are destroyed. Like earlier movies, this one says that politics is a dirty business, but *Advise and Consent* is more interesting, sophisticated, and morally complex than its predecessors. The human side of politics is clear; the majority leader and the Senate regulars are good men who live by a code of honor, even if that code is morally ambiguous. Nobody is pure, not the president or the secretary of state or the clean-cut young senator, not the left or the right, yet some are well-intentioned and play the game with honor. Pidgeon's majority leader and Ayres's vice president give the film moral weight because we like them and trust them. *Advise and Consent* also provides painless instruction on the way the political process works. The repartee between the majority leader and his mistress provides a distinctly grown-up perspective on politics, and the filmmakers also use a group of diplomats' wives in the gallery to explain how the Senate operates.

The *New York Times* dismissed *Advise and Consent* as a cynical movie about dishonorable men, including the president.[3] Critic Pauline Kael wrote it off as a "mindless 'inside' story of Washington shenanigans" and an "overwrought melodrama,"[4] but other critics liked it, noting the accurate depiction of the workings of the Senate. As in many political films, the melodrama was there for entertainment, but it turned out to be the weak point of the film, while the political machinations and procedures were stronger. Still, they would not have been as interesting without the moral conflict introduced by the melodrama.

Real-life politicians took a great interest in *Advise and Consent.* Although Martin Luther King refused an offer to play a senator, three real-life senators did appear in it, and President Kennedy entertained the filmmakers at the White House while the movie was being made. Some senators did not like the final product, however. "I don't think it will be wholesome for either our people or those abroad," declared Strom Thurmond.[5] As usual, the real-life politicians overreacted. *Advise and Consent* not only gave a strong sense of how politics worked, it also insisted that most politicians were decent men. Mr. Anderson's Washington of 1962, however, was different from the city that Mr. Smith visited in 1939. Politics had become more complicated, and innocence was no longer allowed to triumph.

Advise and Consent also anticipated the vicious personality-focused politics of the 1990s, as did another political film of the 1960s. Less melodramatic, *The Best Man* (1964) was sharper and more contemporary—and holds up better—thanks to Franklin Schaffner's direction and Gore Vidal's adaptation of his own play. The scene is a convention to select a presidential nominee, implicitly to succeed Lyndon Johnson, since the film's titles play over portraits of all the presidents through Johnson. Bill Russell (Henry Fonda again) is the intellectual former secretary of state, an Adlai Stevenson–style liberal and presumably the best man. His wife (Margaret Leighton), an independent and intellectual woman, rallies to his side, like Hepburn in *State of the Union,* setting aside marital problems for the greater cause. "Politics make strange bedfellows," she wryly comments. Russell's opponent, Joe Kantwell (Cliff Robertson), is a ruthless ideologue and true believer who combines the image of John Kennedy with the politics of Richard Nixon. Kantwell is scornfully dismissed for having built his career on the pursuit of "an imaginary Communist mafia," an indication of how much American and Hollywood politics had changed in just ten years.

The unscrupulous Kantwell threatens to reveal that Russell once had a nervous breakdown unless he withdraws from the race. Russell's supporters urge him to retaliate by accusing Kantwell of being a homosexual. Russell is incredulous ("That ugly wife, those ugly children!") and refuses to smear his opponent, insisting that he wants to win the nomination because of his stand on political issues. Small corruptions, he insists, destroy character. Russell himself, however, has misled the public about his "happy" marriage, given speeches he has not read ("I'll surprise myself"), and manipulated the press.

If Kantwell embodies the ruthless ideologue and Russell the conscientious liberal, ex-president Art Hockstadter represents political pragmatism. Lee Tracy was nominated for an Academy Award for best supporting actor for his portrayal of this Truman-like politician who declares that he does not personally care whether Kantwell "has carnal knowledge of a McCormick reaper," but demands that Russell use whatever he has got against his opponent. "Power is not a toy we give to children," the ex-president explains. "It's a weapon and a strong man uses it." Disdaining Russell's squeamishness, he asserts that "to want power is corruption already" and that "there are no ends" [to justify means]. It is normal to fool the people, Hockstadter warns Kantwell, but it is "serious when you start fooling yourself." Hockstadter fails to persuade Kantwell to back down, however, and when Russell still will not fight back, he refuses to support him. To stop Kantwell, Russell ultimately martyrs himself by withdrawing from competition and releasing his delegates with a request that they vote for a third candidate. "Men without faces tend to get elected president, and power or personal responsibility tends to fill in the features," he assures us. These may be the best men, but the conclusion is subverted by the film's clear prejudice in favor of Russell/Fonda, the man who is too good for politics.

In an era of increasing interest in politics, *The Best Man* caught enough of the excitement of the game to engage mild public interest and win mixed reviews, although most critics pointed out that Russell/Fonda was altogether too scrupulous and that the film's ends/means morality was less than profound.[6] The State Department worried about the reaction of Soviet audiences to such a cynical portrait of American politics, but director Schaffner dismissed this concern, saying that the Soviets "don't understand politics," by which he presumably meant electoral politics, as in *The Best Man*.[7]

Like *Advise and Consent, The Best Man* was an inside view of politics. Both films played on its seaminess, featuring blackmail based, disturbingly, on homosexuality, but in both films, the political institutions finally worked, and the process and system triumphed. Both films also disparaged ideologues and lauded team players. And in both, Henry Fonda played the good man with a tainted past who had to give up politics, although his character in *The Best Man* did so more decisively.

Like *State of the Union* (1948), *The Best Man* set out the choice between personal integrity and political ambition and opted for integrity. Such martyrdom to idealism "is a central liberal dramatic tradition," according to Richard Maltby,[8] but the choice would have been stronger if Russell's stand on political issues had been clearer rather than simply "good" by implication and in comparison to the abhorrent politics of his opponents. *The Best Man* cynically rejects politics as dirty and hypocritical, thus reinforcing the Hollywood cliché. The Fonda character does not even trust the public enough to appeal to them, as a Capra hero would have done, and his aloofness gives the film an overall tone of elitism and condescension toward politics, perhaps reflecting the attitude of its privileged author, Gore Vidal, who himself dropped out of politics after an unsuccessful congressional candidacy. This elitism is mitigated by the suspicion that perhaps Russell/Fonda is not the best man after all; he seems rather too good, too self-consciously superior. In the end, we are instructed that the probable nominee will live up to his position and all will be well, a reassuring conclusion that has been confirmed by any number of real-life presidents.

Finally, it should be noted that these films—and most others of the 1960s—carried on the male focus of political movies. Women continued to play supporting roles as wives, not even attaining the political stature of Jean Arthur's aide in *Mr. Smith Goes to Washington*. The decade's movies did produce one woman president, although *Kisses for My President* (1964), a 1930s-style sex comedy, focused on "first husband" Fred MacMurray. Homosexuals fared even worse. The weakening of the production code made it possible for movies to feature homosexuality, but only as a seamy secret.

From *Dr. No* to *Dr. Strangelove*

These traditional Hollywood political films contrast with a new genre of political films that emerged in the 1960s, the political thriller. The political content of these films was often high, although their intention was usually more to entertain than to educate. They nevertheless reflected the concerns of the times and shaped the public understanding of then-current issues.

John Frankenheimer's *The Manchurian Candidate* (1962) was one of the first and most successful of these political thrillers. A brainwashed veteran of the Korean War (Laurence Harvey) is programmed to assassinate on command—but who? Meanwhile, a gravel-voiced McCarthy type (James Gregory) rabble-rouses, declaring he has "lists" of Communists in government agencies, declaring that they number fifty-seven when he glimpses the "57 Varieties" label on a bottle of Heinz ketchup. Linking the two men is the veteran's mother, who is also the demagogue's wife and mastermind (Angela Lansbury in the role of a very untraditional woman). A shocking conclusion reveals that the Communist agent who controls the programmed assassin is his mother. The right-wing demagogue turns out to be a front for subversion, a nice twist and one that was courageous in 1962. Frankenheimer's brilliant film brought the cycle of anti-Communist movies to an end by adding complexity and confusion to everybody's motives, simultaneously establishing the thriller as a major form for political movies.

Although the politics of the 1960s is remembered as liberal, or even radical, one of the most durable movie symbols of the era was neither, but did reflect the general fear of nuclear war and the Kennedy administration's reliance on CIA intervention. James Bond was a British secret agent created by novelist Ian Fleming, whose books President Kennedy enjoyed. The first Bond movie, *Dr. No* (1962), was such a hit that a dozen more followed, with Sean Connery and later other actors as the suave spy. The political content of these films was simplistic at best, but it suited the political mood of the nation. Film scholar Joan Mellen declares the Bond movies "the key image of the decade," reflecting the "macho politics" of the Kennedy era,[9] as superspy Bond foils villainous plots for world domination or destruction. To some extent, the Bond movies were a vestige of the cold war, but their view was somewhat more complex in that the Soviet Union was not always the enemy. More often, the menace was an evil genius like Dr. No who played the superpowers off against each other, thus expressing the public's fear that something might go wrong in the delicate balance of power and bring apocalypse. The solution in these films was always provided by the superhero. All we had to do, they suggested, was let the CIA or the British secret service take care of business, a notion that was shared by the Kennedy administration with its penchant for brisk and brutal intervention by the CIA or Special Forces and international brinkmanship. Some real-life CIA plots, like the attempted assassination of Cuban premier Fidel Castro, went even further than the Bond movies, in which action was mostly defensive rather than offensive.

The Bond films and many copycat movies were spoofs that toyed with international disaster, but other motion pictures of the era took the subject seriously, suggesting that worldwide disaster might come not from evil enemies but from within. Some even suggested that the final holocaust could result from an accident. These were the movies that most clearly brought Hollywood into the politics of the 1960s.

The first, *Seven Days in May* (1964), was a thriller written by Rod Serling, best known today for his *Twilight Zone* TV series, and directed by John Frankenheimer. In this movie, a wise, liberal president (Fredric March) signs a nuclear nonproliferation treaty with the Soviet Union, but a group of right-wing generals, led by Burt Lancaster, plots a coup. A junior officer (Kirk Douglas) loyal to the president reveals the conspiracy, but the president is incredulous. Eventually he acts to entrap the treacherous generals and denounce them to the nation in a televised press conference. With the help of the loyal officer, his cynical White House staff, and, presumably, the television-viewing public, the president foils the coup. The twist in Serling and Frankenheimer's thriller was the way they turned American paranoia inside out, suggesting that the threat could come from within and from the right. They also suggested a political role for the public through the president's televised appeal, an unusual message in American political films other than those of Frank Capra. *Seven Days in May* did well at the box office and was praised by most critics. Arthur Knight was excited to see Hollywood, "the sleeping giant . . . waking up again" and dealing with contemporary issues after the escapism of the 1950s.[10] But despite its reassuring message that the system worked, politicians worried about the impression *Seven Days in May* would give abroad, demanding that the export version be clearly labeled "fictional," lest "ignorant foreigners" think such right-wing coups were possible in the United States.[11]

In *Fail Safe* (1964), directed by Sidney Lumet and written by the formerly blacklisted Walter Bernstein, the threat results from a technological accident: an American bomber heads for Moscow because of a mechanical glitch. As in *Seven Days in May,* however, levelheaded men solve the problem. The president, reassuringly played by Henry Fonda, negotiates his way out of the mess, finally ordering U.S. planes to bomb New York City to assure the Russians of fair play and to avoid wider destruction. Rational men capable of thinking the unthinkable—as strategists of nuclear war were doing at the time—somehow made even the sacrifice of New York seem necessary. Some critics praised *Fail Safe* for showing how "intelligent men trying to use their wits and their techniques correct an error,"[12] but others thought the movie was platitudinous, and it stirred little enthusiasm at the box office. *Fail Safe* also suffered from comparison to another, more devastating film about nuclear war that made all other movies on the subject seem naive.

Dr. Strangelove or: How I Learned to Stop Worrying and Love the Bomb (1964), directed and coauthored by Stanley Kubrick, was a critical and box office hit even though it proclaimed that the world had gone mad and was bound for destruction. *Strangelove* opens with a lyrical scene of a bomber being refueled in midair, perhaps an allusion to a similar scene in *Strategic Air Command* (1955), but this time "Try a Little Tenderness" is the musical accompaniment and the tone is satirical, providing a suitable prologue to Kubrick's scathing movie. During a simple military exercise, a fleet of American bombers is sent toward the Soviet Union, but some of the bombers do not respond to a command to return to base. It turns out that an insane Air Force general (Sterling Hayden) has initiated a real attack on the Soviet Union. He hopes to force the president (Peter Sellers) to proceed with the assault rather than suffer Soviet retaliation. The president orders the general to send the coded call-back orders to the planes, but he refuses. The president sends the army to seize the general's base, but the general tells his men they are under attack by subversives in American uniforms. While the battle at the base goes on, the bombers get closer and closer to their target and the president summons his cabinet to the war room. As the tension builds, Kubrick cuts between the base, the president in the war room, and a bomber commanded by Major Kong (Slim Pickens).

One of the generals in the war room (George C. Scott) advises an all-out preemptive attack, but the president calls the Soviet ambassador to the war room instead and uses the hotline to warn the Russian premier, who informs him that a secret doomsday device will destroy the entire world if the Soviet Union is attacked. Confronted with apocalypse, the two leaders cooperate in shooting down the American bombers—all except the one piloted by Major Kong. Damaged in the attack, Kong's plane flies too low for radar detection and proceeds to its target to the tune of "When Johnny Comes Marching Home." Meanwhile Dr. Strangelove (Peter Sellers in another role) arrives in the war room. Speaking in a heavy German accent and giving Nazi salutes with a gloved hand he cannot control, Strangelove advises the president and cabinet on survival after the holocaust, raving about life in caves and mines, drooling over his planned male-female ratio, and referring to the president as "Mein Fuehrer" in a caricature of German expatriates who had become American defense experts. Major Kong's B-52 gets through, however, and the film ends in lyrical shots of mushroom clouds accompanied by "We'll Meet Again," the sentimental World War II song.

Dr. Strangelove is relentlessly cynical and satirical with no completely sympathetic characters. Scientists and the military take the toughest beating. Science is represented by the mad Nazi, Dr. Strangelove, and the military is embodied by the generals played by George C. Scott ("war is too important to be left to politicians") and Sterling Hayden, a lunatic who is convinced that everybody is after his "precious bodily fluids." Major Kong, the ingenious cowboy pilot, would have been the hero in any conventional movie, but cheering for him in this movie would mean rooting for apocalypse. *Strangelove* does not even offer a reasonable liberal as hero. The president is well meaning but ineffectual. So is his military counterpart, a visiting British officer (Peter Sellers again) attempting to stop the insane general. Liberal faith in good men—even a rational president willing to communicate with the Soviets—is dismissed as derisively as is conservative faith in the military. And *Strangelove* attacks technology as well as human folly and fallibility. Slick machines, without hearts or minds, go out of control in the hands of insane, careless, or incompetent humans. The U.S. Air Force denied that such accidents could happen, but Terry Southern, one of the film's authors, declared that its intent was "to blast smugness . . . over a foolproof system which may not be."[13]

Most disturbingly, *Strangelove* issued a warning without offering any hope of salvation. *Seven Days in May* and *Fail Safe* also condemned the military and expressed concern about the safety of technology, but they offered human heroes and a political system that worked. *Strangelove*'s condemnation was more sweeping and offered no hope at all. "It is not war that has been laughed to scorn," critic Pauline Kael wrote, "but the possibility of sane action."[14] The *Washington Post* reviewer worried that "no communist could dream of a more effective anti-American film to spread abroad than this one,"[15] but critics conceded the brilliance of the film, and its skillful combination of comedy and politics made it a popular hit. *Strangelove* won Academy Award nominations (but no Oscars) for best picture, director, writers, and actor (Sellers), the first political film to gain such approval since the 1940s.

Not since the sci-fi films of the 1950s had the consequences of nuclear technology been so directly addressed. *Strangelove, Fail Safe, Seven Days in May,* and, earlier, *On the Beach* played to and expressed public concern about nuclear war and kept the subject on the nation's agenda. They helped shape a generation's attitudes, and they may have contributed to Lyndon B. Johnson's electoral victory in 1964. Johnson presented himself as the "peace candidate," whereas his right-wing Republican opponent, Barry Goldwater, an officer in the U.S. Air Force Reserve, was portrayed as a warmonger and virtual Strangelove.

But even as America worried about nuclear war, it moved toward détente, and so did Hollywood. *Fail Safe* suggested we could negotiate with the Russians, while *Strangelove* sent up the hotline and satirized the Soviets as viciously as it did our own leaders, but both movies helped to modify the old 1950s image of evil Communists, as did other films of the 1960s. *Doctor Zhivago* (1965), for example, was a romantic tale of the Russian Revolution in which all Communists were Stalinist villains, but the eponymous hero

(Omar Sharif) remained resolutely sympathetic with the revolution. Meanwhile, a contemporary comedy, *The Russians Are Coming! The Russians Are Coming!* (1966), delivered a message of reconciliation. A Soviet submarine runs aground in New England and its crew members are perceived as invaders by wacky villagers. "I do not wish to hate anybody," says the handsome Russian (John Phillip Law) to the pretty American (Eva Marie Saint). "It doesn't make sense to hate people," she agrees.

John Wayne's War

Although the war in Vietnam loomed large in the consciousness and politics of the nation by the late 1960s, Hollywood avoided the subject. *The Quiet American* (1958) and *The Ugly American* (1963) anticipated the Vietnam quagmire and Brian De Palma's *Greetings* (1968) was an antiestablishment comedy about draft dodging. But most filmmakers avoided Vietnam, because war films had rarely been commercially successful and because public opinion on the war was deeply divided. Taking a position on a phenomenon still in progress is particularly risky because events may alter both the outcome and public attitudes about it. Besides, television news of the war satisfied the curiosity of most people and made fictional treatments look silly. As a consequence, Vietnam did not get to Hollywood until the war was over—except in one movie, *The Green Berets* (1968).

John Wayne got to the Vietnamese battlefield a decade ahead of other filmmakers when he codirected an old-fashioned, patriotic prowar film that could just as well have been about World War II. *The Green Berets* begins with a black officer's didactic lecture to trainees who are about to don the famous berets of the Special Forces. A white officer (Aldo Ray) explains that the Chinese and Russians are already involved in the conflict, but a visiting liberal journalist (David Janssen) asks skeptical questions. Their instructive exchanges occupy most of the first third of the movie. When the scene shifts to Vietnam, every trite convention of the old war movies is dragged out, including orphans, mascots, painful efforts at comedy, and a scavenger (Jim Hutton). But this middle third of the movie is even more like one of Wayne's westerns, with the Vietcong attacking the Green Beret base like Indians laying siege to a frontier fort. Portrayed as yellow savages, they strip white bodies and brutalize villagers, although a sympathetic South Vietnamese (George Takei) functions as the "good Indian." The liberal reporter is converted by all this, denouncing his biased publisher and proposing to quit his job to join the army's public relations team, but the Green Beret commander (John Wayne) insists that the reporter has a higher duty. He must keep his job and take the truth to the American people. The final third of the movie is a *Mission*

Impossible–style caper, with a team of Green Beret guerrillas infiltrating enemy territory to beat the Vietcong at their own game. "You're what this is all about," Wayne tells the Vietnamese orphan-mascot as the movie ends with the sun setting over the ocean—in the east (from their perspective in Vietnam).

The Green Berets is a long, cliché-ridden lecture in defense of the war. It is the sort of movie in which you know, as soon as you are introduced to them, which supporting actors will die and in which even the violence is reassuringly old-fashioned. The box office pull of John Wayne and his film's cozy invocation of tradition were enough to generate a profit for the film despite bad reviews and the protests of antiwar activists. Wayne was sufficiently politically committed that he may not have cared as much about profits as about the message, however, which could account for the most transparently propagandistic American movie since the pro-Russian films of the 1940s. At any rate, the message was too late to matter, coming just as the Tet offensive showed the strength of the enemy. Public opinion turned against the war, and Lyndon Johnson decided not to run for reelection.

The Coming of the Counterculture

Social change was in the wind in America in the 1960s—and in the movies of the era. Besides concerns about nuclear holocaust and wars in foreign lands, racism and an emerging counterculture became popular subjects for filmmakers.

With a few honorable exceptions, filmmakers had avoided the subjects of race and racism since *The Birth of a Nation,* but the civil rights movement of the 1950s and 1960s and the black pride movement that followed helped get these subjects back in the movies. Liberal filmmakers like Stanley Kramer made movies like *Guess Who's Coming to Dinner* (1967), calling for tolerance. The star-power of actors like Sidney Poitier helped to make movies with racial themes profitable, from *The Defiant Ones* (1958) to *In the Heat of the Night* (1967). By the 1970s, black filmmakers were making movies like *Cotton Comes to Harlem* (1970) with all-black casts—a huge advance in the treatment of race on film from *The Birth of a Nation* or even *Guess Who's Coming to Dinner.* These films and the evolving portrait of race in American movies are discussed in detail in Chapter 13.

Native Americans were also treated better in the films of the 1960s, although 1950s films like *Broken Arrow* had started the trend. Director John Ford made up for his past portraits of bloodthirsty savages with *Cheyenne Autumn* (1964). Far more radically, blacklist victim Abraham Polonsky suggested in *Tell Them Willie Boy Is Here* (1969) that Indians and other minorities should go their own separatist way, trusting no one, least of all white liberals. The film centers on a manhunt with a sheriff (Robert Redford) chasing an American Indian who is wanted for a killing. An impending presidential visit turns a posse and the press into a frenzied mob. The white liberal schoolmarm who would have brought reconciliation in earlier films, is shown here to be silly, ineffectual, and condescending in her wish to care for the Indians. *Little Big Man* and *Soldier Blue* (both 1970) continued the revision of American history by interpreting the fate of the Indians as genocide; both films also alluded to the American involvement in Vietnam.

These films about race reflected and contributed to the emergence of a youthful counterculture in America and elsewhere. With roots in the beatniks of the 1950s and the student protests of the 1960s, as well as the civil rights and antiwar movements, the counterculture was an antimaterialist, youth-oriented phenomenon that expressed itself politically as the New Left and socially as the flower children, or hippies.

The first movie to catch the spirit of this counterculture may have been *Bonnie and Clyde* (1967), a box office success that was denounced by some critics for romanticizing violence. Based on the exploits of two real-life Depression criminals, the film follows two young people (Faye Dunaway and Warren Beatty) as they drift into crime, partly as an act of rebellion against their elders. At one point, Bonnie and Clyde are welcomed as heroes in a migrant camp reminiscent of the one in *The Grapes of Wrath,* but overall, this movie is socially reflective rather than explicitly political. Many saw it as an allegory of youthful disaffection and rebellion against authority in the 1960s. *The Graduate* (1967), a big box office and critical hit directed by Mike Nichols, played on the same theme.

Wild in the Streets (1968) took the generational conflict one step further in the tale of a rock star who uses his popularity to gain political power as young people take over the country. The voting age and then the age for office-holding are reduced to fourteen. Adults are sent to "retirement" camps. In the end, yet another youth coup is plotted as seven-year-olds prepare to rebel against their teenage elders. *Wild in the Streets* managed to simultaneously exploit and send up the youth culture, which was already turning sour.

In *Easy Rider* (1969), the counterculture's biggest box office hit, two hippies (Dennis Hopper and Peter Fonda) judge the state of the nation during a motorcycle odyssey enhanced by drugs. Fonda's character, portrayed in saintly fashion, bestows approval on people who live freely and independently, but admits in the end that he and his friend, if not his generation and the country, have failed: "We blew it." Although *Easy Rider* criticizes conformity, materialism, and authority, it is less political than it seemed at the time. Its most revolutionary effect in 1969 was to demonstrate to the big studios that an independent production and a film about the counterculture could make money.

But by 1968, the counterculture was falling apart. It was becoming clear that drugs led to addiction instead of liberation. The Manson family made communes a nightmare. Martin Luther King Jr. was murdered, and the civil rights movement was fragmented by calls for black power and cultural separatism. The hopefulness of the antiwar movement was shattered by the assassination of Robert Kennedy and riots at the 1968 Democratic convention in Chicago. Richard Nixon was elected president.

Perhaps the film that best summed up counterculture politics and its demise was *Medium Cool* (1969), a low-budget, independent production directed by left-leaning cinematographer Haskell Wexler. A TV news crew films an auto accident as the movie begins. Only after they have shot their footage do they call for help for the victims, establishing one of Wexler's themes, the exploitative nature of the media. John (Robert Forster), the cameraman, senses the coldness of his work and feels alienated from it, as he does from his playboy lifestyle. He films a passionate group of black militants and quits his job when he learns that his station is turning over his footage to law-enforcement officers. Meanwhile, apparently longing for a traditional family relationship, he gets involved with an Appalachian woman and her son. The boy disappears, and the couple searches for him on the violent streets of Chicago during the 1968 Democratic convention.

Wexler set his film in Chicago so the story could be played out with the convention as a backdrop, and the street conflict in the film is real-life footage. Wexler, a known radical, and his crew were hassled by police during the making of the movie, but the footage they got makes a remarkable blend of fact and fiction, successfully heightening the tension of the film as we hear one of his crew shouting, "Watch out, Haskell. This is for real!" It was real enough that the Department of Justice requisitioned Wexler's footage during its investigation of the riots. *Medium Cool* ends somewhat gratuitously in an auto crash, with the camera pulling back to reveal Wexler and his crew filming the wreck, a self-conscious application of his point about the disengagement of the media. This disengagement, or failure to connect, was the central point of *Medium Cool,* not black militancy, street riots, or convention politics, all of which were in the film only as background details. Wexler was saying that traditional politics had failed and there was no salvation for his protagonists.

The critics were divided about *Medium* Cool. Some gave it raves ("technically brilliant," "a kind of cinematic *Guernica*,") but others dismissed it ("awkward and even pretentious . . . a slashing indictment of car driving").[16] Audiences made *Medium* Cool a box office success, however. Its immediacy pulled them in, compensating for its virtually nonexistent plot with the sheer intensity of the moment, and its sense of outrage and alienation was perfectly in tune with the mood of 1969. Many people considered *Medium Cool* the only truly contemporary film of the era.

The success of *Easy Rider* and *Medium Cool* sparked the interest of the studios, which tried to cash in on the counterculture in 1970 with movies about student protest, including *The Strawberry Statement* (1970) and *Getting Straight* (1970). Other films addressed the antiwar sympathies of the era. Franklin Schaffner's highly entertaining *Planet of the Apes* (1968) and its sequels depicted life on earth after a nuclear holocaust, with apes ruling and human beings reduced to slaves. *Patton* (1969), written by Francis Ford Coppola and also directed by Schaffner, presented the World War II general as a sort of mad genius, useful in war but in need of containment by calmer superiors. *M*A*S*H* (1970), directed by Robert Altman, and *Catch-22* (1970), directed by Mike Nichols from Joseph Heller's novel, both made vicious fun of the military, while *Johnny Got His Gun* (1971), written and directed by blacklist victim Dalton Trumbo, delivered a more serious antiwar message about a paraplegic veteran of World War I. Trumbo's film was the least popular of these. Audiences were prepared to laugh cynically at war, but not to examine its consequences too closely.

Besides these films, *Joe* (1970), about a bigoted blue-collar worker who is both attracted and repelled by the counterculture, and *WUSA* (1970), about a right-wing radio station, dealt with fascism in contemporary America. Jane Fonda, Peter Boyle, and Donald Sutherland made *Steelyard Blues* (1972), an antiauthoritarian comedy about a group of 1960s rebels. And a French film about political assassination in Greece, *Z* (1968), directed by Constantin Costa-Gavras, won the Academy Award for best foreign film and ranked fifth in box office receipts for 1970.

9

The 1970s

Cynicism, Paranoia, War and Anticapitalism

All the President's Men (1976)

The 1970s started with President Nixon's invasion of Cambodia and the most widespread antiwar demonstrations of the era. Despite the unpopularity of the war, Nixon enjoyed a landslide reelection victory in 1972—only to face the protracted agony of the Watergate scandal. His 1973 resignation put the uninspired Gerald Ford into the White House and began an era of almost total disillusionment with politics. The political activism of the 1960s gave way to what Tom Wolfe labeled the "Me Decade."[1] Self-interest and political apathy replaced involvement.

As a disillusioned nation celebrated its bicentennial, voters rejected Washington insider Ford and elected Jimmy Carter. A peanut farmer and moderate Democrat, President Carter's modesty appealed to the voters, but not enough to prevent his defeat by conservative Republican Ronald Reagan in 1980. In short, the 1970s took America from Nixon and Cambodia to Ford, Carter, and a prolonged hostage crisis in Iran, concluding with a genuine Hollywood actor in the White House. Few decades have seen so much change, and the films of the era reflect its turbulence.

The film industry also experienced huge changes in the 1970s, as the big studios declined and independent filmmakers gained clout. The studios suffered record losses between 1969 and 1972. A substantial number of political films were released during this time, but they were not sufficiently linked with financial losses to discourage further productions. Some, like *Che!* (1969), an awful film about the Cuban revolutionary, lost money. Others— including *Easy Rider, Medium Cool*, and *Z*—were sufficiently profitable to make the studios take notice, while big productions like *Hello, Dolly!* lost more money than most of the political films cost, so the studios were not totally discouraged and independent filmmakers were positively encouraged.

Most other movies of the 1970s, however, were not at all worried about politics. This was the time of the new blockbusters and a new generation of filmmakers like Francis Ford Coppola, Steven Spielberg, and George Lucas. They learned filmmaking in universities rather than in studios, they were committed to entertaining, and they seemed content to express themselves within traditional genres. These young men and others thrived in a Hollywood where producing a movie depended less on studios than on packaging a deal and putting together investors. They had spectacular early successes that gave them enormous freedom on later projects. Some say they saved the industry.

Coppola's *Godfather* (1972 and 1974) successes were the beginning, but Spielberg's *Jaws* (1975) was the first real blockbuster, shooting to the top of *Variety*'s chart of "Box Office Champions." Although it was primarily a horror film, *Jaws* commented briefly on politics when the mayor of the shark-threatened resort forces the police chief to keep the beaches open so business

144

will not suffer. Spielberg went on to make *Close Encounters of the Third Kind* (1977), *Raiders of the Lost Ark* (1981), and *E.T.* (1982), all of which contained only minimal explicit political comment. Lucas started with *American Graffiti* (1973), and then went on to make *Star Wars* (1977), and its equally successful sequels.

The lack of political content in all these films was seen by some critics as a sort of conservatism, as was their reliance on individual heroes. One radical film journal even went so far as to condemn *Star Wars* as a fascist, militaristic movie because of its hierarchies of sex, race, class, and species, complaining that only the humans, not the Wookies or the robots, got medals for their heroism.[2] Still, Lucas's humans did at least take action to overthrow the "evil empire" (a phrase later used by President Reagan).

These movies were only mildly and probably unintentionally conservative, however, in comparison with other films of the time. Clint Eastwood played a cop in *Dirty Harry* (1971) and its sequels, all of which violently condemn permissiveness and liberalism. Charles Bronson got a vigilante's revenge on urban criminals in *Death Wish* (1974). In movies of this sort, danger and injustice were all around, often in the form of menacing minorities or poor people, but government was tied up by bleeding-heart regulations, so the only solution was to go beyond the law. Meanwhile, horror movies made a comeback, often as slashers, playing on fear and isolation. Disaster movies also fed paranoia, although sometimes in these films people worked together to rise above a crisis and save themselves. On a slightly more positive note, Sylvester Stallone's *Rocky* (1976) updated the American dream of the average guy winning out, a theme Stallone would reiterate with astounding success in seemingly endless sequels.

Meanwhile, audiences were also changing. By 1976, 76 percent of filmgoers were under the age of thirty, a figure that has declined only slightly since then. The number of theaters shrank to 13,500, although multiscreen complexes would soon bring the number up again. The good news for Hollywood was that weekly attendance was creeping up, reaching 18.4 million in 1976 after having bottomed out at 17.7 million in 1970. Film production also increased in 1976, with 353 films released, the most since 1950. The most lasting impact, however, was to be the persistent preponderance of young people in audiences, people who were far more interested in entertainment than in serious analytical or political films.

Mr. Redford Goes to Washington

But while the output of political films at the end of the 1960s and the beginning of the 1970s was high, Hollywood's approach to politics remained cautious except in the hands of independents like Haskell Wexler and Europeans like Costa-Gavras. Many of the films of this highly political era dealt delicately or indirectly with contemporary issues. Antiwar movies, for example, were set during wars other than the one in which the country was then engaged. Virtually no movies dealt directly with the political process except *The Man* (1972), featuring James Earl Jones as America's first black president. *The Man* was a 1960s-style political melodrama, but 1972 also brought another film with a more contemporary political perspective.

Robert Redford was the star, producer, and prime mover in *The Candidate* (1972), the first and best film of the 1970s to deal with political campaigns and a classic example of a high content/high intent political film. Although *The Candidate* uncannily anticipated the career of California governor Edmund G. "Jerry" Brown, writer Jeremy Larner and director Michael Ritchie based it on their experiences in the 1970 campaign of John Tunney, a Kennedyesque senator from California. Several incidents in the film were drawn from the Tunney campaign, and the senator was allowed to okay the script "so it wouldn't be a knife job on him," according to Ritchie.[3]

The Candidate begins on election night in an unnamed state, as a losing candidate addresses his supporters. His manager, Marvin Lucas (Peter Boyle), is already on his way to another campaign, showing a colleague a photo of young Bill McKay (Robert Redford) in *Time* magazine. Lucas is warned that McKay could not possibly beat Crocker Jarmon (Don Porter), the powerful incumbent senator from California, but he nevertheless visits McKay in his ramshackle poverty law office. From McKay's talk to his staff, we learn of the good causes the handsome son of a former governor works on, but he tells Lucas that he is happy with what he is doing and not interested in politics.

"You're happy?" Lucas asks. "Okay. Clams are happy. You saved some trees, you got a clinic opened. Does that make you feel good? Meanwhile, Jarmon sits on his committees and carves up the land, the oil, the taxes." Tempted, McKay asks "What's in it" for Lucas, the professional manager, who murmurs something about "an air card, a phone card, a thousand dollars a week." It is only a job to him, he says, but he appeals to McKay, the crusader, by offering him a forum for his causes and by promising him that he will lose the election. "Of course you'll have to register," McKay's wife warns as he agrees. Like many post-1960s activists, McKay is an idealist and a crusader, but he is naive and suspicious of traditional politics.

In the beginning, the campaign is forthright and issue-oriented as McKay bluntly answers questions on controversial issues like abortion and busing at his first press conference. "Jesus!" a reporter exclaims. "That's a first," another declares as McKay admits he does not know enough to answer a question. But when he says he would fire the Board of Regents of the University

146

of California only to be told that senators do not have that power, McKay begins to recognize his need to be briefed on issues, and he grows more dependent on his manager and staff.

Lucas takes the candidate to a media consultant who is enthusiastic about McKay's youth and virility as contrasted with the age and weariness of his opponent. The voters, he says, will look at Jarmon and think "the Crock . . . can't get it up anymore." So the media packaging begins, first with a haircut, then with new suits and ties, and finally with carefully filmed and edited television ads. In the first ads, McKay talks about issues, but when he sees the results, he realizes that issues do not work in commercials, and so do we. The edited, music-backed ads are much better. "You're showing your face," the media man explains. "That's what we have to sell first." McKay keeps trying to talk about the issues as he is filmed meeting people, but the results are incoherent. "Maybe we can use a line or two out of context," sighs the consultant.

Nobody else wants to run against Jarmon, and McKay wins his party primary easily, but then, manipulated by the professional manager and his opinion polls, he begins to want to win the election. "You're only reaching the people who agree with you already," Lucas says; "you're gonna lose." "But I'm supposed to lose," the candidate replies. "Yeah," says the manager, "but if you keep going this way, you won't only lose, you'll be humiliated, and so will your ideas." We can see that McKay is being manipulated, but we are seduced along with him. Soon he is making all the compromises necessary to win, rehearsing for press conferences and softening his tone on issues. We watch as his advance men prepare a rally, cynically guaranteeing a crowd by scheduling the event during the busy lunch hour and blocking off streets. Eventually, McKay grows so accustomed to being packaged that when he goes on television he points at his coat and asks whether to button it or not. Told to change his tie, he first asks why, then gives up with a resigned "Never mind."

The Candidate deftly introduces the power of the media with footage of McKay at a big banquet with real-life political leaders. As our candidate rises to give his maiden speech, however, the TV lights are switched off and a voice in the background says, "Okay, we got all we need." Later, McKay tries to get some free coverage, changing his schedule to rush to a forest fire in Malibu. "It's perfect," his breathless staff says, showing no concern about the disaster. When he gets there, McKay begins talking about environmental policy, but he is interrupted when his powerful opponent arrives by helicopter and the press dashes away to question him. Jarmon makes the power of incumbency clear with the reminder that he chairs a Senate committee and has a direct line to the president. He promises to act immediately as McKay smiles ruefully.

As the campaign grows more desperate, McKay is persuaded to swallow his pride and solicit the support of his father, the ex-governor, whose politics disgust him. "Did you really run your own [campaign]?" the son asks the father (Melvyn Douglas) as they walk in the woods, groping for reconciliation. "Shit, yes," the old man says. "What's it like to campaign in this state these days?" "I wouldn't know," his son answers. When the young McKay debates his opponent, he grows frustrated with the glib platitudes he has been instructed to mouth and returns to his old style, bringing up tough issues they have not discussed. Chastised by his staff and demoralized after losing the debate, his spirits are revived when his father arrives to endorse him. "Son," the old man says, "you're a politician"—the ultimate insult to young McKay. Still thinking about the debate, the candidate wonders "if anyone understood what I was trying to do." "Don't worry, son," his father says not very reassuringly. "It won't make any difference."

Eventually, the campaign completely swallows the candidate. He follows directions, not knowing where he is or what he is doing, and he has little real contact with people. His campaign staff has grown so large that he does not know them all. Groupies in search of autographs and sex treat him like a star, while strangers slug him or harangue him, even in toilets. He seldom argues with his aides, and when he does, he loses. He becomes an automaton, doing whatever they tell him. "I don't know what her name is, but she's sending a check," he reports after carrying out an order to phone a contributor.

McKay's campaign finally gains momentum and gels, however. At a meeting with the leader of the Teamsters' union, McKay the former activist re-emerges as he condemns the union for what it has done to the farmworkers, but the leader endorses him anyway, and at a rally of the union members McKay gives the speech that ignites the campaign. "There has to be a better way," he cries. In rhythmic references to the division between black and white, old and young, rich and poor, he demands change without being specific. It is a media speech, but it works. The upturn is accompanied by a stirring musical crescendo—the same music that underscores Crocker Jarmon's moving, patriotic speeches. The two candidates have become alike. The campaign rushes on, full of incidents that illustrate the humor, cynicism, intensity, and excitement of politics as well as its techniques, from advertising to getting out the vote. McKay is stunned, however, when he wins. "What do we do now?" he asks his manager, but before he gets the answer, he is swept away by cheering supporters. The door closes, and the camera lingers on an empty room.

The Candidate did not set box offices afire, but it turned a profit and advanced the careers of Robert Redford, Michael Ritchie, and Jeremy Larner, who won an Oscar for his script. Most reviewers liked the film, although

Andrew Sarris denounced its "winning is losing puerilities."[4] Vincent Canby agreed, commenting on its "perverse and puritanical" view of politics while conceding that *The Candidate* was "one of the few truly funny American political comedies ever made" and praising its style for being "as nervous and frenetic as the campaign itself."[5] Even politicians were impressed with *The Candidate*. California's Jerry Brown allegedly wanted to buy advertising time for his campaign during its television broadcast, but was dissuaded by his staff, who thought the public would misunderstand. Brown and others liked the movie's humor and appreciated its depiction of campaign techniques and of the seductive power of politics.

From advertising to winning endorsements and cajoling key groups, *The Candidate* is a veritable campaign primer, deficient only in its treatment of fund-raising. This movie catches the spirit of a campaign and the way it sweeps away the candidate and everybody around him. We watch McKay sell out, but we cheer him on because we want him to win. We laugh at the cynicism of the campaigners and of the "now what?" ending, but the cynicism is softened by the casting of Robert Redford as the candidate. He may be naive, but he means well, and in the end, we still like him, which makes it easier for us to understand how decent people get drawn into the political process and forget their good intentions.

"What do we do now?" asked McKay when he won the election. In 1979, *The Seduction of Joe Tynan* answered his question. Alan Alda, who wrote the script, is Senator Joe Tynan, a good New York liberal. The film lets us know this with an opening montage featuring a busload of black kids and an array of Washington monuments right out of *Mr. Smith Goes to Washington*. We next see Tynan alone in the Senate speaking about hunger, a scene that tells us he cares while others do not. At home that night, he romps in bed with his wife, Ellie (Barbara Harris), gleefully celebrating his success: "I got the works bill passed! I've got clout!"

The realities of politics are introduced in the next scene, when Senator Birney (Melvyn Douglas), a conservative from Louisiana, asks a favor of Tynan. The president has nominated a racist from Birney's state to fill a vacancy on the Supreme Court, and the Senate must now approve the nominee. Birney wants the nomination approved so as to eliminate the man as a potential opponent. "Vote against him if you like," he says; "just don't start a crusade." Tynan agrees as a personal favor to his elder, and we support this mild compromise because, thanks to the fine acting of Melvyn Douglas, we share Tynan's sympathy for the old man.

Joe next meets Karen Traynor (Meryl Streep), a southern labor lawyer, counsel for a black group, and daughter of a powerful politician. Wanting Joe to lead the opposition to the judicial nomination, Karen seduces him into it with an enticing description of what this move could mean to his career. All he has to do is use some film footage of the nominee making a racist speech. "When I think of the splash you could make with this piece of film, I get weak in the knees," she gushes, quickly adding "of course it's the right thing to do." The seduction is soon sexual as well as political.

They succeed in blocking the nomination and the media report a victory for Joe Tynan. His staff prepares to press his advantage, hiring a speech and video coach to polish up his act, planning visits to newspaper editorial boards, and preparing a direct mail campaign. By this time Joe and Karen have gone their separate ways, but Joe's wife is increasingly repelled by her husband's unrelenting absorption in politics, or perhaps she just feels left out. "When were you going to tell me you were running for president?" she asks. "At the inaugural ball?" But for the moment, Joe is only positioning himself for a candidacy, angling to give a crucial speech at a party convention. He attains this modest goal, but Ellie seems about to leave him even as the convention crowd chants, "We want Joe!" He gazes at Ellie from the convention podium. Her mouth quivers. Is it a smile? Will she stay? The ending is ambiguous, but most viewers think she will.

Karen seduces Joe sexually, but she also plays on his ego and ambition, thus seducing him with the prospect of success as well. Joe is not a victim, however. He is an active and enthusiastic participant in both seductions, and he has few qualms about breaking his word to Senator Birney and destroying a nice old man. The treachery of the hero is mitigated, of course, by the racism of the judicial nominee and by the senility of the old man. Besides, we like Tynan/Alda.

The Seduction of Joe Tynan raises the issues of compromise and ambition and makes audiences understand Tynan's position and even feel sympathy for him. Joe's future remains unclear, however. "After a while," warns a colleague who has decided not to run for another term, "you forget why you're here. You just try to hang on to clout." Joe will not walk away from politics like his honorable colleague or like the candidates in *State of the Union* and *The Best Man,* but can he stay and still retain his integrity? That question is left unanswered.

The Seduction of Joe Tynan won mixed reviews, but did fairly well at the box office, thanks at least in part to Alda's popularity. The *New Yorker* derided the movie's "have a nice day" politics and called the film "overwrought, airless and pious."[6] Feminists approved of the presence of strong women with careers, but expressed disappointment that their ultimate function was to support the male. For all its shortcomings, however, *Joe Tynan* reflects political reality. More than most films about politics, it rings true on the personal costs of political life, its small compromises, and its corruptions.

The process is convincingly portrayed without resorting to dirty little secrets as in *Advise and Consent* and *The Best Man,* thus keeping the melodrama within the realm of credibility. *Joe Tynan*'s great strength, like that of *The Candidate,* is its feel for politics and politicians. Bill McKay and Joe Tynan face the horrors and carry on. They may sell out, but we understand why because the movies make sure we continue to like them. However cynical these movies are, they are more realistic than other movies about politics because they keep their politicians human. Their view may be less than reassuring, but their truthfulness is an advance for political movies.

Paranoia

These films marked a change in the way movies portrayed politics. Before World War II, filmmakers insisted that individuals could make a difference; heroes and heroines could fight the system and win, often by calling on the support of "the people." But after the war, movies emphasized the corrupting nature of power: good men became evil (*All The King's Men, A Lion Is in the Streets*) or had to walk away from politics to preserve their honor *(State of the Union, Viva Zapata!).* Still later, individuals had to adapt to the system and play as members of the team *(Advise and Consent, The Best Man).* But in *The Candidate* and *Joe Tynan,* the system was bigger than the individuals. The process itself dominates, sweeping individuals along with it. As entertaining and seductive as these movies were, their message about politics was less than empowering.

Their portrayal of politicians being overwhelmed by the system was mild, however, compared to the political messages of other films of the mid-1970s. Francis Ford Coppola followed *The Godfather* (1972) with *The Godfather, Part II* (1974), an even bleaker view of American society in which his Mafia family goes corporate and falls apart. Meanwhile, Roman Polanski's *Chinatown* (1974) took up corrupt politics in Los Angeles. In all three movies, economic interests dominated and politicians were mere puppets.

Executive Action (1973), based on the works of conspiracy theorist Mark Lane and written by Dalton Trumbo, was even more paranoid with its theory that a right-wing conspiracy had President John F. Kennedy assassinated to prevent his family from perpetuating itself in power and moving the country to the left. Newsreel footage and factual details made *Executive Action* seem realistic, but too much didactic dialogue defeated it with critics and at the box office.

Executive Action ends with an ominous report of the deaths of eighteen material witnesses within three years of Kennedy's assassination, a phenomenon that also inspired *The Parallax View* (1974). In this film, a crusading reporter (Warren Beatty) stumbles onto a corporate assassination bureau when he notices that all the witnesses to a political killing are being eliminated. He infiltrates the Parallax Corporation, which at first seems to be training him as an assassin but later sets him up as the fall guy for another agent. The film begins and ends with investigative commissions dismissing charges of conspiracy in assassinations and concluding that the killer (in both cases the wrong man) acted alone, exactly as the Warren Commission did after the Kennedy assassination. With its ominous music, dark lighting, and obscure villain, *The Parallax View* was basically updating the political thriller, but its hero was not merely co-opted, like Bill McKay in *The Candidate;* he was destroyed by the system. Critics liked the movie, but despite its production values and star, *The Parallax View* failed at the box office.

Political paranoia continued in *Three Days of the Condor* (1975), directed by Sydney Pollack and coauthored by Lorenzo Semple Jr., one of the scenarists of *The Parallax View*. Robert Redford plays a scruffy CIA researcher who chances on some dangerous information that results in his entire office being wiped out, a massacre he escapes only by a fluke. When he phones his superiors, they promise him safety if he comes in, but when the friend sent to reassure him is murdered, he grows wary. Isolated and able to trust no one, he decides to take his story to the *New York Times*. This promises a happy ending until a CIA operative (Cliff Robertson) says to Redford, "How do you know they'll print it?" The doubt in Redford's face leaves us uncertain about the film's ending. Is even the *New York Times* controlled? *Condor* became one of the all-time political box office hits, undoubtedly assisted by the star power of Robert Redford.

All the President's Men (1976), another well-made Redford film, was even more successful, however. Although it was presented as a thriller, audiences consciously saw it as a political movie, high in both political content and intent. Fascinated by the story of Nixon's fall from power, Redford acquired the rights to the book by Bob Woodward and Carl Bernstein. He then recruited director Alan Pakula (*The Parallax View*), who gave his films an ominous quality through the clever use of lighting, editing, and music.

The filmmakers faced a problem, however, when they set out to make a movie of events that were so recent. Audiences had followed the story in newspapers, watched the Senate hearings on television, and heard Nixon deny his involvement, and they had made a best seller of the book by the young *Washington Post* reporters who started the Watergate investigation. The filmmakers were gambling that the nation was sufficiently obsessed with the story to make their movie a success, too. But as Pakula said, the story consisted of "one phone call after another. How do you make that interesting?"[7] With megastars Robert Redford and Dustin Hoffman in the lead roles, the filmmakers decided to play the story as a thriller. *All the President's Men* could not be a whodunit, of course, since the public already knew the answer. It was more of a how-they-done-it, focusing on the reporters and how they gradually and painstakingly got their story.

The action begins with the Watergate burglary, a story assigned to junior *Washington Post* reporter Bob Woodward (Redford). Carl Bernstein (Dustin Hoffman) muscles in as coauthor, and when their story looks bigger than burglary, editor Ben Bradlee (Jason Robards Jr.) resists demands to put a national reporter on it. The big-time editors and reporters, we are told, would be less likely to dig into the story because they have been co-opted by their subjects, lunching at the same posh restaurants as the president's men. This battle between the little guys and the elite puts us firmly on the side of the young reporters and their tough editor. They experience self-doubt when other papers ignore the story, missing the security of pack journalism, but they persist.

Pakula's filming techniques constantly isolate and dwarf the reporters. As they drive away from the newspaper building, for example, their car seems to be swallowed up by the city. As they plow through reams of research material at the Library of Congress, the camera looks down on them, making them appear to the audience as tiny figures encircled by an endless maze, an image that suggests the impossibility of their huge task. The sound track, too, constantly underlines their isolation with ominous music.

The two reporters gradually get their story not from the president's men but from low- and middle-level workers in the Campaign to Re-Elect the President (CREEP)—except for "Deep Throat," the mysterious high-level informant whose face is only dimly shown and who insists on secret meetings. Like the Parallax Corporation or the CIA in *Three Days of the Condor,* CREEP is powerful, unapproachable, and somehow dangerous. The low-level informants are terrified, and even Deep Throat is obviously fearful. Film technique makes this fear palpable when Deep Throat meets Woodward deep inside a murky parking garage in a scene complete with creepy footsteps and thriller lighting. But while the investigation takes place in half-light and long shots with high camera angles, the revelations take place in the bright newsroom, with the camera closer and lower. Pakula said the "hard light of truth is in that newsroom; no shadows there."[8] At the end of the movie, we hear the guns saluting Nixon's inauguration on a television set in the newsroom, but the shots are gradually drowned out by the clacking of a lone Teletype pounding out reports of the conviction of the president's men. But viewers know that by telling the truth to the people, two little guys will bring down the president and his men—a more upbeat ending than even Capra provided, and this time the story was true.

The critics were almost unanimously ecstatic about *All the President's Men*, praising its accurate treatment of journalism although mainly admiring it as a thriller. Vincent Canby called it "the thinking man's *Jaws*."[9] Woodward and Bernstein became role models for American youth as journalism schools turned away applicants. Only Sylvester Stallone's *Rocky*, another movie about a little guy making good, beat *All the President's Men* at the box office in 1976. No other purely political film has done better at the box office than this one, which ranked as one of *Variety*'s "Box Office Champions" through the 1980s. Audiences responded to a well-made film with big stars, but they must also have wanted to relive the recent trauma of Watergate and learn more about it. The film was nominated for Academy Awards for best film and direction. Goldman won an Oscar for his script, and Jason Robards took the award for supporting actor.

All the President's Men told us that politics is corrupt and that bad men can gain great power, but it also said that brave individuals, a free press, and public opinion can bring the evil men down, a traditional Hollywood view. Whereas *The Parallax View* suggested that evil was all pervasive, *President's Men* reassured us that wickedness could be exposed and defeated. *Condor*'s faith in the integrity of the press was vindicated. Yet the message of *All the President's Men* was not entirely comforting. Our heroes are transparently ambitious and careerist. They publish their findings knowing innocent people will be hurt, and the movie does not justify their action. They manipulate people and use their colleagues, ultimately making a big mistake about the confirmation of some information. Yet if two junior reporters have to save the country all by themselves, surely democratic institutions and the press are working imperfectly. If the young reporters or their stubbornly courageous editor had been diverted, the defense of democracy would have failed. Finally, playing the story as a thriller implied an ominous, evil power although it remained undefined. What were the CREEP workers so frightened of and what actually happened to them? Who were the president's men and what exactly did they do? Their actions may have been an accumulation of small corruptions not entirely unlike those practiced by the reporters, but Pakula made them seem purely malign, perhaps even worse than they were. The president's men became a faceless conspiracy like the Parallax Corporation. This treatment, however, probably had more to do with making an entertaining and profitable movie than with sending a message.

Nevertheless, this film sent a powerful message. According to scriptwriter William Goldman, Ronald Reagan thought that *All the President's Men* "cost Gerald Ford the presidency against Jimmy Carter, because the film's release in April of '76 and its long run flushed to the surface again all the realities of Watergate that the Republicans had tried so hard to bury. We are talking,"

Goldman boasted, "about a movie that . . . just might have changed the entire course of American history."[10] Appropriately, it was the first film screened in the Carter White House.

Reagan and Goldman notwithstanding, Sylvester Stallone's *Rocky*, also released in 1976, may have had as much to do with Carter's election as *All the President's Men*. Both movies were about little guys who became heroes, just as Carter rose from the obscurity of Georgia politics to the presidency. Like movie politicians from Mr. Smith onward, Carter presented himself as a nonpolitician, carrying his own luggage, sleeping in the homes of voters, and swearing never to tell a lie; and the nation longed for a nonpolitician like Jimmy Carter in 1976.

Later in the decade, *The China Syndrome* (1979) continued the theme of paranoia and interest in the media. And like *All the President's Men*, this movie also had a direct impact on public policy. *The China Syndrome* was independently made by IPC, the Bruce Gilbert–Jane Fonda production company responsible for other Fonda films of the era. Like those movies, it suffered from what might be called the Fonda syndrome, raising an important issue but delivering a timid message. Although inspired by the death of nuclear power worker Karen Silkwood, director and coauthor James Bridges changed the story line so as to emphasize TV news as much as nuclear energy. Instead of a blue-collar worker like Karen Silkwood, Fonda played a glamorous TV reporter.

Kimberly Wells (Fonda) covers light stories but longs to do hard news. She is given a chance to do a series on nuclear energy, although initially it looks more like promotion than news. By chance, she and her crew are present at a power plant during an "incident," and her aggressive freelance cameraman (Michael Douglas) films the event surreptitiously. They rush back to the station with their scoop, but when the power company denies that anything unusual happened, the station manager refuses to let Kimberly air the story. Confident that the TV station will not air anything detrimental to its capitalist partner, the hot-tempered cameraman steals the film.

Kimberly goes looking for the photographer and the film so she can give it back to the station manager and save her job. In a bar near the power plant, she meets Godell (Jack Lemmon), the engineer who was in charge at the time of the accident. He is nervous about talking to her, but he is also attracted to her, and she uses her good looks to get him to open up. Gradually, his worries about a company cover-up come out.

Godell starts out as a true believer in nuclear power and his company. When his coworker, an uneducated twenty-five-year company man (Wilfred Brimley), says he is afraid the investigators will attribute the accident to human error and make him the scapegoat, Godell is incredulous. "What makes you think they're looking for a scapegoat?" he asks. "Tradition," answers the company man. When the shallow investigation concludes with a cover-up, the appalled Godell begins poking around and discovers falsified safety checks that prove the accident was more serious than the company has admitted. The power company rejects Godell's charges and has Kimberly's report suppressed with the collusion of her television station. New safety checks would cost too much, the company says, and might delay the licensing of a new plant at even greater cost. Kimberly and her activist cameraman arrange for Godell to give evidence at hearings on the licensing of the new plant and arrange for their soundman to deliver their videotaped evidence to support him, but the soundman, like Karen Silkwood, is killed in an auto accident. Desperate, Godell seizes the control room of his plant and sends for Kimberly and her cameraman to broadcast his statement. Above them in a glass booth, a company executive oozes evil as he watches their preparations. By the time they go on the air, Godell is so nervous that he comes off as a nut. The police antiterrorist squad breaks in and kills him, and at that very moment another nuclear accident begins.

Even as the power plant shakes and rattles, the company mounts a new cover-up, blaming it all on the dead Godell. Kimberly asks Godell's coworker, the company man, whether management's allegations about his friend are true. He pauses, and then says the company is wrong, that Godell was a good man. As the film ends, we assume the truth has come out, although a note of ambiguity is introduced when the movie takes us back to the television studio and the news broadcast is interrupted by an advertisement for microwave ovens.

Predictably, the nuclear power industry tried to discredit *The China Syndrome* even before it was released, but two weeks after it opened, an accident at Pennsylvania's Three Mile Island nuclear plant spectacularly gave the movie both credibility and publicity. The film was advertised as a thriller, but the coincidence of Three Mile Island gave emphasis to what would otherwise have seemed a timid message. Thanks to the free publicity, heavy advertising, generally good reviews, three Oscar nominations, and many public appearances by Fonda, Douglas, and Lemmon, all of whom agreed with the movie's message, *The China Syndrome* did well at the box office.

In addition to foreseeable criticism from the nuclear power industry, the harshest reviews of this film came from the left, which flayed *The China Syndrome* for choosing entertainment over political substance, trivializing the opposition to nuclear energy, ignoring the problems of blue-collar workers, showing too much faith in the media, and substituting individual for collective action.[11] In the end, the film's heroes are not against nuclear power; they just want to tell the public the truth. Good people stand up and speak out, another reassuring conclusion along the lines of *Mr. Smith Goes to Washington* and *All the President's Men. The China Syndrome* implies that telling the truth about the accidents will be enough to mobilize the public and precipitate government action. And in a way it was. This popular and entertaining movie, considerably aided by the coincidence of Three Mile Island, added impetus to the long years of organizing, demonstrating, and lobbying that ended the construction of nuclear power plants in America.

Revenge of the Blacklist

In addition to political thrillers and movies like *The Candidate,* the mid-1970s brought a modest revival of the Old Left. As the civil rights and anti-war movements reached their culmination, the Old Left found itself rehabilitated. Activists who had been blacklisted and spurned in the 1950s became the new heroes and heroines, and the old witch hunt virtually reversed itself as HUAC's collaborators and friendly witnesses fell into disrepute. Lillian Hellman, Dalton Trumbo, Arthur Miller, and others who had been harassed became cultural icons, and the Old Left got its revenge in the movies, too.

In the grand Hollywood tradition, however, the first of these films, *The Way We Were* (1973), was more romantic than political. Star casting and an eye toward prospective profits may have led to the toning down of the political content originally intended by director Sydney Pollack and writer Arthur Laurents, who adapted his own novel.

Katie (Barbra Streisand) is a student activist in the 1930s. As president of the Young Communists League, she is serious and committed, even fanatical, and she works her way through college, too. The rich, handsome Hubbell (Robert Redford), however, is just out for a good time. Katie, who is Jewish, dismisses Hubbell as a rich WASP twit until one of his short stories is read aloud in class. "In a way he was like the country he lived in," the story begins. "Everything came too easily." Later, during World War II, the two meet again and fall in love. They end up in Hollywood, where he is a scriptwriter and she is an activist housewife. When Katie joins the House Un-American Activities Committee (HUAC) protests, they separate, and the movie ends when they accidentally meet later in New York City. She is handing out ban-the-bomb literature, and he is taking his new WASP wife into the Plaza Hotel. Katie reports that she, too, has remarried, and they part nostalgically.

The romantic stars made *The Way We Were* a box office hit, but most reviewers criticized its soft politics, which reduced the movie to a melodrama of doomed love. In scenes that were cut from the movie at the last minute, Katie is called to testify before HUAC and must choose between naming names or refusing to do so and hurting Hubbell's career. She refuses and loses him for the sake of her politics. Had audiences seen this version, we might have wished the wimpy Hubbell good riddance, but instead we see Katie giving up Robert Redford just to stand on a street corner and hand out leaflets.

Nor surprisingly, the political theme of *The Way We Were* was lost on most audiences, but if its backers and makers played safe with their investment, those of *The Front* (1976) were more forthright. The writer, director, and several actors in *The Front* were blacklisted themselves, a fact that was noted in the film's end credits and that surely added to its credibility.

In this film, a blacklisted TV scriptwriter (Michael Murphy) asks his friend Howard (Woody Allen) to "front" for him. This means that Howard will put his name on the writer's scripts and deal with producers in the writer's stead in return for a fee. Howard agrees because he needs the money, and soon he is serving as a front for other blacklisted writers as well and enjoying wealth and fame. The workings of the blacklist are seen not only through Howard's dealings with the writers he fronts for, but also through pressures on Hecky Brown (Zero Mostel), a comic. Claiming innocence of left-wing activities, Hecky is pressured to spy on Howard and others, loses his job, and ultimately kills himself.

The investigators then subpoena Howard. He has no politics and is outraged at being wrongly accused, but he cannot inform because he would lose his stable of writers. The investigators demand names—any names, even the dead, even Hecky Brown. One of the writers Howard fronts for explains that all the persecutors really want is to prove they can make Howard submit—a belief widely shared by HUAC's critics. During the hearing, Howard balks at naming his dead friend Hecky, declaring that he does not recognize the committee's right to "ask those kind of questions and furthermore you can all go fuck yourselves." He walks out, and the film ends with him being taken to prison for contempt. A crowd cheers, his left-wing writers pat him on the back, and he wins back his liberal girlfriend. The front has become a hero and "Young at Heart" plays on the sound track ("Fairy tales can come true, it can happen to you . . .").

The Front got mixed notices from critics, many of whom found it unsatisfactory as either political analysis or comedy. The harshest criticisms were from the left for taking blacklisting too lightly, particularly through the comic "intrusion . . . of the classic Woody Allen character, the Jewish schlemiel."[12] Pauline Kael thought it was a "slightly archaic" movie about a common man standing up for what was right, "like the heroes of the forties wartime movies written by those who were later blacklisted."[13] Audiences, however, liked *The Front*, and it was more successful at the box office than a film with tougher politics might have been.

The Front described the workings of the blacklist and left no doubt that it was bad. If anything, the movie oversimplified this evil by caricaturing the investigators. To the film's credit, however, not all of its blacklist victims were as innocent as Hecky and Howard. Still, *The Front* offered little real understanding of why the blacklist existed, and even its terrible impact on individuals was obscured by what most audiences took as a happy ending, despite the film's implication that it was fantasy. Casting Woody Allen in the lead also weakened *The Front*, instantly making it "a Woody Allen movie." Howard learned, grew, and finally took action, yet because of Allen's presence the audience perceived the movie as a comedy, straining for laughs even when they were not there.

The Way We Were and *The Front* illustrate how political messages can be subverted or obscured by Hollywood's imperative to find an audience and make money. Both films took on political subjects, and then backed away, the former toward romance and the latter toward comedy. Both films would have been stronger if the motives of their main characters had been more clearly political, but their actions were either unfathomable or explained by love and loyalty. On the other hand, the romance and comedy found audiences, which tougher politics might not have done.

Although *Julia* (1977) was not explicitly about the blacklist, it must have been sweet revenge for HUAC critic Lillian Hellman, who wrote the book, *Pentimento*, that included the story on which this film was based. Directed by Fred Zinnemann, *Julia* starred Jane Fonda and Vanessa Redgrave, both of whom, like Hellman, had suffered career setbacks because of their politics. Julia (Redgrave) is an antifascist student activist and a committed revolutionary in Nazi Germany. She asks her friend Lillian (Fonda) to help her by smuggling money for the resistance, an act of danger and bravery, especially for someone like Lillian who is not directly involved. Lillian undertakes the mission out of personal loyalty rather than political commitment, and matures in the process. The politically conscious Julia is the moral center of the film and her commitment is strongly justified by her antifascism. Lillian, on the other hand, exhibits the naiveté of some people who associated with left-wing causes in the 1930s, suggesting that HUAC exaggerated their subversiveness. Perhaps more notable, however, was the fact that women were heroines rather than marginal characters in this film. By giving both women a firm basis for their actions and by letting us see Lillian mature, *Julia* provided a politically stronger condemnation of HUAC and the blacklist than either *The Way We Were* or *The Front*. Significantly, this film about friendship, bravery, and political commmitment—neither a romance nor a comedy—was a popular and critical success and won three Oscars.

Disillusionment

Whatever their shortcomings, *The Way We Were, The Front, Julia,* and *All the President's Men* acknowledged the potential for honorable individual action. *The Candidate* and the political thrillers of the 1970s had argued that such action was futile against the overpowering corruption of the system, but their heroes were willing to join the struggle, and at least there was a central power that could be opposed, even if defeat was inevitable.

Other movies of the decade revealed a deeper disillusionment, perhaps more accurately reflecting the spirit of the times. Beloved political leaders had been killed. The civil rights, antiwar, and women's movements of the 1960s and 1970s had fallen apart. Political action seemed useless to many liberals after the defeat of George McGovern and the reelection of Richard Nixon in 1972. Watergate, Nixon's resignation, and Gerald Ford's presidency only exacerbated the disillusionment, as did the fall of Saigon in 1975. Crime, violence, urban decay, and racial polarization were on the rise, and the environmental and sexual liberation movements seemed more personal than political. The country diffidently celebrated its bicentennial in 1976 as the little-known antipolitician Jimmy Carter was elected president. Not surprisingly, movies reflected the nation's disillusionment.

During this period, Warren Beatty, one of Hollywood's most politically active stars, produced, coauthored (with Robert Towne), and starred in *Shampoo* (1975), directed by Hal Ashby. Although this is not primarily a political movie, its climactic scene takes place at a political banquet and it uses constant television commentary on the 1968 election of Richard Nixon as a backdrop. Beatty said his movie was "about the intermingling of political and sexual hypocrisy,"[14] comparing Nixon's public behavior with our own private behavior.

Director Robert Altman showed similar disillusionment in *Nashville* (1975), using the country-and-western music capital as a microcosm of American society. Altman had taken on the military in *M*A*S*H* (1970) and made corporate businessmen the villains in his "western," *McCabe and Mrs. Miller* (1971). *Nashville* was more overtly political, although most viewers were unsure just what the message was. Like Altman's other films of the 1970s, it destroyed all expectations with its multicharacter structure and chaotic plot, yet it managed to remain profoundly humanist.

No less than twenty-four characters crisscross through *Nashville*. Their lives are a country-and-western version of Tom Wolfe's "Me Decade" as they dash around trying to attain or keep hold of stardom. "The whole piece," scriptwriter Joan Tewkesbury said, "was about people who were trying to do the best job they could with the equipment they had in this dumb kind of social structure."[15] As in *Shampoo,* politics provides a backdrop for the hustling in *Nashville.* Hal Philip Walker is the unseen "Replacement Party" candidate for president. A roving sound truck constantly announces his vaguely populist proposals, including a new national anthem "that people can sing." An advance man (Michael Murphy), reminiscent of the campaign manager in *The Candidate,* is in Nashville lining up stars to support Walker at a big concert. All twenty-four characters come together at the rally, and the movie climaxes when an assassin who apparently panics while waiting to kill Hal Philip Walker murders one of them, a country megastar. The film ends as an aspiring country singer picks up the microphone and sings "It Don't Worry Me," an antipolitical song that says we will all survive no matter what.

Audiences were mystified by *Nashville,* probably because of its chaotic structure, and its box office was mediocre, but the film was nominated for five Academy Awards, and critics raved about it. Some complained about its ending, however, and Tewkesbury admitted that the assassination was added at Altman's request.[16] Such occurrences were on Americans' minds at the time, and this one pointed up the randomness of violence in our society, but as an ending, it may have been more convenient than political. The basic mood of *Nashville* was pessimistic, the film had no political answers, and only a few honorable characters offered hope for the future.

Martin Scorsese's *Taxi Driver* (1976) was even bleaker. This film's protagonist, Travis Bickle (Robert De Niro), is an unstable Vietnam vet who is drawn to politics by his infatuation with a campaign worker (Cybill Shepherd), who ignores him. To get attention or revenge, he plans to assassinate her candidate, but he is diverted by his obsession with a child prostitute (Jodie Foster) and ends up wreaking bloody havoc on her pimp (Harvey Keitel). Politics is a separate world in this movie, irrelevant to the hell Travis lives in. Like the beautiful campaign worker, politics is hypocritical and uncaring, incapable of providing salvation. Travis wreaks his crazy vengeance not on the politician, however, but on the pimp, a more deserving target. This grim, antipolitical movie was allegedly an inspiration to John Hinckley, who attempted to assassinate President Ronald Reagan to gain the attention of Jodie Foster.

Network (1976) featured yet another crazy man and yet another assassination. Directed by Sidney Lumet and written by Paddy Chayefsky, *Network* was a huge popular and critical hit, with four Oscars and five more nominations, for although it was as cynical as *Nashville* and *Taxi Driver,* audiences found it more entertaining. "I'm mad as hell and I'm not going to take this any more!" cries a TV anchorman (Peter Finch) when he is fired. He threatens to commit suicide on live television and becomes a cult hero. The network sees it has a good thing going and unscrupulously takes advantage of the newsman's insanity by giving him his own show. The programming executive (Faye Dunaway) will broadcast anything that will get good ratings, including a sort of terrorist-of-the-week show. She is encouraged and rewarded by the vicious, unscrupulous network president (Robert Duvall), but even he is subordinate to the chairman of the board (Ned Beatty). Preaching like a revivalist converting sinners, the chairman warns the obsessed anchorman to contain his rabble-rousing because corporations like the one that owns the network have replaced nations and now rule the world.

Network's "I'm mad as hell" slogan gave the film a populist tone, but its contempt for television audiences did not manifest faith in the public. In fact, *Network* offered no hope at all. Like other movies of the 1970s, including both *Godfather* films, *Chinatown*, *The Parallax View*, and *Shampoo*, *Network* saw politics and politicians as less powerful than corporations, a more radical and distressing political analysis than that offered by earlier films. Even more distressing, these movies refused to offer even a glimmer of hope.

Hollywood Discovers Vietnam

Among the most painful topics for Americans in the 1960s and 1970s was the war in Vietnam. Hollywood largely avoided this subject except for John Wayne's *The Green Berets* (1968) and some films of the early 1970s for which the war functioned as background. In *American Graffiti*, for example, the war was seen as a part of growing up. In *Nashville,* an edgy Vietnam vet who could have been an assassin turns out to be a hero. And in *Taxi Driver,* it is a crazed veteran who explodes into horrific violence. But it was not until after the fall of Saigon in 1975 and the election of President Carter in 1976 that Hollywood contemplated Vietnam seriously.

The first such effort, *Twilight's Last Gleaming* (1977), was a thriller along the lines of *Fail Safe,* offering a left-wing explanation of the war. Director Robert Aldrich, one of Hollywood's most consistent liberals, had previously made the pro-Indian *Apache* (1954) and the antiwar, anticlass *Attack* (1956).[17] Lawrence Dell (Burt Lancaster), the protagonist in *Twilight's Last Gleaming,* is a renegade general but, contrary to convention, he is a liberal rather than a fascist, and he wants the American people to know the truth about U.S. involvement in Vietnam. Drummed out of the air force and railroaded into prison for his fanaticism, he escapes with two other inmates, seizes a Strategic Air Command (SAC) missile silo, and threatens to launch the missiles unless the president makes public the minutes of a National Security Council meeting that will tell all. A sympathetic president (Charles Durning) prepares to do so, but his advisers oppose him, and when he goes to the silo to bring the renegade general out, both men are gunned down. In the words of Dell's associate, the men who control the system would sacrifice even the president rather than "blow their gig."

162

The general and the president act as they do for clear, unambiguous reasons: they are good men who want the people to know the truth. In earlier movies, the good guys usually won when the people learned the truth. Here, as in other 1970s movies, the truth never comes out and the good guys lose, but at least the movie tells us such heroes do exist. The film's chilling conclusion gains nuance and a certain ambiguity from good casting and fine acting, but audiences and critics were unenthusiastic.

Other movies about the war followed. *Rolling Thunder* (1977) featured a Vietnam vet using skills acquired in the war to wreak vengeance at home. *Big Wednesday* (1978) was about three surfers, one of whom was drafted and sent to Vietnam. The effects of the war were taken up in *Who'll Stop the Rain* (1978), which suggested that America had corrupted itself through its involvement in Vietnam, as a disillusioned journalist, criminals, crooked federal agents, and relatively innocent bystanders fight over the spoils—drugs, in this case.

Go Tell the Spartans (1978) and *The Boys in Company* C (1978) were the first combat films about Vietnam since *The Green Berets,* although neither was as old-fashioned as that film. *Go Tell the Spartans* takes place in the early days when Americans are just advisers in Vietnam, but one of them (Burt Lancaster again) begins to doubt the worthiness of the cause. Sidney J. Furie's *The Boys in Company C,* however, was a combat film with a difference.

Like a World War II movie, *The Boys in Company C* follows a cross section of American men—including a black, a big-city Italian, a hippie, and a good ol' country boy—through training and their first month in Vietnam, but we soon learn that this is like no other movie war. Within a day of arriving in Vietnam, one takes heroin, another deals drugs, and a third blows up a general's trailer. Their officers are tyrants interested only in body counts, the enemy is an unseen terror, and the South Vietnamese officers are corrupt. The movie, however, makes a point of including some good Vietnamese civilians who are befriended by the streetwise black soldier who, albeit reluctantly, becomes the informal leader of Company C.

The men are ordered to lose a soccer match to a Vietnamese team in order to boost the morale of their allies. In return, Company C will be taken off combat duty and sent on a soccer tour. The catch is that they have to keep losing. They refuse and return to the front, preferring to take their chances rather than become part of the all-pervasive corruption. *The Boys in Company C* does not, however, say that fighting to win is the best alternative. Rather, it honors those who refuse to sell out, whether they fight or desert, and especially if they are loyal to their peers.

Unfortunately, this fine little movie was overshadowed by Hollywood's first big star-studded productions on Vietnam. *The Deer Hunter* and *Coming*

Home swept the 1978 Oscars and cleaned up at the box office. These two films were also widely, if somewhat unfairly, perceived as representing the right- and left-wing perspectives on the war.

The Deer Hunter, written by Deric Washburn and directed by Michael Cimino, is about a group of working-class men who leave their industrial hometown to go to war. They do so out of a sense of duty, without questioning why and with no particular prejudices either for or against the war. The camaraderie of their life at home gives way to the brutality, chaos, confusion, and pervasive evil of the war. When they are taken prisoner, everything centers on their struggle for survival. Before they escape, their evil Vietcong captors force the men to play a brutal game of Russian roulette. Having lived through incredible degradation, some of the young men return to their community, but they are ineradicably altered by what they have gone through, and they have difficulty adjusting.

Michael (Robert De Niro), the leader of the group and an avid deer hunter, no longer takes pleasure in hunting. He returns to Saigon just before its fall to try to save Nick (Christopher Walken), who has become obsessed with the game of Russian roulette he learned from the Vietcong and now plays before an audience for money. The game becomes a symbol of American involvement in Vietnam, and it also reveals that its South Vietnamese audience and gamblers are just as vile and bloodthirsty as the Vietcong. Nick finally loses and Michael returns to their hometown, where the film ends with the surviving buddies sadly singing "God Bless America."

Although *The Deer Hunter* was a popular and critical hit, many people perceived it as a right-wing film because of its failure to question the war and its uniformly racist portrait of Asians. The film is oblivious to the impact of the war on the Vietnamese, in effect blaming them and absolving Americans of any responsibility. The game of Russian roulette is an effective dramatic device, but it also symbolizes the Asians' contempt for human life. Director Cimino, who declared *The Deer Hunter* an antiwar film because "any good picture about war is an antiwar picture," saw the Russian roulette as a symbol of the pointlessness of war.[18] For him, the theme of the film was how war destroys individuals and communities. Having seen the ravages of war, Michael no longer enjoys hunting deer. Even the singing of "God Bless America" can be seen as ironic, as the singers try to convince themselves that they still believe the lyrics. But while the pro- or antiwar sentiments of *The Deer Hunter* can be debated, it is clear in the film that the Vietnamese are the bad guys and Cimino's working-class Americans are innocent of responsibility. Cimino deserves credit for making a movie about the men who really fought the war, yet he seemed condescending to his working-class heroes, who are incapable of articulating their thoughts and oblivious to the politics of the war. *The Deer Hunter* might have been a more right-wing film if Cimino had shown authentic working-class men with authentic attitudes about the war.

In contrast to Cimino's epic of working-class men, *Coming Home* (1978) focuses on the middle-class wife of an officer. Initiated by Jane Fonda and Bruce Gilbert, *Coming Home* was directed by Hal Ashby, photographed by Haskell Wexler, and written by Waldo Salt, Robert C. Jones, and Nancy Dowd. The message these liberals put together was very different from Cimino's but almost as muddled.

Jane Fonda plays Sally, whose officer husband (Bruce Dern) is sent to Vietnam. Sally at first dreads being left alone, but after a while she feels liberated. She gets a sports car and a house on the beach and starts working with paraplegics. Soon she meets and falls in love with Luke (Jon Voight), a veteran who is opposed to the war. Like many Fonda characters, Sally is naive in the beginning, but she grows and learns and, as Gilbert Adair has written, "turns into Jane Fonda."[19] Despite his disabilities, Luke furthers the cause by helping her achieve her first orgasm. They have happy times and play at the beach. Sally's husband, Bob, is mentally unbalanced when he comes home from Vietnam. She tries to reconcile with him, but in his stressed-out state, she cannot reach him. When the meddlesome FBI tells Bob that Sally has been involved with an antiwar activist in his absence, he loses control, menacingly confronting the lovers, but ultimately turns away, defeated and in despair, to end it all by swimming out to sea to die.

Like *The Best Years of Our Lives*, *Coming Home* was about adapting. Luke is the model, coming to terms with a bad war by opposing it. In so doing, he becomes a complete, caring human being, able to help Sally to adjust. Bob, on the other hand, is unable to adapt his traditional military values to new circumstances. Too rigid to change, he chooses death. It could have been worse for Bob; an earlier draft of the script had him sniping at freeway traffic. As an antiwar movie, *Coming Home* could have convinced few. Apparently the filmmakers thought they could make their point best by fudging the politics and playing up the romance. Perhaps they were right, for although some critics disdained this film as superficial, it did well at the box office and won Academy Awards for best actress, actor, and screenplay.

Meanwhile, Hollywood eagerly awaited the definitive film on the war in Vietnam from Francis Ford Coppola, America's hottest contemporary director after his *Godfather* successes. The anticipation was heightened when Coppola was nearly bankrupted by prodigious production problems in the Philippines, for unlike *The Deer Hunter* and *Coming Home*, all of *Apocalypse Now* (1979) was to be set in Vietnam.

Based on Joseph Conrad's novel *Heart of Darkness*, Coppola's movie follows Willard (Martin Sheen) on his mission to find and kill Kurtz (Marlon Brando), a rogue American officer who is fighting the enemy on its own terms. During his journey, Willard runs into a cavalry officer addicted to surfing who leads a helicopter raid on an innocent village in search of the perfect wave. Later, Willard's crew panics and slaughters a boatload of Vietnamese who also turn out to be innocent. As their adventures continue, Willard and his men witness American troops going berserk over a *Playboy* show imported for their entertainment, reiterating the uniqueness of this war and sending up Bob Hope's renowned troop shows. After all this, when Willard finally arrives at Kurtz's bizarre encampment, the arguments of the renegade leader and his admirers in favor of their mad methods seem relatively persuasive. In the end, Willard has to decide whether to eliminate Kurtz, join him, or replace him. The film makes all these alternatives seem credible.

Critics and audiences were stunned by *Apocalypse Now*, for Coppola's nightmare of Vietnam was more surrealistic than realistic. Reviews of the movie were mixed, as both left and right criticized the confusing (or confused) politics of the film, and despite eight Academy Award nominations, *Apocalypse Now* won only for sound and cinematography. Coppola's film nevertheless did well at the box office, surpassing the other war movies to join *Variety*'s top 100 "Box Office Champions." Despite their reservations, the critics generally agreed that *Apocalypse Now* successfully communicated the horror of the war. Better than other films, it suggested the war's otherworldliness, its confusion of good and evil, and its contagious, destructive madness. Yet *Apocalypse Now* could also be read as a defense of that destructiveness because of Kurtz's claim that he was driven to extreme action by the atrocities of the Vietcong. In fact, Kurtz's justification of his behavior seemed to be the point of *Apocalypse Now,* not only because the role of Kurtz was played by a superstar but also because the character was the subject of the quest that took up two hours of the film.[20] This interpretation was undercut, however, by Kurtz's apparent madness, Brando's low-key performance, and the apparent innocence of the Vietnamese civilians in the earlier scenes. The meeting with Kurtz is an anticlimactic and unsatisfying conclusion to Willard's journey, but the events leading up to the meeting help explain Kurtz's actions and the view of Vietnam as a quagmire, making clear the reasons for deeper and deeper U.S. involvement and excess.

All of these films about Vietnam made money and some were big hits, but Hollywood soon turned away from the war. Bad reviews and box office worries played a part in this disenchantment, but the nature of the war seemed the primary reason. The complexity of the situation in Vietnam was difficult to catch in fiction films, especially when people had seen so much news footage on TV. The Vietnam War also remained a very painful subject, not only because America lost, but also because the reasons for involvement had never been clear. Hollywood liked simpler wars, like World War II, in which our reasons for fighting were clear, but in the brief cycle of movies about Vietnam, few offered an explanation. *Apocalypse Now* contemplated the deepening American involvement and its increasing irrationality, but on the whole these films focused on the impact of the war on the individuals who fought it and on its effect on American society. Except for a handful of characters in *The Boys in Company C* and *Coming Home* who survived with their honor and their sanity intact, these movies unanimously concluded that the war screwed everybody up, a message that was basically antiwar. In this at least, the Vietnam movies were well within the Hollywood tradition—most war films made during peacetime are antiwar. But even the antiwar message was obscured by the films' focus on individuals, a sure way to defuse political content, since every issue is personalized and therefore not necessarily applicable to American society as a whole. Meanwhile, other issues caught the film industry's limited political attention.

Labor Unions and Corporate Power

America sank deeper into disillusionment and apathy through the 1970s, but even as the nation as a whole turned away from politics, Hollywood continued in one of its most political periods, taking on not only Vietnam, but also a variety of other issues. This was partly due to the coming of age of filmmakers whose political consciousness had been shaped by the 1960s, but changes in the corporate structure of the film industry were also a factor. Larger corporations absorbed most of the big studios in the 1970s. The last to retain its independence was Columbia, which fell to Coca-Cola in 1982. Initially, the corporate studios made fewer films, but as the size of audiences and the number of cinemas increased, so did the number of movies.

The nature of production had changed, however. Making a movie increasingly depended on packaging writers, directors, actors, and others into a "deal." Such deals were still initiated by studios, but independent producers, agents, directors, actors, and writers also put together deals and took them to studios, which then acted as investors or distributors. Independent funding eventually became easier with the evolution of cable television and videocassettes as sources of revenue. In short, the role of the studios had changed: movies could now be made without them. Both *Coming Home* and *Apocalypse Now,* for example, were independent productions, as were many other films of the era. Perhaps the increased independence of filmmakers accounts for a little flurry of prolabor and anticorporate films as the decade ended.

Hollywood has never shown sustained interest in the working class. Movies have always been more likely to center on lawyers, architects, teachers, doctors, or the idle rich. Working-class characters were more common in the early silent movies, and Warner Bros. featured them often enough to earn the label "the workingman's studio" in the 1930s. But by the 1950s and 1960s, working-class people had become an endangered species in the movies, despite an occasional *Marty* (1955) or *Joe* (1970).

Union members fared even worse[21] because the studios fought a long battle against the unionization of their own workers. Even after that battle ended, unions were rarely favorably treated in American movies. *The Grapes of Wrath* sided with the workers, but stopped short of the enthusiastic unionism of Steinbeck's novel. Outright prounion films like the suppressed *Salt of the Earth* were rare, and union corruption as in *Big Jim McLain* and *On the Waterfront* was more common. Given Hollywood history, the number of films about workers and unions that appeared in the late 1970s and early 1980s was remarkable. Interestingly, Hollywood took up this topic as union membership was in decline and labor conflict was becoming a thing of the past. Like Vietnam, it was a safe subject by the time the movies got around to it.

Director Hal Ashby's *Bound For Glory* (1976) was about real-life folk singer Woody Guthrie's travels with migrant farmworkers in 1936, but the treatment and the casting of David Carradine in the lead reduced the movie's hero to a moody agitator who did not seem to care much about the people he stirred up. Factory workers took center stage in *Blue Collar* (1978) and *F.I.S.T.* (1978), although neither film had anything good to say about unions. Paul Schrader's *Blue Collar* powerfully conveyed the alienation and frustration of assembly-line workers, but it soon turned into a grim caper movie as three autoworkers rob their corrupt union and then turn against one another. Norman Jewison directed *F.I.S.T.*, but the movie seemed to have been more heavily influenced by Sylvester Stallone, its coauthor and star, who plays the Hoffa-style leader of the union whose initials give the film its title. *F.I.S.T.* begins with a righteous strike that effectively makes the case for unions. The idealistic young hero joins up, grows more involved, and rises to leadership, but he ultimately betrays both his workers and his union as the film reiterates one of Hollywood's favorite political themes: power corrupts.

Despite movies like these and public antagonism to unions, one of the big hits of 1979 was the prounion *Norma Rae*, independently produced and directed by one of Hollywood's most consistent liberals, Martin Ritt. *Norma Rae* did well at the box office, picked up two Academy Awards, and was praised by most critics. Based on the true story of a woman textile worker and union organizer, *Norma Rae* was released just as the effort to unionize the southern textile mills came to a head, helping to publicize the workers' call for a national boycott against J.P. Stevens, one of the biggest companies. Both the boycott and the movie had happy endings.

Norma Rae (Sally Field), a naive and apathetic single parent who works in the mills, is recruited by Reuben, a northern union organizer (Ron Liebman) whom the other workers shun. Under his guidance, she develops into an effective grassroots organizer and leader. Their relationship is at the center of the film, but although movie tradition leads us to expect them to have an affair, they do not. Their cultural and class differences are driven home by the difficulties she faces as she becomes more involved in the fight for unionization. He is on his own, free to leave when he likes, but her roots are in the community and the personal pressures on her are enormous. Her family turns on her, and the factory managers try to isolate her as a troublemaker. In the end, however, the workers vote to join the union and Norma Rae is triumphant. Reuben packs up his files and moves on to his next project, leaving her in charge.

The upbeat ending ignored the tough battles to negotiate a contract and control the union that lay ahead, but the strengths of *Norma Rae* outweighed this weakness. Better than most films *Norma Rae* communicated the need for unions and the personal and political difficulties of organizing them. *Norma Rae* gave too much credit to two individuals, a shortcoming it had in common with most American political films, but unlike most, it stressed that by working together and taking action, average people could take care of themselves.

Being There (1979), written by Jerzy Kosinski from his novel and directed by Hal Ashby, takes us from the shop floor to corporate boardrooms. Chance Gardener, played with brilliant reserve by Peter Sellers, is a retarded illiterate who has lived all his life on the estate of a wealthy benefactor, watching television and tending the garden. When his protector dies, Chance is turned out on the streets, but he is unable to discern the difference between television and reality. When street toughs harass him, he tries to make them go away by changing the channel on the TV remove control he carries. He walks into the street and is hit by a limousine. Its passenger, Eve Rand (Shirley MacLaine), takes him to her mansion for treatment, apparently worried about a lawsuit.

Eve's husband, Benjamin (Melvyn Douglas yet again and even better), is a dying megaindustrialist, one of the men who run the country. He is impressed by Chance, whose rare comments either are noncommittal, and so taken as agreement, or refer to gardening, in which case they are taken metaphorically. The Rands introduce Chance to their circle, and he comes to be seen as some kind of authority. His cool reserve and his gardening comments, which everyone takes as metaphors, make him an instant celebrity when he appears on a television talk show. Rand introduces Chance to his protégé, the president of the United States, who is delighted with what he takes as Chance's optimistic advice about the economy: "As long as the roots are not severed, all will be well in the garden. . . . There will be growth in the spring." Rand's corporate colleagues choose the imbecilic Chance as their next presidential candidate. Meanwhile, Chance wanders into the wintry garden. The film ends as he crosses a pond, walking on water.

Sellers was nominated for an Academy Award for his portrayal of Chance, and Melvyn Douglas won a well-deserved Oscar for his supporting role, but although the movie was a box office success, some critics were put off by the absurdity of *Being There*. Intended as devastating satire, the film came across as ominous rather than funny. People were unsure about its message and some even took Chance's final walk on water literally rather than ironically. Like *Network*, *Being There* was a condemnation of television, which numbs people's minds and creates instant celebrities who do not deserve respect. Both films also insisted that businessmen, not politicians, ran America.

Being There was only one of many movies of the late 1970s and early 1980s featuring the pervasive influence of business, perhaps reflecting Hollywood's greater independence as well as its anxiety about its own corporate status. Jane Fonda starred in a whole string of antibusiness movies during this period: *Fun with Dick and Jane* (1977), *Comes a Horseman* (1978), *The Electric Horseman* (1979), *The China Syndrome* (1979), and *Nine to Five* (1980). But a film that was itself a debacle for the businesses of Hollywood capped off the antibusiness films of the 1970s.

Michael Cimino's anticapitalist *Heaven's Gate* (1980) is about the nineteenth-century range wars in Wyoming, during which land barons, aided by hired thugs and the army, brutally crush immigrant settlers. Cimino's dazzling technique directs our sympathy to the heroic immigrants, whose community is movingly portrayed, but a dearth of dialogue and an obscurely motivated hero (Kris Kristofferson) make *Heaven's Gate* too dependent on images. The critics panned it as boring, pretentious, and overlong, and distributors withdrew the film before many people could see it. *Heaven's Gate* deserved better because of its visual beauty as well as its revisionist view of the history of the West. Its anticapitalism also suggested that the interpretation of Cimino's earlier work, *The Deer Hunter*, as right-wing was unfair. *Heaven's Gate* cost $44 million and brought in less than $2 million, ruining Cimino's career and leading film financiers to assert greater control over filmmakers—an ironic achievement for an anticapitalist film.

The few defenders of *Heaven's Gate* argued that the film bombed because the American people were not prepared to see the truth about their history. But truth or not, a whole string of films through the 1970s—from *The Candidate* to *All the President's Men*, *Network*, *Being There*, and most of Jane Fonda's films—had already proved that audiences were perfectly willing to accept cynicism, paranoia, and corporate skulduggery.

10

The 1980s

New Patriotism, Old Reds, and a Return to Vietnam in the Age of Reagan

Platoon (1986)

Republican presidents Ronald Reagan and George H.W. Bush presided over the United States through the 1980s, as the country appeared to turn to the right. Observers in other countries found it hard to understand how America could prefer a second-rate actor like Ronald Reagan to Jimmy Carter, but for many Americans Reagan represented optimism and hope over Carter's pessimism and malaise. International politics played a part, too, when Carter proved unable to resolve a lengthy stalemate over hostages in Iran. Electing Reagan, Americans protested the hostage crisis, rejected the Carter style, endorsed a reduction in government, and moved to the right, but they also expressed nostalgia for their own past. Reagan was part of that past, having appeared on movie and television screens since 1937. His familiarity, his likable personality, and his very presence were reassuring. So was his rhetoric of traditional values and patriotism. Reagan offered simple, old-fashioned answers and an unflinching faith in America that people longed for.

More than any other president, Reagan saw America and the world through a movie lens, making frequent references to films and even citing scenes from movies as if they were real-life events. His language was often drawn from film. For him, the Soviet Union was the "evil empire"—as in *Star Wars*—and his concept of an umbrellalike missile defense for the United States took the name of that film. Like many Americans, he understood his country and the world through the movies, seeing fewer shades of gray than his predecessor and communicating in simple, straightforward, and reassuring words.

Worries about his lack of experience in foreign affairs were soon swept away by a wave of patriotism. The joyous return of the Iranian hostages on the day of his inauguration launched the revival of American pride and patriotism. Reagan called for a renewal of American power and boosted the nation's military might with massive increases in military spending. Carter's foreign policy emphasis on human rights was replaced by interventionism. Reagan bombed Beirut, sent troops into Lebanon, and loosed the U.S. Marines on the tiny island of Grenada. He intervened in El Salvador and Nicaragua, supporting the Contra counterrevolutionaries. He sent U.S. jets to raid Libya, which he claimed was the headquarters of world terrorism. Many Americans approved these actions—and some of the movies of the era reflected that approval.

Meanwhile, Reagan reduced taxes, cut social programs, and ran up huge deficits to fund military spending. Vice President George H.W. Bush, succeeding Reagan as president in 1988, continued his domestic and international policies, enjoying significant early victories. The cold war ended when the Berlin Wall fell and the Soviet Union collapsed. Then, when Iraq occupied Kuwait in 1991, Bush showed decisive world leadership by building a coalition to free Kuwait and contain Iraq. But Bush was no Ronald

172

Reagan. Lacking his predecessor's charisma and good luck and with the nation blaming him for a recession, Bush was defeated in 1992 by Demo-·crat Bill Clinton.

But despite the nation's apparent move to the right in presidential elections in the 1980s, the films of the decade were as politically diverse as in preceding decades, perhaps even more so. As independent film production increased, films with liberal messages seemed to proliferate, perhaps in reaction to Reagan and the move to the right. Other movies, however, reflected the conservatism of the decade, emphasizing traditional values and patriotism. Sylvester Stallone's *Rocky* movies, for example, were old-fashioned stories based on traditional values; other films of the 1980s exemplified the resurgence of patriotism along with these values.

A Warmed-Up Cold War and New Patriotism

Reaganite movies did not come into their own until after his 1984 reelection, but the trend started in 1982 with Sylvester Stallone's *First Blood,* for which the *Rocky* movies and *F.I.S.T.* had paved the way. John Rambo (Stallone), a former Green Beret and winner of the Congressional Medal of Honor, is an alienated, itinerant Vietnam vet searching for a buddy who survived the war. After learning that his friend has died of Agent Orange–induced cancer, the distraught Rambo wanders around, looking like a cross between a hippie and a Hell's Angel. Not surprisingly, a small-town sheriff (Brian Dennehy) orders him to move on and drives him to the outskirts of town. Rambo, who does not like being told what to do, starts back into town. The two men fight, and Rambo is arrested. In jail, he becomes a victim of police brutality. With visions of Vietnam in his head, Rambo goes berserk and breaks out, fleeing to the woods.

A posse pursues Rambo along with the National Guard and state police. Rambo kills the bad cops but only wounds others, declaring, "Out here I'm the law!" His old Green Beret commander (Richard Crenna) tries to talk the surrounded Rambo into surrendering. "Do you want a war you can't win?" he asks. Explaining the film's title, Rambo replies, "They drew first blood—not me":

> It wasn't my war. You asked me, I didn't ask you. And I did what I had to do to win, but somebody wouldn't let us win. And I come back to the world, and I see all those maggots at the airport, protesting me, calling me a baby-killer and all kinds of vile crap. Who are they to protest me, huh? Back there I could fly a gunship, I could drive a tank. I was in charge of million-dollar equipment. Back here I can't even hold a job.

First Blood condemned the maltreatment of Vietnam vets, a message with which few would disagree, but the real point of this film was action. Although critics laughed at the movie, Stallone laughed last: *First Blood* was a box-office smash, and Stallone followed it with two *Rambo* sequels.

The next Reaganite movie was *Red Dawn* (1984), directed by John Milius, who wrote *Apocalypse Now*. When Russian, Cuban, and Nicaraguan Communists invade a small Colorado town, the Wolverines, a group of teenagers who resemble the partisans in World War II movies, resist the attackers. The mayor of the town, who collaborates with the Communists, represents politicians. The teenagers run rings around the occupying army for a while, but they finally sacrifice themselves in a kamikaze-style mission. The movie closes with a shot of Partisan Rock, a monument to the heroes of the resistance.

"Movies like *Red Dawn* are rapidly preparing America for World War III," said the chairman of the National Coalition on Television Violence, denouncing its 134 acts of violence per hour and labeling it "the most violent film ever seen."[1] Dismissed by critics as a mediocre action movie, *Red Dawn* was nevertheless a box office hit. "The ferocity of the American people," director John Milius smugly observed, "has always been underestimated."[2] But action rather than politics probably accounts for the popularity of his film. *Red Dawn* was anti-Communist, but only because Communists were convenient enemies; the bad guys had no perceivable political ideology and could just as easily have been from outer space. The inclusion of Latinos among the invaders distinguished *Red Dawn* from the anti-Communist movies of the 1950s, but otherwise it was no more politically sophisticated. Ultimately, it was more individualistic than anti-Communist.

Although it is hard to take the politics of *Red Dawn* seriously, the movie set precedents that other films would soon follow. It revived Communists as convenient enemies, and it proved the marketability of posturing patriots as heroes. Few movies had fallen back on these old stereotypes since the 1950s. After the Cuban missile crisis in 1962, America and the Soviet Union had moved toward détente, and so did the movies. Superpatriot heroes and Communist villains were out of style during the cynical 1960s and 1970s, but in the 1980s, Ronald Reagan made patriotism and anti-Communism okay again, and *Red Dawn* proved they were good box office.

Once unleashed, Reaganite cinema became even cruder. *First Blood* and *Red Dawn* seem sophisticated compared to what followed. *Missing in Action* (1984) and *Invasion U.S.A.* (1985) were raw action flicks starring Chuck Norris, a wooden actor but a supple stuntman. In *Missing in Action,* Norris plays an escaped prisoner of war who returns to Vietnam with an American senator who is investigating allegations about American soldiers missing in action (MIAs). Discredited by the evil Vietnamese and disowned by the

174

American politician, the hero wreaks havoc on various enemy encampments, prisons, and convoys, saves the MIAs, and brings them back to Ho Chi Minh City to repudiate the Vietnamese liars. Not surprisingly, critics did not take *Missing in Action* seriously. Like other Chuck Norris movies, however, it did well at the box office despite its lack of tension, credibility, and excitement.

In Norris's other hit, *Invasion U.S.A.,* he plays an ex-CIA agent who comes out of retirement to stop a Russian "invasion" of Florida. Diabolical Communists in various disguises slaughter Cuban refugees, ghetto dwellers, Christmas shoppers, and families in suburban homes, stirring up distrust and unrest and turning people against one another. "America has not been invaded by a foreign enemy in nearly two hundred years," the Communist villain sneers. "Look at them . . . soft, spineless, decadent. They don't even understand the nature of their own freedom or how we will use it against them. They are their own worst enemies." The movie confirms this analysis when cowardly FBI agents phone in sick and spoiled citizens whine about rationing. The "tide of terror" turns into a "threat to democracy," with demands for martial law and the suspension of the Constitution, but happily, the hero stops the invaders single-handedly. Thanks in part to a larger budget, *Invasion U.S.A.* was better than *Missing in Action,* although neither of Norris's popular movies really had much to say about politics. International tensions were merely an excuse for violent action, feeding Reaganite anti-Communism.

Rambo's return was almost as crude, but *Rambo: First Blood Part II* (1985), written by Sylvester Stallone, was even more popular than the Reaganite movies that preceded it. John Rambo (Stallone again) wins a pardon for his earlier rampage in the woods when he accepts an assignment to find American MIAs in Vietnam. "Do we get to win this time?" Rambo asks his former Green Beret commander (Richard Crenna). He is only supposed to photograph the MIAs for evidence, but he tries to bring one back. The helicopter sent to pick him up abandons them, and the Vietnamese and their Russian advisers capture and torture Rambo. He escapes, slaughters the enemy, frees the MIAs, and leads—or drags—them to safety. He trashes the headquarters of the U.S. mission when he gets back and warns its bureaucratic chief to find the rest of the MIAs or risk the wrath of Rambo. This movie places the blame for the continued captivity of the MIAs squarely on the U.S. government, which first declined to win the war and then refused to pay war reparations to Vietnam in exchange for the MIAs.

In a promotional video for *Rambo,* Stallone, unlike most filmmakers, was forthright in declaring his movie political. "I hope to establish a character that can represent a certain section of the American consciousness," he said, "and through the entertainment [I also hope to] be educational. . . . More than being just a fighting man, [Rambo] represents the entire fighting force."

Stallone also claimed that his movie was part of the "pre-stages of a true historical event" in which the existence of the MIAs would be verified. "It's no big secret," he declared. "Vietnam wants reparations from us. We don't want to pay all those billions," possibly because "our officials are being paid off." Movies like *Rambo* were popular, Stallone asserted, "because the people are on to something. There's a thirst for verification."[3]

Despite derisive reviews and Stallone's pretensions, *Rambo* was a big hit even though the action was perfunctory. David Morell, author of the novel on which *First Blood* was based, dismissed *Rambo* as "a cartoon. On military bases," Morell said, "they show it as a comedy."[4] Others took it more seriously, though few critics liked it. David Halberstam labeled Stallone "a cinematic Joseph McCarthy" for his assertions about the existence of the MIAs and for conveying the "exact reverse of the real message of the Vietnam War."[5] President Ronald Reagan, on the other hand, admired Stallone's message. "After seeing *Rambo* last night," he joked during a terrorist crisis, "I know what to do next time this happens." He failed to comment on *Rambo*'s contention of U.S. government complacency in freeing the MIAs, however. Stallone concluded his *Rambo* films with *Rambo III* in 1988, in which our hero invades Afghanistan. By this time, however, audiences were losing interest.

Anti-Communism also was a theme of *Rocky IV* and *White Nights* (both 1985). Stallone wrapped himself in the flag for his fourth Rocky film, in which the boxing hero comes out of retirement to defeat a Soviet fighter produced by biochemical engineering rather than old-fashioned hard work. The fight takes place in Moscow, where a hostile crowd of Communists ends up cheering Rocky as he calls for international understanding in a concluding speech that attempts to mitigate the anti-Communism of the rest of the film. It was the only one of the new cold war films to fail at the box office. *White Nights* was more successful thanks to the presence of Mikhail Baryshnikov and the direction of Taylor Hackford. An airliner makes an emergency landing in Soviet territory, and a Russian ballet dancer (Baryshnikov) who has defected to the United States is taken captive. He escapes with a black American tap dancer (Gregory Hines) who has defected to the Soviets. Director Hackford played down his movie's politics, claiming it was "only realistic about artistic freedom," but Baryshnikov was more accurate when he said, "this film is politically right wing and patriotic."[6]

Iron Eagle, Heartbreak Ridge, and *Top Gun* (all 1986) soon added to what the Soviet press labeled "war-nography." In *Iron Eagle,* an American teenager flies to the rescue of his father, whose plane has been shot down over North Africa. The movie praises President Reagan as "this guy who don't take no shit from no gimpy country," but Reagan's government fails to save the captive pilot, forcing the teenager to do the job himself. *Heartbreak Ridge* featured a tough career soldier (Clint Eastwood) making men of his trainees, who are ultimately tested in the triumphant invasion of Grenada, a tiny island in the Caribbean.

Top Gun topped them both, though, at least at the box office, becoming the biggest ticket seller of 1986. Maverick (Tom Cruise), the young pilot who must become "top gun," is obsessed by the memory of his father, who was shot down under mysterious circumstances over Southeast Asia. It turns out that Dad was a hero, but details of his death have been kept secret for political reasons. Maverick ultimately proves himself in a skirmish with an unnamed enemy whose pilots fly Russian-made MIGs. *Top Gun* takes such confrontations for granted, beginning with U.S. and enemy jets playing tag and ending in real combat. Lest the audience worry that this incident might trigger World War III, we are told "the other side denied the incident." The implication that this sort of thing is a daily occurrence may have worried some viewers—all the more so because the U.S. Navy wholeheartedly endorsed and cooperated in the making of this picture. *Top Gun* is a throwback to old-fashioned war movies, no longer calling for calm vigilance, as did *Strategic Air Command* in 1955, but advocating confrontational machismo instead. Slick and shallow, it was the essence of Reaganite cinema.

This same strutting self-confidence ran through all the patriotic movies of the Reagan years, but as in other Hollywood eras, this was not the only vision. Although these films seem to exemplify the decade, they were in the minority. Hollywood also produced films about working people and mainstream politics. In fact, films with a conservative perspective were a minority.

Workers, Farmers, Fishermen—and Stockbrokers

In contrast to these patriotic films, another group of movies of the 1980s addressed the economic and political situation of working people, from coal miners and nuclear power workers to farmers, fishermen—and stockbrokers.

Silkwood (1983), directed by Mike Nichols and written by Nora Ephron and Alice Arlen, was about women, workers, and unions, corporate capitalism, and the dangers of nuclear power. *Silkwood* was stronger than *The China Syndrome* or *Norma Rae* on these issues, but it was also edgier. Karen Silkwood (Meryl Streep) is a blue-collar worker and single parent like Norma Rae, but her awakening is slower and far less ecstatic. Karen and her coworkers at a nuclear processing plant are ignorant and confused about their personal lives as well as the dangers they are exposed to at work. Even when they become concerned about their safety in the plant, they value their jobs too much to make their concerns public—except for Karen. She becomes an activist on their safety issues, complaining to coworkers, the company, and outsiders. Unlike the inspired, self-sacrificing Norma Rae, however, Karen is a cranky sort of activist. Silkwood never makes it clear whether her commitment is genuine or she just enjoys challenging authority and stirring things up. Her union encourages her activism, but the local union officials are as clueless as she is about how to proceed, and the national union organizers are so culturally and geographically distant that we cannot tell whether they really care about her or are just using her as a tool to organize other workers. Karen agitates about the safety issue until it is discovered that she and her house are contaminated with radioactive material, apparently planted by the company to suggest that she has manufactured the crisis. Then, while on her way to give evidence of falsified safety records to the New York Times, she is killed in an auto wreck. Here the movie hedges: ominous headlights behind her suggest murder, but a postscript to the film notes that there was evidence of drugs in her blood, implying that she might have died accidentally.

Silkwood was nominated for four Academy Awards, but did less well at the box office than Norma Rae and The China Syndrome. Historical accuracy became a key issue in otherwise mostly good reviews, with the New York Times criticizing the movie in an editorial and the Village Voice persuasively denouncing the film as a slur on Karen Silkwood.[7] The filmmakers invited such criticism by using a true story about a woman who had become a folk hero of the left, although as the Voice pointed out, they also had the advantage of five years of free publicity, including stories of the massive damage suit against Silkwood's employers.

Silkwood also made itself vulnerable to criticism by its refusal to take sides. It was ambiguous about Karen's character and motivations, the good faith of the union, the culpability of the company, and even her death. The movie kept its focus on working-class characters who did not blossom like Norma Rae but remained minimally articulate and self-aware and therefore less sympathetic than the white-collar professionals of The China Syndrome. Silkwood bravely let the audience decide about the characters, allowing Karen Silkwood to be more human than the usual heroine. For some, particularly the partisans of the real-life Silkwood, that made for an unsatisfying film with no point of view. Without knowing whether Karen's death was murder or a drug-induced accident, audiences could not be angry with the culprits or sad at the tragedy.

In 1984, the focus shifted from blue-collar laborers to rural workers in what came to be known as "the farm trilogy." Places in the Heart, The River, and Country all featured beleaguered small farmers fighting the elements and the banks, and they all featured strong women. Places in the Heart starred Sally Field as another plucky heroine who overcomes adversity, this time with the help of a child, a blind lodger, and an itinerant black. Places in the

Heart was less political than the other two farm movies, however, because it was safely set in the past and because it was mainly about brave human beings triumphing over adversity by determination and hard work. The most popular of the farm movies, it won Oscars for Sally Field and scriptwriter Robert Benton.

The River was also about a determined individual, but although Tom Garvey (Mel Gibson) is determined, he is unable to save his farm by himself. His wife Mae (Sissy Spacek) is the real backbone of the family, working the farm on her own when Tom goes to the city to scab in a steel mill, a moving sequence that manages to communicate both why scabbing is bad and why people do it. But determination and hard work are not enough to save the farm. A greedy agribusinessman pressures the state to build a dam to irrigate his massive holdings and hires down-and-out farmers to break up the levee Tom has built to protect his land, but in the end the farmers turn on the agribusinessman and help the small farmer in a scene reminiscent of the ditch sequence in *Our Daily Bread*. The loser is unperturbed, however. "We'll win in the end," he says, "because we can outlast you." Nominated for four Academy Awards, *The River* was a modest success despite criticism of its sentimentality.

Country was the least sentimental of the farm movies; its small farmers are even more reserved and inarticulate than Karen Silkwood and her friends. Director Richard Pearce distanced them from us with few close-ups and little sentimentality. Just as we suspect that Karen Silkwood might be a trouble-maker rather than a true believer, here we wonder if the farmers' difficulties are their own fault. Again, a strong woman (Jessica Lange) holds her farm family together as her husband (Sam Shepard) crumbles when their government loan is called in. They win at least a stay of execution, however, when she organizes the neighboring farmers to resist the government. As in *The River,* collective action saves the day, although we are not sure for how long. Like Field and Spacek, Jessica Lange was nominated for an Academy Award for her performance, but *Country*'s unsentimental restraint appealed less to audiences than did the other farm movies.

Although far from radical, all three of these movies were critical of American farm policy. Inspired by foreclosures on small farms that were much in the news in the early 1980s, these movies may have taken on the subject after it was too late to affect the policy, just as the movies about Vietnam had come too late to affect the war. Of the three films, only *Country* seemed to address government policy directly, but its makers were nervous enough about its politics in the year of Reagan's reelection that they refused benefit showings for political causes to avoid "politicizing the film" and insisted that its "villain [was] not the Reagan administration," but monolithic bureaucracy and "government apathy."[8]

A little later in the decade, small farmers battled big developers in another part of the country in *The Milagro Beanfield War* (1988), directed by Robert Redford, one of America's most political filmmakers. His entertaining film, which mixed Capra and magical realism, may have been a little too whimsical for most audiences, but it was one of the first to feature a southwestern United States setting and a range of positive Latino characters as well as a different sort of political battle.

Fishermen rather than farmers fight government in *Alamo Bay* (1985), directed by Louis Malle and written by Alice Arlen, coauthor of *Silkwood*. "We defend everybody all over the world, but there ain't no protection for any American, and that ain't right," declares one fisherman, Pierce (Ed Harris), when hardworking Vietnamese immigrants drive him and other white shrimp fishermen out of business in the recession-struck Gulf of Mexico. Another (Amy Madigan) tries to save her small business by trading with the Vietnamese, but the Ku Klux Klan takes advantage of the white fishermen's frustration to foment violence. Thanks to the resolve of Malle and Arlen, we sympathize with the immigrants but also understand the frustration of the white fishermen.

John Sayles, perhaps America's preeminent independent filmmaker, took audiences to the coal mines of West Virginia in the 1920s in *Matewan* (1987). Chris Cooper plays a union organizer encouraging white and black miners to join together to fight the repressive coal companies and their strikebreaking thugs. Beautifully filmed by Haskell Wexler, *Matewan* is a powerful and moving evocation of the plight of the miners and the divisive, brutal tactics of the mine owners, although its sympathy for the miners is so complete that at times it seems simplistic and one-sided.

Alamo Bay and *Matewan* are perceptive studies of the situation confronted by the people at the bottom of America's economic heap. Like the equally reserved *Silkwood* and *Country*, they resolutely reject easy solutions. Together, these films constitute an indictment of American capitalism—a message audiences may not have wanted to hear in the age of Reagan. *Norma Rae, The China Syndrome,* and *The River* shared the liberalism of these movies, although these films, along with *Places in the Heart,* were far more affirmative about the possibility of taking action. All of these movies focused on workers, whether on farms and shrimp boats or in mines, mills, and power plants, at a time when yuppies were capturing the nation's attention. These films also featured strong women, making them feminist in varying degrees, even as the equal rights amendment failed to win ratification.

The appearance of these movies in such times was largely due to the new independence of filmmakers. Only *The River* was produced by one of the old studios (Columbia), although big studios were involved to some degree in most of the others. But the reception of these films suggested that the country was not as deeply conservative as its enthusiasm for Ronald Reagan seemed to indicate. Most of these movies were favorably reviewed, and all but *Alamo Bay* were honored with Academy Awards or nominations. Some were box office hits as well.

But the biggest hit in this minigenre of films about capitalism was *Wall Street* (1987). Like the other movies, *Wall Street* was critical of capitalism—more powerfully and explicitly than the others—but its primary capitalist character was such a potent creation that he is probably better remembered than the movie's overall anticapitalist message. Directed by Oliver Stone, *Wall Street* features Michael Douglas in the Oscar-winning role of Gordon Gekko, a ruthless Wall Street broker. The sleek Gekko revels in his work, wheeling and dealing, buying and selling, insider trading and corporate raiding, because "it's all about bucks." In the most famous scene in the movie, Gekko declares "Greed is good!" as he lectures enraptured shareholders. Charlie Sheen plays Bud, Gekko's protégé, and it is through his eyes that we see the battle between good, represented by Bud's working-class father (Martin Sheen), and evil, represented by the greedy Gekko. But as Roger Ebert observed: "The movie's real target isn't Wall Street criminals who break the law. Stone's target is the value system that places profits and wealth and the Deal above any other consideration. His film is an attack on an atmosphere of financial competitiveness so ferocious that ethics are simply irrelevant."[9]

Electoral Politics, Courts, and Bureaucracy

As political—or politicized—as the films of the 1980s were, few focused on electoral politics or government like the films of Robert Redford in the 1970s or Frank Capra in the 1940s, and none found the audiences of those films.

The courts and the legal system, on the other hand, received more cinematic scrutiny in this decade than in most others, perhaps because they were safer subjects or just because crime always pays at the movies. Robert Redford played a reforming prison warden in *Brubaker* (1980), but the movie's central political theme had to do with compromise. Urged to make concessions to the conservative powers-that-be, Brubaker refuses and ultimately loses. Since Robert Redford plays Brubaker, we take his side and accept the movie's condemnation of compromises. Sidney Lumet examined pervasive police corruption in *Prince of the City* (1981), featuring informers as heroes. *The Verdict* (1982) reiterated Lumet's faith in the jury system as a desperate attorney (Paul Newman) defeats corrupt judges, lawyers, doctors, and hospital administrators.

The U.S. Supreme Court took center stage in Ronald Neame's considerably lighter *First Monday in October* (1981), which also raised the issue of compromise. Here Jill Clayburgh plays the first woman member of the Court, a conservative antipornography campaigner from California's Orange County. Walter Matthau is her liberal antagonist, a justice committed to free speech even if it is smutty. The workings of the Court are instructively presented, and the antagonists debate the meaning of the First Amendment credibly if simplistically. A crisis arises when the integrity of the conservative justice is impugned by the revelation that her late husband helped cover up the secrets of an ominous corporation. She prepares to resign, but her liberal colleague talks her out of it, despite their ideological disagreements.

First Monday is reminiscent of a Tracy–Hepburn movie, but it barely touches on romance. The ideological rivalry of the Clayburgh and Matthau characters develops instead into a solid working relationship, as the movie lauds rational debate among honorable people. *First Monday* reiterates the big-bad-business theme, but its main message is that decent people can have differing views and that these views need not be based on self-interest or corruption. Above all, the movie respects Court politics and tells us that the system works. Given the public antagonism to liberal judges dating back to the civil and criminal rights decisions of the 1950s and 1960s, the movie seemed a virtual defense of the courts. *First Monday in October* was innocuous, but unlike many American political films, it respected politics and the people who participate in it. The critics were unenthusiastic, but the movie had respectable box office results thanks to its optimism, its cast, and its good timing: *First Monday* was released just as President Reagan appointed Sandra Day O'Connor, an Arizona conservative, as the first woman justice of the U.S. Supreme Court.

Less optimistic but more in keeping with popular prejudice was Peter Hyams's *The Star Chamber* (1983), with Michael Douglas as a young, liberal judge frustrated by the legal loopholes used by attorneys to get their guilty clients off. Another judge (Hal Holbrook) introduces him to the Star Chamber, a group of renegade judges who take the law into their own hands by hiring hit men to murder criminals who have avoided punishment through legal niceties. After unleashing the Star Chamber on an innocent man, the young liberal has second thoughts, however, and betrays the vigilante judges. Torn between action sequences to hold audience interest and its political themes, the message of *The Star Chamber* is ambivalent at best. First it says that protecting defendants subverts justice, giving approval to the Star Chamber's punishment of wrongdoers, all of whom happen to be members of minority groups or of the lower class and who also happen to be so repulsive that they seem to deserve what they get. Perhaps to minimize offense, the filmmakers include a woman and a black in the avenging Star

Chamber. In the end, however, this judicial elite gets its comeuppance, too. Only the young judge and the black cop who break up the Star Chamber come off well. All things considered, this is a law-and-order movie, covering its exploitation of social prejudice and lust for vengeance with a liberal gloss, condemning and then upholding the system, but never resolving the question of whether the law gives too much or too little protection to those accused of crime.

Another film of the 1980s touched on politics more obliquely itself, but was expected to make a big splash in real-life politics. *The Right Stuff* (1983), adapted from Tom Wolfe's best seller and directed by Philip Kaufman, was about America's first astronauts, one of whom, John Glenn, was a senator and a serious contender for the Democratic presidential nomination in 1984.

The Right Stuff contrasts the men who became astronauts with test pilot Chuck Yeager (Sam Shepard), who did not, making it clear that he is too much of an individual to jump through hoops and conform, as the others willingly do. In the movie, John Glenn (Ed Harris) and the other astronauts attain success by compromise and conformity, but we know they have kept their integrity. They have the right stuff, especially in contrast with the crude reporters, foolish politicians, and offensive hangers-on with whom the movie surrounds its heroes.

President Reagan and Glenn's Democratic opponents feared that *The Right Stuff* would provide the astronaut's candidacy with a powerful send-off, but both the movie and the campaign flopped. Although Glenn ultimately comes off well in *The Right Stuff,* the movie was not enough to save his presidential campaign. Some film industry people thought association with the politician jinxed the film, because "no one would pay to see a movie they thought was a political polemic."[10] Unenthusiastic reviews and the movie's reluctance to play the astronauts as either buffoons or heroes did not help either, and the movie failed financially.

Another group of films of the 1980s addressed concerns about technology and nuclear war. John Badham's *WarGames* (1983) and *Short Circuit* (1986) and Marshall Brickman's *The Manhattan Project* (1986) played to youthful audiences by featuring teenage heroes, but unlike the confrontational, patriotic *Top Gun* and *Iron Eagle,* these films expressed liberal concern about nuclear apocalypse. The threat in all three films comes from uncontrollable technology, and, in all three, teenage nerds—considerably more credible heroes than the beefcakes of the other movies—avert disaster. These films also raised the issue of accidental nuclear war, a subject that had been ignored since the 1960s, although they did so mainly as a premise for action and entertainment. Critics were unimpressed, but *WarGames,* at least, was a box office hit.

Protocol (1984), directed by Herbert Ross and written by Buck Henry, was also a popular success. Almost a "Ms. Smith Goes to Washington," it centers on Sunny Ann Davis (Goldie Hawn), a Washington cocktail waitress who accidentally foils an assassin. The Arab potentate she saves takes a fancy to her, and the State Department cynically offers her as a pawn in negotiations for a military base. Sunny, who has never voted, becomes a protocol officer and does a fast study of American government, which is presented in a montage of Washington reminiscent of Mr. Smith's arrival or our introduction to Joe Tynan. But when Sunny travels to the Middle East, her visit precipitates a coup d'état and a scandal. Testifying before a congressional committee investigating "Sunnygate," the heroine refuses to blame the bureaucrats who set her up. "I'm responsible," she declares. When Congress acts, "it has a direct effect on we the people's lives, so if we don't—I mean if I don't—know what you're up to, and if I don't holler and scream when I think you're doing it wrong, and if I just mind my own business and don't vote or care, then I just get what I deserve, so now that I'm Sunny Davis, a private citizen, again, you're going to have to watch out for me, 'cause I'm gonna be watching all you . . . like a hawk." Sunny gets the guy and is elected to Congress, too. The critics derided *Protocol,* but audiences liked the comedy, and they also may have liked the movie's trite, but positive, message of individual responsibility. As familiar from old movies as the president himself, the message fits almost as well with Reaganite philosophy as did *Rambo* or *Top Gun.* It was even antigovernment in the same way Reagan was, mistrusting bureaucrats and Congress in particular.

Another movie of the era focused more explicitly and seriously on politics, but was less successful than *Protocol.* In Sidney Lumet's *Power* (1986), Richard Gere is a political media wizard who tells clients, "My job is to get you in. Then you do whatever your conscience tells you to do." Using opinion polls and clever TV ads, he cynically packages candidates to fit what the public wants. He is finally disillusioned, however, when he discovers he is being used by Arab oil sheiks seeking to block solar energy legislation. Confronting an idealistic young candidate being managed by a rival media man, the campaign consultant denounces his own profession and tells the budding politician to say what he really believes. He does, and he gets more votes than expected, although he still does not win. The film ends with "The Stars and Stripes Forever" playing as the camera pans over video equipment and computers—the new tools of politics.

Like Lumet's *Network, Power* was over-the-top, but while *Network* succeeded as black comedy, *Power* was just melodrama. The villains of *Power* are neither funny nor credible, and the good guys are incredibly naive. Director Lumet and writer David Himmelstein ignore the fact that politicians have always manipulated voters, blaming the sad state of the nation almost entirely on new technology and gullibility of the public. All politicians in the film are willing dupes, except for one female governor (Michael Learned). *Power*'s insights into the techniques used by media consultants were instructive, but the movie grossly exaggerated their influence. Critics panned it and audiences ignored it, despite the popular successes of Lumet's other films.

Old and New Left Nostalgia in the Age of Reagan

While patriotic films from *Rambo* to *Top Gun* seemed to catch the conservative spirit of the 1980s, the decade also produced a surprising number of films with liberal themes and characters, heroes, and stories of the political left.

Most prominent of these was Warren Beatty's *Reds* (1981). Long one of Hollywood's most politically active stars, Beatty used his box office clout and success as a producer to make one of America's most important political films. He was the film's star, director, producer, and coauthor. The subject of *Reds* is John Reed, the left-wing journalist whose books about his experiences in the Mexican and Russian revolutions were classics and who was the only American ever to be honored by burial in the Kremlin Wall. Beatty had been interested in Reed since a visit to Russia in the 1960s, when aging revolutionaries told him he looked like the writer.

We meet Reed as he offends a social gathering in Portland, Oregon, with his left-wing views and meets Louise Bryant (Diane Keaton), a local woman who feels stifled by provincial society. She wants to write and shows Reed her work. He invites her to return to New York with him. "What as?" she asks, fearing she will still be trapped in a subordinate role when independence is what she most desires. She goes with him, however, and joins an exciting society of left-wing artists and intellectuals in Greenwich Village.

Reed is driven by his political commitment, constantly dashing off somewhere to write about and sometimes participate in political events. Bryant complains, impatiently condemning his need for "another shot of limelight." When she has an affair, they get married and settle down in a cozy cottage with a puppy. But he is still peripatetic, and she is still discontented. Finally, she leaves him to go to France, where she writes unsuccessfully about World War I. Reed follows and persuades her to join him in Russia, where the revolution is under way. Caught up in the spirit of events, they share the excitement of the revolution, of which they eventually become a part. *Reds* evokes the chaos of that conflict as well as the intoxicating meetings of workers, so we are with Reed when he rises to speak at a turbulent rally. "We'll join you in revolution!" he proclaims on behalf of American workers. At the end of his speech, the crowd separates Reed and Bryant. They struggle toward each other, and at the film's midpoint they make love while outside a marching crowd sings the rousing "Internationale." Political, professional, and personal commitments come together in one glorious—or ludicrous—moment.

Reed and Bryant return to America. She lectures; he writes his classic *Ten Days That Shook the World*. Reed joins one of the contending Communist factions and prepares to return to Russia to have it recognized as the official party in America. "You're not a politician," Louise protests. "You're a writer. . . . You're an artist." He goes anyway, and the party orders him to stay and work on propaganda. He finds that his old friend Emma Goldman (Maureen Stapleton) has grown disillusioned with the revolution. "The dream is dying," she sighs. "The centralized state has all the power. They're putting anarchists like me in jail, exterminating all dissenters." "What did you think, anyway?" Reed responds. "It was going to work right away?" The party sends him on a tour to speak on behalf of American workers in support of the revolution. When a party official edits his speech, he is offended. "You don't rewrite what I write," he insists, repeating one of his catch phrases and reminding us he is an artist.

Reed seems to be growing disillusioned, but before further political developments occur, we return to Louise, now determined to join him. Getting into revolutionary Russia is difficult, however, and she makes a Zhivago-like journey through the snowy wastes of Finland. The lovers rush toward each other through yet another crowd and are tearfully reunited. Reed promptly falls ill. He promises Louise they will go on together and again she asks, "What as?" "Comrades," he says, and dies.

Beatty's emphasis on the personal life of his protagonists was a concession to Hollywood tradition that made his lavish epic more romantic than political. John and Louise could almost be Rhett and Scarlett. Unlike *Gone with the Wind*, however, *Reds* is true except for a few incidents. Reed and Bryant were real American radicals, members of a group whose history, unlike that of the landed aristocracy of the antebellum South, had been ignored by Hollywood. *Reds* also was distinguished by Beatty's innovative use of "witnesses"—real people, some of them famous, whose reminiscences about Reed are interspersed throughout the film, giving Beatty's epic resonance and credibility and making it more than a romance. Their disagreements and confusion warn that memory, and therefore history, are fallible. "I'd forgotten all about them," one witness says of Reed and Bryant. "Were they socialists?" The witnesses validate some parts of *Reds* and challenge others, but even their disagreements strengthen the movie by reminding us that the film itself is just one interpretation of history.

Beatty claimed his film was "reclaiming history" by telling a story about the left when it was still a viable force in American politics or, as he put it, at the last historical moment before America's ideology "hardened."[11] One critic dismissed his efforts as "nostalgia of the left,"[12] but nostalgia or not, *Reds* dealt with a history that had been lost for most Americans. The antiwar movement of World War I, the American Socialist and Communist parties and their factions, the Wobblies, Eugene Debs, Emma Goldman, and Big Bill Haywood are a part of our past, and we should know about them, whether or not we share their values.

Reds was far from purely left-wing in its point of view, however. The movie had it both ways, leaning Red in its choice of heroes and heroines and its initial romantic view of the Russian Revolution, but anti-Red in its ultimate portrait of Soviet totalitarianism. The film withheld final judgment by implying rather than explicitly stating Reed's disillusionment. On another level, *Reds* had it both ways by emphasizing the individualism of people who advocated collective politics, not only by focusing on their personal lives but by insisting on artistic integrity ("You don't rewrite what I write.").

Reds never made the political values of its characters clear, nor did it define the class conflict on which real-life politics in both the United States and Russia then centered. It was a more personal than political film, although it was at its most trite when it dwelled on the purely personal with its quaint cottage, cute puppy, and clumsy man in the kitchen. This was presumably a commercial choice made by Beatty; screenwriter Trevor Griffiths's original script was more political than romantic. But at least *Reds* respected politics as an important part of its characters' lives, and unlike most American films, it also showed the importance of work in people's lives. Indeed, the greatest strength of *Reds* may be its presentation of the way personal lives blend with work, careers, and politics. And *Reds* was more complex and willing to question than most movies about politics. The witnesses and the positive picture of the Russian Revolution and America's radical past also were worthwhile contributions.

The reviews of *Reds* were generally good, although many pointed out that Beatty's politics were more cautious than radical. The *New York Times* called it old-fashioned American optimism, about "as ideological as the puppy."[13] Andrew Sarris was more enthusiastic, praising *Reds* as an "open-minded historical inquiry" with the "clang of paradox and contradiction."[14] With twelve Academy Award nominations, *Reds* looked set to dominate the 1981 Oscars, but it won awards only for Best Director, Cinematography, and Supporting Actress (Stapleton). On accepting his own award, Beatty thanked Paramount and Gulf and Western, which then owned Paramount, as capitalists willing "to finance a three-and-a-half-hour romance which attempts to reveal for the first time just something of the beginnings of American socialism and American communism" and gave credit to the "freedom of expression that we have in American society and the lack of censorship we have from the government or the people who put up the money."[15] But despite three Oscars and good reviews, Beatty's very expensive picture was a financial failure. Audiences did not like the witness technique as much as critics did, and many found the film long, boring, and even silly.

Despite the financial disappointment of *Reds,* American filmmakers continued to make political movies, but not on such a grand scale—and even less ambitious political movies had difficulty finding investors. Sidney Lumet's *Daniel* (1983), a thorny examination of left-wing history, was produced by the artists themselves with no studio assistance at all. Lumet had been directing political movies since making *Twelve Angry Men* in 1957. He dealt with informers in *A View from the Bridge* (1961), nuclear war in *Fail Safe* (1964), feminism in *The Group* (1966), police corruption in *Serpico* (1973) and *Prince of the City* (1981), homosexuality in *Dog Day Afternoon* (1975), and corporate control of television in *Network* (1976). All these movies treated controversial issues in complex and interesting ways, rarely oversimplifying, resorting to clichés, or making their messages unnecessarily obvious. Lumet shunned the "political" label, however. Even *Daniel,* he claimed, was simply "about parents and children and the damage people do without meaning to."[16]

Daniel (Timothy Hutton) is the son of the Isaacsons, Jewish Communists who, like the real-life Rosenbergs, are executed as Soviet agents. The story of their death is told from their son's point of view, connecting the two generations and showing how one affects the other. Daniel is disillusioned, alienated, and apolitical, cruel to his young wife, harsh to his adoptive family, and impatient with his neurotic sister. While he retreats deeper and deeper into himself, his sister tries drugs and then political activism. He hates the memory of their parents while she venerates it, but in the end she goes insane and commits suicide whereas Daniel finally makes peace with himself and his memories and takes a step toward political commitment by joining an antiwar demonstration.

Like *Reds, Daniel* restores a part of the history of the left by showing its rallies and concerts as well as its paranoia and persecution. The Isaacsons's guilt or innocence is never clear in the film, although their apparent poverty and innocent activism make them seem unlikely spies. Whether innocent or merely complicit, however, their children were damaged, and Lumet claimed that this was the subject of his movie. His point was that the parents' commitment beyond the family destroyed the children. This gloomy view of family psychology contradicted the affirmative ending of his movie, however. Daniel's wife and child are with him as he joins the antiwar demonstration. Commitment had separated Daniel from his parents, yet for him it is salvation, perhaps because he embraces it with his family.

Like Lumet's other films, *Daniel* was dark and depressing, with complex characters, few of whom were likable. That did not keep audiences away from Lumet's earlier movies, but *Daniel* was more political, despite the director's denials. Critics picked at its family neuroses and exploitation of the Rosenbergs. Some thought the family melodrama muddled its politics. "Political movies are damned if they do, and damned if they don't," observed Andrew Sarris.[17] If they make their political point clear, people may dislike the message or its obviousness, but if the point is not clear, people find the film muddled and confusing.

Lumet followed *Daniel* with *Running on Empty* in 1988. Judd Hirsh and Christine Lahti portray radicals who, in the 1960s, blew up a lab that made napalm, unintentionally killing a janitor. They have been on the run from the FBI ever since, repeatedly uprooting their children out of sheer paranoia or when the FBI closes in. The film's crisis occurs when their son (River Phoenix) approaches high-school graduation and must choose between joining his family in their next move or going on with his life and a career as a musician. But although past political actions set up the situation, *Running on Empty* is not really about politics. Even more than *Daniel,* it is about families and the repercussions of past acts. The message of both films could be read as a warning against radical action, despite Lumet's liberal reputation. Despite its fine cast and good acting, reviews of *Running on Empty* were mixed (some critics loved the movie whereas others found it melodramatic and simplistic), and audiences ignored it. Although nostalgia was a theme of the Reagan years, *Reds, Daniel,* and *Running on Empty* suggest that audiences were not nostalgic about America's left-wing history—even though all three movies emphasized powerful personal stories as well as political themes.

Another little group of movies dealt with the activists of the 1960s and 1970s more gently, though not much more successfully as far as critics and audiences were concerned. Milos Forman's *Hair,* a counterculture musical about the 1960s, was belatedly filmed in 1979, and several filmmakers took up the stories of 1960s activists and idealists as they matured. The fates of three Harvard students of the 1960s are assessed in *A Small Circle of Friends* (1980), but this movie attributes the past activism of the trio to personal relations rather than to politics, thus trivializing the political involvement of a whole generation.

The Return of the Secaucus Seven (1980) focused on the reunion of a group of 1960s activists who were once arrested in Secaucus, New Jersey, en route to an antiwar demonstration in Washington, D.C. Followers rather than leaders, the seven were marginal to the antiwar movement and yet were affected by it. Writer and director John Sayles made the limits of his characters' political involvement clear, but without belittling 1960s activism. *The*

Big Chill (1983), directed by Lawrence Kasdan, was a strikingly similar film—some said a rip-off—about a weekend reunion of 1960s pals, but it reached a much larger audience. The group reunites because of the suicide of its dominant member. These idealists of that decade have sold out, however, to become career-oriented professionals. Their friend's death symbolizes the death of the values of the 1960s. *1969* (1988), written and directed by Ernest Thompson, may have unintentionally contributed to the death of those values. Robert Downey Jr. and Kiefer Sutherland play 1960s college students caught up in the counterculture and antiwar movement. They return to their small hometown and clash melodramatically with their families. Critics derided *1969*'s phony sense of place and time as well as its shallow politics.

Hair, A Small Circle of Friends, The Return of the Secaucus Seven, The Big Chill, and *1969* all looked back nostalgically on the 1960s, but the popular and entertaining *Big Chill* most clearly defined the 1980s attitude toward that generation. These movies were about shattered dreams and aging, not politics. Their characters represented the attitudes of many of their generation, and their stories should be told, but among these films only *Secaucus Seven* managed to treat the politics of the 1960s with respect and accuracy. Other films derided, trivialized, and finally scorned the activism and social concern of the period.

Some of the movies that looked to previous political eras, however, showed respect for political commitment. *Reds* made commitment seem exciting and rewarding while admitting its costs. The psychological price of involvement was higher in *Daniel,* but in the end it was seen as a means of salvation. Even the films that look back to the 1960s mourn the loss of commitment. It seemed that in the 1980s, people missed commitment even though they were too fearful, cynical, or self-absorbed to believe in it anymore. They did not flock to these films, however. *Reds* was a critical success, but only *The Big Chill* was a box office hit. Perhaps its portrait of sold-out idealists made it more in tune with its times than the other movies.

America and the Third World

Except for films about wars, few American movies in the twentieth century dealt with international politics. After Vietnam, America grew cautious about its international role, grappling with the limits of power and struggling toward a foreign policy that emphasized détente, human rights, and a new respect for the third world. Under President Jimmy Carter, the nation turned almost isolationist. Because of Vietnam jitters, neoisolationism, and Carter's support of human rights and nonintervention, the United States stood by as two of its authoritarian allies, the shah of Iran and President Anastasio Somoza of Nicaragua, were overthrown. A guerrilla war started in El Salvador. Another war was under way in Angola, and unrest was increasing in South Africa. (Two films with international directors and writers, *Cry Freedom* [1987] and *A Dry White Season* [1989], dealt with that subject.) In 1980, the Soviet Union invaded Afghanistan, but the United States took no action. When Ronald Reagan became president, however, American foreign policy changed. Human rights were of little concern; interventionism was back. This change soon showed up in the movies, with most filmmakers firmly opposed to Reagan's foreign policy, especially as applied to Latin America. Their movies were among the most critical ever made about America and its foreign policy, yet some were popular and critical successes.

Hollywood, like the nation, ignored Latin America for a long time, venturing south of the border only occasionally for a big movie like *Juarez* or *Viva Zapata!* or for settings for costume epics and musicals. The movies also ignored Hispanic-Americans, except for occasional appearances as stereotypical bandits, whores, maids, or venal generals. Then the revolutions in Nicaragua and El Salvador and the growing assertiveness of America's huge Hispanic population pushed Latin America back into the national consciousness.

In the 1980s, more Hispanics showed up in the movies. *Zoot Suit* (1981) told the story of the Sleepy Lagoon murders and the anti-Mexican riots in Los Angeles during World War II. *The Border* (1981), coauthored by Deric Washburn (*The Deer Hunter*) and director Tony Richardson, shifted the focus to an Anglo immigration officer (Jack Nicholson) on the Mexican border. The exploitation and corruption of the border are seen through his tired, cynical eyes, but he at least tries to help a Mexican girl (Elpidia Carrillo).

By contrast, *El Norte* (1983) was a low-budget production filmed in Spanish and featuring unknown actors. Told from the point of view of two young Guatemalan immigrants to the United States, according to director and coauthor Gregory Nava, the film focused on their personal story because "an overtly political film . . . would have put off too many people. As it is, left, right, and center seem to like it and political people can easily make the connections."[18] *El Norte* left little doubt that the immigrants were refugees from an oppressive system or that they were exploited once they arrived in this country, but by understating their case, Nava and coauthor Anna Thomas made viewers sympathetic to the immigrants without giving offense. They rejected suggestions to cast stars like Robbie Benson and Brooke Shields in the leads and to make the protagonists lovers rather than brother and sister because such compromises, although they would have made it easier to raise money for the independent production, would have blurred the film's focus. The writers' judgment proved valid. *El Norte* won good reviews and was a small-scale hit.

Movies set in Latin America itself were more popular than border stories, however, especially when they featured big stars and plenty of action. *Missing* (1982) was the first of these and also Costa-Gavras's first American production in English. A Greek-born citizen of France and one of the world's finest and most political directors, Costa-Gavras first examined American involvement in Latin America in *State of Siege* (1973), the story of the kidnapping of a CIA agent (Yves Montand) by Uruguay's Tupamaro guerrillas, but *Missing* was a more accessible, traditional film that reached a much bigger audience.

In *Missing,* Charlie Horman (John Shea), a nice young American living in Chile with his wife Beth (Sissy Spacek), disappears in the aftermath of the coup that brought down the popularly elected Marxist government of Salvador Allende. When Beth and the American embassy cannot find him, Charlie's father Ed (Jack Lemmon), an all-American conservative, arrives, suspecting that his son got himself into trouble with his political dabbling. But he gradually comes to share Beth's belief that the American bureaucrats are duplicitous and that Charlie has disappeared not because of anything he did, but because he was with a tourist friend in the town that was the base for American involvement in the coup and he saw too much.

After visiting a stadium full of political prisoners and a morgue full of bodies, Ed confronts the American officials. They confirm that Charlie has been killed by the Chilean military. Ed is outraged. "I do not think that they would dare do a thing like that unless an American official co-signed the kill order," he says. "Why would we want him dead?" the ambassador asks. "Probably because he knew of our involvement in the coup," Ed answers, calling the ambassador's denial "a bald-faced lie." A CIA man effectively admits complicity in Charlie's death, telling Ed that his "kid . . . was a snoop" who deserved what he got. "If you hadn't been personally involved," the ambassador explains to Ed, "you'd have been sitting at home, complacent and more or less oblivious to all this. This mission is pledged to protect American interests. . . . There are over three thousand U.S. firms doing business down here. Those are American interests. In other words, your interests. I'm concerned with the preservation of a way of life."

Until this scene, Costa-Gavras exercised uncharacteristic restraint in making his political points. Charlie is clearly a harmless do-gooder caught up in the violence of Latin American politics. Ed is a skeptical father who gradually learns about the brutality of the coup and becomes aware of American complicity. As we follow Ed through the learning process, we come to share his rage. U.S. officials, the film tells us, have helped overthrow a foreign government, lied to their own citizens, and possibly approved of the death of an innocent American.

Missing was a box office hit and nominated for several Academy Awards, winning for best script. Mixed reviews praised the film's pacing and performances, but some thought its politics were too blatant whereas others objected to its conclusions. Like *Silkwood, Missing* was based on a true story, and also like that movie, it was attacked for distorting the record. The State Department denied the movie's allegations, whereas a left-leaning critic condemned Costa-Gavras for focusing on individuals, saying it was odd "to see a European filmmaker falling into . . . one of the ways Americans hide from the concrete realities of the rest of the world."[19]

Missing would have been strengthened by the presence of one or two strong Chilean characters to point out the devastating impact of the coup on them, but Costa-Gavras chose characters with whom Americans would identify. Focusing on Chileans would have diverted attention from his primary concern, American involvement. It also could have reduced the conflict to Chilean good guys and American bad guys, which would not have been as persuasive to American audiences as the all-American confrontation he chose instead. Through these characters and dramatic devices, Costa-Gavras conveyed the extent of American involvement in the coup. *Missing* did what a political movie should do: it entertained people and it made a point. The controversy over the film's interpretation of historical fact only confirmed its power.

Critics raised similar objections to *Under Fire* (1983), another film about U.S. involvement in Latin America seen through the eyes of Americans. Photographer Russell Price (Nick Nolte) joins his friends Alex (Gene Hackman) and Claire (Joanne Cassidy) in Nicaragua, where the Sandinista revolutionaries are about to overthrow Somoza, a right-wing dictator. Alex leaves for a job as a network anchorman; Russell and Claire become lovers and grow sympathetic to the revolution, which the film tells us is totally justifiable. When the rebels need to persuade the media and the people that their recently deceased leader is alive, they ask Russell to fake a photo of the leader. Considering it a violation of his journalistic integrity, he first resists, then gives in, sure that the revolution is a worthy cause. Then he discovers that some photos he shot at the rebel camp are being used by the CIA to identify rebel activists so they can be captured and killed. As Somoza's regime collapses, Alex returns to Nicaragua and demands that Russell arrange an interview with the (dead) rebel leader. Before the request can be dealt with, Somoza's national guard shoots Alex. Russell photographs the killing, and the film suggests that the anchorman's death outrages the American public, resulting in the withdrawal of U.S. support for Somoza and affecting the revolution, as the photographer had hoped his fake picture would.

Under Fire clearly sides with the rebels, but an antirevolutionary perspective is forcefully stated by a CIA agent (Jean-Louis Trintignant) and a mercenary (Ed Harris). All revolutions turn to dictatorships, they tell the idealistic journalists, so what difference does the revolution make? More insultingly, the mercenary says that the journalists are paid to do their jobs, just like him. "See you in Thailand," he says as the film ends.

Under Fire, like *Missing,* was about Americans, not Latinos. None of its central characters was Nicaraguan, just as none of *Missing*'s was Chilean. Another Hollywood element in *Under Fire* was the implication that the revolution was dependent on a single heroic leader. In fact, the Sandinistas won with collective leadership, but that is harder to film. *Under Fire* was more successful as a treatise on journalists under pressure, trying to come to terms with their own power and to use it for good rather than have it used by malefactors (like the CIA agent). Russell must make a moral choice between professional ethics and good politics (helping the revolutionaries). He chooses politics, but the film refused to make his choice so obvious as to obscure its difficulty or to stifle argument about it.

Under Fire was a success in Europe, but flopped in the United States. Some critics thought its subject was too much in the news at the moment. Others thought the movie failed because it was anti-American. "The film may be the only American movie in recent decades to side with a foreign government against which the United States has aligned itself," declared the *New York Times.* Roger Spottiswoode, the British director of *Under Fire,* insisted that the film was not anti-American, however. "It is a film against American policy in Central America. . . . In that sense it's got political content," but "it's an exciting story and it has lots of different levels other than the political one."[20] Supporters of American foreign policy nevertheless condemned *Under Fire*'s bias, whereas critics on the left denounced its portrait of a "one-dimensional Third World where the natives pull liberal heartstrings—until they get reckless."[21]

If being about a contemporary issue and opposing U.S. policy were the first two strikes against *Under Fire,* its treatment of journalists may have been the third. The press was highly critical of the film for justifying the fakery of the photograph. Labeling Russell's ruse "Rambo-think in reverse," Enrique Fernandez condemned the movie for saying "it's okay to lie for the left."[22] Vincent Canby called *Under Fire* "absolutely absurd" for oversimplifying the success of a revolution and for adding to public mistrust of the press.[23] Pauline Kael, however, said other journalists unconsciously do the same sort of thing Russell did.[24]

Kiss of the Spider Woman (1985), a joint U.S./Brazilian production, presented a Latin American perspective on revolutionary politics. Brazilian Hector Babenco directed this adaptation of Manuel Puig's novel in English with an

194

American cast. The story is set in a South American prison, where a homosexual, Luis Molina (William Hurt), befriends a revolutionary, Valentin Arregui, (Raul Julia). Molina is an apolitical romantic who survives prison by reenacting movies, including a fascist melodrama that appalls his cellmate. When Molina is freed, he carries out a political act on the instructions of his revolutionary friend. His motive is romantic, rather than political, and he is used by both the police and the revolutionaries, but he achieves fulfillment by his commitment. Meanwhile, Valentin, still in prison, has learned to dream in order to survive. The roles have been reversed. In a way, *Spider Woman* is cynical about politics, yet the love and pride of the self-sacrificing Molina make a superficially meaningless act heroic.

Spider Woman had nothing to say about U.S. involvement in Latin American politics, but other films did. In *Latino* (1985), directed by Haskell Wexler (*Medium Cool*), Green Beret Eddie Guerrero (Robert Beltran) is sent to train Nicaraguan counterrevolutionaries, a job he comes to dislike. His Nicaraguan lover adds to his doubts about the U.S. role in Nicaragua, and the sweet but determined farmers of a Sandinista co-op provide a sharp contrast to the crude, antirevolutionary contras. Eddie becomes so disillusioned that he allows himself to be taken captive on a raid. The army has sent Chicanos like Eddie to Central America because they can pass as natives if captured, but he violates orders, keeping the dog tag that will identify him as an American and reveal U.S. involvement in the conflict. Although well meaning, *Latino* was too obvious. Even critics who were sympathetic with its politics panned it. "I guess I'm damning it," David Edelstein wrote, "for not stirring people up the way a hack right-wing action flick does—for forgetting that, in American movies, it's not enough to tell the truth."[25]

Salvador (1986) did what Edelstein seemed to want from *Latino:* communicating the chaos and horror of revolution and stirring things up. In fact, *Salvador* looked more like a right-wing movie than the left-wing movie it was. Oliver Stone (*Wall Street*) directed and coauthored this low-budget production with Richard Boyle, the gonzo journalist whose story it tells. Boyle (James Wood) seems to have been present at every highly publicized atrocity of the long war in El Salvador, including the assassination of Archbishop Oscar Romero and the murder of three nuns. Through it all, he drinks, takes drugs, mistreats women, abuses his responsibility, and disappoints those who trust him. He is such an offensive character that his conversion to the revolutionary cause lessens its credibility, but he also prevents the politics of *Salvador* from seeming pious. The film's reverential treatment of the rebels in their quiet camps strains belief, however, as does Boyle's one speech explicitly denouncing U.S. policy. Boyle's disgust when the rebels kill some prisoners is an attempt to provide balance, but *Salvador* is still less balanced than even *Missing* or *Under Fire*. It ends with Boyle and his Salvadoran lover being led off in handcuffs—by U.S. immigration officers. "The man who made this movie is no gentle persuader hoping to cast a wide net out in the mainstream," wrote one offended critic.[26] *Salvador* is sometimes crude and simple-minded, but Stone's no-holds-barred filmmaking leaves a powerful impression.

Romero (1989) dealt with some of the same subjects, but less forcefully and entertainingly. John Duigan's film is a biopic about Salvadoran archbishop Oscar Romero (Raul Julia), telling of his disillusionment with the Salvadoran government, his radicalization, and finally his assassination. Produced by Paulist Pictures, which is associated with a Catholic order of teachers, the film was a little too reverent for its own good, but it did record a piece of history. So did *The Old Gringo* (1989), featuring Gregory Peck, Jane Fonda, and Jimmy Smits caught up in Pancho Villa's Mexican revolution. *Washington Post* critic Hal Hinson dismissed it as "grandly scaled folly . . . with overblown revolutionary nonsense."[27] Other critics agreed.

The failures of these movies might have discouraged the making of others on the subject, but at least they offered an alternative to the conservative, superpatriot films of the Reagan era, although they were considerably less popular.

Return to Vietnam

Another set of films provided a more popular and powerful counterpoint to *Rambo* and *Top Gun*, as filmmakers—most notably Oliver Stone—returned to the subject of Vietnam.

Stone's *Platoon* (1986) was less overtly political than *Salvador*, his earlier film. *Platoon* is a tough, gritty movie about American soldiers in Vietnam. Based on the director's own experiences, the film is filled with powerful images of the horror of that war. Compared to *Apocalypse Now* and *The Deer Hunter*, *Platoon* is unpretentious and down-to-earth. It deals with the ways the war affected a small group of men, rather than attempting to communicate a bigger message.

"You volunteered for this shit, man?" declares a black soldier on discovering that Chris Taylor (Charlie Sheen) is in Vietnam because he felt the fighting should not be left to "poor kids." "You got to be rich in the first place to think like that!" the soldier scoffs. In a series of terrifying patrols and battles, two sergeants struggle for "possession" of young Taylor's soul. Barnes (Tom Berenger) is a scarred, gung-ho soldier driven to win at any cost and furious at the constraints imposed on the fighters by the politicians. "Our captain Ahab," Taylor calls him. Elias (Willem Dafoe) is a mellow, dope-smoking progressive. When Taylor asks if he believes in what he is doing, Elias says he did in

1965, but "Now. . . . no. . . . We're gonna lose this war. . . . We been kickin' other people's asses for so long I figure it's time we got ours kicked."

Throughout his harrowing film, Stone focuses relentlessly and respectfully on the men who actually fought the war, the grunts. "They're poor, they're the unwanted, yet they're fighting for our society and our freedom," Chris observes at the beginning, but by the end, he is saying, "we did not fight the enemy, we fought ourselves and the enemy was in us." Like earlier movies about Vietnam, *Platoon* pays little attention to what we did to the Vietnamese and makes no effort to analyze the reasons for the war. Such restraint is surprising from the maker of *Salvador,* but by focusing on the real horrors of fighting the war rather than its politics, Stone broadened his audience and made his point more strongly. More than in most political films, music underscored the message of *Platoon,* with Samuel Barber's sad "Adagio for Strings" setting its mournful tone.

Dedicating his film to "the men who fought and died in Vietnam," Stone said, "I'd like [Vietnam vets] to see it and feel it and walk out and say never again."[28] Many vets and other viewers seem to have done so. "We didn't set out to make an anti-war film," producer Arnold Kopelson said, but "if, through *Platoon,* the public perceives Vietnam as a war America shouldn't have got involved in, then it may raise their consciousness about what's going on in Nicaragua."[29]

Praised by the critics, *Platoon* was a big box office hit and won four Academy Awards, including Best Picture and Best Direction. The success of *Platoon* came as a surprise to many, who found its politics dramatically out of sync with the patriotic conservatism of the Reagan era. Among the most surprised were the Hollywood studios that had refused to finance *Platoon,* a mistake they might have avoided if they had noted the success of *The Killing Fields* (1984), an earlier, equally powerful film about the conflict in Southeast Asia that was produced by a British company.

Three more Vietnam films by great directors followed, though none was entirely successful as a film or at the box office. Barry Levinson directed *Good Morning, Vietnam* (1987), Stanley Kubrick directed *Full Metal Jacket* (1987), another British production, and Brian De Palma directed *Casualties of War* (1989). All told stories of Vietnam from the perspective of troops similar to those in *Platoon,* and all emphasized the moral ambiguities and horrors of that war.

A Decade of Diverse Messages

In retrospect and even at the time, movies like *Rambo* and *Top Gun* seemed to dominate the 1980s and the era of Reagan. Certainly they were popular with audiences, if not critics. But other films with very different messages also were offered. Some, like *Missing* and *Platoon,* were very successful and stand the test of time better than the superpatriotic films. Most remarkably, these films succeeded partly because they seemed to beat the Stallone-Norris-Eastwood movies at their own game, with tough and realistic action. They also suggested that the American public was willing to contemplate the harsh realities of international involvement rather than simply to fantasize about some sort of revenge victory.

Reaganite films were box office hits, but movies from *Reds* to *Silkwood, Salvador,* and *Daniel* examined politics from another perspective. Many addressed tough issues, presented complex characters, and refused to offer facile solutions. Political commitment, these movies asserted, was difficult but worthwhile. Some films, of course, continued to manifest naive faith in the system, the people, or the press, but these movies were fewer in number than in previous eras. Several advocated activism even as the country grew apathetic and self-centered. Even the increasingly youthful audience and rising production costs—averaging $16 million in 1986 with half again as much for promotion—did not discourage the making of serious films about politics. With cable television, videocassettes, and an increasing number of movie theaters providing new outlets, revenues, and investors for filmmakers, independent production increased, and the 1980s ranks with the 1930s as one of the most fertile eras for political films.

11

The 1990s and Beyond 9/11

Primary Colors (1998)

As the 1990s began, Republican George H.W. Bush had succeeded Ronald Reagan in the White House. His administration reached its apogee in the successful Gulf War of 1991, for which Bush masterfully built an international coalition, although he ended the war without bringing down Saddam Hussein. His popularity soared but soon collapsed as a recession hit the economy and Bush seemed unable to cope. Quoting Clint Eastwood's Dirty Harry, Bush had declared "Read my lips, no new taxes" when he first ran for president, then raised taxes in the face of recession. His movie quote came back to haunt him in the 1992 election, when he was decisively beaten by Bill Clinton. Besides being the first baby boomer to become president, Clinton was the darling of Hollywood, and the Clinton White House virtually became Hollywood East for a succession of filmmakers and movie stars. He would also become the implicit subject of several films of the 1990s.

The final decade of the millennium also brought a paradox with respect to film and politics. After the vapidity of many of the films of the 1980s and growing corporatism in the film industry, healthy skepticism about the prospects was probably in order. Would filmmakers deign to create challenging, more explicitly political films, or would the growing chains of ever-larger multiplexes be consigned to sequels of "high-concept" remakes of television sitcoms? Or could the two perhaps coexist?

Writing in *The Nation* at the decade's end, Jon Clark noted, "Everyone in Hollywood agrees on one thing: The studios are reluctant to make political or even serious pictures. For moviemakers, being called 'political' is often the kiss of death."[1] Although reasonably compelling and politically charged movies such as *Wag the Dog* (1997), *Bulworth* (1998), and *Primary Colors* (1998) did manage to emerge, they were financial flops despite boasting big stars, big directors, and big studio marketing machinery.

Clark had a point; of the top twenty films of the decade, only the maudlin *Forrest Gump* (1994) and the neowestern *Dances with Wolves* (1990) might charitably be categorized as overtly political films. Far more popular were romantic blockbusters like *Titanic* (1997) and special-effects-laden fantasy epics like *Jurassic Park* (1993) and the *Star Wars* sequel *Phantom Menace* (1999). Indeed, special effects were perhaps the signature feature of the decade's films, and critics frequently bemoaned the preeminence of "FX" razzle-dazzle over storytelling substance. Independent movies became more noticeable but also more conventional (see Chapter 3), but even if movies like Robert Altman's *The Player* (1992), *Usual Suspects* (1995), and *Memento* (2000) did not necessarily evoke overtly political themes and messages, they did veer significantly from the mind-numbing status quo of the standard Hollywood product of the decade.

Key Political Films of the 1990s

Nevertheless, the decade did produce a significant canon of explicitly political films that, if lacking in measurable impact upon the political system, certainly added to its lexicon. Thematically, the most interesting overtly political films—those with obvious political content and what seemed to be intentional messages—reflected a deep cynicism about the political system and its institutions. To the extent they were partisan vehicles, the tenor of the decade was definitely askew toward the liberal side of the aisle, as political movies with coherently conservative themes were few, if any. Such films shared screen space with vapid, yet sometimes more entertaining (and generally more financially successful) movies that used political institutions for their human interest value, much as media coverage of political events (i.e., the Clinton impeachment saga) seemed to. Even so, as the corporate, politically safe product flooded the screens in the 1990s, there were opportunities for the moviegoing public to take in more challenging fare.

The leading contender for the decade's touchstone political film must be *Wag the Dog* (1997), a movie whose tagline was "truth, justice, and special effects." Featuring two of the generation's biggest stars in Dustin Hoffman and Robert De Niro, director Barry Levinson's creation was a brilliant mixture of Hollywood and Washington, D.C. Shot in just twenty-nine days with a small budget, the scattershot story begins with a president who is accused of molesting a Girl Scout ("Firefly Girl") in the Oval Office just eleven days before the next election. In order to divert the public's attention from the scandal, the president's spin doctor (De Niro) enlists a Hollywood producer (Hoffman) to create a fake war. The resulting pseudowar with Albania (!) is waged via press release, music video, and war memorabilia in a movie that was always both absurd and frighteningly plausible. In its mixture of political insight and comedy, the film echoed some of the best political satires, from *Dr. Strangelove* (1964) to *The Mouse That Roared* (1959).

When *Wag the Dog* was released, it was viewed as uncannily prescient because of the proximity of the Lewinsky scandal. President Clinton, in fact, was accused of "wagging the dog"—diverting the media and public attention with a foreign policy initiative—when he ordered missile attacks on a chemical weapons plant in Sudan and a terrorist training camp in Afghanistan. (Of course, such charges were vigorously denied by the Clinton administration.) In retrospect, however, the film was perhaps even more precisely predictive of the second Iraqi war. In the movie, war with Albania is said to be necessary because of "links to extremist Muslim groups" and weapons of mass destruction (a "suitcase bomb") that did not exist. The ostensible motive of the terrorists: "They want to destroy our way of life!"

(In fact, *Wag the Dog* was based on a book whose premise was that the first Iraqi war was staged by President George H.W. Bush and Saddam Hussein.)

As eerily plausible and prescient as *Wag the Dog* seemed to be, its deeper meaning was perhaps even more salient. As the action progresses, the machinations of the Hollywood professionals become more important (and seem more intelligent) than those of the politicos. Perhaps no other movie had effectively investigated the growing similarities between the two worlds and the indispensability of images and sound bytes in American politics.

Another election satire, *Bulworth* (1998), finds Warren Beatty playing the title character, a U.S. senator who is deeply depressed. He takes out a large insurance policy on himself and arranges his own assassination. Going for days without food or sleep and increasingly despondent, Bulworth arrives drunk to give a scheduled speech to an African-American group in Los Angeles. Instead of delivering his prepared speech, Bulworth starts speaking what he honestly believes, most of it shocking his audience (not to mention his campaign manager). Quickly, the senator gains attention for telling it like it is, even as he begins immersing himself in hip-hop culture and falling in love with an African-American woman. As he becomes a political phenomenon and regains his will to live, however, the assassination plot is still in motion.

Bulworth, while certainly satirical and cynical, was a different type of film than *Wag the Dog*. Much of the film's humor lay is in the juxtaposition of the formerly stodgy Bulworth and the hip-hop culture—he even starts rapping his political speeches. But the political premise was much more conventional: *Bulworth* came from a long line of films that implied that if only liberal or populist politicians would speak the truth, they would somehow be more popular. Still, it was novel to see a movie character explaining why Americans do not have national health insurance (because of payoffs by insurance companies) and how the Medicare program is more efficient than private health insurance companies. *Bulworth* was essentially a novel, albeit entertaining, vehicle for liberal ideology.

Although neither movie was a resounding hit, of the two, *Wag the Dog* was much more successful financially (it ran five weeks, with a $43 million domestic gross) than *Bulworth* (three weeks, $26 million). By contrast, the twentieth most popular film of the decade, *Toy Story* (1995), grossed $192 million. Both *Wag the Dog* and *Bulworth* gained notoriety among critics and the media, *Wag the Dog* for its presumed connection to President Clinton and *Bulworth* primarily for controversy over its racial imagery. Perhaps movies that suggest that the voters (and therefore, moviegoers) are idiots for believing the bald-faced lies of their elected representatives are poor commercial propositions.

202

Bob Roberts (1992) also presented a fictional senatorial candidate and election. Tim Robbins (who also wrote and directed) starred in the title role as a candidate from Pennsylvania. Candidate Roberts is a slick and ingratiating pol, who touts ill-defined support for symbolic issues such as national pride and family values. Espousing "rebel conservativism," he plays guitar and sings counterprotest songs like "Times Are Changin' Back" and "This Land Was Made for Me." Behind the scenes, though, we are allowed to see that Roberts is really a cynical, mudslinging manipulator. His campaign exploits many of the techniques of (successful) modern campaigns. Presented as a pseudodocumentary, *Bob Roberts* garnered nearly unanimous critical praise, but flopped miserably at the box office, grossing less than $5 million. Robbins next failed to make much of a splash with *Cradle Will Rock* (1999), which with an adamantly liberal slant explored the relationship between art and politics during the Great Depression. Robbins also played a right-wing terrorist in the not-so-thrilling thriller *Arlington Road* (1999), a movie that some critics said was the first to invoke the bombing of the federal building in Oklahoma City in 1995.

If *Wag the Dog* was the boldest overtly political movie of the decade, the brashest had to be Oliver Stone's *Natural Born Killers* (1994). In what someday might be regarded as Stone's masterwork, the relationship between the news media and politics was explored in a way as twisted yet as spot-on as *Wag the Dog*'s look at Hollywood. The film depicted the story of two young lovers, Mickey (Woody Harrelson) and Mallory (Juliette Lewis), who go on an ultraviolent killing spree. A television reporter (Robert Downey Jr.) from a show called *American Maniacs* follows them and the pair becomes a cause célèbre.

Released about the time of the societal fascination with the O.J. Simpson trial, *Killers* explored the discomforting symbiosis between the media and violence in American culture. The movie was much more about how the media (and everyday Americans) reacted to the idea of Mickey and Mallory than it was about their bloodthirstiness. In that respect, it shared the harrowing near-plausibility of *Wag the Dog*. With popular television shows like *Cops* and *America's Most Wanted* on the air, not to mention the Simpson trial spectacle, how unlikely was a pair of celebrated mass murderers?

Unlike *Wag the Dog*, though, *Killers* was directed in an utterly surreal way. Included were uses of animated sequences, black-and-white photography, a multitude of color lenses, and even a mock sitcom sequence that "explained" Mickey and Mallory. Stone threw a passel cinematographic tricks at this movie to highlight its garish message of the extent to which violence is idolized in American mass culture. Said film critic Roger Ebert, "Once we were shocked that the Romans threw Christians to the lions. Now we figure out a way to recycle the format into a TV show. That's what *Natural Born Killers* is all about."[2] Some critics found the movie gratuitous in its shocking approach, and audiences tended to shy away: the film barely managed to break even.

After Stone, John Sayles is perhaps America's most consistently political director, with strong messages about politics in almost all his films. In the 1990s, Sayles delivered *City of Hope* (1991), *Lone Star* (1996), *Men with Guns* (1997), and *Limbo* (1999), and he later directed *Sunshine State* (2003) and *Casa de los Babys* (2003). All his films deal at least tangentially with class and gender politics; many address issues of race as well. Other themes include political protest and apathy, the labor movement, the politics of property development, international exploitation, and local politics. Sayles writes, directs, and edits all his films, none of which cost much to make and none of which, unfortunately, has ever reached a large audience. The films, however, do well as independent cinema playing in art houses, and, partly because of their low budgets, they make money—at least enough for Sayles to go on to his next film.

His films of the 1990s tended to emphasize personal vision of politics; *Sunshine State*, for example, focused on the effects of Florida real estate development on the lives of several interconnected characters. Said Sayles, "Our movies are political in that they deal with how people affect each other, and how governments affect people and how people affect governments, but they are not ideological. I would say they just recognize that there are politics involved in a lot of things."[3] However, in 2004 Sayles came back to more overtly political fare with *Silver State*, his fifteenth feature film. Featuring Chris Cooper as a gubernatorial candidate (with the politically loaded name of Richard Pilager) who looks and sounds an awful lot like George W. Bush, *Silver State* is a tongue-in-cheek, satirical look at contemporary elections.

Candidate Pilager stands for "honesty, integrity, and articulacy (sic)," but in reality fronts for moneyed interests. However, *Silver State* was primarily hung around a much less captivating character, a down-at-his-heels journalist named Danny O'Brien (Danny Huston) who stumbles onto a complicated conspiracy that fails to surprise or enlighten the audience. Richard Dreyfuss contributed a convincing portrayal of Pilager's slick campaign manager, but on the whole *Silver State* feels too hollow to convince us of any underlying truths.

The Cold War Reheated

The 1990s were a decade that witnessed rapid political change. Foremost, the Soviet Union and its East European empire crumbled. Many observers credited this surprising development to the firm defense policies of Ronald

Reagan, although others attributed it to the long history of American commitment to the cold war. Still others believe that the Soviet Union toppled from the sheer weight of its own corruption. Oddly, perhaps, the dissolution of the "evil empire" was not popular subject matter for the decade's film. As one critic expressed it, "the end of the cold war . . . created a grievous villain vacuum in Armageddon-mongering fiction."[4]

In fact, even as the Soviet Union fell apart, several box office successes reverted to the cold war for the familiar enemy, including the box office smash *The Hunt for Red October* (1990), *Crimson Tide* (1995), and the far less commercially successful *Russia House* (1990). Compared to the images of cold, efficient, malignant power delivered by the Reaganesque films of the previous decade, the Soviet enemy portrayed in these films is technologically inferior, self-doubting, and in fact seeking to aid American efforts to counter its military and political might. Collectively, the films seem to devalue the dismantling of the Soviet empire, as the villains they portray seem less than a worthy adversary of a superpower.

Red October, based on a novel by the generally conservative Tom Clancy, features Alec Baldwin as Clancy's CIA action hero, Jack Ryan (a role that Harrison Ford would less successfully reprise in *Patriot Games*, 1992, and *Clear and Present Danger*, 1994). Ryan is brought aboard an American submarine when U.S. intelligence learns that a Soviet sub commander, Marko Ramius (Sean Connery), has steered his sub (Red October) off course toward American shores. The film is primarily a highly effective suspense movie, but while certainly evincing the competence and effectiveness of American military and intelligence prowess, it also manages to cast the Soviet system as somewhat bumbling even as the Soviet commander—who seeks to defect to the United States—is provided a noble sheen by Connery.

Another submarine tale, *Crimson Tide* suffers from the lack of a coherent, compelling villain. Instead of the evil empire, submarine officers portrayed by Gene Hackman and Denzel Washington must contend with a breakaway group of Russian forces that have seized missile silos from the former USSR. Much of the plot revolves around the tensions between Hackman's and Washington's characters, but the film also portrays the former übervillain of Soviet military might as less imposing than earlier films might have. Similarly, *Russia House* (based on a novel by more liberal-leaning—and British—author John Le Carré), although it operates on a much more human and dramatic level than the submarine stories, provides us with a Soviet system that is militarily deficient and crying for assistance in its own defeat. Sean Connery plays a British author who is given secret data about the Soviet missile system: Russian rockets "suck instead of blow . . . and can't hit Nevada on a clear day," as a CIA agent comments. A critical success on the strength of the dramatic performances by Connery and Michelle Pfeiffer (the Soviet "leak"), the film was not a big success at the box office, perhaps because it failed to portray the kind of villainy to which American audiences could relate. From where would the next generation of supervillains come?

A decade before the events of September 11, 2001, with the credibility of the Soviet Union as an ominous threat in rapid decline, Hollywood began to look toward terrorism and terrorists as stand-ins for the role of villainous international threats to American security. Although Russians—specifically, nuclear weapons from the former Soviet Union—as well as generic Latin Americans (*Toy Soldiers*, 1991), Kazakhstanis (*Air Force One*, 1997), and even Irishmen (*Patriot Games*, 1992) were occasionally demonized as terrorist threats, the evildoer of choice tended to be Arabic. In popular movies like *Navy Seals* (1990), *True Lies* (1994), and *Executive Decision* (1996), "Middle Eastern," "Islamic," or "Arab" terrorists posed the threats that American action heroes had to defuse. In *Under Siege* (1992), white terrorists threaten to sell nuclear arms to Arab nations, while a frenzied Arab mob creates the backdrop for *Rules of Engagement* (2000).

In all likelihood, the makers of these films did not intend to single out Arabs as innately evil, and the generic Middle Eastern villains were merely a convenient choice to replace the hastily exited Soviet heavies. However, research conducted by media critic Jack Sheehan indicates that, far from being a recent development, the vilification of Arabs is a long-standing Hollywood tradition. Reviewing more than 900 movies produced since 1900, Sheehan found that nearly all presented a negative stereotype of Arabs (typically as brutal, heartless, uncivilized "others" bent on terrorizing civilized Westerners), whereas only twelve movies transmitted what could be construed to be a positive image.[5] (One of the few exceptions was *Three Kings* (1999), which we discuss later in this chapter.)

The crude stereotyping might be less potentially injurious if film portrayals of Arabs as ordinary people were more commonplace. "Stereotyping and demonizing of the Arab or Muslim by American film has been so complete and so successful that film critics, most Americans and social commentators have barely noticed," notes one Arab studies scholar.[6] Furthermore, the heritage of Arab-bashing creates difficulties when the use of Arab antagonists is truly appropriate. *The Siege* (1998) envisioned a realistic terrorist scenario where an extremist Islamic group threatens to bomb New York City—eerily prescient, of course, of the September 11 attacks. What differentiated *The Siege* from the vast majority of films using Arabs as villainous elements was that it sought to provide insight into the attitudes, backgrounds, and history of Islamic extremists. It also presented other Arabs in a positive light, including an Arab-American agent who participates in the investigation of the threat.

Actually, *The Siege* was not so much a movie about terrorism as a meditation on the effects on civil liberties that terrorism poses. According to director Ed Zwick, *The Siege* is "very much about what civil liberties are we
prepared to sacrifice for the sake of prosecuting a war [against] an unseen
enemy? Are we willing to abnegate certain privileges and rights? privacy?
speech? whatever? assembly? for the sake of actually dealing with something that's very pernicious and has been the plague of every other country
but America for the last thirty years?"[7]

However, the film was largely lost on American audiences, who perhaps
confused it with yet another Arab terrorist action flick. Ironically, it also
suffered from criticism that it was anti-Arab, an accusation that might have
been less tenable had it not been released amid so many movies that actually
do seek to mindlessly vilify Arabs.

The War That Keeps On Giving . . .

Although the cold war seemingly vanished in the wake of the collapse of
the Soviet system, filmmakers continued to mine the Vietnam War. Oliver
Stone, already noted for *Platoon* (1986), opened the decade with *Born on
the Fourth of July* (December 1989, but viewed primarily in 1990). Whereas
Platoon sought to explore the nature of the war itself, *Fourth of July* examined the war's domestic impacts. Up-and-coming megastar Tom Cruise portrays Ron Kovic, a paraplegic Vietnam vet who wrote a memoir about his
experiences. The use of Cruise, who to some represented an American ideal,
was effective in selling the film's message of the horror of war. Kovic is
transformed from an all-American boy (hence the film's title), to a patheti-
cally crippled soldier (his paraplegic's therapy is depicted in detail), to an
angry opponent of the war. Some critics, however, began to sense that the
war's cinematic novelty had been depleted: "Because there have now been
so many films about Vietnam, because we've seen so many innocent villagers gunned down, so many accidental deaths, so much tragedy and pain,
unless a radically different perspective is presented . . . a numbing sense of
familiarity sets in," wrote Hal Hinson of the *Washington Post*.[8] Nevertheless, perhaps due to Cruise's participation and performance, the film was a
smash financial success.

Stone's third Vietnam film, *Heaven and Earth* (1993), sews up the logical
conclusion to his first two efforts: it explores the war's effect on the Vietnamese
—and focuses on a woman instead of on the men in combat. The book is
based on the two-volume autobiography of Le Ly Hayslip, a Vietnamese
woman. Running nearly two and a half hours, the film lacks the excitement
of battle scenes, as Hayslip tends to be a passive victim of the war's brutal-

ization of her country and, ultimately, herself. Lacking a bankable Hollywood star—Hayslip is portrayed by a Vietnamese-American college student—the film was a financial flop whose material some critics found inappropriate for Stone's typically frenetic style of direction.

Arguably the biggest Vietnam War movie of the decade, however, did not actually take the war as its theme. Directed by Robert Zemeckis, a relatively obscure protégé of Steven Spielberg, *Forrest Gump* (1994) followed the fictional life of a mentally handicapped man. The film literally inserts Gump's life into a panoply of latter twentieth-century American history, using digital effects to enable him, among other things, to teach the "real" Elvis Presley how to dance and to meet the "real" Lyndon Johnson at the White House on-screen. However, it is the Vietnam War that serves as the pivotal event in the film's narrative, as most of the film seems to constitute a string of disjointed vignettes.

Gump, played by American icon-in-the-making Tom Hanks, fights heroically in the Vietnam War. Befriending a black soldier who will die in combat, he valiantly saves another soldier by carrying him through miles of jungle brush. He is awarded a Medal of Honor by President Johnson, yet also manages to energize a massive antiwar protest. Essentially, Gump, whose everyman status is elevated by Hanks's own, comes to signify everything that is good about America, even under the worst of circumstances. Viewers are allowed to feel good about every recent aspect of American history, including race relations, the war, and war protests . . . even George Wallace and paraplegics become easier to take. This quality of the movie, along with the eerily impressive special effects, helps explain *Gump*'s stunning success at the box office (it grossed $679 million), as well as a few critical accusations of pandering to "maudlin sentiment."[9] The film is not prowar so much as it is unabashedly and relentlessly pro-American. If life is indeed a "box of chocolates," according to its hero's adage, in *Gump* it is a box of diet chocolates that can readily be both had and eaten.

After ignoring the subject of World War II for years, Hollywood turned once again to that war during the 1990s. The best of the lot, Steven Spielberg's *Saving Private Ryan* (1998), was one of the most-seen films of the decade. Mixing detailed realism in battle scenes with time-tested war movie stereotypes, Spielberg's film is an unabashedly patriotic ode to the fighters of the "last good war." The film's enormous popularity helped to inspire a new wave of recognition for veterans of the war. Tom Hanks starred as the regular guy—a Midwestern schoolteacher—who leads a platoon of young soldiers in search of Private Ryan. Although the soldiers are occasionally frightened, they never question their participation in the war, as soldiers in a typical Vietnam War movie would.

Spielberg also tapped into the horrors of World War II with *Schindler's List* (1993), which documented the heroic actions of an otherwise ordinary Polish businessman in rescuing Jews from extermination at the hands of the Nazis. Without disparaging *Schindler's List*, which received high critical praise and an Academy Award for Best Picture, it bears noting that American audiences seem to take to movies about foreign political heroes more readily than those about heroes of their own country. They have demonstrated their interest in films that document the shaking-up of the political systems of other countries, such as *Gandhi, Evita, Michael Collins, In the Name of the Father*, and *Cry Freedom*, yet an American movie about slavery has yet to achieve much popularity.

The most original, if not also the very best war movie of the decade, *Three Kings* (1999) was one of the few major motion pictures to address the first Gulf War. Near the war's end, three American soldiers (bankable star George Clooney, Mark Wahlberg, and Ice Cube) learn that a cache of confiscated gold bullion is hidden in an obscure Iraqi encampment. What might have been a simple reworking of a similarly plotted World War II movie, *Kelly's Heroes* (1970), becomes much more interesting when the trio discovers that Iraqis are being slaughtered as the American military retreats. The film was thus, on one level, an explicit critique of the Bush administration's prosecution of the war.

Of greater interest, however, was how director David O. Russell drew the central characters of this first post-Vietnam American war. Clooney, Wahlberg, and Ice Cube portrayed soldiers, not conscripts, who are at once "bored, opportunistic, confused about a war they never got a chance to fight properly, and dangerously impulsive."[10] Their enemies, moreover, were not inscrutable demons (as the Vietnamese were frequently portrayed, even in antiwar films), but were instead depicted as human beings with their own problems and agendas.

Three Kings also set itself apart with its energetic style. The ante of active camerawork offered by Vietnam War movies like *Platoon* was raised considerably by Russell's visually striking, rapidly cutting eye that helped the audience buy the sense of random chaos in which these characters must make life-and-death decisions. Lens filters kept the Middle Eastern desert looking menacing, yet banal. Surprisingly, audiences responded well to a movie that seemed to undercut an American military victory, and *Three Kings* grossed more than $60 million domestically (as well as another $40 million internationally).

A later effort, *Black Hawk Down* (2001), was an even more downbeat war movie that depicted the ill-fated American military mission in Mogadishu, Somalia, in 1992. Director Ridley Scott (the *Alien* franchise) achieved a stunningly realistic depiction of urban combat. As in *Three Kings*, the soldiers in *Black Hawk Down* learn that they are fighting only for themselves and their buddies; the script implies that the political decision makers in the Clinton administration are to blame for their predicament. *Black Hawk Down* generated some criticism because of the way that Somalis were depicted—largely as targets in a shooting gallery. In fact, over a thousand Somalis were killed during the battle depicted in the film. A curious footnote: when *Black Hawk Down* was screened in Mogadishu (a bootleg version, shown outdoors) in 2002, the Somali audience cheered as American helicopters crashed and soldiers died.

Presidential Characters

As no decade of film before it, the 1990s were focused on the United States. Fictional presidents were featured or figured prominently in at least a dozen popular movies, while biographical (and quasi-biographical) films of Richard Nixon, Bill Clinton, and John Kennedy were also released. What many of these films shared was emphasis on the personal lives of presidents (real or imagined). To a certain extent, this tendency mirrored reality, as the Clinton presidency was characterized by unprecedented interest in chief executive "affairs." But many of these films preceded the Lewinsky and related scandals, as did both *Dave* (1993) and *The American President* (1995).

Cinematic fascination with the president is scarcely a product solely of the decade in question. Americans generally tend to be more aware of and interested in presidential politics than those at any other level, perhaps due in part to the myth of the all-powerful president. Popular movies about fictional presidents can speak volumes about American perceptions of themselves and their country.

Both *Dave* and *The American President* in broad strokes resembled Capra-like fantasies about the presidency. At the surface, both were romantic comedies or light dramas that explored the idea of a president's social life. In *Dave*, Kevin Kline plays a small-town businessman whose uncanny resemblance to the incumbent president results in his summons to Washington to cover for the president, who has suffered a heart attack while engaging in an extramarital affair. À la Capra, Dave turns out to be a ceaselessly honest, everyday guy who, when thrust into a corrupt system, becomes a force for good—that is, when he's not getting emotionally involved with the president's wife, who has become estranged from her husband due to his lack of character in all matters.

On a political level, *Dave* betrays a hopelessly simplistic and perhaps even purposely naive view of the presidency that might make Capra blush. When a budget shortfall threatens homeless shelters, Dave summons his entire cabinet, snaps his fingers, and, voila, increases social spending and balances the budget (with a little help from his small-town buddy, an accountant). In case the left-of-center bent is not obvious (the screenwriter was a Democratic delegate at the 1980 national convention), Dave successfully rebuffs the evil machinations of the real president's right-wing aide. To the extent—and here is the big question—that the audience took Dave seriously, the movie reinforced the idea of the all-powerful president as well as the Capra ideal of the efficacy of one man versus the corrupt system. The painless politics it espoused was, as the *Washington Post* noted, "an attempt to reheat the American pie and hand around the slices, a form of gentle jingoism equivalent to playing the national anthem at ball games."[11] Yet *Dave* maintained a mainly lighthearted and occasionally satiric sensibility. Oliver Stone, fresh from directing his *JFK* conspiracy film, appears in a cameo role to proclaim that Dave is part of a conspiracy.

The American President, although it was not without a host of lighthearted moments, has a somewhat more serious tone. Michael Douglas portrays Andrew Shepherd, a liberal president who is up for reelection. He also happens to be a widower who meets an attractive, capable environmental lobbyist named Sydney Wade (Annette Bening). Sparks fly. The plot thickens when Shepherd's right-wing opponent uses the affair (which has become public knowledge) as an election issue. As we would expect any fictional president to do, Shepherd successfully rebuffs the attack, protects gun control and the environment, and manages to keep the girl and live happily ever after.

Like Dave, this fictional president is obviously liberal, but this time with big-city style and attitude. (Neither is identified as a Democrat, however, apparently so as not to alienate Republican audiences.) When accused of being an American Civil Liberties Union (ACLU) member, Shepherd barks to his opponent, "Yes, I am a card-carrying member of the ACLU. But the more important question is: Why aren't you, Bob?" in a way that might provide comfort to liberal audiences. The system is again portrayed as corrupt, but this president knows how to make the deals that preserve his integrity and his political goals. In fact, arriving as it did when the Clinton administration was embattled and feeble, the film's message seemed to be aimed at Clinton. As president, Michael Douglas does not care what the polls say—he does the right (liberal) thing! Go left, young man!!

The American President came across as a little more sophisticated about political realities than *Dave*—President Shepherd has to make deals—but equally naive about the presidency. Both placed Capraesque faith in the efficacy of personal character to trump political reality. But the broad comic and romantic appeal of both films was probably more responsible for their sizable financial successes. Neither *Dave* nor *The American President* was of itself likely to have any measurable impact on moviegoers; conjointly with many other movies that also embodied a simplistic view of the presidency, however, they may have helped mold our expectations of the office.

Another fictional presidency or rather, pair of presidencies was the subject of the gentle screwball comedy *My Fellow Americans* (1994). Jack Lemmon and James Garner play two former U.S. presidents; Russel P. Kramer (Lemmon) is a stuffy, conservative Republican and Matt Douglas (Garner) is an amorous, liberal Democrat. (There is also a vice president who resembles Dan Quayle.) When the incumbent president (Dan Ackroyd) is hit with a bribery scandal, he tries to frame Kramer and Douglas. The two wind up on the lam and (you would never guess it) eventually learn to appreciate each other's company and values. Although essentially a harmless romp, *My Fellow Americans*, like many films that address political icons, deftly reconciled the differences between ideologies with personal warmth and humor.

The myth of the all-powerful president was revisited at absurd new extremes in two other fictional presidencies in *Independence Day* (1996) and *Air Force One* (1997). In *Independence Day*, an alien force invades planet Earth. Likable actor Bill Pullman portrays the president, who, along with a ramshackle group of other survivors of the alien attack, personally joins the battle by flying a fighter jet. *Independence Day*, suffice it to say, was not overly concerned with any sort of realism. It was a zesty, self-consciously silly pastiche of B-movie clichés dating from *War of the Worlds* (1953) up to approximately *Star Wars* (1977). Beyond the flying heroics of the president, the movie also managed to mix in a little jingoism: with the entire world under attack, it is the Americans who have the brains and the moxie to defeat the evil aliens. These aliens are so evil that they forgo the usual posturing as friendly explorers and start nuking American cities from the get-go. (It may have been comforting to some viewers to see the rest of the world actually applauding an American military action.) However, although it reinforced implausible expectations about the presidency, *Independence Day* was such a cartoon that only the most naive viewer would confuse its lazy plotting for a political message.

Mars Attacks (1996), released at roughly the same time, was essentially the same movie taken to its logical cartoonish conclusion and was therefore something of an antidote for those taken aback by the gleeful simplemindedness of *Independence Day*. Directed by visual maestro Tim Burton (*Edward Scissorhands, Beetlejuice*), it was said to be based on a series of bubblegum cards that were issued in the 1950s. The aliens microwave Congress and just about everything else in sight, with little point other than sheer cinematic fun . . . which, unfortunately, the movie oddly lacks. As president, Jack Nicholson adds little to what might have been a hilarious turn. Once the audience was amused by the quirky aliens and the cardboard cast of "heroes," there was little left to captivate.

Air Force One featured yet another president with vast military experience and expertise. Harrison Ford was cast as President James Marshall, a Vietnam combat hero whose plane is hijacked by a Kazakhstani terrorist (Gary Oldham, an old hand at playing crazies of all races). Needless to say, the president's combat savvy pays off and Marshall dispatches the villain in due course. Apart from the reprise of the president-as-action-hero concept first seen in *Independence Day*, this film included Glenn Close as the vice president who must grapple with the terrorist's demands. To its credit, the film let Close act with dignity and the audience-preferred level of toughness, perhaps helping to sell the idea of a female candidate to upcoming electorates. The movie itself was predictable, forgettable fun that did not really trample on any provocative political airspace. Yet the decade's message of the all-powerful president was once again affirmed in one of the most popular films of the decade.

Less fictive, yet not necessarily true-to-life films about the presidency addressed the life of Richard Nixon and the death of John F. Kennedy. Oliver Stone's *JFK* (1991) was the premier overtly political film event of the decade, grossing over $70 million domestically. The title notwithstanding, the film was actually about a conspiracy to assassinate Kennedy and its cover-up; the president himself was presented as an ideal of liberalism. (*JFK* implied that Kennedy had plans to withdraw American troops from Vietnam). Directed with Stone's trademark, extremely active camera (and liberal use of color filters), the movie was an intense experience fraught with compelling performances by an outstanding cast (Kevin Costner, Sissy Spacek, Joe Pesci, Donald Sutherland, Gary Oldman).

But *JFK* raised a fascinating and disturbing paradox as a political film. In portraying the conspiracy to murder a president, Stone took extreme liberties with the factual evidence of such a conspiracy. In the words of film critic Roger Ebert, the narrator of the film (upon whose book the film is loosely based), former New Orleans district attorney Jim Garrison, "was a loose cannon who attracted crackpot conspiracy theories the way a dog draws fleas."[12] Yet Garrison's theories, as well as others, were depicted as factual amid a backdrop of legitimately disturbing aspects of the Kennedy assassination. Was *JFK* therefore fiction? Docudrama? Propaganda?

Whatever else it was, *JFK* was indubitably controversial. Stone was and is frequently vilified for distorting the truth, if not lying outright about the subject matter of *JFK*. One problem is that any film based on historical subject matter contains historical inaccuracy, particularly—those like *JFK*—that address inherently mysterious or ambiguous subjects. According to film historian Roger Rosenstone, "Film will always include images that are at once invented and true. True in that they symbolize, condense or summarize larger amounts of data, true in that they impart an overall meaning of the past that can be verified, documented or reasonably argued." From this standpoint, a film like *JFK* can be interpreted as a hypothesis about historical events, what Rosenstone calls "historical intervention in that it's provoking you to at least consider what might have happened, not to give you a definitive history."[13]

Such interpretations are perhaps sufficient for film critics and scholars, but what about the audience? Does a film like *JFK*, for example, lead to unwarranted mistrust of government and/or the judicial system? Perhaps not . . . most viewers attending a movie like *JFK* are already armed with perceptual screens, and many may have read the reviews of the movie, which in the case of *JFK* tended to emphasize its lack of historical accuracy. Those enamored of conspiracy theories, of course, were already converted to the film's point of view. But what Stone's film did do, unequivocally, was to focus public interest and debate on a politically charged subject. It even spurred the release of previously sealed files by means of a congressional resolution signed by President George H.W. Bush. This was no mean feat in a mass cultural environment replete with other distractions. Film scholar William Romanowski states that the controversy about *JFK* "demonstrated how effective a motion picture can be as a transmitter of knowledge, history, and culture."[14]

Stone continued in a similar, although somewhat less controversial vein with his biopic of Richard M. Nixon, *Nixon* (1995). Although an outspoken liberal like Stone might have been expected to deliver a brutal caricature of the scandal-ridden Republican president, *Nixon* was actually a fairly evenhanded and conventional Hollywood-style biography. Unfortunately, some of the same aggressive filmmaking techniques that made the shocking substance of *JFK* all the more compelling tended not to coalesce as effectively with the more staid narrative of Nixon's life. Nixon, after all, had an undistinguished upbringing, and winning and losing elections does not make for compelling cinema; Anthony Hopkins, familiar to many filmgoers in his role as psycho killer Hannibal Lecter, gave a heroic effort in the title role, but did not really look or sound like the man.

Stone provoked by creating some fictionalized scenes that developed a theory of Richard Nixon's personality: essentially a lonely man who felt unloved from childhood onward. Like *JFK*, *Nixon* received criticism from those who felt it was too far afield with the historical record. Unlike its predecessor, however, *Nixon* failed to stir much public response, grossing much less than the $50 million cost of making the three-hours-plus movie.

An interesting footnote to *Nixon* that fell largely by the wayside, *Dick*

(1999) was a farcical romp that answered the cinematic question: what if the famous eighteen-minute gap in the Watergate tapes had involved two teen-age girls? A curious combination of teen comedy and broad political satire, *Dick* featured Michelle Williams and Kirsten Dunst as two teens who stray from their tour group while visiting the White House; the pair stumbles into the Oval Office and hilarity ensues. Unfortunately, for all of its relentlessly cute put-ons of Nixon's presidency, *Dick* was not particularly funny and failed to recoup even half of its miniscule $13 million budget. Some critics, how-ever, liked its ability to "make particular aspects of the recent American past comprehensible to those too young to have lived them."[15]

Another quasi-historical presidential film was one of the more interesting overtly political movies of the decade, *Primary Colors* (1998). Based on the best-selling roman à clef by Joe Klein (who originally published it anony-mously), *Primary Colors* concerns the 1992 presidential campaign of one southern candidate who is notorious for his appetites. In other words, it was is a thinly veiled interpretation of Bill Clinton's run for the presidency. The film, while notably even less accurate than either *JFK* or *Nixon* (it may even have given *Dick* competition in that regard), provided a stunningly insightful look at what made Clinton both such an effective candidate and a troubled president. Directed by Hollywood veteran Mike Nichols (perhaps best known for *The Graduate*, 1967), *Primary Colors* was most captivating when star John Travolta, in his role as Governor Jack Stanton, was, in effect, imitating Bill Clinton. In a series of campaign vignettes, Travolta/Clinton mingles iras-cible personal charm with keen political and policy instinct in a way we would imagine the real Clinton doing.

Unfortunately, the film's insights seemed to end with the remarkable take on Clinton, the human being. As a chronicle of the political process that en-abled him to gain power, the film had little to offer. The second half of the movie got bogged down in an improbable scenario that saw one of Governor Stanton's aides become suicidal over their leader's "selling out." That might not have been so improbable if the selling out in question did not involve "go-ing negative" in a political campaign. In this way, the film far more closely resembled *Dave* and *The American President* than, say, *The Candidate*, in its sentimental understanding of the political process. Although the film raised a discernible amount of media hubbub, the public was less than enthralled and the movie failed to earn back much more than half of its $65 million budget.

High Crimes and Misdemeanors

The 1990s also saw a high tide of fictional suspense movies centered on the presidency, frequently involving miscreant presidents. *In the Line of Fire*

(1993) was a generally effective thriller, starring Clint Eastwood as a Secret Service man whose career has been marred by his failure to protect President Kennedy in Dallas. John Malkovich portrayed the current president's would-be assassin. Although by no means a film with a particular political point to make—the focus was on the action and Eastwood's struggle to redeem himself—the movie adequately reflected the reality of a presidential election. Eastwood's character, of course, was in the tradition of his *Dirty Harry* anti-hero; he snubs the bureaucracy and throws the procedure book away at a footfall. The film also included some murky talk that the country is no longer what it used to be and that its flag has fallen but this was not a resonant message. *In the Line of Fire* was one of the top-grossing movies of 1993 and received critical praise as an example of effective Hollywood storytelling.

In *Clear and Present Danger* (1994), Harrison Ford reprised his role as author Tom Clancy's superspy, Jack Ryan. The film had nothing to do with *Schenk v. United States*, the Supreme Court ruling that free speech could be limited if its exercise presented a "clear and present danger." Ryan is called in to clean up a murder spree on a yacht that has possible connections to the president (a vaguely Reagan-looking Donald Moffat). The action proceeds down to South America, where a stereotypical Colombian drug warlord is holding Americans—who were fighting a secret war—captive. What ensues is a fairly gripping if by-the-numbers suspense movie.

Interestingly, however, the script betrayed little of author Clancy's right-wing worldview because Ford demanded it be moderated, which was achieved by bringing in a more liberal coauthor.[16] In the original script, the Reagan-like president is not vilified, whereas in the film he is exposed by Ryan in testimony before Congress. The film seemed to be the cinematic answer to the Iran-Contra affair: this time, the president does not skate away quite so easily. This episode illustrated how stars with leverage can affect the political messages a film delivers.

Murder at 1600 (1997) and *Absolute Power* (1997) are two movies that seemed to be inspired by the Clinton administration. In each, the president is implicated in murder. In *Murder at 1600*, Wesley Snipes portrayed detective Harlan Regis of the Washington, D.C., police force called in to investigate the murder of a striking blond woman in the White House. A formulaic thriller that happened to be set in the president's residence, *Murder* did not say much except to underscore that the president could be a very bad man. The president is scarcely on screen, in part because the audience is expected to think he is guilty of something.

Absolute Power was an equally forgettable exploration of presidential evildoing. Directed by Clint Eastwood and starring Gene Hackman, it involved a career burglar (Eastwood) who happens upon a murder scene that involves . . . the president! Although perhaps only hardcore right-wingers would somehow implicate Clinton on the basis of this pedestrian thriller, *Absolute Power* did seem to pander to that sensibility. As critic Charles Taylor wrote, "Even the queasy, unpleasant tone . . . is perfect for conservatives, since they get to be titillated by the sex and violence . . . and take a shocked attitude toward it."[17]

Taken collectively, these movies were most intriguing in that they were released around the time that the Clinton administration was being accused of murdering aide Vince Foster. To the extent that they make such a scenario more plausible, such films exacerbated an extraordinary (and ultimately groundless) attack on the White House.

Congressional Acts

A few films of the 1990s had congressional settings. From the first, Hollywood has viewed Congress as a corrupt institution, ripe for saving by a principled individual—much as Americans tend to view Congress dimly, but usually admire their own representative. No exception to the rule, *The Distinguished Gentleman* (1992) featured star Eddie Murphy as Thomas Jefferson Johnson, a con man who dupes his way into Congress when an incumbent dies. For a farce, the film actually conveyed some of the actual trappings of the legislative process, including the importance of sitting on certain committees, the role of Political Action Committees (PACs), and the struggle over freshman office space. The film's plot also turned on a real policy issue, the link between high-voltage transmission lines and cancer.

Produced by Marty Kaplan, a former speechwriter for Democratic presidential candidate Walter Mondale, *The Distinguished Gentleman* was loosely based on actual events—particularly scandals in the U.S. Congress. But despite its veneer of factualness, the movie provided only a dumb parody of legislative wrongdoing. When Johnson gets to Washington, he looks to exploit the system for his own betterment. Immediately, he is able to sell his votes (to the highest bidder, of course). "With all this money coming from both sides," asks Congressman Johnson, "how could anything ever get done?" The answer, from a hooked-up lobbyist: "It doesn't."

Thus *The Distinguished Gentleman* made *Mr. Smith Goes to Washington* seem positively nuanced in its depiction of Congress and its faults. (In fact, the film's press release actually referred to Eddie Murphy as "the Jimmy Stewart of the Nineties.") When Johnson meets and becomes enamored of a pretty young lobbyist whose child may have gotten cancer by means of close proximity to power lines, he just cannot help but straighten up, fly right, and in so doing expose the corrupt institution for what it is. The movie was only a modest financial success and was generally pounded by critics for its in-sipid storytelling.

Just over ten years later, *Legally Blonde 2: Red, White, and Blonde* (2003) covered the same tired ground as *The Distinguished Gentleman*. The sequel to a funnier comedy featuring Reese Witherspoon as Elle Woods, a deceptively dim-looking blonde law student, *Legally Blonde 2* inserted the same character into Congress as an aide to a congresswoman (Sally Field). The aide's mission is to convince Congress to stop testing cosmetics on animals. In the ensuing hilarity, Elle learns the truth about democracy and how self-serving Congress is. Critically panned in large part for its hackneyed plotting, the movie grossed a more than respectable $90 million. Together, *Legally Blonde 2* and *The Distinguished Gentleman* helped to compound public misapprehension of Congress and did so in a way that was only marginally entertaining.

Legal Matters

Some of the best overtly political films of the decade focused on the American legal system and related policy issues. Director Milos Forman's *The People vs. Larry Flynt* (1996) was a biography of *Hustler* magazine publisher Larry Flynt. Although the film covered Flynt's entire life, at its heart was Flynt's obscenity trial in 1987. Flynt's magazine published a cartoon that depicted conservative televangelist Jerry Falwell as an incestuous drunk, and Falwell sued for $40 million in damages. After the film first familiarizes us with Flynt's crudeness, it next traces the progress of the suit all the way to the Supreme Court. Edward Norton, in the role of Flynt's attorney, provides a compelling oral argument and gamely banters with the Court (itself rarely a cinematic setting). The film was as effective as any at relating the logic and importance of the First Amendment guarantee of free speech in a democratic society.

Civil Action (1998) depicted the experiences of real-life trial lawyer Jan Schlictmann (John Travolta), who evolves from a self-interested ambulance chaser into a public interest attorney. The film focused on a lawsuit brought against multinational corporations for polluting a Massachusetts town. Instead of milking this story for a predictable Hollywood storyline, *Civil Action* luxuriated in the ambiguities and complexities of high-stakes civil litigation. It also avoided the tendency of movies—particularly those set in the legal system—to separate the courtroom into good guys and bad guys, searching instead for how and why the winners win and the losers lose. As Roger Ebert wrote, *Civil Action* is "like John Grisham for grownups."[18] Due to its high-profile cast, *Civil Action* was expensive to make and failed to recoup its $60 million budget at the domestic box office.

218

Perhaps the most compelling film of the decade with a legal system setting was *The Insider* (1999). Directed by Michael Mann (a director better known for action films like *Heat*) the movie made the true story of a scientist for a tobacco company, Jeffrey Wigand, feel like a gripping suspense yarn—without compromising the politically charged material. Instead of the conventional Hollywood claptrap about a little guy who takes on the system and wins, *The Insider* gave serious consideration to the notion that everyone in a legal conflict has an agenda, the media included. A star-studded cast (including Russell Crowe as Wigand and Al Pacino as CBS news producer Lowell Bergman) was given ample room to fill in the shadows between black and white. Director Mann made characteristically good use of lighting (and frequently, the lack thereof) to give the proceedings a healthy tinge of suspense.[19] Despite seven Oscar nominations (including Best Picture and Crowe for Best Actor), *The Insider* actually lost money, which probably did not improve the prospects for future intelligent, politically charged film projects.

Citizen Ruth (1996) was an independently produced look at both sides of the abortion debate from a heavily satiric perspective. It starred Laura Dern as Ruth, an indigent drug abuser (she "huffs" toxic fumes from various kinds of spray cans) who gets pregnant and may or may not want an abortion. But the film was really about lampooning the extremists on both sides of the abortion issue, who are soundly and equally ridiculed throughout *Citizen Ruth*. Antiabortionists are depicted as hymn-singing "baby savers" while abortion rights activists are lesbians who sing New Age hymns to the moon. And so on. For sadly, once the movie has made it clear that extremists on both sides are dogmatic nutcases, *Citizen Ruth*'s zany plot sounds funnier than it really is. By pulling its punches with a cop-out ending and granting equal time to all zealots, the movie fails to take any clear position. Although it garnered some critical praise, *Ruth* died at the box office.

A more successful film by the same director as *Ruth* (Alexander Payne) defied easy categorization. *Election* (1999) would seem to be an intentionally political film because its subject matter is a high school student council election. Matthew Broderick stars as civics teacher Jim McAllister, who very much wants one student, Tracy Flick, to lose the election, since her affair with one of his colleagues resulted in scandal. Meanwhile, unhappy at home, McAllister is embarking on an affair of his own with a family friend. His efforts to make Tracy lose the election ultimately result in personal and professional humiliation. Although *Election* was hilarious for its send-ups of high school personalities (and perhaps the banality of teaching high school civics), it did not try to present a pointed satire of the American political system. Most of the dark humor revolved around the foibles of its characters' personalities, although the election itself was broadly presented as a farce.

Political Science Fiction

Several science fiction films of the 1990s seemed to resonate politically. If there was a single unifying theme of the decade's sci-fi, it was a sense of alienation fueled by the perception that the outside world and all its institutions were a facade for a darker, mind-numbing force that commanded conformity from all humanity. This seemed to be the idea behind such popular fantasies as *The Truman Show* (1998), *The Matrix* (1999), the more recent *Minority Report* (2002), and the lesser-known *Dark City* (1991). A far more comedic entry, *Men in Black* (1996), also touched on a similar vein.

In *The Truman Show*, Jim Carey plays the title role of a man, Truman Burbank, who is blissfully unaware that his entire life is a TV show watched by millions every day. When Truman discovers the truth, he becomes outraged and seeks to flee the giant set in which he has been living, which does not sit well with the corporate giant behind the TV show of his life. The show's director and Truman's personal manipulator, Christof (Ed Harris), seeks to keep Truman imprisoned.

The Truman Show was interesting for the way it presaged and critiqued the American obsession with reality television—people keep watching Truman's life with voyeuristic gusto, even though nothing interesting happens. Its premise, that one's life is lived in a glass jar for the amusement of others, was captivating at the outset. Unfortunately, the movie never got too far beyond its premise, devolving into an action piece. Its life-affirming, Hollywood stock ending (yes, Truman escapes!) was far less original than its beginning. The outcome implied that no matter how artificial our world may seem, individualism can emerge triumphant.

Beyond the endless *Star Wars* sequels, perhaps the science fiction smash of the decade was *The Matrix* (1999). Keanu Reeves plays Neo, a computer hacker who is led to believe that reality as he and everyone on earth knows it is a collective dream fed by a massive computer system known as The Matrix. The Matrix imprisons humanity in a dream state as it sucks the life force out of its bodies. A group of rebels contacts Neo and informs him that he must play a role in defeating the Matrix.

The Matrix was a surprise megahit produced, written, and directed by two relative unknowns, Andy and Larry Wachowski. Much of its appeal was doubtlessly found in the groundbreaking digitalized special effects used for its action sequences—the movie was a natural for the then newly popular, home theater audio-video systems. But the theme of alienation and ennui spawned by a consumer society also seemed to strike a collective nerve. One British critic reasoned that the *The Matrix* and its two sequels might reflect the "widespread feeling of helplessness in the U.S."[20]

Unfortunately, the potential for exploring that theme was largely squandered in favor of mind-numbing action sequences in the sequels, *The Matrix Reloaded* (2003) and *The Matrix Revolutions* (2003), which tended in long stretches to resemble long video games rather than movies. Although both movies were financial successes (due in large part to international box office receipts), perhaps the unabashed use of Cadillac product placements ran against the grain of selling alienation from mass society.

Dark City (1998), a much smaller picture (budget: a mere $27 million) than *The Matrix* trilogy, featured a nearly identical premise. John Murdoch (Rufus Sewell) is an amnesiac who awakens to learn that he may be a serial killer. Murdoch learns that a mysterious group called the Strangers controls the entire city. Through a process called the Tuning, the Strangers can manipulate time and physical space. *Dark City* followed Murdoch's efforts to thwart the Strangers and discover his own identity.

Although it resembled *The Matrix* in its theme of alienation amid a world of facades, *Dark City* had an entirely different look and feel. Thanks to the remarkable visual world created by George Liddle and Patrick Tatopoulos, the film luxuriated in a timeless sense of foreboding that invoked Fritz Lang's silent classic, *Metropolis*. *Dark City* also operated on a more personal level than the *Matrix* series, which may have muted its effect as a political vehicle. It never caught on with mass audiences, either, barely recouping its original budget in domestic and international box office.

A much bigger financial success was the comic book adaptation *Men in Black* (1997). Yet again, life on earth is but a veneer for another "real" world. In this one, aliens of all sorts reside on and frequently visit earth. It is the duty of government agents, played by Will Smith and Tommy Lee Jones, to keep this alien influx a secret from earthlings. *Men in Black* was a harmless if amusing high-tech farce, and the aliens are generally lovable CGI (computer-generated imagery) creations. The film's satire was directed at other movies more than at real political institutions. A sequel, *Men in Black II* (2002), was less successful both critically and financially.

September 11, 2001, and Beyond

As we will discuss in Chapter 12, the specter of the September 11 terrorist attacks and the ensuing war with Iraq dealt the new millennium a unique opportunity for the political documentary film, such as *Fahrenheit 9/11* (2004), to become a new political force. The extent to which such films will remain in the public's frequently short attention span is an open question, as is the film's possible impact on the 2004 election. For its part, Hollywood was not particularly quick to exploit the terrorist attacks, although, as we have seen, the selection of Arab terrorists had become common long before 2001. At least one film, the forgettable Arnold Schwarzenegger thriller *Collateral Damage* (2001), was delayed for several months because its subject matter involved a terrorist plot.

Although it was produced before these films, perhaps the most explicit fictional link to the September 11 attacks was *The Sum of All Fears* (2002). Another film version of a Tom Clancy/Jack Ryan novel, *The Sum of All Fears* featured young star Ben Affleck in the role played previously by Harrison Ford and Alec Baldwin. A group of terrorists in Russia are able to obtain nuclear weapons from the former USSR; the novelty of this film is that they detonate such a device in Baltimore. Beyond that chilling link to the contemporary fear associated with terrorism, however, *The Sum of All Fears* had little to do with the subject matter of terrorism or even weapons of mass destruction. The plot rests on the dubious (and perhaps tired) proposition that Americans and Russians still distrust one another enough to risk nuclear war. How audiences might connect the dots between the explosion in Baltimore and real threats of terrorism is an intriguing question. At any rate, despite a cool response from most critics, *The Sum of All Fears* did reasonably brisk business at the box office.

Apocalyptic threats were also the hook for another post-9/11 thriller, *The Day After Tomorrow* (2004). In this update of the old disaster film genre, global warming takes an unexpected and extreme turn for the worse; New York City is flooded and flash-frozen while tornadoes destroy Los Angeles. One scientist, Adrian Hall (Dennis Quaid), is onto the debacle but not before cataclysm is set in motion. The film includes a president and vice president who are suspiciously reminiscent of George W. Bush and Dick Cheney, and filmmaker Roland Emmerick (who also directed *Independence Day*) has stated that the movie is in part a critique of the environmental policies of the Bush administration. (Even after the tornadoes wipe out Los Angeles, the president refuses to change his mind about global warming!)

Although scientists largely pooh-poohed the way the threat of global warming is portrayed in the film, the German-born Emmerick intended it as a warning: "The American people are good people. It's the government that needs to be more honest. I'm just holding up a mirror. I'm saying in this film that this could happen if you don't change."[21] Part of a long lineage of disaster and science fiction films that posit dystopian futures as the result of human failures, *The Day After Tomorrow* was not a memorable addition to that canon because its characters and plotting were so two-dimensional. The movie, however, did spark political discussion about global warming, and critics of the theory of global warming feared that the enormously popular film would add an irrational element to the environmental policy debate.

Although few movies explored more traditional beliefs, Mel Gibson's *The Passion of the Christ* attracted more viewers than almost any of the political movies and more than three times as many as *Fahrenheit 9/11*. *The Passion* focused on the torture of Christ in the final two hours of his life. Although it reflected a distinctively traditional theological view of its subject matter, it did not pursue political themes. It was intended to be a literal reenactment—in a sense, a documentary—of the death of Jesus Christ, as told by the Bible. However, its immense popularity (along with the conservative ideology of its maker) seemed to signal a sociocultural statement.

The biggest specific controversy that arose with the film's release, however, was sparked by allegations that it blamed Jews for the death of Jesus. Although critics predicted that a new outbreak of anti-Semitism would occur, little if any racial conflict seemed to ensue. The more resonant impact of the film was the possibility that it might inspire a spate of religiously themed movies. Its success provided fodder for conservative social critics, who saw affirmation of their belief in the public's desire for traditional values in the movies. The extent to which future projects would embody that thought and/or exploit the success of *The Passion* remains unknown at this time.

Approaching the midpoint of the decade, the bigger question is whether the popularity of such serious and politically charged films as *Fahrenheit 9/11* and *The Passion* would have a salient impact on the film industry or constitute yet another passing fad. According to one industry insider, "because of the success of [*9/11* and *The Passion*], Hollywood is re-evaluating how it views both religion and politics. There's been a cultural and paradigm shift in the perception of these movies by Hollywood and the audiences."[22] Other observers question the public's attention span for such weighty fare once the war and the 2004 election are distant memories. And as the future of politics and film is imagined, it is important to bear in mind that both *Fahrenheit 9/11* and *The Passion* are in large part so successful because ultimately they entertain. The recent past of popular film is littered with serious movies with provocative messages that were unsuccessful primarily because they failed to do just that.

Retrospectively (and excluding *Fahrenheit 9/11*), as a decade, the 1990s (and the adjoining years) provided little basis for hope that Hollywood would commit itself to making thoughtful overtly political movies. The best efforts in that regard were generally independent films or box office flops and frequently both. Although much is sometimes made of a liberal Hollywood agenda, relatively few movies pursued leftist causes very openly. On the other hand, even fewer projected a traditional or conservative point of view. As always, the best political films managed to be politically pointed yet entertaining with a minimum of dogma.

Political Films by Topic

12

True Lies?

The Rise of Political Documentaries

The Atomic Cafe (1982)

Perhaps the most startling development in popular film during the past decade was the improbable ascent of the documentary film. Although documentaries have been an important art form since the dawn of motion pictures, until the contemporary era they have not been a significant commercial force. In fact, none of the top ten most popular (nonmusical) documentaries of all time was produced before 1989, when filmmaker and political raconteur Michael Moore's groundbreaking *Roger and Me* was released. By contrast, eight of the top ten were released after the year 2000 (Table 12.1).

But what exactly is a documentary? There is no set, universally agreed-upon definition of the term. We might say that a documentary is intended to be nonfictional and therefore factual. Documentaries are also inherently propagandistic, in that they seek to persuade the audience of some "truth." But the recent history of documentary filmmaking and its success challenges even this basic description.

Many of the earliest movies were in essence documentaries, as filmmakers simply turned their cameras on anything that was happening—before the conventions of filming fictional pieces had been developed. Soon, however, documentary filmmakers began toying with making documentaries films that, while not "untrue," certainly manipulated reality to make their subjects more interesting and compelling. An early landmark documentary, *Nanook of the North* (1922), contained scenes of Eskimo life that appeared to be "real," but were in fact staged by director Robert Flaherty, including sets designed to enable the use of filmmaking equipment. But although these kinds of techniques made documentaries more entertaining, they were not commercial successes and were not intended to be.

Documentaries became a little more commercial—and more controversial—in the 1960s and 1970s when several reached small audiences, mostly in art houses and later on television or videotape. Emile D'Antonio's *Point of Order* (1964) taught a new generation about McCarthyism, using television film footage of the Army-McCarthy hearings. D'Antonio followed *Point of Order* with *In the Year of the Pig* (1968), a movie about the Vietnam War, and *Milhouse* (1971), about President Richard Nixon. Both were more polemical, more controversial, and less successful than *Point of Order.* Frederick Wiseman, surely the dean of American documentarists, launched his series of documentaries about American institutions with *Titicut Follies* (1967), about a mental institution, followed by *High School* (1968), *Law and Order* (1969), *Hospital* (1970), and many others right up to *Public Housing* (1997) and beyond. None of Wiseman's films had narration. He just let the cameras roll and allowed the denizens of the institutions to speak for themselves.

In the 1970s, Barbet Schroeder's *General Idi Amin Dada* (1974), about an African dictator, David Halpern's *Hollywood on Trial* (1976), about Holly-

Table 12.1

Top Ten Grossing Documentaries of All Time

Title	Studio	Lifetime gross	/ Theater	Opening	/ Theaters	Date
Fahrenheit 9/11	Lions	$118,002,561	2,011	$23,920,637	868	6/23/04
Bowling for Columbine	UA	$21,576,018	248	$209,148	8	10/11/02
Winged Migration	SPC	$11,689,053	202	$33,128	1	4/18/03
Super Size Me	IDP	$10,349,135	230	$516,641	41	5/7/04
Hoop Dreams	FL	$7,830,611	262	$18,396	3	10/14/94
Tupac: Resurrection	Paramount	$7,718,961	804	$4,632,847	801	11/14/03
Roger & Me	WB	$6,706,368	265	$80,253	4	12/22/89
Spellbound	Think	$5,728,581	117	$17,508	1	4/30/03
Touching the Void	IFC	$4,593,598	137	$96,973	5	1/23/04
The Fog of War	SPC	$4,198,566	261	$41,449	3	12/19/03

wood and House Un-American Activities Committee (HUAC), and Barbara Kopple's *Harlan County USA* (1977), about unions in the coal mines, all found small audiences. *Hearts and Minds* (1974), directed by Peter Davis, found a somewhat wider audience, made a bigger splash—and won an Oscar for Best Documentary. The title reflected the unsuccessful U.S. strategy of trying to win "the hearts and minds" of the Vietnamese people in order to win the Vietnam War. Davis featured interviews of participants in the war, filmed comments of political and military leaders, and news footage of the war to make his points. Hal Erickson reports that

> the film was briefly withdrawn from distribution when . . . [an] advisor to President Johnson insisted that the advisor's reputation had been damaged and demanded that the two minutes featuring [him] on-camera be deleted. More controversy arose when *Hearts and Minds* won the Best Documentary Oscar, whereupon the Academy issued a statement—read during the awards ceremony by Frank Sinatra—that it did not condone or advocate the volatile statements made by the producers during their acceptance speech.[1]

The audiences for all these documentaries were small, mostly young, and liberal to radical. In their own small way, the documentaries contributed to the movements of the 1960s and 1970s, confirming what some already believed and adding believers among the previously uninitiated (mostly college students). As the 1960s and 1970s turned into the 1980s and the "me generation," interest in documentaries like these waned, but precedents had been set for today's documentary filmmakers.

While the documentaries of the 1960s and 1970s attempted to tell their stories and make their points in a reasonably entertaining way, more recent documentaries have further blurred the distinction between the imperatives of entertaining the audience with a story (as conventional movies do) and the factual quality traditionally associated with documentaries. *The Atomic Café* (1982) successfully strung together old "documentary" footage in the form of government-issued films about nuclear radiation. A rerelease in the early 1970s of a 1930s pseudodocumentary about the evils of marijuana, *Reefer Madness* (1938) had demonstrated the entertainment value of old propaganda films. The old scenes in *Atomic Café,* including such absurdities as schoolchildren being asked to "duck and cover" under their desks (to music) in order to survive a nuclear attack, were at once comedic and helped the filmmakers ridicule the idea of nuclear war. Although only very modestly successful at the box office, the film turned a profit, won an Oscar, and nurtured the notion among filmmakers that a documentary could both entertain and make a political point. As Combs and Combs note, "by appealing to our higher emotions through humor . . . they gave political propaganda a whole new impetus toward light-hearted satire and parody."[2]

The Thin Blue Line (1988) was a riveting film that further whittled down the distinction between documentary and other movies. The movie explores the 1976 murder of a Dallas policeman for which drifter Randall Adams was convicted and sentenced to death. Director Errol Morris used a mix of traditional documentary interviews and staged scenes that, cleverly strung together in an almost surreal way, turned the story into a highly engrossing mystery. The music of avant-garde composer Philip Glass underscored the mood of the film, which led the viewer to question the official story of the murder. The repetition of a staged reenactment of the crime, the incongruous official story, and the hypnotic score combined to create an effective challenge to Adams's guilt. In fact, the movie was so successful that it resulted in Adams's release from prison the same year it was released—a rare example of a political film achieving an observable and specific political result. Beyond that, *The Thin Blue Line* left the viewer with the clear implication that the "official story" was not always to be trusted—even in capital murder cases.

Roger and Me (1989) introduced the world to Michael Moore, a folksy-looking and -talking, unabashedly liberal political provocateur. Moore's movie traced his efforts to contact General Motors CEO Roger Smith about the fate of the filmmaker's hometown of Flint, Michigan. But that search was only a ruse with which to tie together the movie's exploration of economic despair in Flint. With *Roger and Me,* Moore discovered a way to improve upon *The Atomic Café;* rather than just using old footage that was entertaining and politically provocative in its absurdity, Moore plumbed the city of Flint for contemporary scenes that achieved the same purpose even more effectively. As captured by Moore on film, Flint's economic woes yielded a panoply of emotions, including pathos (a family is evicted just before Christmas), humor (a woman tries to make a living skinning rabbits and selling their hides), and disgust (various political and economic leaders appear to be indifferent to the fate of those affected by the city's poor economy). Moore himself appeared throughout the film, interviewing luckless citizens and (especially) trying to find Roger Smith. Taken as a whole, the film was an effective piece of political polemic; Moore made no pretense of objectivity and therefore did not try to present any balance in his indictment of Flint's (and by extension, perhaps, America's) political and economic elite.

Moore's film was, by documentary standards at least, a smash success, grossing nearly $7 million on a budget of less than $200,000. But perhaps more so than any documentary that preceded it, *Roger and Me* also created a hailstorm of politically pointed criticism that set the pattern for his subsequent films. Critics charged that the movie was propaganda (true) and that it manipulated the facts and the people in the film to achieve its political ends (also true). Moore's defenders pointed out that *all* movies rearrange and manipulate "facts" to make their stories coherent and their messages clear. By combining entertaining vignettes and his own brash but personable character, Moore had created a new form of documentary with the potential to both entertain and, possibly, shape the public's political imagination.

Moore produced and directed a couple of other less critically and financially successful films in the 1990s, including *The Big One* (1992), a critique of corporate America, but once again struck both gold and a political nerve with his release of *Bowling for Columbine* (2003). An exploration of the violence wrought by guns in America, *Columbine* represented a refinement and expansion of the documentary techniques that had made *Roger and Me* such a success–and also fomented increased political controversy.

The title was taken from the fact that the two high school students who were responsible for the massacre of students at Columbine High School had been bowling the morning of the shootings. The incident at Columbine was only a starting point, as the film took a wide-ranging look at guns and violence in American society. Compared to *Roger and Me,* though, *Bowling for Columbine* took some pains to be more thoughtful even if it was not particularly objective. The film probed the American plague of gun violence from a variety of angles; filmmaker Moore seemed genuinely unable to come up with a clear explanation for the problem of gun violence, although he did not hesitate to identify some likely villains along the way: gun fanatics, militia members, guns and ammunition manufacturers and sellers, and (particularly) the National Rifle Association (NRA) and its leadership were allowed to indict themselves with their own simplemindedness. For example, James Nichols—brother of one of the men convicted for the Oklahoma City bombing —argues passionately, if not semipsychotically, that one must be armed to fight for a political cause . . . but admits that he has never even heard of Gandhi and the idea of nonviolent political action. Yet the film never explicitly advocated gun control as the answer to the problems it explored.

Like *Roger and Me, Columbine* was both thought-provoking and extremely entertaining. It also used Moore's folksy presence and exploited the weaker moments of the individuals he chose to vilify. Moore threw in old documentary footage (à la *Atomic Café*) of a 1950s TV commercial for a toy gun that sounds real, an animation sequence that resembled the popular cartoon show *South Park,* and even some acts of what might be called performance art (for example, he took survivors of the Columbine incident to meet with K-Mart executives in an effort to stop selling ammunition). Moore also managed to provide a critique of welfare reform policy as he explored a tragic shooting by a first-grader whose single mother was at work most of the day to earn a meager wage.

Although very popular at the box office by documentary standards and praised by most film critics, *Bowling for Columbine* predicated the same kind of critical and political melee that *Roger and Me* had sparked, but with much more volume. It certainly fomented debate in media circles. Critics pointed out that Moore had manipulated images and events to make his point and that he unfairly accosted celebrities like Charleston Heston (president of the NRA) and Dick Clark (who owned the restaurant where the first-grader's mother worked). More generally, such critics were alleging that Moore's film was *not a documentary.* There is definitely some validity to this assertion, as *Bowling for Columbine* was unabashedly critical of American society, particularly with respect to the ownership and use of guns. In essence, like *Roger and Me,* it was a polemic that sought to lead viewers to conclude that something about Americans and guns was fundamentally askew.

The question that follows, however, is to what extent "documentary" is a truly meaningful category of film. As we have seen, the trajectory for contemporary documentaries is the increasing emphasis on entertainment and narrative over the supposedly more traditional approach of "just the facts." But from the beginning, documentary filmmakers have selected aspects of reality to tell their stories, the version of the truth that they sought to tell. Is any other approach even possible? Consider how the unedited, unplanned eighty-one-second videotaping of the 1991 Rodney King beating resulted in a hung jury for the policemen who were accused of beating him, in part because the two sides in the courtroom were able to create widely convincing yet totally disparate interpretations of the same factual footage. Filmmakers, in any event, are not about to start releasing unedited videotape . . . and *Bowling for Columbine* proved to be a relatively tame affair compared to Moore's next production.

Although *Bowling for Columbine* smashed all previous box office records for documentaries with $21.5 million in gross receipts, nobody anticipated the juggernaut that Moore's next "documentary," *Fahrenheit 9/11* (2004) would prove to be. *Columbine,* for all its success and media attention, was actually viewed in just a paltry 248 cinemas nationwide—*Fahrenheit* was shown in more than *two thousand* theaters and became the first documentary to actually take the top position in weekly box office ticket sales. The political debate it sparked was also perhaps the most vociferous and voluminous ever created by an overtly political film and, given its proximity to the 2004 elections, potentially the most efficacious. *9/11* became a political football even before its release when the subsidiary of the Disney Corporation with which Moore had contracted to produce the film declined to release it. It was ultimately released independently (by executives from Disney), but the controversy played right into Moore's hands as free publicity for his film.

A searing indictment of the war in Iraq and the Bush administration's role in its initiation, *9/11* represented the culmination of the elements of the quasi-documentary approach Moore had honed with his previous films. Rather than relying as much on amusing stunts and the insertion of his camera-friendly provocateur persona, in *9/11* Moore took his documentary approach back almost full circle. Abandoning to an extent the "kitchen sink" potpourri of techniques and scenarios thrown at viewers in *Bowling for Columbine,* he let his subjects' own images both amuse and alienate his audience. President Bush is seen reading a book to a group of schoolchildren during the minutes immediately after being informed of the September 11 attacks. He is seen playing golf after making tough-guy comments about terrorism. He and his staff are seen preening before making on-camera appearances.

One can agree or disagree with its politics, but *Fahrenheit 9/11* made political reality seem . . . like a movie! The behind-the-scenes shots of politicians looking all too human were exactly what we have come to expect in a regular movie. The insertion of old *Dragnet* television scenes harked back to the "goofing" on the law in *Reefer Madness,* and other scenes that scoff at the danger posed by Iraq were reminiscent of *The Atomic Café.* Moore's deft editing of September 11 footage, never actually showing the buildings under attack, only the onlooking crowd and the sounds of the attack (with a blank screen), was truly captivating. Although the film lost momentum near its end, interviews with the mother of a dead American soldier comprised both a minimystery (when we meet the woman, we sense that something is troubling her deeply) and tragedy (when we learn he has died in Iraq).

This approach, therefore, was anything but artless. Moore (and his crew), for example, obviously combed through hours of film footage to find the most unfavorable footage of Bush and his administration, the sort of scenes that mainstream media would traditionally shy from if only in the name of decorum. And he linked these images to his thesis about the war and its illegitimacy, in part by lacing the film with disturbing footage of the prosecution of the war itself. Amazingly, this linkage was achieved in a way that—although clearly upsetting to his opponents—did not necessarily make an audience feel manipulated, particularly those sympathetic to its viewpoint. In short, *Fahrenheit 9/11* was both a modern masterpiece of political propaganda and a movie with an unprecedented, very specific political objective. Moore timed the release of the film (and its subsequent early release on DVD) to coincide with the presidential election of 2004. Extremely pointed interviews in the film suggested that viewers might want to consider voting against the president.

At the box office, *9/11* was a staggering success. It shattered the old mark set by *Columbine* by grossing over $100 million in its first month of release, based on estimated ticket sales of more than 12 million, and remained among the top five releases for more than a month. Public opinion polls revealed that 8 percent of American adults had seen the film as of July 11, 2004, and that an additional 18 percent planned to see it at a theater and another 30 percent planned to see it on video.[3] Clearly, *9/11* had the potential to affect both support for the war in Iraq and the outcome of the 2004 election, even if contemporary research findings about the effects of film on political behavior seemed to suggest otherwise.

The political fallout from *9/11* was and is on a level unmatched by modern films. In anticipation of criticism from defenders of the president and the war itself, Moore created a "war room" that would deal with accusations of inaccuracy. However, this time Moore's critics were not only from the political opposition. Even some liberals who generally agreed with Moore's view of the Iraqi war faulted him for manipulating his audience and taking liberties with the images of Bush and others in the film. Others took a more sympathetic view, asserting that although Moore may have used crass and even unfair methods to make his case, these are the precise methods by which his political opposition (in other media) has thrived. Wrote one commentator, "Moore is such a fitting adversary to the current administration—and its mainstream media chorus of approval—because he knows how to speak in precisely the same vocabulary of sensation, sound bites and sheer emotionalism that the [Bush administration] uses to promote its policies."[4]

Fahrenheit 9/11 in many ways embodied a "natural experiment" for exploring the relationship between film and politics. It was as overtly a political film as was imaginable, to which record numbers of voters and politically active individuals were exposed. Its context seemed to embody a perfect storm of a controversial war, an upcoming election, and the growing conflation of reality and cinematic imagery (also seen in so-called reality television). Would it have any measurable or verifiable effect on political events, or did it merely serve mainly to preach to the choir, exerting little sway on those not already predisposed to its point of view?

Public interest in political documentary film seemed on the increase. Even before the success of *Fahrenheit 9/11* seemed to spill over onto other politically charged documentaries, Errol Morris's documentary *The Fog of War* (2004) was a modest sensation, winning an Oscar and generating a fair amount of political discussion. The film was essentially a straight interview with former Defense Secretary Robert McNamara, focusing on his role in the Vietnam War. Errol Morris invented a special device called the "Interrotron" that allowed the interviewee to look directly into the camera and see the interviewer (Morris) rather than the camera. The device was said to relax the interview subject and also make the audience feel closer to the interview. Although it was not nearly as innovative and seductive as Morris's *Thin Blue Line*, *The Fog of War* did implicitly raise eerie parallels between what

McNamara believes were the mistakes of the Vietnam War and the war in Iraq. Without the latter conflict as a backdrop, it seems doubtful that *The Fog of War* would have created much of a stir, nor would it have become the tenth most financially successful documentary in American film history.

Another war-related documentary that attracted some viewers, *Control Room* (2004) explored the Arab-language television network, Al-Jazeera. Directed by an Egyptian-American, the film went behind the scenes at the network to provide American audiences with a view of the Arab media. Although it was relatively low-key about making a message, like *The Fog of War* the film had obvious implications for the Iraqi war, questioning the role of journalists as "objective" participants. The film helped viewers understand how the expectations of the audience help shape the news that they see. "It benefits Al-Jazeera to play to Arab nationalism, because that's their audience," says an American Marine press representative in the film, "just like Fox plays to American patriotism. . . . That's their demographic audience and that's what [their viewers] want to see." However, the audience for this challenging release was limited to small cinemas and never more than seventy-five of them nationally.

Another very recent documentary-like film, *Super Size Me* (2004), was a much bigger box office draw. Director Morgan Spurlock expanded on Michael Moore's participant-observer tactics by basing the entire film on his own single stunt. In *Super Size Me,* he eats nothing but McDonald's food for an entire month as the film chronicles his subsequent health problems. The message was pretty clear—junk food is bad for one's health—but the stunt made the message a lot more palatable (but not appetizing!). Audiences ate up this act to the tune of more than $10 million in box office gross, making *Super Size Me* the fourth most popular documentary. The film's release appeared to have had the immediate political impact of causing the McDonald's Corporation to announce the end of its "super size" option, although that connection was denied by McDonald's.

Several more intensely political documentaries were released in 2004, including *Outfoxed: Rupert Murdoch's War on Journalism,* a film that sought to expose the right-wing bias of the publishing mogul's Fox Network news, and *The Hunting of the President,* a filmed version of the book by Joe Conason and Gene Lyons (subtitled *The Ten-Year Campaign to Destroy Bill and Hillary Clinton).* Both films emerged from openly liberal Democratic sources that did little to efface their partisan origins. Neither was greeted with a great deal of commercial interest; both were screened in only a few cities (although *Outfoxed* was quickly made available on DVD). The lack of public interest —despite generally rosy reviews—for these straightforwardly deadpan partisan statements seemed to suggest limits to the phenomenal expansion of the documentary in the modern cinema.

13

Film and the Politics of Race
The Minority Report

Bamboozled (2000)

As in every other aspect of American life, the mix of racial politics and film has been volatile, resulting in a rich and complex history. The depiction of minorities in popular movies has generally been both reflective of social and political reality and occasionally intended to send political messages. But the study of minorities in the movies is fraught with complexities. What constitutes a "minority film"? Must such films (1) be directed by minorities, (2) feature many minority actors, (3) emphasize race-related social and political issues, and/or (4) be created primarily for minority audiences? With respect to the political impact of movies, do movies create or reflect racial conflict and other outcomes?

In this chapter, we focus selectively on the evolution of films by and about African-Americans. One rationale for this approach is that race relations betweens whites and blacks have proved to be the most enduring conflict in American society—as well as the one most often depicted in popular movies. We focus on films and events from the latter part of the twentieth century, as this era represents the most interesting and most widely viewed part of the cinematic landscape. These films include both reflections of race relations and efforts that create more pointed political messages about race relations. Certainly volumes could be devoted to the study of other racial minority groups, although the way popular movies have treated other minorities parallels the way they have treated African-Americans.

From the onset, the relationship between film and the African-Americans politics has been problematic. *The Birth of a Nation,* as discussed in Chapter 4, created such outrage that Hollywood was loath to address race relations directly for decades. Subsequent films shied from its depiction of blacks as threatening savages, so instead blacks were almost universally depicted as demeaning caricatures in early films, including happy, shiftless Uncle Toms, kind but witless Mammy servants (as in *Gone with the Wind*), dancing fools, and the like. At the same time, independent black directors and producers were creating an alternative cinema, albeit for a very small audience. Oscar Micheaux, for example, working with extremely limited resources, created more than forty movies between 1919 and 1948.[1] However, such films were ultimately no match for Hollywood, which would not distribute films by budding black independent filmmakers and trumped them with richly produced all-black musicals.

The 1960s and 1970s: Hollywood Discovers Minorities

Race relations and the war in Vietnam dominated the politics of the 1960s, yet Hollywood avoided both issues until late in the decade, apparently assuming that an issue that polarized the nation would offend too many people

238

to turn a profit. The same rationale had applied to films about race since the tumultuous response to *The Birth of a Nation,* although there had been honorable exceptions in the late 1940s (*Pinky, Home of the Brave, Intruder in the Dust*) and 1950s (*The Defiant Ones, Imitation of Life*). The powerlessness of blacks in popular films mirrored that in the political system itself.

In the 1960s, however, Hollywood discovered that race could sell tickets. Minority issues were hot, and a vaguely liberal national consensus on civil rights had developed; as long as filmmakers played safely within that consensus, they could appear controversial yet please the majority. This trend accelerated when the film industry belatedly noticed that minorities themselves constituted a substantial potential audience. A decade of civil rights activism had prepared audiences to accept a greater and more realistic presence of blacks in Hollywood films.

One of the first successful films dealing with race was Alan Pakula's *To Kill a Mockingbird* (1962), with Gregory Peck as a brave lawyer defending a black man accused of rape in a small southern town. *In the Heat of the Night* (1967), directed by Norman Jewison, was an even bigger hit. The story of a racist southern sheriff (Rod Steiger) and a northern black lawman (Sidney Poitier) who are forced to work together, *In the Heat of the Night* ridiculed the southerner's racist attitude toward the clearly superior black cop. The film was an all-round hit, winning Academy Awards for best motion picture, script, and actor (Steiger) and later spawning a TV series.

Another contender in the 1967 Oscar race was also antiracist: Stanley Kramer's *Guess Who's Coming to Dinner,* which starred Katharine Hepburn and Spencer Tracy as parents whose daughter is about to marry a black doctor (Sidney Poitier). Audiences loved this comedy, and both Hepburn and the script won Oscars, but critics were hard on the movie, pointing out that the problems of its affluent families were irrelevant in an era of ghetto riots. To their credit, such movies condemned white racism, but most did so in a sanitized way calculated not to offend white audiences. The racist characters were such crude caricatures that whites could join in the condemnation without feeling guilt about their own racial sensibilities. The liberalism of these films was thus well within the national consensus of the time. Yet such films may have paved the way to even greater racial tolerance.

Poitier was ridiculed for playing cuddly, acceptable blacks in his 1960s films, yet his screen presence surely helped prepare white audiences for integration, even if some whites were shocked when they found out that not all blacks were like Sidney Poitier. This fact became abundantly apparent in a spate of 1970s films that featured nearly all-black casts and plenty of action. Loosely labeled "blaxploitation" movies, these films featured a new "Superspade" stereotype: a suave but tough black hero "who lived a violent life in pursuits of black women, white sex, quick money, easy success, and a cheap joint, among other pleasures."[2] This stereotype was politically empowering, but also socially demeaning and ultimately a dead end for blacks in the movies.

The mold was set by independently produced *Sweet Sweetback's Baadasssss Song* (1970s). Shot on a shoestring budget in South Central Los Angeles, it is the story of a sex-show performer (Sweetback, played by director Marvin van Peebles) who witnesses the beating of black revolutionaries by white cops. In turn, Sweetback roughs up the cops and must then live on the run—indulging in sex and violence and outsmarting the dimwitted white police manhunt. The movie was a minor sensation, grossing over $10 million and providing the impetus for a score of Hollywood copycat efforts. (The story of the film's creation is the subject of a 2004 quasi documentary, *Baadasssss!*) *Sweetback* and movies of its ilk projected an empowered, if flawed, black male amid a corrupt, mostly white political system.

Subsequent movies like *Shaft* (1971) and its sequels, *Shaft's Big Score* (1972) and *Shaft in Africa* (1973), as well as *Superfly* (1972) and *Coffy* (1973) demonstrated that blaxploitation flicks—and therefore, movies that featured black characters and themes—could attract a crossover (white) audience, even if their political messages were muddled in the emphasis on sex, drugs, and violence. Critics denounced their "reverse racism," since the (white) man was often portrayed as weak, corrupt, and stupid, but black and white audiences were drawn by the action as well as the mystique of the Superspade stereotype. Suddenly, black was very cool at the box office. *Coffy* and its follow-up *Foxy Brown* (1974) even demonstrated that black women could join in on the action. The success of the blaxploitation craze was short-lived, however, and the spate of copycat and sequel black action films died out.

The Politics of Black and White in the 1980s

Racial politics was still a hot topic in America in the 1980s, but filmmakers pretty much steered clear of it. John Sayles touched on it in *Matewan* (1987), however, and a few other filmmakers also addressed America's most persistent political challenge.

Ragtime (1981), for example, based on E.L. Doctorow's panoramic historical novel of turn-of-the-century America, featured a variety of characters and political themes in elaborately interwoven stories. Director Milos Forman chose to focus on a mild-mannered young black man, Coalhouse (Howard E. Rollins Jr.), who is driven to radical revenge after white racists destroy his car. With no recourse in the law, he resorts to violence. A black attorney refuses to help Coalhouse on the persuasive grounds that other clients have greater needs, and Booker T. Washington (Moses Gunn) makes a strong case for his own pacifist tactics, but *Ragtime* stays resolutely on the side of Coalhouse as well as its other nonconformist, antiauthoritarian characters.

Ragtime's treatment of the subject of race was very different from that of Sidney Poitier's movies of the 1960s. Despite the film's historical setting, Coalhouse is an up-to-date character, proud and stubborn, with a chip on his shoulder, insistent on his rights, unwilling to placate whites on any terms. Unfortunately, whatever message *Ragtime* meant to send was lost in obscure motivations and a confusion of subplots. From Coalhouse's (he leads a break-in of magnate J.P. Morgan's home) extreme actions to his shooting death on the order of a seemingly decent police commissioner (James Cagney), *Ragtime* provided few clues to the characters' motivations. Despite fine performances, this distancing kept audiences from identifying with the characters, and *Ragtime*'s rich and beautiful evocation of the American past was not enough to sustain it. Critics and audiences were unenthusiastic, and although the movie was nominated for five Academy Awards, it won none. It is still worth viewing, however.

Mississippi Burning (1988), directed by Alan Parker and written by Chris Gerolmo, was a tougher and more forthright film about the politics of race, set in Mississippi in 1964. Based on the true story of the FBI investigation of the disappearance of three young civil rights workers (one black and two white), the movie conveyed a strong sense of the tension in a small southern town caught up in the civil rights battles of the 1960s. Gene Hackman and Willem Dafoe portray two very different FBI men, with Hackman as the cautious, good-ol'-boy southerner and the younger Dafoe as a more aggressive outsider. Their challenge as investigators is to get anybody—black or white—in the tight little town to talk about what happened. Whites, many of whom may have been complicit in the murders, keep to themselves. Blacks keep silent out of fear. One who refuses to talk to the agents is nevertheless beaten by local Klansmen. But as Roger Ebert pointed out, one of the strengths of this film was that "there are no great villains and sadistic torturers in this film, only banal little racists with a vicious streak."[3] Although some critics condemned the film for focusing on white FBI agents when blacks were the real heroes of the era, *Mississippi Burning* got mostly rave reviews and won several Academy Award nominations.

Costa-Gavras's film *Betrayed* (1988), scripted by Joe Eszterhas, touched on a similar but more contemporary subject less successfully. Debra Winger plays an undercover FBI agent assigned to investigate white supremacists—but she falls in love with the prime suspect (Tom Berenger). Reviewers condemned the movie, as they did *Mississippi Burning,* for dealing with racism by focusing on white characters, but while some critics thought *Mississippi*

241

Burning was redeemed by its script, acting, and sense of place, others dismissed *Betrayed* for the heavy-handedness of its message.

Spike Lee, the preeminent African-American director of his or perhaps any era, brought racial politics in America completely up to date in *Do the Right Thing* (1989), which he wrote, directed, and starred in. An array of black and white characters interact at a pizzeria in New York's Bedford-Stuyvesant neighborhood on a single, oppressively hot summer day. An Italian family runs the pizzeria, survivors of an era when the neighborhood was predominantly Italian. Now it is black and poor, and a minor disagreement between the pizzeria owner and one of the black residents results in racial insults, slurs, and eventually violence, provoked by heat, poverty, and the insecurities of the neighborhood's varied residents. Lee's high-energy film was funny, moving, and provocative at the same time, with some sympathy and understanding for all its characters. Hal Hinson of the *Washington Post* called *Do the Right Thing* "a moral workout. At once a plea for tolerance and a rationale for violent opposition, the film embraces both its patron saints, Martin Luther King and Malcolm X, then invites us to hassle out the contradictions."[4] Some audiences were elated by the ambiguity of this film's message, whereas others were frustrated. Spike Lee accepted both reactions, declaring, "All we can do is present the problems."[5] Although only modestly successful at the box office ($26 million gross), *Do the Right Thing* captured some awards, two Oscar nominations, and lots of media attention.

Lee himself became a significant film artist and political figure with the success of *Do the Right Thing.* He had burst on the scene three years earlier with an independently produced hit, *She's Gotta Have It* (1986), which demonstrated both his directing skills and his ability to make financially successful movies about blacks and black themes. Lee skillfully parlayed this success in a way that enabled and inspired other black artists—actors, directors, and others—to succeed also. He also was and is extremely visible and outspoken, becoming a prominent, if often controversial, spokesperson for black concerns about film. Unlike many other directors (black and white), Lee is able to make movies with racial subjects and themes that, instead of reflecting social and political reality, create an alternative vision that frequently constitutes an alternative to Hollywood stereotypes, although not always a coherent race-related message. Even as the popular and critical attraction to his films has been inconsistent, Lee has been adamantly reluctant to pigeonhole his political message.

Directed by Edward Zwick, *Glory* (1989), on the other hand, had a more straightforward message. Kevin Jarre's script told the story of a regiment of black soldiers led by white officers in the Civil War. Seen through the eyes of the white officer (Matthew Broderick), *Glory* was criticized as yet another film about race told from a white perspective. But powerful performances from Denzel Washington and Morgan Freeman as black soldiers provide balance. During the war, blacks were not fully trusted by either side, and black soldiers were thought to be too undisciplined and unreliable to be effective. The 54th Regiment of Massachusetts Volunteer Infantry, made up of free northern blacks as well as escaped slaves, fought bravely in some of the bloodiest battles of the war, disproving the prejudice against them. As a result, the North recruited more black troops, and the added manpower was crucial to winning the war. Another issue in the film is that the black troops received lower pay than the white troops. When the black soldiers refuse to accept their unequal paychecks, their white officers join them, producing a bond between them that contributes to their success. The distance between the races, however, is never glossed over. *Glory* opened to good reviews, and won Academy Awards for soundtrack and supporting actor Denzel Washington, only the second of three African-American actors ever to win that award.

The 1990s: The Emergence of Black Directors and Blaxploitation Revisited

The 1990s inaugurated some significant new trends in black cinema, although black films never attained truly consistent and widespread commercial success. Inspired and enabled by the success of Spike Lee, African-American directors attained modest success with a series of chronicles of life in South Central Los Angeles—the impoverished black community of Southern California. Most prominently, African-American director John Singleton created *Boyz N the Hood* (1991), a gritty narrative about young blacks coming to grips with the realities of the prospects they face. White characters are generally portrayed as bigoted and as hindrances to black advancement. The film received several Oscar nominations and established Singleton as a candidate to join Spike Lee as a preeminent black filmmaker.

Working a similar vein, twin African-American directors Albert and Allen Hughes created *Menace II Society* (1992). Another effective exploration of life in the Los Angeles ghetto, *Menace* was even less hopeful about the prospects for young urban blacks than was *Boyz N the Hood*. But neither Singleton nor the Hughes brothers were successful in carving out subsequent releases that would expand upon their visions of black America. Both wound up as part of the recent blaxploitation revival, with Singleton remaking *Shaft* (2000) and the Hughes brothers creating their *Dead Presidents* (1995) heist flick. Although both Singleton and the Hughes brothers demonstrated great potential in their subsequent releases, they did not match the critical and commercial success that their initial filmmaking forays had represented.

Instead of heralding the advent of a vital new African-American cinema, racially distinctive cinema in the 1990s for the most part was treading water. A host of heist movies, reminiscent of the politically neutered blaxploitation era, emerged. *New Jack City* (1991) helped cut the mold. Mario Van Peebles, son of the director of *Sweet Sweetback's Baadasssss Song,* directed this entertaining crime-genre film with a mostly black cast. Whereas in the old blaxploitation movies the villains were generally white, in *New Jack City* the bad guys are black—and so are many of the cops who are after them. Although this and similar films introduced a new generation of filmgoers to the blaxploitation concept, they did little to advance a political agenda for black films.

Spike Lee remained the standard bearer for politically provocative African-American film. His *Malcolm X* (1992) was a hard-nosed, three-dimensional biography of the political activist. It also propelled Denzel Washington (in the title role) to fame as a crossover star. Far from a Hollywood glamorization of the fiery orator, *Malcolm X* explored the complexities and ambiguities of his life in a way that was compelling to mainstream audiences; however, the film is to date Lee's last undisputed critical and commercial triumph, and even the life of Malcolm X he so ably depicted did not result in a definitive direction for black political film.

Everything Is Buddy-Buddy

Race relations, as depicted in American cinema in the 1980s and 1990s, were frequently represented in what came to be known as an interracial variation of "buddy movies." Typically, such films entailed an "odd couple"—a white and a black, frequently policemen—whose exploits were entertaining and also innocuous. The comedy revolved around the juxtaposition of stereotypical white and black social behaviors. The smash hit *48 Hrs* was a typical example and perhaps a progenitor of this minigenre. Circumstances oblige a white police officer (Nick Nolte) and a black convict (upcoming star Eddie Murphy) to work together to solve a crime. *48 Hrs* was a generally mindless crime romp; the real appeal of the movie (and its sequel) was the contrasting of a stereotypically white character with a black counterpart.

The success of *48 Hrs* meant that the same formula would be repeated numerous times in the 1990s in such popular releases as *Beverly Hills Cop* (1984) and *Lethal Weapon* (1988) and their various sequels. Although these very popular series and a host of derivative knockoffs did not seek to say anything beyond their superficial (yet frequently entertaining) action sequences, they did seem to imply an ultimately cozy relationship between the races that exceeded any social reality of the era. Hollywood seemed intent on smoothing over the social reality of race relations in the United States.

The fact that the black and white characters were typecast as so incompatible initially itself pointed to the idealization of race relations that such movies projected. Yet audiences clearly enjoyed many of these buddy movies, so perhaps a charitable interpretation is that they may have helped engender a more tolerant, if not necessarily enlightened, relationship between the races.

The black and white buddy concept was pushed to extremes by white director Quentin Tarantino's hugely popular *Pulp Fiction* (1994). *Pulp Fiction* is a loosely strung-together series of vignettes that feature phenomenally cool criminals. One of the central stories involves two supercool criminals portrayed by white actor John Travolta and black actor Samuel L. Jackson. The script calls for Jackson, particularly, to make frequent use of the offensive term *nigger,* albeit in a self-consciously hip way. Spike Lee criticized Tarantino for exploiting the term (which Tarantino also used frequently in his 1997 blaxploitation update, *Jackie Brown*), setting off a public feud between the two directors. The incident pointed to the greater issue of the political sensitivity of contemporary white directors' portrayal of black issues.

In *Driving Miss Daisy* (1989), for example, a grumpy old southern white woman is paired with a black chauffeur. Although they begin at odds with each other, by the end of the drama they realize what good friends they have become and how much they have in common. Immensely popular at the box office (and awarded the Best Picture Oscar award), the film seemed to project a liberal message of racial tolerance. But one critic, writing about *The Human Stain* (2003), in which Anthony Hopkins portrays an African-American passing as white, observed that such movies (like the buddy flicks) constitute "intellectual and moral comfort food. . . . They do not challenge the oddly soothing traditional template of racial thinking—the premise, which is increasingly a myth, that there are two and only two brightly delineated racial identities."[6] *The Human Stain* died at the box office, but offered a much more nuanced portrayal of race relations than many films that touch upon the subject.

A few more challenging films were offered by white directors in the 1990s. Steven Spielberg, who had explored racial issues before with *The Color Purple* (1986), directed *Amistad* (1997), a dramatization of the aftermath of a revolt by slaves on a ship bound for America in 1839. *Amistad* generated significant controversy on several fronts: Spielberg was accused of plagiarizing the script from a black author (the charge was settled out of court), and historians complained that he had taken too many liberties with the historical record. Although *Amistad* is somewhat compelling as entertainment, one critic wrote that it "quickly turns into another courtroom drama where the noble white people must save helpless black people."[7] By Spielberg's lofty standards of profitability, *Amistad* was a flop, barely earning its $40 million budget in domestic receipts.

Another history-based effort, Jonathan Demme's *Beloved* (1998) was an adaptation of a fact-based novel by black author Toni Morrison. The film received critical praise as a gripping depiction of the lives of ex-slaves after the Civil War, in part due to standout performances by stars Oprah Winfrey and Danny Glover. Yet it failed to recoup even half of its $53 million budget at the box office. Nonetheless, within the economic history of race in Hollywood, *Beloved* was significant for bringing to screen a famous literary novel by an African-American female author and for being produced by an African-American woman (Winfrey).

The Future of Black Films

The 1990s ended with what was perhaps Spike Lee's most racially provocative film yet, *Bamboozled* (2000). Lee explored racial stereotyping and exploitation in television and film in an over-the-top tale of a black, Harvard-educated television networking programmer, Pierre Delacroix (Damon Wayans), who tries to create a television show so offensive that he will be fired. Instead, *The ManTan Minstrel Show*—in which black performers perform racially demeaning slapstick in blackface—becomes a hugely popular hit, leaving Delacroix to defend himself as its creator. To call *Bamboozled* a satire is a gross understatement, and it is not an easy film to watch; aside from its cringe-inducing evocations of minstrel humor, Lee chose to shoot the film in digital video—consistent with the medium of television he is skewering, but also wearying. And as the plot progresses, it veers deeply into melodrama and away from the caustic satire it began with.

Nonetheless, *Bamboozled* contained many insightfully hilarious scenes as well as a serious political conversation. Critical reaction varied widely; Stephen Holden of the *New York Times* praised it: "In going where few have dared to tread, *Bamboozled* is an almost oxymoronic entity, an important Hollywood movie. Its shelf life may not be long, nor will it probably be a big hit, since the laughter it provokes is the kind that makes you squirm. But that's what good satire is supposed to do. Out of discomfort can come insight."[8] But many other critics considered *Bamboozled* an undisciplined and incoherent mess, and audiences avoided it.

A few recent films succeeded on the basis of telling stories with largely black casts that explored less stereotyped portrayals of black Americans. *Soul Food* (1997) tells the story of an extended black family in Chicago as seen through the eyes of its young narrator. Much of the drama revolves around the lives of the boy's mother and her two sisters, who are competing with each other on various levels. The movie was a modest crossover hit, and although it did not project an explicit political agenda, it did familiarize audiences with more realistic images of black families than are typically found in Hollywood films.

Another film that avoided black stereotypes was *Barbershop* (2002), which takes place at a barbershop with a primarily black clientele. The owner, Calvin (Ice Cube), sells the shop to a seedy character who intends to turn it into a strip club, and the action occurs on its last day of business. Most of the film centers on the conversations of the barbers and their clientele. Although not a film intended to make a political statement, *Barbershop* did arouse political controversy because of a comedic monologue by one of the barbers (played by Cedric the Entertainer) that invokes negative opinions about Rosa Parks, Rodney King, and O.J. Simpson. Some black leaders (notably the Reverend Jesse Jackson) argued that the film denigrated Rosa Parks by suggesting that her fame was somewhat undeserved and that the movie thus demonstrated the lack of appreciation for civil rights pioneers among young black Americans. The film's producers defended the scene, arguing that the lines were spoken by a character who is clearly the clown of the barbershop. If nothing else, the controversy demonstrated how political fissures in the black community make it difficult for even low-key films with black casts to succeed without race becoming an issue.

A 2003 movie with obvious political content, *Head of State,* spoofed race relations during the Bush administration's tenure. A weakly received political satire imagining comedian Chris Rock as president, the film's punch, such as it was, derived from how unlike the actual officeholder Rock's president was. It included scenes instructing fuddy-duddy white Washington how to dance, or "be black," as did that year's more lucrative *Bringing Down the House.* Both films relied on a seemingly outdated notion of race relations, with blacks teaching whites how to loosen up, and whites bestowing political or economic power on blacks for self-serving purposes masked as charitable.

On the whole, films with black political themes have been rare, and those that have fared well in the Hollywood environment are even rarer. Far more commonly, mainstream movies have featured blacks in stereotypical roles such as jokers, minstrels, sidekicks, and villains. A few black actors (such as Denzel Washington, Morgan Freeman, and Laurence Fishburne) and even fewer black actresses have transcended the constraints imposed by Hollywood to appear in films that more or less ignore race. At the creative level, Spike Lee remains perhaps the only African-American director with the cachet to delve into racially pointed political subject matter, and even his mainstream appeal seems to have ebbed. Although Hollywood's reluctance to take risks with black-themed films is a major obstacle, contemporary black political film seems mired and rudderless in the same way that black political leadership is. It may therefore be generally regarded as a reflection of the shifting sands of racial reality rather than a visionary beacon.

247

One interesting side note: A spate of recent films reprised paranoid political conspiracy thrillers of the 1970s like *The Parallax View* and *Three Days of the Condor.* Among these new films were *Enemy of the State* (1998), *Bait* (2000), and *The Manchurian Candidate* (2004). There were two key differences between the two eras' versions of this subgenre: this time around, African-American actors played the lead roles, and the conspiracies were driven by personal rather than institutional forces. As Roger Ebert says of *Enemy of the State:* "It's not the government that is the enemy, this movie argues, so much as bureaucrats and demagogues who use the power of the government to gain their own ends and cover their own tracks."[9] All three movies created paranoia around excessive governmental surveillance technology. By casting black male leads, the films suggested that a black voice crying conspiracy or speaking out against government intrusion may carry greater legitimacy than a white actor trying to convey the same message. Presumably, white stars are so thoroughly identified with the corruption of power and the confusion between political and Hollywood celebrity that it takes a black "truth teller" to achieve any credibility in the film's suspense. These films also suggested that in a terror-filled world, Hollywood suspects audiences would rather see a black male panic—a more familiar movie theme than white male uncertainty, given who for the most part holds the actual reins of national security.

Finally, a small cadre of black directors has emerged that has more or less successfully created films primarily geared to black audiences. Although the audience for these films is quite small, these directors may become more influential in the coming years. Ethiopian-born Haile Gerima, for example, directed *Sankofa* (1993), which explores the violent past of the African slave trade as a means of making a political point about the present. (*Sankofa* is an African word meaning "We must go back and reclaim our past so we can move forward, so we understand why and how we came to be who we are today.")[10] In the film, Mona, a black female model (Oyafunmike Ogunlano), finds herself reliving the past as a slave named Shala and participating in a slave revolt on an American plantation. Ultimately, Mona/Shala returns to the present profoundly changed by her experience. The *New York Times* noted that "*Sankofa* asks its audience to enter a different moral universe, one that slavery created."[11] Although shown almost exclusively in cinemas in black neighborhoods, *Sankofa* turned a handsome profit and demonstrated that a market exists for political black-themed films. Whether such films could make an impact on larger, crossover audiences remains an open question.

14

Women, Politics, and Film

All About Eve?

Elizabeth Ann Haas, PhD

The Contender (2000)

To consider the role of women and politics in American film inherently requires an expanded definition of what we mean by *political* because, historically, films expressly about the political process or government institutions rarely feature significant women characters. In most overtly ("pure") political films, women tend to melt into the background of a supporting role. They perform the cliché "behind every great man stands a woman." In general, their minimal importance in overtly political films speaks to women's political and economic subordination in a patriarchal society. In particular, it speaks to men's dominance in an industry as financially profitable as filmmaking.

Yet it would be a mistake to assume that the dearth of important female roles in pure political films means that women are irrelevant to these movies. Despite their subordinate role, and in some ways because of it, women are inseparable from any history of film, including any account of the intersection between politics and movies.

To begin with, it is worth noting generally that women have played more substantial, wide-ranging roles throughout the film industry than is commonly recognized. As recent revisionist accounts document, many female directors, writers, and producers enjoyed vibrant careers before the 1930s and the advent of the rigidly controlled studio system of film production. Recent efforts like the Turner Classic Movies series A Salute to Women Film Pioneers and the biography *Without Lying Down: Frances Marion and the Powerful Women of Early Hollywood* have begun to resurrect figures like Marion, once Hollywood's highest-paid screenwriter, and directors Alice Guy Blaché, Nell Shipman, and Lois Weber. Focus on their careers and salvaged "lost" films reveals that from the beginning of feature filmmaking women were forging an American cinematic legacy behind as well as in front of the camera. In fact, according to one film scholar, "There were more women working in the industry before 1920 than at any other time in history. More than 100 women directed films during the silent era."[1]

For the topic of women and politics in American film, the significance of this unearthed record affects our understanding of trends like the following: between 1910 and 1923 five separate versions of *Salome* were produced, and between 1917 and 1934 three versions of *Cleopatra* found their way to the screen. As early politically relevant films go, these stories stand out for dramatizing the myths and facts of two notorious yet mighty women at a time when the acceptability of women in American public places, from city streets to city hall, was undergoing epic change. Both stories show women exerting political power: Cleopatra is queen of Egypt, entangled in alliances partly romantic and partly political, while biblical Salome dances for King Herod in order that he do her bidding and behead John the Baptist, the wish of Salome's mother, the new queen. That these films equate female power undeniably political in its effect with sexual allure and also proved popular enough to support several remakes reflects widespread interest in and fear of women's shifting social, economic, and ultimately political place in American life during the first part of the century. They also point to a pattern consistent within Hollywood history: women on screen almost always represent sex. Whether they are queen or empowered to behead a man simply by shaking some booty, their significance almost always depends on sex.

Given the prominence of women in the industry during these years and their imminent eclipse from the scene, the recurrence of these stories may also hint at male attitudes toward women working within the industry itself.

At the same time, from the mid-1910s through the mid-1920s, director Lois Weber made films on political subjects like capital punishment and governmental corruption as well as on gender-defined topics such as birth control, prostitution, promiscuity, and abortion. Her moralizing films, unique in both form and content, tackled in more contemporary and transparent terms the sorts of issues that lay beneath the surface of the popularity of the historical dramas *Salome* and *Cleopatra.* Her work also sparked more controversy. In the pre-Hays Code days of her career, her movies prompted censorship hearings with the police shutting several of them down, events that only furthered her commercial success.

The more lucrative the movie business proved to be, however, the less able were women like Weber to maintain their stake in it. After all, women did not even have the right to vote until 1920, by which time Hollywood was on its way to becoming a virtual monopoly controlled by the executives of the top eight studios, none of them women. As a result, women's choices of film topics, like those important to Weber, ceased to have an advocate. The groundbreaking influence of these pioneers was subsequently erased from the archives when their films were lost or credited to other, usually male, directors. Such was the fate of Guy Blaché, who spent years of her life trying to set the record straight on her early film accomplishments. Only now, some forty years after her unmarked death in Mahwah, New Jersey, is she recognized as the first director ever to film a narrative story.[2]

Additionally, it is easy to see that despite the neglect of official film histories, women are everywhere in films, even when they have not exerted any direct control over their production. Given women's relative lack of political and economic status and their minimal impact on the actual production of films, we must look to the politics of the image and the "socially reflective" film to understand the significance of women within the topic of film and politics. That is, until the contemporary period, the political significance of women and film lies primarily in the images of women that films have generated as those images reinforce or challenge the prevailing social order, fulfill stereotypes or transcend them.

The following survey of the changing image of woman in American film looks at how mainstream movies reflect and shape values and attitudes about women. The list of films and defining images is highly selective, some might say idiosyncratically so, and of course incomplete. Moreover, the broad phrase "image of woman" usually refers to white, middle- and upper-class women—the fictional ideal Hollywood most often projects on screen.

Early Cinema

Precinematic inventions like Thomas Edison's Kinetoscope offered Americans their first glimpse of independently moving images. What did customers see when they stuck their noses into the soundless wooden cabinets? A man comically sneezing, a strongman flexing his muscles, boxers duking it out in a ring. Other favorite subjects befitting the peep-show quality of the single-viewer machines: women performing exotic dances, women scantily clad, women doing a partial striptease.

As this list suggests, many of the early films showed quotidian events: in *What Happened on Twenty-Third Street* (1902), a young woman on a busy street walks over a subway grate and must straighten out her billowing skirt. As that seemingly mundane example also implies, these early moving images expressed a theme of gender difference: women performing in sexually charged situations for an audience perceived as predominantly male. Though women themselves patronized the Kinetoscope arcades and later the Nickelodeon theaters, many notable early films featuring women obviously anticipated men as their customers and screened voyeuristic images of women accordingly. Films like *Pull Down the Curtains, Suzie* (1904) openly invoked the gender divide implicit in the anonymous viewer (voyeuristic) setting of this new entertainment: as Suzie leaves her companion to go into her room to change, he watches her disrobe from the street below her window.

By 1920 the silent movies had expanded in length to dramatize stories with characters and plot. At the same time, women were agitating for the right to vote and urban America was expanding as a site of industry, consumerism, and immigration both foreign and domestic as people from the country moved to the cities for work. The movies reflected and influenced this time of potential political chaos when staid nineteenth-century Victorian values and agrarian lifestyles gave way to modernity and what writer F. Scott Fitzgerald so famously dubbed the "Jazz Age."

The New Woman

This era's movies represent the shift away from an ideal of femininity as maternal, religiously pious, and submissive—the type of woman promoted in D.W. Griffith movies like *The Birth of a Nation* (1914) and *Way Down East* (1920). In those movies, women protected their chastity at all cost, wore long heavy skirts, swept floors, prepared meals, prayed, and did not do much else. *The Birth of a Nation* even equates America's national identity with the virginity and racial purity of a female character by requiring she kill herself rather than risk being raped by a renegade black soldier, then pinning her self-sacrifice to the "birthed" nation's new order of racial segregation. By 1920, the New Woman had arrived on screen. Popularized at the end of the previous century, the term *New Woman* referred to educated, ambitious women weary of their circumscribed place in society, namely the home. The New Woman advocated political and social emancipation for women, smoked in public, and wore less cumbersome clothing—baring arms and knees!—as she forayed into the city to shop and, increasingly, to work and live. This New Woman ushered three female types to the screen, as evidenced by the following popular films.

The Vamp

A Fool There Was (1915) brings to life a woman so completely lacking in the Victorian virtues of sexual restraint and obedience to men that her very presence is poisonous. The title refers to the lead male character, a fool of a man seduced by the New Woman presented in the guise of the female archetype, the vamp—short for vampire. The heartless vamp wants money and social status and will do anything to get them. Not yet thoroughly modern in appearance, she wears tightly wrapped long dresses and has kohl-lined eyes. The vamp look is nonetheless exotic as played by Theda Bara—considered by some the first true movie star—who made her career in this role. She would go on to star as both Cleopatra (1917) and Salome (1918). Bara's entire filmography—including *The Devil's Daughter* (1915), *Sin* (1915), *Siren of Hell* (1915), *The Vixen* (1916), *When a Woman Sins* (1918), *The She Devil* (1918)—telegraphs the era's obsession with female morality.

A Fool There Was, a huge hit for the fledgling Fox studio, dramatizes the rise and fall of the socially and politically prominent John Schuyler, newly tapped presidential envoy to England. Voyaging there without his wife and daughter, he falls prey to the unscrupulous vamp, so called because her surreal power to mesmerize men literally drains them of will. Her hypnotic power, carnal appetite, and unbowed attitude toward men appear as supernaturally evil. Still, what makes her emblematic of the New Woman is her explicitly sexual characterization and an unsentimental attitude succinctly expressed when she receives a gift of roses: after a brief whiff, she giddily shreds them to bits. Even more New Womanish is Schuyler's sister-in-law, who advises his wife to divorce him—a rare bit of advice for a woman to offer in those days of low divorce rates. Scenes depicting the vamp's decadence juxtaposed with Schuyler's rapid physical decay, a sign of his helpless addiction to her sexual favors, remain notable in a plot otherwise confusing for contemporary audiences to follow.

The Femme Fatale

More than a decade later, in 1927, F.W. Murnau directed *Sunrise* with a similar New-Woman-as-vamp theme, this time with a twist: the vamp hails from the city and the object of her seduction is an unassuming country boy. As a representative of the new cityscape's electric lights, tall buildings, and open-all-night atmosphere, this New Woman is more grounded in a recognizable reality. More femme fatale than vampire, she completely embodies the Jazz Age style with her androgynous bobbed hair, short dresses, and aggressive sexuality. The femme fatale seduces the rube and urges him to murder his wife, sell his property, and live the high life with her in the big city. The vivid contrast between city and country scenes and Murnau's evocative use of light and shadow make *Sunrise* an engaging film to watch even now.

The Flapper

A more benign version of the New Woman than either the vamp or the femme fatale, the flapper also earned plenty of screen time during this period. Fun-loving but not at all manipulative, enjoying clothes and unconventional behavior like dancing and drinking in speakeasies, the 1920s flapper inherited her spirit from the women who came before her flexing their political muscle. Suffragists won passage of the Nineteenth Amendment, earning women the right to vote; women leaders of the temperance movement helped to ratify the Volstead Act, the prohibition on alcohol. The flapper exploited women's greater freedom to have a good time.

Clara Bow famously became the first "It" girl playing a flapper in *It* (1927). The term *it* was code for sex appeal, but the girls who had "it" were less venal than either the femme fatale or the venomous vamp yet every bit the New Woman icon. In one telling scene, the flapper, preparing for a date, takes a modest dress, snips it here and there, adds a few decorative flourishes, and suddenly she's the very picture of "it": fashionable, free-spirited, flirtatious, and confident. The film was so popular that even today film and style magazines use the term *it* to refer to the ineffable cachet of newly popular stars. While men and women can both have "it," women especially wanted "it" because despite the liberties newly afforded women, from voting to drinking in mixed company, they were still primarily defined in relation to men. They were good girls if they had fun without leading men on; they were bad girls if they had fun with more than one man at a time. The films of this era (and beyond in many instances) reward good girls with marriage and punish bad girls by exiling them from marriage and the social circle.

From Flapper to Shop Girl

With the stock market crash and onset of the Depression, the movies looked to a more somber image of woman in the "social problem" film. The New Woman's loose sexual mores and style-conscious worldliness hardened into the dreary shopgirl or mill worker down on her luck. The movies dared not offer only escapist fantasies about self-indulgent characters without risk of alienating audiences who were experiencing wrenching economic distress. The modern woman therefore could not be viewed as simply enjoying the high life as either conniving seductress or lighthearted flapper anymore; she suffered and scraped to get by.

With the advent of the talkies in the 1930s, the movies as we now know them came to the fore of popular mass entertainment. Many evolving genres required certain parts for women: the gangster picture's gun moll, the musical's chorine, the women's picture's self-sacrificing mother, the screwball comedy's fast-talking romantic partner, the horror film's innocent victim. Not all but many of these parts were clearly incidental to the film's biggest themes. From getting her face smashed with a grapefruit by a hoodlum in the gangster classic *The Public Enemy* (1931) to playing love interest to both man and ape in *King Kong* (1933), the woman in popular Depression-era genres frequently had very little of substance to do. She reacted but she did not instigate. Films about social problems like unwed mothers, crime, and financially ruined families, however, often put women center stage, a symbol of endurance. These characters arguably stood as a rebuke to the New Woman who thought she could carouse all she wanted, paying little heed to the consequences of her behavior.

Four notable films starring Joan Crawford demonstrate this particular ideological shift regarding women's behavior. In 1928, Crawford gave a star-making performance in the silent film *Our Dancing Daughters,* a film so popular it spawned two more featuring virtually the same cast: *Our Modern Maidens* (1929) and *Our Blushing Brides* (1930). The quintessential high society flapper role of Diana put Crawford's chorus girl's legs to work dancing the Charleston in breathless party scenes. After watching Diana whip off her party dress to continue dancing in her slip, one male admirer asks, "You want to take all of life, don't you?" She responds, "Yes—all! I want to hold out my hands and catch at it." Her biggest dilemmas are choosing what dazzling dress to don and whether to wed her boyfriend. Marriage, she fears, would spoil her fun.

Only two years later, Crawford filmed the grim melodrama *Paid* (1930). Stripped of Diana's glamorous wardrobe, no-expenses-spared parties, and frivolous friendships, Crawford plays modest shopgirl Mary Turner, framed for a crime she did not commit. After three years in prison, she is freed but has turned into a hard-hearted criminal bent on revenge against the men who set her up, promising, "You're going to pay for everything I'm losing in life." Within two years the typical Crawford part has gone from carefree clothes-horse to bitter working-class girl, who spends at least part of each film in dreary smock-dresses, scrubbing floors and swearing to change her lot in life, not simply endure it. In *Possessed* (1931), she escapes dismal factory life on the arm of a rising but married political star. He keeps her in diamonds and furs but finds he must choose between her and his career, knowing that either a divorce or word of an affair would sink his campaign. The movie rewards her adultery when he chooses to forsake his pursuit of public office to keep her. (When the Hays Code went into effect a few years later to regulate movie morality, this rewarded sin would not make it past the censors.)

The reversal in fortune Crawford's characters undergo from *Our Dancing Daughters* to *Paid* and the opening of *Possessed* is the actual plot of *Dance, Fools, Dance* (1931). In this film, Crawford plays Bonnie Jordan, a typical flapper, wealthy and fun-loving. When her father loses his fortune in the stock market crash, Bonnie must trade her dancing togs for a reporter's notebook to earn her own living. Life is no longer hers to simply reach out her hands and "catch at"; now the dispossessed flapper must put those hands to work. Throughout the film, Bonnie's previous high-hat lifestyle proves useful to her investigative work and allows the film to have it both ways: it can revel in her former high-class sensibility and display conspicuous consumption while also showing the Depression's brutal, equalizing effect on her and people of her class. Also cast adrift by her father's bankruptcy, her brother, not as lucky as Bonnie, falls hard into a world of gangland theft and murder. While investigating a crime, Bonnie discovers her brother's plight but too late to save him. The film ends when Bonnie marries a man from her old life. He appreciates her anew for the lessons she has learned in self-reliance. After toppling her from her socioeconomic pinnacle and dramatizing her fall, the film at last rewards her for hard work and honest intent.

The Working Woman

The theme of working women recurred in many of the films produced in this period and extended into the era of World War II, when women took over work on railroads and in shipyards, steel plants, and other war industries as men went to fight with the armed forces overseas. The government campaigned for women to work these jobs with posters displaying "Rosie the Riveter" images of women working in men's uniforms at men's jobs. One such poster featured a soldier, a sailor, and a pilot pointing to a poster of a woman worker with the caption, "Their real pin-up girl." Another addressed openly the potential tension caused by women filling jobs formerly reserved for men with a picture of a woman in overalls and headscarf and a man standing protectively beside her: "I'm proud . . . my husband wants me to do my part."[3] With this kind of propaganda, the U.S. government promoted women in blue-collar jobs as patriotic. Meanwhile, women moving into professional careers interested director Frank Capra. One of his overtly politically populist films, the comic-melodramatic *Meet John Doe* (1941), prominently features a woman in the rise and fall of political innocent "John Doe."

To win back her job from the new owner of her newspaper, columnist Ann Mitchell invents in her farewell column a politically and socioeconomically alienated man called John Doe. A stand-in for all those ruined by the Depression, John Doe pledges to kill himself by jumping from a tower on Christmas Eve in protest against "man's inhumanity to man." People respond to his message, and Ann, played by Capra favorite Barbara Stanwyck, keeps her column. Soon John Doe fan clubs spring up everywhere, necessitating the hunt for a real John Doe. Ann discovers Long John Willoughby, a former baseball player turned vagabond, played by Gary Cooper, and turns him into her John Doe. All this pleases her new boss, big businessman strong-arm D.B. Norton, a fascist figure with his own private police squad. He is pleased, that is, until the clubs start to wield potential political influence beyond his control. Norton unmasks Willoughby. When Willoughby's supporters discover his ruse, he climbs the tower to kill himself anyway, feeling powerless to stop the widespread political disillusionment his fakery caused. Meeting him there at midnight, Ann tries to stop him from jumping but faints in his arms. Willoughby confronts Norton on the tower, too, and the film ends ambiguously, with Ann still unconscious and Norton still powerful, still lurking.

Important to the theme of working women, in this film Ann Mitchell dominates the film's storyline and determines the moral development of Willoughby. From casting Willoughby as her John Doe, to writing his speeches and motivating him to believe sincerely in a cause begun only as a publicity gimmick, to crossing Norton despite all the money he has thrown her way, Ann Mitchell is the film's engine. She is the good sport, the go-to gal. Her brains and her pluck set the plot in motion. While suspenseful, the film never turns into a forum on her sexual nature or questions where her political loyalties lie, and thus Ann plays more than prop to the film's male lead. That sign of female

257

proactivity distinguishes the movie from Capra's other political films. A smart movie addressed to smart women as well as men discovering women's competence in the world of work, *Meet John Doe* suggests that the absence of men from their traditional political and social roles was not all bad.

Woman in a World Gone Wrong

Barbara Stanwyck shows a different face of woman popularly on display just before, during, and immediately after World War II in the cycle of movies dubbed "film noir." A phenomenal hit then and a staple of film noir revival festivals today, *Double Indemnity* (1944) features Stanwyck as Phyllis Dietrichson, the quintessential femme fatale of 1940s film noir. A vamp in the tradition of *A Fool There Was* and *Sunrise*, Dietrichson meets life insurance salesman Walter Neff, played by Fred MacMurray. Clad in nothing but a towel and ankle bracelet, she seduces him. Like all femmes fatale, Phyllis resents her marriage and convinces Walter that she is her husband's victim, saying, "He keeps me on a leash so tight I can't breathe." Under the spell of her close-fitting sweaters and gardenia perfume, Neff agrees to murder her husband and help her reap the insurance money.

As if they were romantic partners in a 1930s screwball comedy, Phyllis and Walter match wits verbally, only the subtext to their banter is not just sex but the genre's theme of social alienation. The film's screenwriter and noir novelist, Raymond Chandler, describes the noir attitude as acknowledgement of a world gone wrong, "a world in which long before the atom bomb, civilization had created the machinery for its own destruction and was learning to use it with all the moronic delight of a gangster trying out his first machine gun. The law was something to be manipulated for profit and power. The streets were dark with something more than night."[4]

Through lies and double crosses the doomed lovers meet in director Billy Wilder's famous climax. Filmed in the noir style of extreme light and dark, the film's penultimate scene positions Phyllis as the center of a web cast by the room's shadows and the lines of her blouse. Still unique in film up to that time, Phyllis acting the man's part, pulls a gun from her dress and shoots Walter. In a romantic clutch with him, she admits she never loved him or anybody else. He kills her before hobbling back to the insurance office to confess his crimes, a futile but ennobling act when compared with Phyllis's cold admission.

Duplicitous and castrating, Phyllis epitomizes the self-serving noir woman. Neff laments, "I killed him for money and for a woman. I didn't get the money . . . and I didn't get the woman." But in noir the spider woman derives no pleasure from her wicked ways either. Phyllis is not only antiromantic and greedy in this world gone wrong; she is something even worse in Hollywood's eyes: she is antifamily. Avaricious to the core, she puts no one's needs above her own. Her selfishness extends to her stepdaughter, Lola. While seducing Neff, Phyllis is also seeing Lola's boyfriend behind her back, the ultimate in maternal treachery.

The cautionary tale of the noir femme fatale warns against women assuming greater agency through work on the assembly line or in the office by equating their empowerment in real life with the destruction of the prewar family in movies. Film noir anxiety caused by working women is most pronounced in *Laura* (1944) and *Mildred Pierce* (1945). Both title characters conquer commercially—Laura in advertising, Mildred in the restaurant business—but falter emotionally, with Laura falling for a cad and Mildred Pierce failing as a mother. Like Phyllis, these characters upend traditional expectations that women know their own heart, instinctively care for their children, and put their husbands first. The entire genre's cynicism expresses tacit nostalgia for a time when everyone knew where a woman could be found: in the home, with the children, out of sexual and economic circulation.

Woman on the Verge

By the 1950s, the masculinity-challenging, home-wrecking, noir femme fatale lost momentum on screen. With men back at home and on the job in postwar America, certain strands of Hollywood ideology suggested that women should resume their part as nurturing and faithful. Femininity no longer implied ambition, much less promiscuity, some of that decade's most popular films said. After three decades of women on screen seducing, deceiving, and in rare instances killing men, however, it was too late to close Pandora's box. These mixed messages created a view of women as slightly mad. Neither marriage nor failing to marry enables this postwar woman to cope. Films like *Possessed* (1947), *Harriet Craig* (1950), *Executive Suite* (1954), *A Woman's World* (1954), and *Queen Bee* (1955) stuff women back into the domestic, frequently suburban, realm of submission to their husbands and watch as they panic. The eponymous Harriet Craig works at her housekeeping like a profit-driven corporate executive. Putting so much effort into producing a spotless, perfectly appointed home, however, reaps no profit, only an oppressive hysteria. *Executive Suite*'s Julia Treadway owns a controlling share of stocks in a company whose chief executive has just died. Suicidal over his death and her own spinsterhood, she has the power to decide the man to replace him. A 1940s woman would have boldly set up a man for the job, seduced or murdered him, and acquired the company herself. Treadway, on the other hand, is so distraught over her wasted, unmarried life she breaks down sobbing—on the ledge of the company's top-story office. In *There's Always Tomorrow* (1956), the murderous lovers of *Double Indemnity,* Stanwyck and MacMurray, meet again. This time, he plays a happily married man feeling unappreciated by wife and kids. She plays a single woman from his past who forgoes her own desire for him to steer him back toward the family that needs him, a self-sacrifice unthinkable for a noir woman. In these 1950s dramas, the world of crime and scheming women has been replaced by the corporate boardroom and stay-at-home moms.

The same period witnessed a renewed idealization of the blond bombshell with the hourglass figure. That image of woman replaces the androgynous, at times masculine look of the long, lean, shoulder-padded women of the 1940s. The 1950s female stars share more in common with curvaceous, pre-war sex symbols like the bawdy Mae West in *I'm No Angel* (1933), who quips, "It's not the men in your life that count, it's the life in your men." The 1950s said good-bye to the likes of Crawford and Stanwyck as "It" girls and hello to Betty Grable, Lana Turner, and Marilyn Monroe. The "new look," as magazines dubbed the fashion trend these stars promoted, took advantage of postwar prosperity to use yards of extra material in large poofed skirts, cinched at the waist. These dresses emphasized the so-called wasp figure of exaggerated chest, slim waist, and exaggerated behind. As embodied by Monroe in movies like *Monkey Business* (1952), *How to Marry a Millionaire* (1953), and *The Seven Year Itch* (1955), the sexy woman of the 1950s was also part child, her sexuality endlessly open and available. Her characters regularly delivered lines like this from *The Seven Year Itch*: "There I was with a perfectly strange plumber—and no polish on my toenails." Her ditzy qualities mitigated her sexiness so she posed no threat to the suburbanized, corporate man or even his wife.

The wasp figure promoted by the "new look" took on ironic meaning in another Hollywood female trope of the era: the monstrous woman. Movies like *Attack of the Fifty-Foot Woman* (1958) and *The Wasp Woman* (1959) turned the frustration and hysteria of domestically trapped women inside out. Rather than experiencing the fear and paranoia herself, she projects it onto her own exterior, the better to terrorize others. These films translate her panic into her weapon. While they also clearly point to fears of nature gone berserk in the nuclear age, these films tellingly use women to project that fear.

A comparison was also made between the shape of the nuclear missile, so present in public consciousness after the nuclear bombing of Japan in 1945, and the 1950s screen fashion of the cone-shaped bra. The missile-breasts feature prominently in scenes as diverse as the showgirl musical routines performed by Jane Russell and Monroe in *Gentlemen Prefer Blondes* (1953), Julie Adams's swim scene in *Creature from the Black Lagoon* (1954), and

Janet Leigh disrobing in *Touch of Evil* (1958) and *Psycho* (1960). The missile-bra comparison equates fear of women with fear of the nuclear bomb and suggests that women's sexuality in the wake of the family destroying 1940s femme fatale remains potentially deadly.

Femme Fatale Redux

The 1980s and 1990s occasioned a comeback for the noir femme fatale in some of the era's most popular films: *Body Heat* (1981), *Against All Odds* (1984), *No Way Out* (1987), *Fatal Attraction* (1987), *Basic Instinct* (1992), and *The Last Seduction* (1994). The revival of noir themes that define women as dangerous enigmas invites review of these films' wider political and social context: the "second wave" of feminism. Influenced by the civil rights movement, women in the 1960s and 1970s organized to protest sex discrimination in education, housing, employment, and public spaces. They fought for equal pay and legalization of contraception and abortion, and they marched to support the equal rights amendment (ERA) just as first-wave feminists had marched for the vote more than a half century before. Though the ERA failed, other laws and court rulings did prohibit discrimination on the basis of sex, and women were elected to national office not as widows of congressmen but in their own right for the first time.

Culturally and politically, the United States changed in the wake of this second-wave agitation. Many women did not feel obliged to define themselves socially and sexually through marriage, and they moved into previously off-limits vocations. Men resisted but were expected as never before to shoulder child-rearing and housekeeping duties if for no other reason than to compensate for working women's absence from the home. In this way, second-wave feminism affected both political and personal realms, with women forcing subjects like rape and domestic violence to the fore as part of their movement for greater emancipation and legal rights.

A range of popular movies made just before the noir revival reflected these shifts and celebrated women's independence. *Alice Doesn't Live Here Anymore* (1974) begins by making a widow of Alice, compelling her slow, often comic ascent toward self-sufficiency and self-awareness as a single mother. Set during World War II, the Academy Award–winning drama *Julia* (1977) showed off women practicing political subversion and espionage while cultivating a meaningful relationship with each other, independent of men. *The Turning Point* (1977) compared a lonely but successful ballet star with her friend who sacrificed her own artistic aspirations to become a wife and a mother. *Norma Rae* (1979) showcased a single woman's political awakening without adding romantic entanglement to her evolution, while *Coming Home*

(1978) charted a military wife's evolving political consciousness through a sexual awakening outside her marriage in the era of Vietnam. At the end of the 1970s, *Kramer vs. Kramer* (1979) portrayed divorce and ensuing custody battles as the bitter harvest of the women's movement, yet *An Unmarried Woman* (1978), made only the year before, posed divorce as liberation and the means to women's self-confidence and career fulfillment.

By the 1980s, conservative Republican politicians like Ronald Reagan and anti-ERA leaders like Phyllis Schlafly succeeded in their opposition to the women's movement and the politics of sexual liberation. Strengthened by a rise in Christian fundamentalism, the New Right argued that feminist agitation weakened the moral fiber and anti-Communist strength of the United States. Conservatives claimed that feminism's goals, especially abortion rights, doomed "traditional family values" and that with the family in decline the entire country was sure to follow. This sky-is-falling rhetoric resonated with the American public even though the U.S. economy depended on women in the workforce.

At the same time, independent of gender ideology, baby boomer families discovered that they required two incomes simply to maintain the lifestyle their parents had known and they expected to enjoy themselves. This combination of disparate pressures on women to embark on careers previously denied them or to carry their weight financially while also playing "mom" showed up in the movies in patterns reminiscent of classical Hollywood's response to shifting gender roles and economic upheaval during the Jazz Age and World War II. In general, films of this period punish women for the very pursuits that films of the previous decade honored. Many of them figure into the backlash against feminism, a cultural phenomenon most prominently documented in Susan Faludi's 1991 seminal *Backlash: The Undeclared War Against American Women.*

Fatal Attraction

Despite mostly poor reviews, *Fatal Attraction* was the second highest grossing film of 1987, earned several Academy Award nominations including Best Picture, and became one of the most controversial films in recent movie history. Talk shows talked about it, comedy sketch shows parodied it, and newspapers covered it as news. So popular was the film that its title entered the cultural lexicon as a way to indicate obsession turned pathological, particularly a frustrated single woman's obsession with a man or simply her lack of husband and kids. Independent, professionally successful Alex, played by Glenn Close, embodied the film's controversy and became a litmus test for viewers' opinions of feminism. Whether a viewer hated Alex and cheered her demise or rooted for her against the movie's own obvious allegiances said something about that person's attitude toward feminism. *Fatal Attraction* spawned numerous imitations, from *Single White Female* (1992) and *Hand That Rocks the Cradle* (1992) to *The Crush* (1993) and the recent *Swimfan* (2002). These knockoffs suggested that all females, from teens to nannies, contain the seeds of paranoid obsession about men and psychotic envy of other women who enjoy lives validated by men that the psychos attract but cannot keep. (As perhaps the ultimate sign of cultural significance, *Fatal Attraction* also inspired 1993's movie spoof, *Fatal Instinct*.)

Fatal Attraction presents Dan, played by Michael Douglas, a happily married, successful lawyer living in New York City but contemplating a house in the country. His wife, Beth, played by Anne Archer, is beautiful and kind, so devoted to their young daughter that she allows her to take Dan's place in bed with her while Dan is out walking the family dog. When wife and daughter leave for the weekend, Dan has a sexually heated fling with Alex, a publisher he meets through work. Dan describes their arrangement as "two adults who saw an opportunity and took advantage of it." The masculine-named Alex agrees to play by boys' rules, but when Dan ditches her to resume his role as husband and father, she reneges. "I will not be ignored," she threatens. Desperate for his attention, she attempts suicide, swaying him with her despair, then turning on him violently when his sympathy proves temporary. Pregnant and wanting to have the child against Dan's expectations or wishes, Alex tightens the psychological noose as he tries to escape with his family to the country. In the film's climax, Dan saves Beth from Alex's butcher knife by drowning Alex in the bathtub, only to watch her rise from the tub again ready to kill. Finally Beth shoots Alex in the heart, and the film ends with intimations of a tested but restored family peace.

The film sparked intense public debate. Feminists vehemently criticized its over-the-top vilification of the career-minded independent woman. They saw conservative backlash in the way the film first pitted the black-leather-clad Alex against the softly lit, doe-eyed, stay-at-home Beth, then made it clear that, compared to Beth's assets of a successful husband and adorable child, Alex's professional accomplishments amount to nothing. While the women's movement depended upon women joining forces for the benefit of all, this film marked women as the natural enemy of other women. As feminist critics also pointed out, the film both punishes Alex for expressing her sexual desire and exploits that openness to titillate viewers, while allowing Dan to atone for his sexual indiscretion with choices unavailable to Alex. Dan's abdication of Alex's pregnancy, justified by her psychotic behavior, also seemed to mock women's struggle for reproductive freedom.

Other viewers saw Dan and Beth as smug yuppies, a category coined in the 1980s to refer to young urban professionals. From this perspective, Beth and Dan's self-contained, self-satisfied world deserved destruction by Alex's wrath.[5] Alex's fierce, homicidal characterization thus energizes the film in subversive contrast to the rule-obeying, dependent Beth.

Still other critics saw Alex as the source of irrevocable depravity that the film needed to vanquish in order to end satisfactorily. Director Adrian Lyne's original ending, included on the DVD release, involves planted evidence and Alex turned suicidal again. It hits a much more morally ambiguous note than the Beth versus Alex/good versus bad shoot-out resolution. Test audiences, however, rejected any fate for Alex other than death at the hands of Beth. They seemed to echo the politics of the New Right and its opposition to changing mores and gender dynamics by advocating revenge against Alex and death to the threat she posed to "family."

Alex's horror movie resurrection at film's end compares her to the mesmerizing vamp of *A Fool There Was* and attributes to her desires and motives a supernatural force defiant of any plausible, much less sympathetic, psychology. She is not so much woman wronged or even woman blinded by desire as symbol of evil. As more than one critic has pointed out, her transformation from attractive, confident professional to hysterical shrew, monstrous in her desire, undermines the feminist stands she takes to defend herself within the film.[6] As with the 1940s noir femme fatale, Alex's designs oppose the traditional family, but unlike her "husband and home bore me" predecessors, winning for Alex means stealing domestic bliss for herself. While the old femme fatale wanted no part of such monotony, this one kills for it.

The film's reactionary politics, while still resonant in such issues as the political viability of former first lady Senator Hillary Rodham Clinton, nonetheless now have a dated quality to them. Many contemporary fans value the film for its camp appeal or its visual sumptuousness and sharp direction.

Basic Instinct *and* Disclosure: *The Michael Douglas Factor*

Notorious neonoir films from the early 1990s, *Basic Instinct* and *Disclosure* (both 1994) also demonized productive independent women. The blockbuster hit *Basic Instinct* ignited controversy with its explicit depiction of sex and violence and its bisexual femme fatale. Accused of homophobia and misogyny, the story line provoked protests from gay and lesbian groups before filming had even finished. *Disclosure,* a less commercially successful film, courted feminist outrage by portraying sexual harassment as a matter of women exploiting men. The film posed this peculiar gender reversal despite the famous Supreme Court nomination hearings three years earlier when former employee Anita Hill alleged sexual harassment against Clarence

Thomas in a Senate hearing almost entirely composed of men. *Disclosure* also made the woman the villain and the man her victim, counter to the overwhelming number of actual harassment cases filed in the wake of the landmark Thomas hearings.

Fatal Attraction, Basic Instinct, and *Disclosure* coalesce around male lead Michael Douglas to solidify his acting persona as an everyday guy made to suffer the manipulations of unstable, predatory, but somehow also professionally successful women. As he says in *Disclosure* when asked how he will cope, "Grin and bear it like I usually do and hope it doesn't get any worse." The repeated casting of Douglas underscores the ideology that the movies promote, rendering explicit what might have remained implicit with a different male lead. Each film associates female encroachment on Douglas's character's work domain with persecution of him. In *Fatal Attraction,* Alex's publishing company hires his law firm, providing her the chance to seduce and then terrorize him. In *Basic Instinct,* cynical, trigger-happy cop Nick Curran must interview famous thriller author Catherine Tramell, played by Sharon Stone. Catherine's novels imply she knows more about actual crimes than he does, putting her in charge of their initial encounters. *Disclosure* begins with the symbolic emasculation of computer expert Tom Sanders by setting him up for a promotion that goes instead to the ruthlessly ambitious and sexually rapacious Meredith Johnson, played by Demi Moore.

In their overlapping themes and use of Michael Douglas, this trio of films equates female ambition with virulence to send the message that the goal of harmonious family life and the goal of successful men and women sharing the workplace are mutually exclusive. Women are thus the enemy of men except when women are where the New Right would keep them: in the home, tending the kids.

Working Girls

Other films from the 1980s and 1990s took the theme of working women and made comedy of it. The hugely popular *9 to 5* (1980) is a revenge fantasy in which women working anonymous jobs in giant corporations finally get even. Three assistants, played by Jane Fonda, Lily Tomlin, and Dolly Parton, slave for a male boss played by Dabney Coleman, a "sexist, egotistical, lying, hypocritical bigot." Fed up with his abuse and his habit of taking credit for their ideas, they tie him up at his house and take over the office. Under their management, productivity goes up as they instigate employee-friendly programs like child care, flextime, and job sharing. The film was such a success that it led to the creation of two television situation comedies of the same title, and the theme song provided an Academy Award–nominated hit for Parton. A seemingly frothy exercise in wish fulfillment, this film at heart offers a sharp satire on the topic of chauvinism and the routine use of women in ways inappropriate to the work environment.

Baby Boom (1987) comically addressed the culture's burning question of whether women could "have it all," both demanding career and full-time family, and was popular enough to spur a television series, too. Unlike the female support staff of *9 to 5,* lead character J.C. Wiatt, played by the unlikely Diane Keaton, is the boss of her office. Known as "the tiger lady," J.C. epitomizes the fearsome professional woman forsaking family life for a high-powered career as an advertising executive. Known for her competitive drive, J.C. thrives in a world dominated by men until the day she inherits a long lost cousin's baby and her compulsively ordered life turns chaotic. Comedy derives from the incompatibility of mothering and career success, with J.C. tossing off lines like "I can't have a baby—I have a 12:30 lunch meeting" and "I went to Yale and Harvard, I don't have children." Despite J.C.'s efforts to put up the baby for adoption, her live-in lover dumps both her and their posh DINK lifestyle, the term coined in the 1980s meaning "double income, no kids." The baby thus quashes her love life and jeopardizes her career.

Forced to quit her high-powered position when predictably she decides against adoption, J.C. retreats with the baby to Vermont, where she at last masters the art of mothering and, as a direct consequence, the film implies, falls in love with the local vet. Meanwhile, her type-A personality resurfaces when she invents a recipe for baby applesauce so tasty that she successfully markets it nationwide and gets to reject her old advertising firm's bid to direct her new product's ad campaign. While audiences enjoyed the fantasy, critics were not as enthusiastic, noting the film's heavy-handed message about saving the endangered nuclear family. As one critic acidly put it, "From time to time, Hollywood likes to make movies that assuage some of the guilt that it feels for being such a superficial, unthinking, materialistic behemoth. *Baby Boom* is one of these films—a typically 1980s movie whose essential message is 'making money and living in flash apartments is all well and good, but what we all really want is to have kids and live in an old house making jam.'"[7]

J.C. Wiatt's look in this film is also "typically 1980s": she sports shoulder-padded, exquisitely fitted business suits the better to "pass" as a man in a man's world, the New York advertising scene. When Diane Keaton famously wore men's ties and jackets as part of her *Annie Hall* (1977) clothing ensemble, that look playfully connoted women's struggle for gender parity but within the film's story line amounted to a choice, a fashion whimsy. In the more romantic of the two comedies, *Annie Hall*'s male-inspired attire is a flirtation aid, while the tiger lady's version renders fashion a mandatory uniform. In *Baby Boom,* Keaton's costuming raises the stakes to male impersonation, similar to the shoulder-padded look of 1940s film heroines like Mildred Pierce. Clothing and location cues both say that J.C. becomes a real woman only when she discovers her maternal instincts, flees the city, and ditches the suits. When she gets it all at film's end—baby, man, and business—she forfeits neither family nor wealth, just the office masquerade.

In this respect, *Baby Boom* presents a subtle riff on the earlier *Tootsie* (1982) and *Mr. Mom* (1983), two significant comedies about gender politics featuring men in various degrees of female impersonation. A critical and box office hit, *Tootsie* stars Dustin Hoffman as Michael, an actor unable to get work until he auditions in drag for a female lead in a soap opera. (The fallacy here is that women can gain employment more easily than men can in this post-ERA era, one of the fears promulgated by the anti-ERA lobby.) Throughout the film, Michael-as-Dorothy endures the come-ons and belittlement of reliable chauvinist Dabney Coleman while playing mother, confidante, and friend to numerous characters. His trials as Dorothy lead Michael to reveal his identity at the end by declaring that being a woman has made him a better man. *Mr. Mom* follows a similar trajectory when Michael Keaton's character, Jack, loses his job, dons an apron, and takes over the household while his wife goes to work full-time. Like J.C. Wiatt's transformation in *Baby Boom,* Jack's drag performance is not literal but supposes that men and women, work and home are so at odds with each other that leaving one realm to succeed in the other requires an identity change nearly that drastic. Though not as well known as *Tootsie, Mr. Mom* sends a similar message about learning new respect for women. It stresses more emphatically, however, the financial imperatives that dictate the divide between running a household and holding down a job when Jack's overworked wife becomes as absent from the home as he was before turning into Mr. Mom. When neither spouse gets it all, the ending implicitly gives a thumbs-down to an economy that demands such an unhappy trade-off of its workers, regardless of gender.

Drag of a different sort plays a key part in *Working Girl* (1988) when a secretary masquerades as her upper-class boss. The not-so-subtle reference of the title to prostitution remains a subtext in this romantic comedy that is more interested in issues of class than the divide between family life and career women.

At the film's center is Tess McGill, played by the girlish-voiced Melanie Griffith, a secretary with a working-class pedigree and white-collar ambition. When she discovers that her new boss is a woman, Tess thinks her climb up the corporate ladder will be infinitely easier. Katharine Parker, played with devious glee by Sigourney Weaver, mouths all the right platitudes but proves to be every bit the manipulative user that Tess's male boss was. Tess's illusions about Katharine as a mentor are shattered when Tess discovers

Katharine's plans to use an idea Tess pitched to her and claim credit for herself. When Katharine breaks her leg skiing, Tess sees her opportunity and grabs it by passing herself off as the boss, wearing Katharine's couture clothing and imitating her hairstyle. The transition Tess undergoes from secretary to management by the end of the film is thus as much about knowing how to look successful as it is about having the brains and guts to take charge. To complete the impersonation of business acumen, she must renounce her "working girl" big hair and seductive clothing to adopt the upper-crust style of the low-voiced, porcelain-skinned Katharine with the sculpted face. What is more, she must leave behind her blue-collar neighborhood and friendships.

The film pits Tess against Katharine in the boardroom *and* the bedroom, as Tess slowly falls for Katharine's boyfriend, not realizing who he is. Played by Harrison Ford, Jack Trainer, who is not as enamored of Katharine as she is of him, is attracted by Tess's genuine sweetness and authenticity, qualities that manipulative "tiger lady" Katharine lacks. Unlike the group spirit animating *9 to 5,* this film divides women against each other along the lines of *Fatal Attraction,* suggesting that only one woman is woman enough for both Jack and the job. For one woman to win, the other must lose according to this backlash logic. The film thus lauds Tess's pluck while vilifying Weaver's forceful presence and her aggressive sexuality on humiliating display when she tries to seduce Jack.

Despite or perhaps owing to this rift between Katharine and Tess, the film's closing images of Tess and Jack making a home together suggest an equal partnership between the sexes. Neither character sacrifices for the other as they help each other get coffee and breakfast before heading out to work. The final image seals Tess's triumphant replacement of Katharine: she is now "boss," with her own secretary and a high-rise office with a view. Though Tess makes a point of telling her secretary how fairly she will treat her, *Working Girl*'s comedy relies on ginned-up rivalry between women for its entertainment fuel.

Avenging Angels

If many movies in the 1980s and 1990s counted on audiences to enjoy the sight of women competing with each other for men and jobs, a few unleashed feminine rage squarely at men. *Ms. 45* (1981), *Extremities* (1986), *The Accused* (1988), and *Thelma and Louise* (1991) all concern the problem of justice in the crime of rape. Unlike *Straw Dogs* (1972), which dramatized rape as an insult to the victim's husband and his perceived emasculation through her suffering, or *Deliverance* (1972), which featured a male rape, these films take their female victim's point of view entirely. More importantly, they allot their female protagonists the chance, even obligation, to mete out vengeance. The four movies differ in how far each assault victim is willing to go for reprisal and the means by which she exacts her revenge. The harshest and most excessively violent revenge occurs in the exploitation thriller *Ms. 45,* directed by the controversial Abel Ferrera, and the most attenuated occurs in *Thelma and Louise,* a combination of buddy flick and road movie, directed by Ridley Scott from an Academy Award–winning script by Callie Khouri.

All four of these movies follow in the wake of Susan Brownmiller's watershed book *Against Our Will: Men, Women and Rape,* published in 1975. This comprehensive study defines rape as a crime of coercion and domination of women, reflective of the society in which it occurs, rather than as a strictly violent, sexual act isolated from the public sphere. To rebel against the culture of rape is to struggle against the male dominance that allows men to rape with impunity and encourages a view of women as submissive to men personally and subordinate to men publicly. Such a perspective on rape derives from the second-wave feminist notion that "the personal is the political." The women's movement thus brought rape out of its shroud of secrecy as activists argued against the prevailing idea that rape was a private event that shamed its victims as much as if not more than its perpetrators. Among other effects, these feminist protests resulted in "rape shield" laws that restricted defense attempts to humiliate victims and weaken their cases by airing their sexual histories in court. The aim was to prevent trials from turning into referenda on the issue of whether a victim was "asking for it." These movies all turn on some version of that same question.

Ms. 45 presents two rapes in its first fifteen minutes. A mute woman working at a lowly job in the fashion industry gets raped on her way home from work and then again when she arrives home and catches a burglar mid-robbery. These violations transform her from a meek, subservient creature into a dressed-to-the-nines, gun-toting, one-woman vigilante force, the Avenging Angel of the film's alternate title. A cult favorite, *Ms. 45* is a bloody contribution to the rape-revenge cycle as Thana, played unforgettably by Zoe Tamerlis, starts blowing away almost any man who looks her way. Called "intensely disturbing yet sexy, clever, intelligent, and even funny," *Ms. 45* was not a mainstream hit, and its perspective, presented within the exploitative revenge fantasy genre, did not address a mainstream audience by any means.[8]

Yet the film also comments indirectly on class issues by suggesting that Thana's seamstress job oppresses her almost as much as the violence to her body and the violation of her home. She is a constant victim, poorly dressed, but when she straps on the gun to take charge of her own destiny, Thana also dons sexy clothes, as if she is indeed "asking for it," the faster to attract and kill her offenders. With this transformation of character registered through her come-hither costuming, the film ironically comments on rape court cases in which a woman's clothing can be presented as evidence that no crime actually occurred since a woman dressed in this manner is clearly inviting rape. Thana's muteness drives the power of Tamerlis's performance and implies the inherent defenselessness of women and their relatively voiceless political position within patriarchal culture. This film suggests that as instruments of male-sanctioned power, the police and courts are useless so, to foment change, women must take justice and self-defense into their own hands.

Extremities, based on a successful stage play, also distrusts police willingness and capability to assist women rape victims. The movie dramatizes the plight of a woman survivor of an assault whom the police refuse to help, even though the attacker stole her wallet in his aborted rape attempt. Even as the police deny her further assistance—"If he calls, let us know and we'll send a man round"—the rapist plots his attack on her at home. Played convincingly by former pinup star Farrah Fawcett, Marjorie fights for her life against her attacker, and then turns the tables on him when she captures him and locks him away in her house. Once he is at her mercy, she finds herself paralyzed to turn him in and unable to refrain from torturing him. Despite the film's attempt to let Marjorie's roommates complicate the ethical question of how to treat this criminal, once she cages him, the film runs out of steam. Fawcett won the somewhat astonished praise of critics for her performance, but the film flopped at the box office.

The much more commercially and critically successful *The Accused* presents a twist on these vigilante scenarios by portraying a legal system that first fails its rape victim with a plea bargain for her attackers, then redeems itself by successfully prosecuting a second trial. This film also addresses issues of socioeconomic class by presenting the rape victim, Sarah, as working-class and the setting of her rape a seedy, working-class bar. (Jodie Foster won a Best Actress Academy Award for her role as Sarah.) Sarah, with her rough talk and cheap, provocative style of dress, contrasts with the sophisticated attorney prosecuting her case, Kathryn, played by real-life rape victim Kelly McGillis. (This fact was publicized at the time of the film's release.) When the original trial results in a plea bargain for the rapists, Sarah interrupts a quiet, sophisticated dinner party at Kathryn's tastefully appointed home to accuse Kathryn of selling her out. With license plates reading "Sexy Sadie" and low-slung shirts, Sarah represents the "accused" of the title who must both defend her drunken, flirtatious behavior at the bar and fight for her own case to go forward. Kathryn finally redeems herself by becoming a true advocate for Sarah, validating the system by successfully prosecuting the men who egged on and cheered the rape.

In the presentation of the prosecution's case at the end, the film depicts the rape for the first time, leading some critics to cry exploitation since the graphic scene serves as the film's visual climax, a tacit endorsement of the crime's sexual titillation for viewers. By suppressing the sight of the rape for most of the film, the narrative payoff at the end presents the rape as a visual reward. The film also suggests that sanctioned legal channels can address rape with satisfactory results for the victim, a message contrasting with that of lower-budgeted or independently made films like *Ms. 45* and *I Spit on Your Grave* (1977), which advocate revenge by any means available, the bloodier the better.

The most popular of these films, *Thelma and Louise,* features two rapes, one on-screen, the other off. The on-screen rape occurs when two best friends, a submissive housewife and a waitress at a diner, abandon husband and boy-friend to hit the road for a weekend fishing vacation. They stop at a honky-tonk bar where the married Thelma, played movingly by Geena Davis, flirts with, then gets hit on by a man who knows she is drunk. He takes her out back to the parking lot, but just as the assault begins, Louise, played by flinty-eyed Susan Sarandon, arrives with a gun. (For both actresses this was a name-making film.) She shoots him and the two take off, with the police eventually in pursuit. *Thelma and Louise* implies that a rape in her past motivates Louise's act of extreme violence and her fugitive reaction to the crime. Her past tells her to distrust the police's ability or willingness to believe their self-defense version of events. From experience, she believes that Thelma faced serious trouble in that parking lot.

On the lam, the two shed their hausfrau apparel for roadworthy duds, an outward transformation symbolic of inner evolutions from weak to strong, from subdued to daring, from carefree friends to committed partners. A pa-ternal cop, played by Harvey Keitel, takes their case and comes to care so much about them that by film's end he berates a man for stealing their get-away money. He claims to know the secret truth about Louise's past, the event that haunts her and compels her to run. That he never spells out di-rectly what he "knows" suggests the elusive grip patriarchy still has on these characters even as they blaze a new path for themselves and for the legion of women fans the film attracted.

The film's attitude toward rape is complicated in some respects by Thelma's sexual awakening in a tryst with a hitchhiker the two allow on board with them. An indictment of her unfaithful and abusive husband, Thelma's thrill at the young man's attentions cuts against the story's subplot of Thelma and Louise rejecting the men in their lives and coming to trust only each other. This growing devotion to each other and rebellion against their past social roles, especially as they had been treated and defined by men, invited con-demnation from critics. Many deplored the film as feminist propaganda and antimale. That kind of reaction led other critics to qualify their take on the film's politics. For example, critic Rita Kempley felt compelled to announce: "That's not to say that Thelma and Louise are male-bashers or that the movie is a load of spiteful feminism. . . . This liberating adventure has a woman's perspective, yes, but one that aims to give moviegoers of both sexes an ungirdled good time." [9]

In the end, cornered by the police and clutching each other in the sort of embrace Hollywood reserves for heterosexual couples, the two sail out over a canyon in their convertible and the film freeze-frames them in mid-flight. While manifest destiny remains a driving spirit in traditional westerns, this movie suggests that the only truly liberated space for women is as yet uncharted or, more pessimistically, open to them only in death.

Contemporary Pure Political Films and Women

In the contemporary era, movies featuring both political content and intentional political messages involve major female players usually when gender is one of the ideological issues driving the story. Despite or even owing to the women's movement, the election of women to national office in numbers that defy tokenism, and the overall headway made by women in professions once deemed men-only, movies still entertain the question of what female empowerment means in society and in politics.

Viewed as usurpers of traditional patriarchy and, worse, as having shirked their domestic duties, some women in public life still undergo this sort of scrutiny. Films about campaign politics can dramatize their plight of having to prove themselves both competent and still somehow "all woman" by framing the political process as a testing ground for the fitness of a candidate to command power.

The Contender

In the wake of the sex scandal involving President Bill Clinton, a "pure" political film debuted to ask whether Americans had gone too far in demanding to know every detail of elected officials' personal lives. In *The Contender* (2000), the vice president has died and President Jackson Evans, in a sly performance by Jeff Bridges, decides to secure his place in history by appointing a woman as the new vice president. He chooses Senator Laine Hanson, a perfect contender until it is leaked to the media that in college she participated in group sex. Despite the real-life context of Clinton's extramarital affair, in the film's terms Hanson's gender alone seems to prompt *The Contender*'s guiding question: "Can a slut be president?"

As played by perennial Oscar nominee Joan Allen, Hanson is no-nonsense without being humorless, hardworking and smart without seeming cerebral. (Her build and hairstyle also resemble those of Geraldine Ferraro, running mate to Democratic presidential nominee Walter Mondale in 1984.) Hanson is devoted to her family in a way that forgoes sentimentality. Indeed, the film introduces her having sex with her husband atop an office desk, making it clear that when it comes to a professional life and a sex life she has not compromised in either direction. Yet her down-to-earth qualities also suggest earthiness, a woman who may very well harbor secrets. Besides that, as we have seen, any woman having sex in mainstream American film is automatically suspect.

Once allegations of her past behavior surface, it is open season on Hanson. The press, in all its twenty-four-hour news cycle glory, cannot get enough of the story. Leading the charge against her is Senator Shelly Runyon, a particularly juicy part played by Gary Oldman replete with Nixonian widow's peak and H.R. Haldeman–style thick-rimmed glasses. A member of the opposition party and head of the Senate committee that must clear her nomination, he declares, "I'm not going to confirm a woman just because she's a woman." Then he sets out to destroy her candidacy for pretty much that reason.

Runyon expressly represents the GOP, specifically the branch supporting Richard Nixon's 1960s–1970s silent majority and vice president Dan Quayle's 1980s "family values"—that is, the anti-ERA, antiabortion rights faction. Runyon stands as a renouncement of the 1960s counterculture, symbolized by both Hanson's alleged kinky, "free love" sex and Evans's constant appetite for food, an allusion to the first baby boomer president and man of many appetites, Bill Clinton. If Runyon can prove Hanson's dalliance, he will have shown the American public all it needs to know about a woman: her sexual impurity. If she is guilty of having had unconventional sex, she cannot be counted on to support any other conventional value women still must embody: motherhood, stand-by-your-man rectitude, and sex within marriage only. Distilling a woman's character into a question of her sexual experience is the key code to understanding Republican shorthand. Hollywood, too, relies on that code, only in this film the shorthand is actually deployed in a pure political context, fairly unique in American film.

The plot mirrors the case unfolding against Hanson. News shows air blurry photographs to track the apparent verification of her secret. Hanson neither confirms nor denies the rumor, stating quite succinctly the film's main point: "I simply can't respond to the accusations because it's not okay for them to be made." A bust of Thomas Jefferson in the foreground of several shots and

Allen's costuming in white high-collared shirts against dark jackets suggest colonial-era integrity, while her white sweat-suited jog through Arlington National Cemetery implies her status as sacrificial victim. The film suggests that her right to privacy is not unpatriotic but backed by the nation's own history.

Just as events seem about to bear out Runyon's prediction, "What I say the American people will believe. You know why? I'll have a very big microphone," a Hollywood-style twist occurs to take the heat off Hanson, and it turns out she was not the person caught in those grainy pictures. In this way, the film tries to have it both ways. It wants to point out that questions of sexual conduct are irrelevant to government office while also vouchsafing the purity of its heroine. That her virtue was never really in question undercuts the fact that she withstood the brutal smear campaign so stoically. It rehabilitates her completely as loyal wife and model mother and seems to answer the question "Can a promiscuous woman hold office?" with a sighing "no."

While the film was a box office disappointment, grossing only $17.8 million, critics approved it. Roger Ebert pointed out the film's political context: "When I asked its star, Jeff Bridges, if the plot was a veiled reference to Monicagate, he smiled. 'Veiled?' he said. 'I don't think it's so veiled.' . . . *The Contender* takes sides and is bold about it. Most movies are like puppies that want everyone to pet them."[10]

To a postimpeachment, post-9/11 audience, the film's depiction of the political process as soap opera remains presciently relevant. As the 2004 presidential campaign revived debate over 1960s attitudes and actions in the Vietnam War—even as actual war raged in Iraq—the political process eerily resembled the fight over Hanson's did-she-or-didn't-she sexual past in *The Contender. The Contender* wants audiences to agree that the focus on a politics of personal behavior, orchestrated by politicians and abetted by a hungry media market, takes up too much airtime. By attaching these issues to a female vice presidential nominee, a fiction in American political history, the film suggests that privacy is a particularly feminist concern, hinting at but not fully exploring the related issue of abortion rights. Ultimately, however, the film fails to critique in any meaningful way the feeding frenzy of politics by relying so deeply on a realistic depiction of that frenzy to fuel its plot and titillate viewers. Perhaps that is why the film disappointed audiences in 2000. It mirrored too closely the mediated version of the political process already so omnipresent in American life.

Films with political content and messaging occasionally feature women prominently but not necessarily to make an explicit point about gender. Only indirectly do they question how women should fit into the political arena.

Primary Colors *and* The Manchurian Candidate

Primary Colors (1998) and *The Manchurian Candidate* (2004) are two other pure political films that question the efficacy and integrity of the American political electoral system but more pointedly question the role of women in that system. On the topic of gender, both invoke the image of Hillary Rodham Clinton, the former first lady who went on to become the junior senator from New York. *Primary Colors* treats her with respect in the figure of Susan Stanton, wife of presidential hopeful Jack Stanton. Never venturing beyond the closed door of their bedroom, *Primary Colors* paints the Stantons as well meaning but ultimately flawed, politically driven people. Whether politically motivated people are necessarily flawed, or politics inevitably causes those flaws the film never decides.

Featuring cameos by notable Hollywood Democratic supporters like Rob Reiner, the film recaptures moments from Bill Clinton's actual 1992 primary race, including rumors of Jack's philandering, played with oozy charm by John Travolta. It also mimics reality with a talk show spot by Jack and Susan, played by Emma Thompson as a personally cautious but politically true believer in Stanton. She holds Jack's hand firmly as she defends their marriage, then tosses it aside when the interview ends. More than infidelity, Jack's lies torment Susan. In this she seems more believable than depressing or disingenuous.

The Hillary Clinton references in the 2004 remake of the 1962 paranoid political thriller *The Manchurian Candidate* are more diabolical. Played by Meryl Streep, Eleanor Shaw is mother to Raymond Shaw, the man tapped to be the next vice president after heroic service in the Gulf War; a strategically timed assassination will leave him president. Whereas the political conspiracy in the original film featured Communists in a labyrinthine plan to sabotage the United States not from the political left but from the right, in this film right-wingers pose as liberals to corrode the left from within its own ranks and essentially overrun the government. Substituting corporate America for cold war Communists, this contemporary *Manchurian Candidate* sets up Raymond to be "the first privately owned and operated vice president of the United States." *Manchurian* now stands for Manchurian Global Corp., not Communist China, and Raymond's greedy, self-serving mother provides the key to "owning" him.

Rumors in the entertainment press suggested that Streep channeled Hillary Clinton to portray this overbearing, manipulative monster, and the styling of Streep's appearance in the film alludes to her. Whether true or not, the widespread nature of the rumor means that the mere idea of Hillary Clinton, a lightning rod for political controversy, still terrifies and enthralls Americans.

That Streep's character only mouths the convictions that Clinton purports to believe suggests the ultimate right-wing nightmare: Clinton is a phony, but if so, then she is secretly not a liberal but, more horrifying, a conservative.

Tepidly received at the box office and by reviewers, director Jonathan Demme's *Manchurian Candidate* possibly suffers from the same problem afflicting *The Contender:* its dark worldview is too familiar to be disturbing. With the specter of inflated Halliburton profits hovering over the Iraqi war and the failure to find weapons of mass destruction undermining the original justification for the invasion, the Manchurian Global Corp. plot suggests business as usual. A woman masterminding the conspiracy would not shock anyone familiar with Condoleeza Rice's prominence within George W. Bush's administration.

Conclusion

Women in the movies have most often been consigned to subservient roles, but these roles have evolved with the place of women in the home, the workplace, and beyond. Occasionally those roles have been evocative of equality with and even mastery over men, but more typically the lesson of Hollywood films is that, for women, with great power comes great humiliation or punishment. The number of overtly political movies that prominently feature women in positions of political authority is smaller still, although recent films tend to explore that possibility more regularly than those of the distant past.

15

Afterword

The Candidate (1972)

"I want this picture to be a commentary on modern conditions, stark realism, the problems that confront the average man," says Joel McCrea in the title role in *Sullivan's Travels* (1941). Tired of making movies with titles like *Ants in the Pants,* John L. Sullivan, the rich and famous Hollywood director, disguises himself as a hobo and goes out to research his magnum opus, *Brother, Wherefore Art Thou?* His life on the road is funny at first, but it turns serious when he is mugged, loses his money and his memory, and finds himself truly down and out. After a scuffle in a freight yard, he is convicted of assault and sent to a grim prison farm where life is lightened only by occasional movies shown by a local black church. When he manages to get back to Hollywood, he wants to make only comedies. "There's a lot to be said for making people laugh," Sullivan declares. "Did you know that's all some people have? It isn't much, but it's better than nothing."

With his usual flair, Preston Sturges, the writer and director of *Sullivan's Travels*, was sending up the social conscience films of the Depression. Films, his itinerant director asserts, are supposed to amuse people and take their minds off their troubles. Although Sturges portrayed America's underclass with sympathy, he refused to accept responsibility to help other than by providing momentary diversion. Sturges chose entertainment over educating, helping people understand their society, or providing inspiration or instruction as to how to change it. Entertainment is itself a worthy goal, and *Sullivan's Travels* proved that movies about serious subjects can be entertaining. But *Sullivan's Travels* also summed up Hollywood's attitudes about politics and political movies. American filmmakers are cynical, not only about whether movies should deal with politics, but also about politics itself.

Repeated Messages

Political movies have debated the great issues of the day as the nation debated them, sometimes ahead of the public and sometimes lagging behind, sometimes dissenting and sometimes reinforcing. Regardless of the state of the union, however, some ideas about politics are constantly reiterated by movies. If audiences absorb these repeated messages, their cumulative effect must surely be cynicism and apathy.

Above all, American political films tell us that politics is corrupt. From the Victorian villains of the silent melodramas to the corporate or bureaucratic monsters of latter-day thrillers, politicians and power-holders have been portrayed as greedy, self-interested shysters. Usually, lust for power or personal ambition is their motivation, but sometimes ambition is supplemented or even subsumed by greed, as in the case of the bosses and "interests" of the 1930s movies. Ever since the silents, bad men have used politics for their own economic benefit, although corporations replace individual villains in many of the later movies. This is a more radical analysis, but it usually stops with the single guilty corporation instead of examining the system as a whole. Sometimes, especially in thrillers, an ominous presence lurks "out there," more terrifying because it is not defined. It could be a Communist conspiracy or a corporate cabal, but usually it is more obscure than that, and too big for individuals or even governments to struggle against. Perhaps it is the filmmakers' metaphor for "the system" against which individuals are impotent, yet it seems more specific. Whatever it is, it is pretty scary. And whether the source of corruption in a movie is an individual, a group, or a system, the cinematic view of politics is grim and getting grimmer.

Perhaps corruption is just a convenient source of tension and drama. Perhaps moviemakers are gloomy pessimists or mocking cynics, too self-obsessed, paranoid, or even idealistic to understand or accept the reality of politics. Or maybe politics is as corrupt as they say. But whether they are brainwashing us with fantasy or instructing us in reality, their negative view of politics is unlikely to be empowering. After all, if it takes Robert Redford, Julia Roberts, or Denzel Washington to beat the system, what chance do the rest of us have? And if even they cannot beat it, how can we? Ironically, the most pessimistic movies are often the most radical in that they condemn the system as a whole, yet they help entrench it by discouraging action. Not all movies are fatalistic, however. A few optimistic films show that problems can be solved by great leaders, scrappy individuals, or by appeals to "the people."

From the 1920s through the 1950s, the great leader solution was common. Abraham Lincoln was a favorite, but Franklin D. Roosevelt and others like him also became part of the pantheon. Their pronouncements were treated like the word of God, never questioned or doubted. But even if Lincoln and Roosevelt were as great as the movies portray them, waiting for a leader is not a realistic political strategy, and movies started giving up hope of such saviors as early as 1948, when *State of the Union* told us that good guys could not win. Either they had to walk away from politics to preserve their integrity, or they were destroyed by it. Later, *The Candidate*'s Bill McKay and Jack Stanton (in *Primary Colors*) could not even walk away from it. They were seduced, but the possibility that they could do some good remained. Like the knowledgeable pols of *Advise and Consent*, they would stay and play—a less certain but more realistic view of politics and probably a healthier one.

These movies are still cynical about politicians, however, and there would have been a shortage of heroes if it had not been for the cinematic tradition of the common man rising to meet a challenge. From *Mr. Smith* and *The Grapes of Wrath* to *Norma Rae* and *Erin Brockovich,* ordinary people stumble onto evil and corruption, overcome their fear, and fight the system single-handedly and successfully. These heroes and heroines suggest that action by ordinary people can make a difference; surely this is a more positive message than the one delivered by the fatalistic thrillers or the movies that rely on great leaders.

Such heroes and heroines may be inspiring, but the message of these movies is limited by their tendency to confine problems to a single person, group, or circumstance. But what if the problem is more pervasive? What if a courageous person is not around to take up the cause? Movies rarely present problems with the political system as a whole and they almost never raise issues that are not self-contained. This reduces politics to a need for occasional individual action to regulate an essentially good, smoothly functioning process by pointing out flaws in the form of bad individuals and sometimes bad organizations like gangs, machines, and corporations. Some films—like the paranoid thrillers of the 1970s and the cynical visions of the 1990s—dared to suggest that there was little hope for the future.

Some movies insist that "the people" must be called upon. Once they know the truth, all will be well. Mr. Smith rallied the people, and the journalists of *All the President's Men* and *The China Syndrome* told them the truth about Watergate and nuclear meltdown, although the people did not actually take action in these later movies. This faith in "the people" is as mass-oriented as American movies get. Action is virtually always individual and rarely collective. Despite our democratic ideals, when people get together in American movies, they are more likely to be condemned as a lynch mob than to be praised for their cooperative endeavor. The exceptions are few and far between. *Our Daily Bread, Norma Rae, Reds, Bread and Roses* (2000), and a few other movies attempt to validate the idea of people working and organizing together. *The Grapes of Wrath* features the family and "the people"; *The Last Hurrah* centers on the good ol' boys of the machine. Other movies show friends or coworkers sticking together, as in *The Boys in Company C, Nine to Five,* and *The Right Stuff.* Most of these movies do not go much beyond a stand-by-your-pals message, but at least they are not waiting for Abraham Lincoln or John Wayne to come along.

But whether action is taken by great leaders, individuals, or groups, the motivation in American movies is almost always negative: the bad guys act out of greed or ambition, and the good guys act to stop the bad guys. Except when Abe Lincoln frees the slaves or Woodrow Wilson makes the world safe for democracy, higher motives are rarely expressed. In fact, Lincoln and Wilson acted for a variety of reasons, some of which were not particularly lofty, and by the same token, ordinary people and real-life politicians sometimes act for positive good rather than just to save the nation from bad guys.

This fear of higher motives is partly political and partly artistic. Getting beyond individual motives and issues means getting into ideas—or ideology. Artistically, it is hard to create genuine characters and write credible dialogue that reflect and articulate ideas without seeming to pound in the message with a sledgehammer. Furthermore, any discussion of political ideas beyond accepted democratic values may offend some segment of the audience. Americans are uneasy with ideology, especially any ideology other than their own; most movies respect this attitude by remaining resolutely centrist and issue-oriented.

The exclusion of ideology reduces all motives to self-interest and thus trivializes politics, which ultimately means that politics and politicians are held in contempt. It also means that few American political movies deal with class or with ideas that are out of the mainstream. The right and left usually appear only as caricatures when Hollywood campaigns against fascists, Communists, or the KKK. American political movies support the status quo through this narrowing of the political spectrum and by their insistence that the political process works—albeit in totally unrealistic ways that often involve a heavy dose of deus ex machina. When problems arise, heroic individuals take action and usually succeed.

There are exceptions to this avoidance of ideology, of course, although few American movies stray far from the center. Some lean to the right, stressing individualism and traditional values like self-help, hard work, family, and patriotism, often criticizing moral decline, bureaucracy, and big government, and especially concern about external threats to the nation. Others lean left, emphasizing tolerance and cooperation, criticizing discrimination, conformity, greed, and sometimes capitalism, and they worry about domestic fascism and authoritarianism. Most notable among these are the honorable group of movies that crusaded for racial and sexual equality. Even these are cautious, however, usually preaching that we should be nice to each other, and that minorities and women should behave like white males. Almost invariably, these films individualize and oversimplify. But even though the moderation of movies like *Guess Who's Coming to Dinner* or *Nine to Five* disappointed many, they did push us gently in the right direction.

Innumerable critics have pointed out that political films sometimes seem liberal or even radical because they raise an issue (nuclear peril, racism, corruption) and get us all worked up only to reassure us that heroic individuals, "the people," or the political process itself will make all well in the end. Certainly we ourselves will not have to do anything. Despite the liberal or even radical intent of these films, their net effect is conservative because they reinforce faith in the system, ultimately endorsing rather than criticiz- . ing. If blind faith in the system is not enough to keep us passive, the hope that a hero will come along serves the same purpose. Furthermore, by raising up heroes or letting the system right itself, movies fail to explain larger forces, especially economic ones. Movies that do address these forces are even more despairing, however. They warn us that politics is mean and evil, that it is best avoided because there is not a lot we can do about it, and that if we try to beat these forces, they will smash us. Such films communicate a futility that inspires apathy as effectively as those that reassure us that the system works.

The end results are not encouraging. American political films grapple with problems only to solve them too easily or to predict apocalypse. We end up with "dramas of reassurance"[1] or pessimistic pictures of utter hopelessness, with too few movies suggesting that we can do anything about politics. The gap between the bland happy ending and the bleak tragedy is too great. We need more films somewhere in the middle and more that help us understand our world. Most of all, we need more movies that respect politics as a constructive activity.

Barriers to More Political Films

The cautious messages of American political films are the result of a variety of factors. Like Preston Sturges and his fictional director, American filmmakers are primarily committed to entertaining. When they try to make political points as well, the conflict between the two goals often results in compromises that weaken one or the other or, in some cases, both. But economics, audiences, and the nature of movies as an art form also influence the making of political movies and what they have to say.

Films that criticize the political system are still made, but often they have to be toned down or laced with stars to get the funding in the first place, like *Reds.* Less compromised films such as *Do the Right Thing, Natural Born Killers,* and *Matewan* are made but rarely. These movies were financed on the strength of their well-known star directors.

The conservative orientation of investors is widely believed to have increased as the corporations took over and the power of the studios declined, but, in fact, the collapse of the studio system made it easier for independent filmmakers to develop political projects. They still need lots of money, which means finding investors, however, and they still need the corporate studios to distribute their films. But even the corporate studios invest in political films like *Reds* or the remakes of *The Quiet American* and *The Manchurian Candidate* when they think the films will make money. If such films fail to do so, the fault may lie as much with the audiences as with the bias of the producers.

Audience expectations of escapist entertainment also interfere with the success of serious films. *Wag the Dog* had a lot more to say than *Dave,* but

Dave was closer to what contemporary audiences expect of a movie, and it did far better at the box office, thanks at least in part to a plot that is more amusing than enlightening and a better-funded marketing campaign. Audiences have come to expect not only entertainment, but also slick entertainment. Producers test-market different endings in an effort to find the storyline that makes people feel the best, not the one that rings the most true. The political message of a movie may be played down to avoid offending any major segment of the diverse American audience, or it may be moderated so that as many people as possible will agree with it and buy tickets. Moreover, the ever-increasing reliance on special effects augers against the more complex ideas that political films entail.

The nature of movies as an art form may also moderate their politics. Directors are usually credited with definitively shaping movies, as they have been in this book, but many creative people contribute to the final shape of the film, including writers, producers, cinematographers, editors, designers, and actors. The politics of these individuals may differ, and their perceptions of what audiences want to see, need to be told, or will accept may also vary. Out of the conflict of these differing biases and perceptions comes the movie.

The written script is probably the most important component, but it may be altered or given different emphasis in the process of filming. However forthright the politics of a project is at its inception, it is often muted by the time the concept becomes a movie. Profit-minded filmmakers will seek to please the largest possible audience by deemphasizing the political message. This can be done in all sorts of ways—by revising or deleting dialogue, by cutting political scenes, by emphasizing romance, or by camera placement and casting.

The choice of actors, as we have seen, can radically alter the message of a movie. Known actors and especially stars bring their own personae to parts. *The Front* would have been a different movie without Woody Allen in the lead, as would *JFK* without Kevin Costner or *All the President's Men* without Redford and Hoffman. But while the presence of a star can give tone and resonance to a character, it can also shift the emphasis of a movie. Scripts may be rewritten to suit stars and their images. An actor can also reshape a movie by giving an extraordinary performance that shifts the focus from one character to another and thus alters the balance of the film. Al Pacino and Meryl Streep, for example, accomplish this even in supporting roles.

Casting is just one element of the collaborative art of filmmaking. But casting is not only an artistic choice—it is also a commercial one. Stars bring in audiences and therefore money. Casting a big star may mean compromising the politics of a film in order to ensure ticket sales. Other elements of filmmaking require similar trade-offs and compromises that can affect the political impact of a movie.

Other conventions of American movies also contribute to their individualism. Most focus on heroes, for example, partly because of the star system and partly because of the requirements of melodrama, the standard form of American movies. Melodramas revolve around conflict that must be solved, usually happily and almost always by a hero. That is what we expect and that is what most movies deliver, but these conventions and expectations raise special problems for political filmmakers.

In short, the very nature of the film medium complicates the task of political filmmakers. Add to this the limits placed on films by audience expectations and the need to make a profit and it is easy to see why the messages of political films are frequently muted.

These factors might be sufficient to explain the political caution of filmmakers if movies were made in a vacuum, but they are not. In America even more than elsewhere, politics itself has had an impact on the movies. Besides public protests and demands for censorship, politicians also pay close attention to movies and frequently offer criticism, not to mention dire warnings. A few, including Woodrow Wilson, Franklin Roosevelt, John Kennedy, and above all Ronald Reagan, have enjoyed movies and even given active support to filmmakers. Other politicians worry about foreign reaction to the movie image of America, and many complain about the way the movies caricature their profession—and what the voters must think of them as a result. A few, like the House Un-American Activities Committee (HUAC) investigators and the Justice Department, have done more than criticize and complain.

Reasons to Proceed

Between complaining politicians, protesting audiences, antitrust suits, HUAC, the production code, and the requirements of melodrama, profit, and entertainment, it should not be surprising that American political films are timid. It is more surprising that they are made at all. But even though American filmmakers fear that political content will mean box office poison, they continue to make straightforward political movies. Either they cannot resist the poison or they have developed immunity.

Many political filmmakers have at one time or another felt strongly enough about a political project to work on it even without studio support. Why do filmmakers take such risks? Many are quite simply and genuinely interested in politics. Some are politically committed; one even became president. But in addition to interest and commitment, and often quite separately from either, many filmmakers are or wish to be serious artists. They are not content to make family melodramas or comedy, science fiction, horror, and action movies, although these genres can be serious and do not preclude political content. Indeed, many political films are best described as comedies or action movies and may be intended as little more. But for many filmmakers, serious art requires a serious subject like politics.

Filmmakers are further encouraged to make political movies by the recognition they receive from their colleagues, the critics, and even the public. Political movies make the film industry look serious, even intellectual, so Hollywood takes them seriously and often rewards them with Oscars. Many of the films discussed in this book have been nominated for Academy Awards, and many, from *All Quiet on the Western Front* to *Platoon* and *Born on the Fourth of July,* have won major awards. Oscars do not prove a film's artistic, intellectual, or political merit, but they do give it Hollywood's stamp of approval, improve its box office performance, and provide its makers with clout and credibility for their next project.

Similarly, critics pay special attention to political movies because they deal with "important" themes or because the critics want a chance to say something about politics themselves. Although political movies are often given rough treatment because of their content, the reviews are by no means always bad. The *New York Times* annual list of "Ten Best" movies, for example, has included at least one overtly political film every year since *The Dramatic Life of Abraham Lincoln* appeared on the first list in 1924. Critical praise has been heaped on political movies from *The Birth of a Nation* to *The Insider* and *Wag the Dog.*

Perhaps more surprisingly, the public also takes political films seriously. Far from box office poison, some political films have been popular hits. *The Big Parade* was the highest earning silent film, followed closely by *The Birth of a Nation. Mr. Smith Goes to Washington* was a top box office draw in 1939, as was *The Best Years of Our Lives* in 1947. Stanley Kramer's didactic films almost always did well. *JFK, Forrest Gump,* and *Three Kings* have been box office hits in recent years, and even movies that invoke the political process—albeit crudely—like *Dave* and *The American President* have fared well.

Few overtly political films, however, are blockbusters. Of the top ten grossing movies produced in the 1990s, only *Forrest Gump* addresses political themes in an overt manner. Of course, politically reflective movies like *Independence Day* and *Titanic* were huge successes—but they scarcely provide impetus for the aspiring producer of political films. On the other hand, the runaway success of *Fahrenheit 9/11* suggests that small-budget political films—even documentaries—can provide an attractive return on investment.

A specialized segment of the audience has even learned to look beyond the mainstream of American commercial cinema to independent films, at least partially in search of strong political content. Unfortunately, many viewers have little or no ready access to such films, and the independent film movement seems increasingly co-opted by mainstream values in any event.

Foreign films are another alternative, although their reputation for being stronger and more forthright in their treatment of politics than American movies is exaggerated. Only the best films of other countries reach us; in fact, the tradition of social criticism is no stronger abroad than in the United States. In most countries, it is weaker. "Whether a film like *I Am a Fugitive from a Chain Gang* could be made in any other country," declared British film scholar I.C. Jarvie, "is much to be doubted."[2] Similar statements were made in reference to the production of *Fahrenheit 9/11*.

Strong political films are a tradition, however, in Italy and France. Both countries have produced movies with broader and more penetrating social criticism than almost any American films. Bernardo Bertolucci's *The Conformist* and *1900*, Francesco Rosi's *Christ Stopped at Eboli, Three Brothers*, and *Investigation of a Citizen above Suspicion*, Gillo Pontecorvo's *Burn!* and *Battle of Algiers*, Jean Luc Godard's *La Chinoise* and *Weekend*, Costa-Gavras's *Z* and *State of Siege*, and Louis Malle's *Lacombe, Lucien* make American political films seem pretty weak. The list could go on and filmmakers from other countries, especially Germany and Cuba, could be added, but it is unlikely that proportionately more political films are produced in other nations than in the United States unless the countries are totalitarian and the movies are propaganda.

Europeans may make superior political films in part because their audiences are more sophisticated about politics and their politics is more ideological and analytical than ours. We tolerate views that stray only slightly to the right or left of center, but opinion in Italy and France runs across the whole ideological spectrum, giving filmmakers greater freedom of expression and also providing at least a specialized audience interest. Perhaps because of this diversity of opinion, Europeans argue about politics more than we do and vote in greater numbers than we do, even though they are far more cynical than Americans. Their ideological politics prepares them for newspapers that do not pretend to objectivity, as ours do, and for tendentious movies as well. European filmmakers have also been content to make smaller, cheaper films and to reach smaller audiences. On the other hand, European audiences seem to turn out in large numbers for Hollywood dreck that even American audiences shun.

Italian and French movies are not infinitely superior to ours, however, and audiences there can be just as enthusiastic about American blockbusters as we are, although they are also more likely to admire films like *Heaven's Gate, Under Fire*, or almost any movie by Oliver Stone. Michael Moore was practically deified at the 2004 Cannes Film Festival. But European political filmmakers also voice some of the same complaints as their American counterparts. "Nobody likes political films," says Costa-Gavras, claiming that even when he features big stars he has trouble raising money for his films. He also complains about having to draw in the supposedly sophisticated French audience by promoting his works as thrillers rather than political movies.[3]

The success of a fair number of American political films, as well as the specialized audience that has developed for foreign films and, to a lesser extent, documentaries, suggests that critics are correct in their belief that the film industry has too little faith in audiences. The American tradition of political films is respectable, but the movies could be better. They could be less cautious and superficial. They could be stronger, more complex, and more profound. They could offer a wider variety of political perspectives and analyses. Perhaps most importantly in a democratic political system, they could be more positive about participation and involvement.

Filmmakers and audiences need not give up entertainment to have better political films. Entertainment is the reason we love the movies, but being entertained does not preclude being encouraged to think or even educate. In fact, political and social points can often be most effectively made in traditional entertainment movies because all of us grasp issues better when we see how they affect actual people, even in the movies. Filmmakers should have more faith in their audiences and take more chances with movies about politics. Investors and distributors should support them. The film industry needs to accept, however, that good movies about politics may reach only a segment of the audience, even a subculture. That segment or subculture could be large enough to make a movie profitable, although even good movies about politics are unlikely ever to be blockbusters. If filmmakers and their backers can accept this limitation, they can escape from the compulsion to make consensus movies that offend few and say little. The ideology of entertainment and profit is too deeply entrenched in the American film industry to expect our movies to become politically profound, much less to transform our political system, but brave filmmakers can make more and better movies, and critics and audiences should support them.

The Bottom Line

In Chapter 1 we posed the question of whether all these political messages really mattered. As we noted, the findings of research on the effect of films (and other media) are inconclusive and ambiguous. Certainly evidence exists that movies help shape our orientation to the political world, even if they do not necessarily make us vote for one candidate over another. More important, perhaps, politicians and other participants in the political process act as if movies are extremely important. Debate continues to simmer about who controls the messages movies send and the content of those messages. Dramatically, some commentators suggested that the 2004 presidential election could have turned in part on how many undecided voters viewed *Fahrenheit 9/11* (and whether it affected their votes).

Walter Lippman wrote, "The airy nothings in the realm of essence are efficacious in the existential world when a man, believing it to be true or good, treats the idea as if it were the reality."[4] Can there be any doubt that the "airy nothings" of popular films have affected the political attitudes and actions of countless Americans? The characters portrayed by John Wayne for the most part never existed, yet Newt Gingrich and Arnold Schwarzenegger single him out as an important influence. How many other Americans have been similarly enthralled by the power of film? Similarly, the blurred distinction between acting and holding political office is increasingly perceived as natural and even desirable. The subtle effects of film may not be readily demonstrated empirically, but they permeate the contemporary political world. The question, perhaps, is not how much impact the movies have, but whether any other institution can compete with them.

"Movies can't change a country," Costa-Gavras says, and "it's just as well that it's not that easy."[5] They make a contribution, however. They inform and educate. They provide catharsis, helping us come to terms with our worries and fantasies by acting them out for us. Sometimes they make us feel less alone. Despite their mildness and reassurance, their constant social criticism has helped keep us self-conscious as a nation. They have particularly and rightly condemned intolerance and corruption. Less creditably, they have also told us to rely on leaders and heroes for salvation, ignored the alternative of collective action, and neglected or condemned opinions that stray from the mainstream. Worse, they have disparaged politics in presenting it as evil and corrupting, best avoided by decent people. This image of politics reflects and reinforces popular prejudice, but it helps to entrench alienation and apathy. Movies that reinforce, reassure, or warn us to stay away from politics keep us passive even more effectively than entertainment as pure opiate. No wonder so many critics see movies as a tool through which those who run the country control the rest of us.

Perhaps unfortunately, we seem content to let ourselves be controlled. We love movies. But precisely because we love them, we should take a close look at what they teach us and demand more from them. We cannot expect too much of movies, but they can and should at least keep us thinking and talking.

Appendixes

Appendix 1

An Outtake

A Guide for the Political Analysis of Movies

Here we explore several approaches to writing about movies from a political standpoint. At the outset, it is important to bear in mind that there is no one approach that will suit all purposes and situations. Rather, we hope that the ideas we discuss here will serve as *heuristic* devices—useful, but not ends in themselves—for students who want to (or have to) write about politics and film. As a starting point, we discuss the analysis of an individual film, although you may be interested in writing about several movies that evoke a particular theme. Consistent with the theme of this text, our general purpose will be identifying political messages in movies.

When applied to writing about film, *analysis* is an ambiguous term. Most instructors will expect more from students than a mere review of a movie (although that may be one assignment in some classes). Analysis means going beyond a simple evaluation (review) of a movie to a level of explanation. It may be as straightforward a task as explaining in greater depth and detail your opinion of a film. As William H. Phillips writes in a useful guide on the subject, "Film analysis is a way of explaining what the viewer sees and hears in a film, and how and why the viewer reacts."[1] Comparing and contrasting several films at once provides another analytic springboard, but we will begin with the task of analyzing a single film.

Political analysis means a focus on the political meanings, implications, and messages that a film contains. Because *political* also is an ambiguous term, the burden may fall upon the writer to demonstrate how a film conveys political ideas, events, and values. One consideration to bear in mind is that political analysis, although it may focus exclusively on a movie itself, also may link a film to external events, individuals, and institutions. Similarly, when conducting a political analysis of a film, you may wish to bring political ideology and values to bear upon it. The credibility of such analysis, however, will be enhanced if you openly acknowledge your political background as an influence.

Watching Movies

Although most films students analyze are viewed via DVD on a television screen, the ideal setting is to screen a movie at least once in a cinema with an audience. As we discussed in Chapter 2, moviegoing is a social activity, and you can learn much about a movie from the reactions of fellow attendees—even if they are strangers. Additionally, movies are generally intended to be viewed on a large screen, and some elements of the cinematic art (e.g., the framing of a scene) are much more difficult to appreciate on a small screen. In fact, many DVD versions of popular movies cut out screen space to fit the dimensions of television screens, so when possible, it is preferable to watch a letterboxed (rectangular) version of a film.

Ideally, also, it is best to watch a movie twice before attempting to analyze or write about it. (Of course, this is much easier to do with a DVD player, so some trade-offs are involved!) If you have enough time, the first viewing should be devoted to just enjoying the movie without a great deal of analysis. Keep a notebook handy, though, to jot down first impressions or questions as they pop up. The first screening of a movie will probably mold your initial evaluation; that is, you will know whether and basically why you did or did not like the movie.

Although your personal like or dislike for a movie is quite important, the point of a political film analysis is not merely to review it. So it is essential to maintain a certain amount of distance between your opinion of the movie as entertainment and what it may represent politically. That said, after viewing a movie it is a good idea to reflect upon your opinion. Exactly why did you like or dislike it? What did you like the most? What about the movie bothered you? Confused you? Surprised you? Your answers to these sorts of questions can provide a means of imagining how the movie might affect others and perhaps constitute a springboard for deeper analysis.

After seeing a film once, you should be able to initially categorize it according to the typology of political films discussed in Chapter 1 by determining to what extent political content and intent are embodied in it. Political content is generally easy to identify. Does the movie involve major characters who are politicians or government officials of any type, such as police officers? Is the setting for the film a political institution, such as Congress or the presidency? Are political and social issues debated or part of the setting?

Identifying political intent can be much more challenging. To what extent does the film seem to be intent on sending political messages? Do characters discuss what seem to be political issues? Are political values or ideologies represented in the script? Is the message, if any, clear and straightforward or subtle and/or murky?

If a movie seems to be low in terms of both political content and intent, it may still yield interesting reflections of social and political reality. For example, how does the movie portray characters of different races and gender? How are social classes depicted, if at all? Does the movie seem to judge certain kinds of characters because of their race, class, and so on? Is the movie consistent with prevailing ideas about the economic and social system, or does it question them?

The answer to these and many other possible indicators of political messages may become clearer upon a second viewing of the film, when you can worry less about following the plot and more closely scrutinize the details. A second view also will enable you to study the individual components of the film. You will probably want to take more detailed notes, too.

One convenient way of organizing a political film analysis is to consider the elements of film production discussed in Chapter 2 as they apply to the film you are analyzing. The following sections provide some suggestions along those lines.

Conception

Understanding the conceptual origins of a movie may put it in political perspective. Information about a film's conception may be relatively obvious (e.g., a remake or a sequel) or may require some investigation. Whose idea was the movie? Is it based on a novel or other preexisting source material? Is it based on a true or historical story, or is it purely fictional? After answering these sorts of questions, consider whether they provide any political perspective on the movie.

Production

As discussed in Chapter 2, a film's producers may wield significant influence over its content. Find out which company and individuals controlled its production. Do they have obvious political ties or a history of producing politically significant movies? Is the movie from one of the major Hollywood studios or is it an independent film? What was its budget? The answers to these kinds of questions may provide cues with respect to its political orientation.

Screenplay and Story

At the heart of most political film analyses will be a careful exploration of its content. Presumably at this point, you will already have a good idea if the film carries an overt political message or if it is merely reflective of social and political reality. But how was this message created?

Subject Matter/Genre

Choice of genre can be a significant factor in identifying a film's political messages. If the movie falls clearly into a recognizable genre (western, romantic comedy, etc.), how do its plot and characters square with the expectations that this genre creates? For example, in a western, who are the good and bad guys? How does the movie comment about their goodness or lack thereof? If the movie seems to subvert the genre (perhaps with an unconventional hero or unexpected plot twist), what message does that imply?

If the film's subject matter is openly political, how are political institutions and actors treated? Does the movie tend to fall upon the movie conventions discussed in Chapter 2 (personalization, sugarcoating, the "unlabeled bottle," ambivalence)? Does the story seem to reinforce a particular political ideology or value, and if so, how? Of particular interest here will be the film's ending. Endings typically provide the most compelling judgment of a film's characters (and the ideas they represent). How does the film reconcile the issues it raises?

If the film is based on historical events, how does it appear to comment on those events? Does it represent a departure from popular understanding or does it reinforce conventional wisdom?

Direction

As noted in Chapter 2, direction is commonly thought to constitute the creative centerpiece of modern films. Identify the director of the movie and learn whether he or she has any history of creating politically significant movies. If the director has an avowed political affiliation or ideological orientation, bear this in mind as you view the film. Does the movie you are analyzing contain any obvious trademarks of this director's past works? If it seems to represent a departure from past work, make note of the differences and try to understand why the director has chosen to use a different approach.

Try to determine whether the film takes a formalistic or a realistic approach. If it seems to be formalistic, identify the techniques the director uses to create an alternate reality and how this reality may impinge upon the movie's message. If the film seems to be striving for realism, how is this achieved? Are there any obvious lapses in the film's sense of reality? Do you accept this version of reality? Why or why not? (Be careful—some films create a very "realistic" feeling by using formal and ultimately artificial techniques!)

Try to identify specific aspects of the movie's art that reinforce its political message. In some movies, it will be difficult to identify and to document all these components, so you might need to closely observe a few key scenes that seem to be at the core of the movie's political meaning.

Titles

Opening titles prepare an audience for a film's content. How are the titles in your film consistent with the political themes you have identified?

Sound and Dialogue

Sound may be the most difficult aspect of a film to link to political analysis. William H. Phillips suggests running a scene without the picture so that you can focus on the use of sound.[2] In a book that provides many useful ideas about analyzing films, Timothy Corrigan suggests consideration of the following questions:[3]

- Does the sound ever become more important than the image, and what is the reason for this unusual strategy?
- What role does silence play in the movie?
- Are there sound motifs that identify the characters or actions?
- If you had to pick three key sound sequences from this movie, what would they be and why?

Perhaps the answers to these questions will relate to the political messages you have identified.

Music

Music may be a little easier to link to political message-making, particularly because modern moviemakers are increasingly likely to use rock songs with identifiable lyrics. How do the songs chosen for the soundtrack coincide with (or perhaps provide counterpoint to) a film's political message? Do songs in the movie's soundtrack themselves represent political commentary of some kind? If the soundtrack is mostly instrumental, how does the music reinforce political messaging—are certain characters or events associated with particular musical themes?

Editing/Montage

Although the editing of a movie's individual shots is a key element of the art of a film, it may be difficult in practice to link to political themes. Nevertheless, you should consider how the way a film is put together might contribute to its political impact, if any. Many Hollywood films purposely contain very subtle editing that may be almost undetectable.[4] But more artistically inclined directors typically use editing techniques to heighten the impact of their films. One variable to focus on is a movie's editing pace, which refers to the rhythm of the flow of various shots. Directors will sometimes use a choppy editing technique that typically creates a sense of disorientation or confusion, as opposed to the smoother, invisible approach favored by Hollywood.

Try selecting a critical scene from the movie and carefully observe how it is put together. Is there a long, single shot or is it broken into many shorter ones? How does the cutting contribute to the feeling and meaning of the scene? Here a DVD player will be particularly helpful as you can easily review a given scene any number of times, perhaps using slow motion to help identify its editing.

Composition/Mise-en-scène

Composition also is a typically subtle, yet important component of many movies. The way characters and objects are placed together in the frame of a film allows the director to achieve various sorts of commentary about its contents. Yet even in a formalistic movie, this is often done in such a way as to make us believe the frame occurred naturally. Obviously, composition may vary considerably over the course of a single movie, so you may want to select a critical scene for further analysis. Try using the freeze function of a DVD player to isolate particular compositions. How does the way characters and objects are placed in the scene contribute to the director's evaluation of them? Does this composition seem consistent with the movie's political meanings?

Lighting and Color

We do not normally think about how directors alter and vary lighting in a movie, but as in real life, lighting can do much to affect the mood of a scene or our perception of characters. Dark lighting sets an ominous tone, suggesting danger or corruption; bright lighting seems safe or even happy. One of the easier lighting techniques to analyze is the use of color filters, which can make an entire scene appear to be drenched in a particular color. Does the film include the use of specific colors to comment on its characters and events?

Typically, of course, white and lighter colors will signify goodness, but some directors may counter our expectations with other combinations. Some directors opt to shoot modern movies in black-and-white, in part because of the ways light can be manipulated in that medium. One memorable sequence of Steven Spielberg's *Schindler's List* (1993) is shot in black-and-white, except for a little girl whose red coat is the only color. Spielberg uses these scenes to help establish how the title character begins to see the humanity in the Jewish victims of the German occupation of Poland.

Camera Angles and Placement

Directors use camera angles to accentuate how they want an audience to react to a given scene. Pay particular attention to how good and bad characters are viewed by the camera. When the camera is aimed down on a character, he or she may look threatened or submissive; conversely, if the camera looks up to a character, he or she may look dominating and even threatening. Close-up shots, of course, tend to accentuate the importance of dialogue—these may be parts of the script upon which the director is placing particular emphasis. A more remote camera tends to lessen the importance of the dialogue and focus our attention on action.

Sets, Props, and Special Effects

Careful viewing of the sets, props, and special effects in a movie is an excellent means of discerning whether the director is trying to achieve realism or a more expressive formalism. If the sets do not appear to be particularly realistic, try to imagine what the director is trying to achieve with the artificial setting. It might be part of an effort to make the message of the film less about the specific characters and more allegorical, for example. Special effects, of course, tend to be associated with action films and generally detract from the realism that might be associated with a more serious political message; however, the opposite may be true, as movies like *Natural Born Killers* are rife with artificial elements (animation, extreme camera movement, etc.) that seem intended to heighten the film's messages.

Product Placement

Keep an eye out for recognizable brand names, particularly of consumer products. Do such products seem natural within the setting of the film or are they obvious attempts to help sell the product? Some directors use product placements ironically, perhaps to both comment on consumerism and distance the film from commercialism.

Acting

As discusses in Chapter 2, actors and acting can comprise an important part of a film's political message. Consider, for example, the star power represented by Kevin Costner in *Thirteen Days* (2000). The movie is ostensibly about President Kennedy and the Cuban missile crisis of 1962, but Costner's starring role as Kenneth P. O'Donnell makes it more of a tribute to the skills of the relatively unknown presidential aide. Actors, including their "star" status, roles, and names should be scrutinized carefully for clues about a film's political meaning.

Casting

Casting can provide some obvious cues about political messages. As noted in Chapter 2, some actors (e.g., Tom Hanks) seem to symbolize patriotism or traditional American virtues (as construed by Hollywood, anyway). Others (e.g., Tim Robbins) are clearly identified with a more critical perspective and often participate in films with a similar mindset. It is also possible that an actor or actress will be cast against type (e.g., Tim Robbins in the role of a conservative politician in *Bob Roberts,* 1992).

Characters

Watch especially for roles that represent politicians, elected officials of any kind, bureaucrats, police officers, and other government figures. Are they portrayed sympathetically or as negative stereotypes? Similarly, how are minorities and female characters portrayed, and how are they treated in the storyline?

Names

Be sure to write down the names of key characters because directors often use symbolism in their choices of names. Reflect upon the possible connotations of the characters' names and how the names might relate to the characters' respective roles.

Distribution and Promotion

Take a look at the marketing for the movie—is it being promoted as a political movie or as something else? Is it receiving mass distribution or is it available for viewing only in certain cities (usually New York, Los Angeles, and a few others) and certain types of theaters? The answers to these questions will determine to what extent mass audiences are going to see the movie.

Viewing

If you see the movie in a cinema, try to be aware of how fellow attendees react to various parts of the movie. Is there any applause at key lines? Is there laughter at moments in the film that do not appear to be intentionally funny? Sometimes audiences clap at the end of the movie, which might signal explicit approval of political content in some instances. Consider, too, your own reactions to the movie. Did it make you feel good or bad, happy or sad, hopeful or cynical—particularly with respect to political phenomena?

External Factors

Contemporary students of political films have a trove of riches when it comes to researching how films have interacted with the political world. In addition to the many books and journals that address films and their political significance, the Internet provides a great deal of potentially useful information. Student may use search engines such as google.com to explore how a movie has been received in political terms. Particularly useful general information about movies may be found at sites like imdb.com, allmovie.com, and rottentomatoes.com (which compile movie reviews for all films). These and other sites are compiled in Appendix 2 of this volume. Additionally, many Web sites are devoted to providing information about specific topics that frequently relate to politics and film; an introduction to film-related Web sites is contained in Appendix 2. The Internet also can provide ready access to news, reviews, and commercial information about specific films. Many instructors ask their students to write papers that compare several movies with respect to a specific theme; Web resources can provide an excellent starting point for creating comparisons between films.

Appendix 2

The Net

A Brief Guide to Web-Based Film Resources

GENERAL FILM INFORMATION

These sites contain general information on movies and actors as well as movie reviews. Some sites include box office and business data.

All Movie Guide
www.allmovie.com
    Part of the AMG All Media Guides. Film reviews, plots, and credit information.

American Communication Association—Film
www.americancomm.org/studies/film.html
    Comprehensive portal containing links to sites dedicated to various aspects and genres of film.

Box Office Guru
www.boxofficeguru.com
    This database contains comprehensive box office data on motion pictures released between 1989 and the present.

Internet Movie Database
www.imdb.com
    Extensive information about films—plots, actors, directors, reviews—including such details as bloopers, continuity errors, and alternate versions. IMDbPro is an additional, paid service that provides information about film budgets and box office figures.

Media Resources Center Movie Database
www.lib.berkeley.edu/MRC/moviedb.html
University of California–Berkeley site provides information about specific movies—plots and actors. Also serves as a research starting point for history of specific genres of film and various aspects of film history.

Movie Review Query Engine
www.mrqe.com/lookup
Film review site. Searchable database of published film reviews and similar articles.

Rotten Tomatoes
www.rottentomatoes.com
Film review site. Compiles reviews from various news outlets and features an in-house staff.

FILM JOURNALS AND MAGAZINES

Bright Lights Film Journal
www.brightlightsfilm.com/index.html
Articles about film—history and plot analysis.

Film Quarterly
www.ucpress.edu/journals/fq/
From University of California Press. In-depth, academic-quality articles about various aspects of film: film history, analysis of films, articles on moviemakers, and film theory.

Variety
www.variety.com
Film industry news and gossip. In addition to the entertainment side of Hollywood, *Variety* also covers the business end, reporting weekend and weekly box office figures and studio news.

INDEPENDENT AND GENRE-SPECIFIC FILM SITES

Independent Film at the IMDb
www.indie.imdb.com/index.indie
IMDb's section dedicated to independent films. Film news, plot lines, and other details. Information provided similar to IMDb's main site.

indieWIRE
www.indiewire.com/
Coverage of independent film, including news and film festival coverage.

Political Film Society

www.geocities.com/~polfilms/

Most comprehensive site for overtly political films. Includes political analysis of political films (and nonpolitical films analyzed from a political perspective), reviews, and articles on the political and historical contexts of films featured.

Science Fiction Cinema

www.sciflicks.com/

Includes movie guides, film reviews, and news on science fiction films.

Silent Films

www.uno.edu/~drcom/silents.html

Provides links to various sites on silent films.

Sticking It to the Man

www.stickingittotheman.com/heroes/blaxploitation.html

Guide to the blaxploitation genre, including important films, heroes, and issues in these revolutionary films.

War and Anti-War Films

www.filmsite.org/warfilms.html

History of war and antiwar films in Hollywood as well as internationally. Narrative includes plot lines and actors as well as historical and political contexts of each film mentioned.

World/Independent Film

www.worldfilm.about.com/

Part of the About.com Guides. Features reviews and articles about upcoming independent and world films.

MINORITY AND SPECIAL INTEREST FILMS

African Americans in the Movies

www.lib.berkeley.edu/MRC/AfricanAmBib.html

List of resources on African-Americans in film as well as films with African-American themes.

Black Film Center/Archive

www.indiana.edu/~bfca/

Collection of articles and resources on African-Americans in film, including features on African-American Oscar winners and African-American directors.

Chicanos/Latinos in the Movies
www.lib.berkeley.edu/MRC/LatinoBib.html
List of resources on Latinos in film as well as Latino-themed films.

OutTakes
www.outtakes.net/
Lesbian film reviews.

PopcornQ Movies
www.planetout.com/popcornq/
Articles and reviews focusing on gay film.

Women and Film
www.bama.ua.edu/~mbarrett/filmwsslinks.html
From the women's studies section of the Association of College and Research Libraries. Provides comprehensive listing of related Web resources.

Women in Cinema: A Reference Guide
www.people.virginia.edu/~pm9k/libsci/womFilm.html
Comprehensive reference source including bibliographies, biographies, and reviews.

FILM INDUSTRY ORGANIZATIONS

Academy of Motion Pictures Arts and Sciences
www.oscars.org/index.html

American Film Institute
www.afi.com

British Film Institute
www.bfi.org.uk/

Motion Picture Association of America
www.mpaa.org/

NEWSPAPER FILM REVIEWS

Chicago Sun-Times—Roger Ebert
www.suntimes.com/index/ebert.html
Requires free subscription.

Guardian (UK)—Film
www.film.guardian.co.uk/

The New York Times—Movies
www.nytimes.com/pages/movies/
   Requires free subscription.

The Village Voice—Film
www.villagevoice.com/film/

Appendix 3

Closing Credits
A Political Filmography

Closing Credits: A Political Filmography

Title	Year	Director	Screenwriter	Additional Screenwriter(s)
Abe Lincoln in Illinois	1940	John Cromwell	Grover Jones	
Abraham Lincoln	1930	D.W. Griffith	D.W. Griffith	
Abraham Lincoln, The Dramatic Life of	1924	Phil Rosen	Frances Marion	
Absence of Malice	1981	Sydney Pollack	Kurt Luedtke	
Absolute Power	1997	Clint Eastwood	William Goldman	
Accused, The	1988	Jonathan Kaplan	Tom Toptor	
Advise and Consent	1962	Otto Preminger	Wendell Mayes	
Against All Odds	1984	Taylor Hackford	Eric Hughes	Richard Rush
Air America	1990	Roger Spottiswoode	John Eskow	
Air Force One	1997	Wolfgang Peterson	Andrew W. Marlowe	
Alamo Bay	1985	Louis Malle	Louis Malle	
Alice Doesn't Live Here Anymore	1975	Martin Scorsese	Robert Getchell	
All Quiet on the Western Front	1930	Lewis Milestone	Lewis Milestone et al.	Robert Penn Warren
All the King's Men	1949	Robert Rossen	Robert Rossen	
All the President's Men	1976	Alan Pakula	William Goldman	
America	1924	D.W. Griffith	D.W. Griffith	
American Graffiti	1973	George Lucus	George Lucus	Gloria Katz, Willard Huyck
American Madness	1932	Frank Capra	Robert Riskin	
American President, The	1995	Rob Reiner	Aaron Sorkin	
American Way, The	1986	Maurice Phillips	Scott Roberts	
Amistad	1997	Steven Spielberg	David Franzoni	
And Justice For All	1979	Norman Jewison	Valerie Curtin	Barry Levinson
Annie Hall	1977	Woody Allen	Woody Allen	Marshall Brickman
Apocalypse Now	1979	Francis Ford Coppola	Francis Ford Coppola	John Milius
Arlington Road	1999	Mark Pellington	Ehren Kruger	
Arrowsmith	1931	John Ford	Sidney Howard	
Atomic Café, The	1982	Jane Loader	Jane Loader	K. and P. Rafferty

Film	Year	Director	Screenwriter	Additional Screenwriter(s)
Attack of the Fifty-Foot Woman	1958	Nathan Juran	Mark Hanna	
Baby Boom	1987	Charles Shyer	Nancy Meyers	Charles Shyer
Back to Bataan	1945	Edward Dmytryk	Ben Barzman	Richard H. Landau
Bait	2000	Antoine Fuqua	Adam Scheinman	Andrew Scheinman, T. Gilroy
Bamboozled	2000	Spike Lee	Spike Lee	
Bananas	1971	Woody Allen	Woody Allen	
Barbershop	2002	Tim Story	Mark Brown	Don D. Scott, M. Todd
Basic Instinct	1992	Paul Verhoeven	Joe Esterhaz	
Beau James	1957	Melville Shavelson	Melville Shavelson	Jack Rose
Being There	1979	Hal Ashby	Jerry Kosinski	
Beloved	1998	Jonathan Demme	Akosua Busia	Richard LaGravenese, A. Brooks
Best Man, The	1964	Franklin Shaffner	Gore Vidal	
Best Years of Our Lives, The	1946	William Wyler	Robert Sherwood	
Betrayed	1988	Costa-Gavras	Joe Eszterhas	
Between the Lines	1977	Joan Micklin Silver	Joan Micklin Silver	
Beverly Hills Cop	1984	Martin Brest	Danilo Bach (and story)	Daniel Petrie Jr. (and story)
Big Chill, The	1983	Lawrence Kasdan	Lawrence Kasdan	Barbara Benedeck
Big Jim McLain	1952	Edward Ludwig	James Edward Grant	
Big Parade, The	1925	King Vidor	Lawrence Stallings	Harry Behn
Big Wednesday	1978	John Milius	John Milius	Dennis Aberg
Birth of a Nation, The	1915	D.W. Griffith	D.W. Griffith	Frank E. Woods
Black Hawk Down	2001	Ridely Scott	Ken Nolan	
Black Legion	1937	Archie Mayor	Abem Finkel	William Wister Haines
Blaze	1989	Ron Shelton	Ron Shelton	
Blockade	1938	William Dieterle	John Howard Lawson	
Blow Out	1981	Brian de Palma	Brian de Palma	
Blue Collar	1978	Paul Schraeder	Paul Schraeder	Leonard Schraeder
Bob Roberts	1992	Tim Robbins	Tim Robbins	
Body Heat	1981	Lawrence Kasdan	Lawrence Kasdan	
Border, The	1981	Tony Richardson	Deric Washburn	Walon Green, David Freeman
Born on the Fourth of July	1989	Oliver Stone	Oliver Stone	Ron Kovic

Appendix 3, Table (*continued*)

Film	Year	Director	Screenwriter	Additional Screenwriter(s)
Born Yesterday	1950	George Cukor	Albert Mannheimer	
Born Yesterday	1993	Luis Madoki	Leslie Dixon	
Bound for Glory	1976	Hal Ashby	Robert Getchell	
Bowling for Columbine	2003	Michael Moore	Michael Moore	
Boys in Company C, The	1978	Sidney J. Furie	Sidney J. Furie	Rick Natkin
Boyz N the Hood	1991	John Singleton	John Singleton	
Bread and Roses	2000	Ken Loach	Paul Laverty	
Bringing Down the House	1992	Adam Shankman	Jason Filardi	
Broken Arrow	1950	Delmer Daves	Michael Blankfort (Albert Maltz)	
Brubaker	1980	Stuart Rosenberg	W.D. Richter	
Bulworth	1998	Warren Beatty	Jeremy Pikser	
Candidate, The	1972	Michael Ritchie	Jeremy Larner	
Casa de Las Babys	2003	John Sayles	John Sayles	
Casablanca	1942	Michael Curtiz	Howard Koch	
Casualties of War	1989	Brian de Palma	David Rabe	
Catch 22	1970	Mike Nichols	Buck Henry	
Che!	1969	Richard Fleischner	Michael Wilson	Sy Bartlett
Cheyenne Autumn	1964	John Ford	James R. Webb	
China Syndrome, The	1979	James Bridges	James Bridges	T.S. Bridges, Mike Gray
Chinatown	1974	Roman Polansky	Robert Towne	
Citizen Kane	1941	Orson Welles	Herman Mankiewicz	Orson Welles
Citizen Ruth	1996	Alexander Payne	Alexander Payne	Jim Taylor
City of Hope	1991	John Sayles	John Sayles	
Civil Action, A	1998	Steven Zaillia	Steven Zaillian	
Clear and Present Danger	1994	Phillip Noyce	Donald Stewart	John Millius, Steven Zallian
Cleopatra	1912	Charles L. Gaskill		
Close Encounters of the Third Kind	1977	Steven Spielberg	Steven Spielberg	
Coffy	1973	Jack Hill	Jack Hill	
Collateral Damage	2002	Andrew Davis	David Griffiths	Peter Griffiths

Film	Year	Director	Screenwriter	Additional Screenwriter(s)
Color Purple, The	1985	Steven Spielberg	Menno Meyjes	Robert C. Jones
Coming Home	1978	Hal Ashby	Waldo Salt	John Wexley
Confessions of a Nazi Spy	1939	Anatole Litvak	Milton Krims	
Conspiracy Theory	1997	Richard Donner	Brian Helgeland	
Contender, The	2000	Rod Lurie	Rod Lurie	
Control Room	2004	Jehane Noujame	Jehane Noujame	Julia Bacha
Conversation, The	1974	Francis Ford Coppola	Francis Ford Coppola	
Country	1984	Richard Pearce	Richard Pearce	
Crack: The Big Lie	1987	Mark Jean	Mark Jean	
Cradle Will Rock	1999	Tim Robbins	Tim Robbins	
Creature from the Black Lagoon, The	1954	Jack Arnold	Harry Essex	
Crimson Tide	1995	Tony Scott	Michael Schiffer	
Crisis	1950	Richard Brooks	Richard Brooks	
Crossfire	1947	Edward Dmytryk	John Paxton	
Crowd, The	1928	King Vidor	King Vidor	John V.A. Weaver
Crush, The	1993	Alan Shapiro	Alan Shapiro	
Cry Freedom	1987	Richard Attenborough	John Briley	
Dance, Fools, Dance	1931	Harry Beaumont	Aurania Rouverol	Richard Shayer
Dances with Wolves	1990	Kevin Costner	Michael Blake	
Daniel	1983	Sidney Lumet	E.L. Doctorow	
Dark City	1998	Alex Proyas	Alex Proyas	
Dark Horse, The	1932	Alfred E. Green	Joseph Jackson	Wilson Mizner
Dave	1993	Ivan Reitman	Gary Ross	
Day After Tomorrow	2004	Roland Emmerich	Roland Emmerich	
Days of Glory	1944	Jacques Tourneur	Casey Robinson	
Days of Heaven	1978	Terence Malick	Terence Malick	
Dead Man Walking	1995	Tim Robbins	Tim Robbins	
Dead Zone	1983	David Cronenberg	Jeffrey Boam	
Death Wish	1974	Michael Winner	Wendell Mayes	
Deer Hunter, The	1978	Michael Cimino	Deric Washburn	
Defiant Ones, The	1958	Stanley Kramer	Nathan E. Douglas	H.J. Smith

Appendix 3, Table (continued)

Film	Year	Director	Screenwriter	Additional Screenwriter(s)
Deliverance	1972	John Boorman	James Dickey	
Deterrence	2000	Rod Lurie	Rod Lurie	
Devil's Daughter, The	1915	Frank Powell	Garfield Thompson	
Dick	1999	Andrew Fleming	Sheryl Longin	
Dirty Harry	1971	Don Siegel	John Milius	Harry Julian Fink, R.M. Fink, Dean Risner
Disclosure	1994	Barry Levinson	Michael Crichton	Paul Attanasio
Distinguished Gentleman, The	1992	Jonathan Reynolds	Jonathan Reynolds	
Do the Right Thing	1989	Spike Lee	Spike Lee	
Dog Day Afternoon	1975	Sidney Lumet	Frank Pierson	
Double Indemnity	1944	Billy Wilder	Billy Wilder	
Dr. Strangelove	1964	Stanley Kubrick	Stanley Kubrick	Terry Southern, Peter George
Doctor Zhivago	1965	David Lean	Robert Bolt	
Driving Miss Daisy	1989	Steven Spielberg	Alfred Uhry	
Dry White Season, A	1989	Colin Welland	Euzhan Palcy	
Duck Soup	1933	Leo McCarey	Bert Kalmar et al.	
Easy Rider	1969	Dennis Hopper	Dennis Hopper	Terry Southern
El Norte	1983	Gregory Nava	Gregory Nava	Anna Thomas
Election	1999	Alexander Payne	Alexander Payne	Jim Taylor
Eleni	1985	Peter Yates	Steve Tesich	
Endangered Species	1982	Alan Rudolph	Alan Rudolph	John Binder
Enemy of the State	1998	Tony Scott	David Marconi	
Enforcer, The	1976	James Fargo	Stirling Silliphant	Dean Riesner
Erin Brockovich	2000	Steven Soderbergh	Susannah Grant	
Executive Action	1973	David Miller	Dalton Trumbo	
Executive Decision	1996	Stuart Baird	Jim Thomas	John Thomas
Executive Suite	1954	Robert Wise	Ernest Lehman	
Exodus	1960	Otto Preminger	Dalton Trumbo	
Extremities	1986	Robert M. Young	William Mastrosimone	

Film	Year	Director	Screenwriter	Additional Screenwriter(s)
F.I.S.T.	1978	Norman Jewison	Joe Eszterhas	Sylvester Stallone
Face in the Crowd, A	1957	Elia Kazan	Budd Schulberg	
Fahrenheit 9/11	2004	Michael Moore	Michael Moore	
Fail Safe	1964	Sidney Lumet	Walter Bernstein	
Falcon and the Snowman, The	1985	John Schlesinger	Steven Zaillian	
Falling Down	1993	Joel Schumacher	Ebbe Roe Smith	
Far From Heaven	2002	Todd Haynes	Todd Haynes	
Farmer's Daughter, The	1947	H.C. Potter	Allen Rivkin	Laura Kerr
Fat Man and Little Boy	1989	Roland Joffe	Bruce Robinson	
Fatal Attraction	1987	Adrian Lyne	James Dearden	Nicholas Meyer
First Blood	1982	Ted Kotcheff	Michael Kozoll	William Seckheirn, Sylvester Stallone
First Family	1980	Buck Henry	Buck Henry	
First Lady	1937	Stanley Logan	Rowland Leigh	
First Monday in October	1981	Ronald Neame	Jerome Lawrence	Robert E. Lee
Fog of War, The	2003	Errol Morris	Errol Morris	
Fool There Was, A	1915	Frank Powell	Porter Emerson Browne	
For Whom the Bell Tolls	1943	Sam Wood	Dudley Nicholls	
Forbidden	1932	Frank Capra	Frank Capra	
Foreign Affair	1948	Billy Wilder	Billy Wilder	Charles Brackett
Formula, The	1980	John Avildsen	Steven Shagan	
Forrest Gump	1994	Robert Zemeckis	Eric Roth	
48 Hrs	1982	Walter Hill	Roger Spottiswoode	Larry Gross et al.
Front, The	1976	Martin Ritt	Walter Bernstein	
Full Metal Jacket	1987	Stanley Kubrick	Stanley Kubrick	Gustav Hasford
Fury	1936	Fritz Lang	Fritz Lang	Bartlett Cormack
Gabriel Over the White House	1933	Gregory La Cava	Carey Wilson	Bertram Bloch
Gandhi	1982	Richard Attenborough	John Briley	
Gangs of New York	2002	Martin Scorsese	Jay Cocks	
Gardens of Stone	1987	Francis Ford Coppola	Ron Bass	
General Died at Dawn, The	1936	Lewis Milestone	Clifford Odets	

313

Appendix 3, Table (continued)

Film	Year	Director	Screenwriter	Additional Screenwriter(s)
General Idi Amin Dada	1974	Barbet Schroeder	Barbet Schroeder	
Gentleman's Agreement	1947	Elia Kazan	Moss Hart	
Gentlemen Prefer Blondes	1953	Howard Hawks	Charles Lederer	
Getting Straight	1970	Richard Rush	Robert Kaufman	
Ghosts of Mississippi	1996	Rob Reiner	Lewis Colick	
Giant	1956	George Stevens	Fred Guiol	John Seale Ivan Moffatt
Glass Key, The	1942	Stuart Heisler	Jonathan Lattimer	
Glory	1989	Edward Zwick	Kevin Jarre	
Go Tell the Spartans	1978	Ted Post	Wendell Mayes	
Godfather, The	1972	Francis Ford Coppola	Francis Ford Coppola	
Godfather, The, Part II	1974	Francis Ford Coppola	Mario Puzo	
Gone with the Wind	1939	Victor Fleming	Sidney Howard	
Good Morning Vietnam	1987	Barry Levinson	Mitch Markowitz	
Graduate, The	1967	Mike Nichols	Buck Henry	Calder Willingham
Grand Canyon	1991	Lawrence Kasdan	Meg Kasdan	Lawrence Kasdan
Grapes of Wrath, The	1940	John Ford	Nunnally Johnson	
Great Dictator, The	1940	Charles Chaplin	Charles Chaplin	
Great McGinty, The	1940	Preston Sturges	Preston Sturges	
Great White Hope, The	1970	Martin Ritt	Howard Sackler	
Greed	1923	Erich von Stroheim	Erich von Stroheim	
Green Berets, The	1968	John Wayne, R. Kellog	James Lee Barrett	
Greetings	1968	Brian de Palma	Brian de Palma	
Group, The	1966	Sidney Lumet	Sidney Buchman	
Guess Who's Coming to Dinner	1967	Stanley Kramer	William Rose	
Hail the Conquering Hero	1944	Preston Sturges	Preston Sturges	
Hair	1979	Milos Forman	Michael Weller	
Hand That Rocks the Cradle, The	1992	Curtis Hanson	Amanda Silver	
Harlan County USA	1977	Barbara Kopple	Barbara Kopple	
Harriet Craig	1950	Vincent Sherman	James Gunn	Anne Froelich

Film	Year	Director	Screenwriter	Additional Screenwriter(s)
Head of State	2003	Chris Rock	Chris Rock	
Heartbreak Ridge	1986	Clint Eastwood	James Carbatsos	
Hearts and Minds	1974	Peter Davis	Peter Davis	
Heaven and Earth	1987	Ulli Lommell	Ulli Lommell	
Heaven's Gate	1980	Michael Cimino	Michael Cimino	
Her Honor the Governor	1926	Chet Withey	Doris Anderson	
Hi Mom!	1969	Brian de Palma	Brian de Palma	
High Noon	1952	Fred Zinnemann	Carl Foreman	
High School	1968	Frederick Wiseman	Frederick Wiseman	
Hitler Gang, The	1944	John Farrow	Frances Goodrich	Albert Hackett
Hitler's Children	1943	Edward Dmytryk	Emmett Lavery	
Hitler's Madman	1943	Douglas Sirk	Melvin Levy, Peretz Hirshbein	Doris Molloy
Hoffa	1992	Danny Devito	David Mamet	
Hollywood on Trial	1976	David Helpern	Arnie Reisman	
Home of the Brave	1949	Mark Robson	Carl Foreman	
Honorary Consul, The	1983	John MacKenzie	Christopher Hampton	
Hospital	1970	Frederick Wiseman	Frederick Wiseman	
How to Marry a Millionaire	1953	Jean Negulesco	Nunnally Johnson	
Human Stain, The	2003	Robert Benton	Nicholas Meyer	
Hunt for Red October, The	1990	John McTiernan	Donald Stewart	Larry Ferguson
Hunting of the President, The	2004	Nickolas Perry, H. Thomason	Nickolas Perry	Harry Thomason
I Am a Fugitive from a Chain Gang	1932	Mervyn LeRoy	Sheridan Gibney	Brown Holmes, Robert E. Burns
I Married a Communist	1949	Robert Stevenson	Charles Grayson	Robert Hardy Andrews
I Spit on Your Grave (Day of the Woman)	1978	Meir Zarchi	Meir Zarchi	
I Was a Communist for the FBI	1951	Gordon Douglas	Crane Wilbur	Matt Cvetic
Idiot's Delight	1939	Clarence Brown	Robert E. Sherwood	
Imitation of Life	1959	Douglas Sirk	Eleanore Griffin	
In the Heat of the Night	1967	Norman Jewison	Sterling Silliphant	
In the Line of Fire	1993	Wolfgang Petersen	Jeff McGuire	
In the Year of the Pig	1968	Emile de Antonio		
In This Our Life	1942	John Huston	Howard Koch	

315

Film	Year	Director	Screenwriter	Additional Screenwriter(s)
Independence Day	1996	Roland Emmerich	Roland Emmerich	
Informer, The	1935	John Ford	Dudley Nichols	
Inherit the Wind	1960	Stanley Kramer	Nathan E. Douglas	Harold J. Smith
Insider, The	1999	Michael Mann	Eric Roth	Michael Mann
Intolerance	1916	D.W. Griffith	D.W. Griffith	
Intruder in the Dust	1949	Clarence Brown	Ben Maddow	
Invasion of the Body Snatchers	1956	Don Siegal	Richard Collins	Jack Finney, Daniel Mainwaring, Sam Peckinpah
Invasion U.S.A.	1985	Joseph Zito	James Bruner	
Iron Curtain	1948	William Wellman	Milton Krims	
Iron Eagle	1986	Sidney J. Furie	Sidney J. Furie	Kevin Elders
It	1927	Clarence G. Badger	Elinor Glyn	Hope Loring
JFK	1991	Oliver Stone	Oliver Stone	Zachary Sklar
Joe	1970	John G. Avildson	Norman Wexler	
Johnny Got His Gun	1971	Dalton Trumbo	Dalton Trumbo	
Juarez	1939	William Dieterle	John Huston et al.	
Judgment at Nuremburg	1961	Stanley Kramer	Abby Mann	
Julia	1977	Fred Zinnemann	Alvin Sargent	
Kelly's Heroes	1970	Brian G. Hutton	Troy Kennedy Martin	
Killing Fields, The	1984	Roland Joffe	Bruce Robinson	
King in New York, A	1956	Charles Chaplin	Charles Chaplin	
King Kong	1933	Merian C. Cooper	Merian C. Cooper	Edgar Wallace
Kiss of the Spider Woman	1985	Hector Babenco	Leonard Schrader	
Kramer vs. Kramer	1979	Robert Benton	Robert Benton	
Last Hurrah, The	1958	John Ford	Frank Nugent	
Last Samurai, The	2003	Edward Zwick	John Logan	Edward Zwick, Marshall Herskovitz
Last Seduction, The	1994	John Dahl	Steve Barancik	
Latino	1985	Haskell Wexler	Haskell Wexler	

Film	Year	Director	Screenwriter	Additional Screenwriter(s)
Laura	1944	Otto Preminger	Vera Caspary	Jay Dratler
Law and Order	1969	Frederick Wiseman	Frederick Wiseman	
Legally Blonde 2: Red, White, and Blonde	2003	Charles Herman-Wurmfel	Kate Kondell	
Lethal Weapon	1987	Richard Donner	Shane Black	
Lifeboat	1944	Alfred Hitchcock	John Steinbeck	
Limbo	1999	John Sayles	John Sayles	
Lion Is In the Streets, A	1953	Raoul Walsh	Luther Davis	
Little Big Man	1970	Arthur Penn	Calder Willingham	
Little Drummer Girl, The	1984	George Roy Hill	Loring Madel	
Lone Star	1996	John Sayles	John Sayles	
*M*A*S*H*	1970	Robert Altman	Ring Lardner Jr.	
Malcolm X	1992	Spike Lee	Arnold Perl	
Man on a Tightrope	1953	Elia Kazan	Robert Sherwood	
Man with the Golden Arm, The	1955	Otto Preminger	Walter Newman	Lewis Meltzer
Man, The	1972	Joseph Sargent	Joseph Sargent	
Manchurian Candidate, The	1962	John Frankenheimer	John Frankenheimer	George Axelrod
Manchurian Candidate, The	2004	Jonathan Demme	Daniel Pyne	Dean Gougaris
Manhattan Project, The	1986	Marshall Brickman	Marshall Brickman	Thomas Baum
Marie	1985	Roger Donaldson	John Briley	
Mars Attacks!	1996	Tim Burton	Jonathan Gems	
Matewan	1987	John Sayles	John Sayles	
Matrix Reloaded, The	2003	Andy Wachowski	Larry Wachowski	Andy Wachowski
Matrix Revolutions, The	2003	Andy Wachowski	Larry Wachowski	Andy Wachowski
Matrix, The	1999	Andy Wachowski	Larry Wachowski	Andy Wachowski
Medium Cool	1969	Haskell Wexler	Haskell Wexler	
Meet John Doe	1941	Frank Capra	Robert Riskin	
Men in Black	1997	Barry Sonnenfield	Ed Solomon	
Men with Guns	1997	John Sayles	John Sayles	
Menace II Society	1993	Albert and Allen Hughes	Albert and Allen Hughes	Tyger Williams
Milagro Beanfield War, The	1988	Robert Redford	John Nichols	David Ward
Mildred Pierce	1945	Michael Curtiz	James M. Cain	Ranald MacDougall

317

Film	Year	Director	Screenwriter	Additional Screenwriter(s)
Milhouse	1971	Emile de Antonio	Nicholas St. John	
Missing	1982	Costa-Gavras	Costa-Gavras	Donald Stewart
Missing in Action	1984	Joseph Zito	Joseph Zito	
Mission to Moscow	1943	Michael Curtiz	Howard Koch	
Mission, The	1986	Roland Joffee	Robert Bolt	
Mississippi Burning	1988	Alan Parker	Chris Gerolmo	
Monkey Business	1952	Howard Hawks	Harry Segall	Ben Hecht
Monsieur Verdoux	1947	Charles Chaplin	Charles Chaplin	
Moon Over Parador	1988	Paul Mazursky	Paul Mazursky	Leon Capetanos
Mr. Deeds Goes to Town	1936	Frank Capra	Robert Riskin	
Mr. Mom	1983	Stan Dragoti	John Hughes	
Mr. Smith Goes to Washington	1939	Frank Capra	Sidney Buchman	
Mrs. Miniver	1942	William Wyler	George Froeschel	James Hilton, Jan Struther, Claudine West, Arthur Wimperis
Ms. 45	1981	Abel Ferrara	Nicholas St. John	
Murder at 1600	1997	Dwight H. Little	Wayne Beach	David Hodgin
Music Box	1989	Costa-Gavras	Joe Eszterhas	
My Fellow Americans	1994	Peter Segal	E. Jack Kaplan	Richard Chapman, P. Tolan
My Man Godfrey	1936	Gregory La Cava	Gregory La Cava	Morrie Riskind et al.
My Son John	1952	Leo McCarey	Myles Connelly	
Nanook of the North	1922	Robert J. Flaherty	Robert J. Flaherty	
Nashville	1975	Robert Altman	Joan Tewkesbury	
Natural Born Killers	1994	Oliver Stone	Oliver Stone	David Veloz, Richard Rutowski
Navy Seals	1990	Lewis Teague	Chuck Pfarrer	Gary Goldman
Network	1976	Sidney Lumet	Paddy Chayefsky	
New Jack City	1991	Mario Van Peebles	Thomas Lee Wright	Barry Michael Cooper
Nine to Five	1980	Colin Higgins	Colin Higgins	
1969	1988	Ernest Thompson	Ernest Thompson	

Film	Year	Director	Screenwriter	Additional Screenwriter(s)
Nixon	1995	Oliver Stone	Oliver Stone	Stephen J. Rivele
No Way Out	1987	Roger Donaldson	Robert Garland	
Norma Rae	1979	Martin Ritt	Irving Ravetch	Frank Harriet Jr.
North Star, The	1943	Lewis Milestone	Lillian Hellman	
Old Gringo	1989	Luis Puenzo	Alda Bortnik	Luis Puenzo
On the Beach	1959	Stanley Kramer	John Paxton	James Lee Barrett
On the Waterfront	1954	Elia Kazan	Budd Schulberg	
One, Two, Three	1961	Billy Wilder	Billy Wilder	
Orphans of the Storm	1921	D.W. Griffith	D.W. Griffith	
Our Blushing Brides	1930	Bess Meredyth	John Howard Lawson	
Our Daily Bread	1934	King Vidor	King Vidor	Elizabeth Hill
Our Dancing Daughters	1928	Harry Beaumont	Josephine Lovitt	
Our Modern Maidens	1929	Jack Conway	Marian Ainslee	Ruth Cummings
Outfoxed: Rupert Murdoch's War on Journalism	2004	Robert Greenwald		
P.T. 109	1963	Leslie Martinson	Richard L. Breen	Lucien Hubbard
Paid	1930	Sam Wood	Bayard Veiller	Lorenzo Semple Jr.
Parallax View, The	1974	Alan J. Pakula	David Giler	Benedict Fitzgerald
Passion of Christ, The	2004	Mel Gibson	Mel Gibson	Calder Willingham, J. Thompson
Paths of Glory	1957	Stanley Kubrick	Stanley Kubrick	Donald Stewart
Patriot Games	1992	Phillip Noyce	W. Peter Illif	Edmund H. North
Patton	1969	Franklin Schaffner	Francis Ford Coppola	Morton Fine
Pawnbroker, The	1965	Sidney Lumet	David Friedkin	Larry Karaszewski
People vs. Larry Flynt, The	1996	Milos Forman	Scott Alexander	Harlan Thompson
Phantom President, The	1932	Norman Taurog	Walter de Leon	Dudley Nichols
Pinky	1949	Elia Kazan	Phillip Dunne	
Places in the Heart	1984	Robert Benton	Robert Benton	
Plainsman, The	1936	Cecile B. DeMille	Waldemar Young et al.	
Planet of the Apes	1968	Franklin J. Schaffner	Michael Wilson	Rod Sterling
Platoon	1986	Oliver Stone	Oliver Stone	
Point of Order	1964	Emile de Antonio	Emile de Antonio	Robert Duncan

Appendix 3, Table (continued)

Film	Year	Director	Screenwriter	Additional Screenwriter(s)
Politics	1931	Charles Reiner	Wells Root	
Possessed	1931	Clarence Brown	Edgar Selwyn	
Possessed	1947	Curtis Bernhardt	Ranald MacDougall	Lawrence Menkin
Power	1986	Sidney Lumet	David Himmelstein	
President Vanishes, The	1934	William Wellman	Cary Wilson	Cedric Worth
Primary Colors	1998	Mike Nichols	Elaine May	
Private Files of J. Edgar Hoover, The	1978	Larry Cohen	Larry Cohen	
Protocol	1984	Herbert Ross	Buck Henry	
Public Enemy, The	1931	William A. Wellman	Kubec Glasman	John Bright
Public Housing	1997	Frederick Wiseman	Frederick Wiseman	
Pull Down the Curtains, Suzie	1904			
Pulp Fiction	1994	Quentin Tarantino	Quentin Tarantino	
Queen Bee	1955	Ranald MacDougall	Edna L. Lee	Ranald MacDougall
Quiet American, The	1958	Joseph L. Mankiewicz	Joseph L. Mankiewicz	
Quiet American, The	2002	Phillip Noyce	Robert Schenkkan	
Ragtime	1981	Milos Forman	Michael Weller	
Rally Round the Flag, Boys	1958	Leo McCarey	Leo McCarey	Claude Binyon
Rambo: First Blood, Part II	1985	George Pan Cosmatos	James Cameron	Sylvester Stallone
Rambo III	1988	Peter Macdonald	Sylvester Stallone	
Red Dawn	1984	John Milius	John Milius	Kevin Reynolds
Rebel Without a Cause	1955	Nicholas Ray	Nicholas Ray	Irving Shulman, Stewart Stern
Reds	1981	Warren Beatty	Warren Beatty	Trevor Griffiths
Reefer Madness	1938	Louis Gasnier	Arthur Hoerl	
Return of the Secaucus Seven	1980	John Sayles	John Sayles	
Revolution	1985	Hugh Hudson	Hugh Hudson	
Right Stuff, The	1983	Phillip Kaufman	Phillip Kaufman	
River, The	1984	Mark Rydell	Robert Dillon	Julian Barry
Rocky	1976	Sylvester Stallone	Sylvester Stallone	
Rocky IV	1985	Sylvester Stallone	Sylvester Stallone	
Roger & Me	1989	Michael Moore	Michael Moore	

320

Film	Year	Director	Screenwriter	Additional Screenwriter(s)
Rolling Thunder	1977	John Flynn	Paul Schrader	Heywood Gould
Rollover	1981	Alan J. Pakula	David Shaber	
Romero	1989	John Duigan	John Sacret Young	
Running on Empty	1988	Sidney Lumet	Naomi Foner	
Russia House	1990	Fred Schepisi	Tom Stoppard	
Russians Are Coming!, The	1966	Norman Jewison	William Rose	
Salome	1908	J. Stuart Blackton	Oscar Wilde (play)	Theodore A. Liebler Jr. (scenario)
Salt of the Earth	1954	Herbert Biberman	Michael Wilson	
Salvador	1986	Oliver Stone	Oliver Stone	Richard Boyle
Sankofa	1993	Haile Gerima	Haile Gerima	
Saving Private Ryan	1998	Steven Spielberg	Robert Rodat	Steven Zaillian
Schindler's List	1993	Steven Spielberg	Karl Luedtke	
Sea Hawk, The	1940	Michael Curtiz	Howard Koch	
Secret Honor	1994	Robert Altman	Donald Freed	Arnold Stone
Seduction of Joe Tynan, The	1979	Jerry Schatzberg	Alan Alda	
Senator Was Indiscreet, The	1947	George Kaufman	Charles MacArthur	
Sergeant York	1941	Howard Hawks	Ben Finkel	Harry Chandler
Seven Days in May	1964	John Frankenheimer	Rod Serling	
Seven Year Itch, The	1955	Billy Wilder	Billy Wilder	George Axlerod
Shaft	1971	Gordon Parks Jr.	John D.F. Black	Ernest Tidyman
Shaft in Africa	1973	John Guillermin	Stirling Silliphant	
Shaft's Big Score	1972	Gordon Parks Jr.	Ernest Tidyman	
Shampoo	1975	Hal Ashby	Robert Towne	Warren Beatty
She Devil, The	1918	J. Gordon Edwards	George James Hopkins	
Ship of Fools	1965	Stanley Kramer	Abby Mann	
Short Circuit	1986	John Badham	S.S. Wilson	Brent Maddock
Siege, The	1998	Edward Zwick	Lawrence Wright	
Silkwood	1983	Mike Nichols	Nora Ephron	Alice Arle
Sin	1915	Herbert Brenon	Herbert Brenon	
Single White Female	1992	Barbet Schroeder	Don Roos	
Siren of Hell	1915	Raoul Walsh		
Small Circle of Friends	1980	Rob Cohen	Ezra Sacks	

Appendix 3, Table *(continued)*

Film	Year	Director	Screenwriter	Additional Screenwriter(s)
Soul Food	1997	George Tilman Jr.	George Tilman Jr.	
Soul Man	1986	Steve Miner	Carol Black	
Spy Who Came In from the Cold, The	1966	Martin Ritt	Paul Deb	
Star Chamber, The	1983	Peter Hyams	Peter Hyams	
Star Wars	1977	George Lucas	George Lucas	
State of Siege	1973	Costa-Gavras	Costa-Gavras	Franco Solinas
State of the Union	1948	Frank Capra	Anthony Veiller	Miles Connelly
Steelyard Blues	1972	Alan Myerson	David S. Ward	
Storm Center	1956	Daniel Taradash	Daniel Taradash	
Storm Warning	1950	Stuart Heisler	Daniel Fuchs	Richard Brooks
Strategic Air Command	1955	Anthony Mann	Valentine Davies	Beirne Lay Jr.
Strawberry Statement, The	1970	Stuart Hagmann	Israel Horovitz	
Sullivan's Travels	1941	Preston Sturges	Preston Sturges	
Sum of All Fears, The	2002	Phil Alden Robinson	Paul Attanasio	Daniel Pyne
Sunrise	1927	F.W. Murnau	Carl Mayer	
Sunrise at Campobello	1960	Vincent J. Donohue	Dore Schary	
Sunshine State	2003	John Sayles	John Sayles	
Super Size Me	2004	Morgan Spurlock	Morgan Spurlock	
Superfly	1972	Gordon Parks Jr.	Phillip Fenty	
Sweet Sweetback's Baadasssss Song	1971	Melvin Van Peebles	Melvin Van Peebles	
Swimfan	2002	John Polson	Charles F. Bohl	Phillip Schneider
Taxi Driver	1976	Martin Scorsese	Paul Schrader	
Tell Them Willie Boy Is Here	1969	Abraham Polonsky	Abraham Polonsky	
Tender Comrade	1943	Edward Dmytryk	Dalton Trumbo	
Testament	1983	Lynne Littman	John Sacret Young	
Thelma and Louise	1991	Ridely Scott	Callie Khouri	
There's Always Tomorrow	1956	Douglas Sirk	Ursula Parrott	Bernard C. Shoenfeld
They Won't Forget	1937	Mervyn LeRoy	Robert Rossen	Aben Kandel
Thin Blue Line, The	1988	Errol Morris	Errol Morris	
Thirteen Days	2000	Roger Donaldson	David Self	

Film	Year	Director	Screenwriter	Additional Screenwriter(s)
Three Days of the Condor	1975	Sydney Pollack	Lorenzo Semple Jr.	David Rayfiel
Three Kings	1999	David O. Russell	David O. Russell	John Ridely
Titicut Follies	1967	Frederick Wiseman	Frederick Wiseman	
To Be or Not to Be	1942	Ernest Lubitsch	Edwin Justus Mayer	
To Kill a Mockingbird	1962	Robert Mulligan	Horton Foote	
Tootsie	1982	Sydney Pollack	Don Maguire	Larry Gelbart
Top Gun	1986	Tony Scott	Jim Cash	Jack Epps Jr.
Traffic	2000	Steven Soderbergh	Stephen Gaghan	
True Lies	1994	James Cameron	James Cameron	
Truman Show, The	1998	Peter Weir	Andrew Nichol	
Turning Point, The	1977	Herbert Ross	Arthur Laurents	
Twelve Angry Men	1957	Sidney Lumet	Reginald Rose	
Twilight's Last Gleaming	1977	Robert Aldrich	Ronald Cohen	Edward Huebsh
Ugly American, The	1963	George Englund	Stewart Stern	
Under Fire	1983	Roger Spottiswoode	Ron Shelton	Clayton Frohman
Union Pacific	1939	Cecil B. DeMille	Walter de Leon et al.	
Unmarried Woman, An	1978	Paul Mazursky	Paul Mazursky	
Vanishing American, The	1926	George Seitz	Ethel Doherty	
Verdict, The	1982	Sidney Lumet	Sidney Lumet	
Viva Villa	1934	Jack Conway	Ben Hecht	
Viva Zapata!	1952	Elia Kazan	John Steinbeck	
Vixen, The	1916	J. Gordon Edwards	Mary Murillo	
Wag the Dog	1997	Barry Levinson	Hilary Henkin	David Mamet
Walker	1987	Alex Cox	Rudy Wurlitzer	
Wall Street	1987	Oliver Stone	Dorothy Tristan	John Hancock
WarGames	1983	John Badham	Lawrence Lesker	Walter Parkes
Washington Masquerade	1932	Charles Brabin	John Meehan	Samuel Blythe
Washington Merry-Go-Round, The	1932	James Cruze	Jo Swerling	
Washington Story, The	1952	Robert Pirosh	Robert Pirosh	
Wasp Woman, The	1959	Roger Corman	Leo Gordon	
Watch on the Rhine	1942	Herman Shumlin	Dashiell Hammett	
Way Down East	1920	D.W. Griffith	Anthony Paul Kelly	

Appendix 3, Table (*continued*)

Film	Year	Director	Screenwriter	Additional Screenwriter(s)
Way We Were, The	1973	Sydney Pollack	Arthur Laurents	
What Every Woman Knows	1921	William C. de Mille	Olga Printzlau	J.M. Barrie
What Happened on Twenty-Third Street, New York City	1902			
When a Woman Sins	1918	J. Gordon Edwards	Betta Breuil	
White Nights	1985	Taylor Hackford	James Goldman	Eric Hughes
Who'll Stop the Rain	1978	Karl Reisz	Judith Rascoe	
Wild in the Streets	1968	Barry Shear	Robert Thom	
Wild River	1960	Elia Kazan	Paul Osborn	
Wilson	1944	Henry King	Lamar Trotti	
Windtalkers	2002	John Woo	John Rice	Joe Batteer
Winter Kills	1979	William Richert	William Richert	
Working Girl	1988	Mike Nichols	Kevin Wade	
WUSA	1970	Stuart Rosenberg	Stuart Rosenberg	
Young Mr. Lincoln	1939	John Ford	Lamar Trotti	
Z	1968	Costa-Gavras	Costa-Gavras	
Zoot Suit	1981	Luis Valdez	Luis Valdez	Jorge Sampron

Appendix 4

The Bottom Line
Domestic Gross Receipts by Decade

The following tables include the domestic gross box office receipts for the top grossing films for each decade, along with the top grossing documentary films of all time. Unfortunately, box office data for most of the political films discussed in this book are unavailable; such data are available for the 1990s and later films (see Table 12).

Appendix 4, Table 1

Top Four Grossing Films at the U.S. Box Office, 1909–1919

Gross	Title	Year
$3M	*The Birth of a Nation*	1915
$1M	*Tarzan of the Apes*	1918
$430K	*Traffic in Souls*	1913
$245K	*The Squaw Man*	1914

Source: IMDb Pro.

Appendix 4, Table 2

Top Ten Grossing Films at the U.S. Box Office, 1920–1929

Gross	Title	Year
$9.2M	*The Four Horsemen of the Apocalypse*	1921
$9M	*Ben-Hur: A Tale of the Christ*	1925
$3.8M	*The Covered Wagon*	1923
$3M	*Aloma of the South Seas*	1926
$3M	*The Jazz Singer*	1927
$3M	*Over the Hill to the Poorhouse*	1920
$2.5M	*The Kid*	1921
$1.2M	*Lights of New York*	1928
$921K	*West of Zanzibar*	1928
$704K	*The Unholy Three*	1925

Source: IMDb Pro.

Appendix 4, Table 3

Top Ten Grossing Films at the U.S. Box Office, 1930–1939

Gross	Title	Year
$185M	*Snow White and the Seven Dwarfs*	1937
$14.8M	*The Wizard of Oz*	1939
$12M	*Frankenstein*	1931
$4M	*Ingagi*	1931
$3M	*Top Hat*	1935
$2.3M	*42nd Street*	1933
$2.14M	*Conquest*	1937
$1.8M	*Damaged Lives*	1933
$1.58M	*Parnell*	1937
$1.19M	*Ninotchka*	1939

Source: IMDb Pro.

Appendix 4, Table 4

Top Ten Grossing Films at the U.S. Box Office, 1940–1949

Gross	Title	Year
$103M	*Bambi*	1942
$84.3M	*Pinocchio*	1940
$16.4M	*Sergeant York*	1941
$7.57M	*Meet Me in St. Louis*	1944
$6.8M	*Easter Parade*	1948
$5.2M	*The Yearling*	1946
$4.5M	*Road to Rio*	1947
$4.2M	*Pinky*	1949
$4M	*Dillinger*	1945
$4M	*Buck Privates*	1941

Source: IMDb Pro.

Appendix 4, Table 5

Top Ten Grossing Films at the U.S. Box Office, 1950–1959

Gross	Title	Year
$93.6M	*Lady and the Tramp*	1955
$87.4M	*Peter Pan*	1953
$80M	*The Ten Commandments*	1956
$51.6M	*Sleeping Beauty*	1959
$34.1M	*Cinderella*	1950
$25M	*Some Like It Hot*	1959
$23.8M	*House of Wax*	1953
$21.8M	*The Caine Mutiny*	1954
$21.2M	*Mister Roberts*	1955
$8M	*Annie Get Your Gun*	1950

Source: IMDb Pro.

Appendix 4, Table 6

Top Ten Grossing Films at the U.S. Box Office, 1960–1969

Gross	Title	Year
$153M	*One Hundred and One Dalmatians*	1961
$142M	*The Jungle Book*	1967
$112M	*Doctor Zhivago*	1965
$102M	*Butch Cassidy and the Sundance Kid*	1969
$102M	*Mary Poppins*	1964
$72M	*My Fair Lady*	1964
$56.7M	*2001: A Space Odyssey*	1968
$56.7M	*Guess Who's Coming to Dinner*	1967
$46.3M	*It's a Mad Mad Mad Mad World*	1963
$44.8M	*Let's Make Love*	1960

Source: IMDb Pro.

Appendix 4, Table 7

Top Ten Grossing Films at the U.S. Box Office, 1970–1979

Gross	Title	Year
$461M	*Star Wars*	1977
$260M	*Jaws*	1975
$205M	*The Exorcist*	1973
$187M	*Grease*	1978
$142M	*Saturday Night Fever*	1977
$142M	*Animal House*	1978
$135M	*The Godfather*	1972
$128M	*Close Encounters of the Third Kind*	1977
$127M	*Smokey and the Bandit*	1977
$120M	*Blazing Saddles*	1974

Source: IMDb Pro.

Appendix 4, Table 8

Top Ten Grossing Films at the U.S. Box Office, 1980–1989

Gross	Title	Year
$435M	E.T. the Extra-Terrestrial	1982
$309M	Star Wars: Episode VI—Return of the Jedi	1983
$290M	Star Wars: Episode V—The Empire Strikes Back	1980
$251M	Batman	1989
$242M	Raiders of the Lost Ark	1981
$239M	Ghost Busters	1984
$235M	Beverly Hills Cop	1984
$211M	Back to the Future	1985
$197M	Indiana Jones and the Last Crusade	1989
$180M	Indiana Jones and the Temple of Doom	1984

Source: IMDb Pro.

Appendix 4, Table 9

Top Ten Grossing Films at the U.S. Box Office, 1990–1999

Gross	Title	Year
$601M	Titanic	1997
$431M	Star Wars: Episode I—The Phantom Menace	1999
$357M	Jurassic Park	1993
$330M	Forrest Gump	1994
$328M	The Lion King	1994
$306M	Independence Day	1996
$294M	The Sixth Sense	1999
$286M	Home Alone	1990
$250M	Men in Black	1997
$246M	Toy Story 2	1999

Source: IMDb Pro.

Appendix 4, Table 10

Top Ten Grossing Films at the U.S. Box Office, 2000–2003

Gross	Title	Year
$404M	*Spider-Man*	2002
$377M	*The Lord of the Rings: The Return of the King*	2003
$340M	*The Lord of the Rings: The Two Towers*	2002
$340M	*Finding Nemo*	2003
$318M	*Harry Potter and the Sorcerer's Stone*	2001
$314M	*The Lord of the Rings: The Fellowship of the Ring*	2001
$311M	*Star Wars: Episode II—Attack of the Clones*	2002
$305M	*Pirates of the Caribbean: The Curse of the Black Pearl*	2003
$281M	*The Matrix Reloaded*	2003
$268M	*Shrek*	2001

Source: IMDb Pro.

Appendix 4, Table 11

Domestic Gross Receipts for Political Films of the 1990s and Beyond
(rounded to the nearest million dollars)

Gross	Title	Year
330	*Forrest Gump*	1994
306	*Independence Day*	1996
281	*Matrix Reloaded*	2003
250	*Men in Black*	1996
216	*Saving Private Ryan*	1998
192	*Toy Story*	1995
172	*Air Force One*	1997
171	*Matrix*	1999
146	*True Lies*	1994
139	*The Matrix Revolutions*	2003
132	*Minority Report*	2002
125	*The Truman Show*	1998
122	*Clear and Present Danger*	1994
120	*Hunt for Red October*	1990
118	*Fahrenheit 9/11*	2004
102	*In the Line of Fire*	1993
96	*Schindler's List*	1993
91	*Crimson Tide*	1995
84	*Legally Blonde 2: Red, White, and Blonde*	2003
83	*Under Siege*	1992
83	*Patriot Games*	1992
76	*Conspiracy*	1997
70	*JFK*	1991
68	*Executive Decision*	1996
63	*Dave*	1993
61	*Rules of Engagement*	2000
61	*Three Kings*	1999
60	*The American President*	1995
57	*Civil Action*	1998
50	*Natural Born Killers*	1994
50	*Absolute Power*	1997
47	*The Distinguished Gentleman*	1992
43	*Wag the Dog*	1997
41	*The Siege*	1998
39	*Primary Colors*	1998
37	*Mars Attacks!*	1996
29	*The Insider*	1998
27	*Dark City*	1991
26	*Bulworth*	1998
26	*Murder at 1600*	1997
26	*Memento*	2000
25	*Navy Seals*	1990
23	*Russia House*	1990
22	*My Fellow Americans*	1994
22	*The Player*	1996
22	*Bowling for Columbine*	2002

Appendix 4, Table 11 *(continued)*

Gross	Title	Year
20	*City Hall*	1996
20	*The People vs. Larry Flynt*	1996
15	*Toy Soldiers*	1991
15	*Election*	1999
14	*Nixon*	1995
7	*Roger & Me*	1989
6	*Dick*	1999
6	*Heaven and Earth*	1993
5.5	*Bob Roberts*	1992
< 1	*Citizen Ruth*	1996
< 1	*War at Home*	1996

Notes

Notes to Chapter 1

1. Phillip L. Gianos, *Politics and Politicians in American Film* (Westport, CT: Praeger, 1995).

2. See, for example, Bruce Austin, *Immediate Seating: A Look at Movie Audiences* (Belmont, CA: Wadsworth, 1989).

3. Goldwyn himself sent a few messages. His first film company was publicly committed to "a foundation of intelligence and refinement," and it was Goldwyn, after all, who produced Lillian Hellman's *The Little Foxes* (1941), a bone-chilling tale of capitalist greed, and *The Best Years of Our Lives* (1946), a poignant story of the aftermath of war. He also was responsible for *The North Star* (1943), one of Hollywood's most blatantly pro-Russian films. Apparently Goldwyn was not so much opposed to messages as ambivalent about them. See Ephraim Katz, *The Film Encyclopedia* (New York: Perigee, 1979), p. 491.

4. See, for example, Louis Gianetti, *Understanding Movies* (New York: Prentice Hall, 1996).

5. James E. Combs, *American Political Movies: An Annotated Filmography of Feature Films* (New York: Garland, 1995), p. x.

6. Beverly M. Kelley, *Reel Politik: Political Ideologies in '30s and '40s Films* (Westport, CT: Praeger, 1998).

7. James Combs and Sarah Combs, *Film Propaganda and American Politics: An Analysis and Filmography* (New York: Garland, 1994), p. 8.

8. Dan Nimmo and James E. Combs. *Mediated Political Realities* (New York: Longman, 1983).

9. Murray Edelman, *The Symbolic Uses of Politics* (Champaign: University of Illinois Press, 1964).

10. Nimmo and Combs, p. 105.

11. Gianos, p. xii.

12. Nimmo and Combs, p. 105.

13. Dan Leab, "Blacks in American Cinema," in *The Political Companion to American Film,* ed. Gary Crowdus (Chicago: Lakeview Press, 1994), p. 46.

14. Nimmo and Combs, p. 106.

15. Nimmo and Combs, p. 108.

16. See, for example, Susan Faludi, *Backlash: The Undeclared War Against American Women* (New York: Anchor Books/Doubleday, 1992).

17. Gianos, pp. 4–8.

18. William S. Cohen and Gary Hart, "TV's Treatment of Washington—It's Capital Punishment" *TV Guide,* August 24, 1985.

19. Andy Rooney, "Anything You Say, Senator Ewing," *San Francisco Chronicle,* September 29, 1985.

20. For a succinct summary of the research on the effects of mass media on political behavior, see, for example, Doris A. Graber, *Mass Media and American Politics,* 6th ed. (Washington, DC: CQ Press, 2001), pp. 195–225, or David A. Paletz, *The Media in American Politics: Contents and Consequences* (New York: Longman, 1999), pp. 103–113.

21. Sharon Waxman, "Two Americas of 'Fahrenheit' and 'Passion,'" *New York Times,* July 13, 2004.

22. Namkung Young, "A Motivational Study of Moviegoers: A Q-Methodological Approach." *Q-Methodology and Theory* 4 (1999): 182–207.

23. William Stephenson, "Applications of Communication Theory: Immediate Experience of Movies," *Operant Subjectivity* 1 (1978): 96–116.

Notes to Chapter 2

1. www.moviegeek.homestead.com/files/featprod1.htm.

2. Walid Habboub, "Movieball," 2004, www.boxofficeprophets.com/column/index.cfm?columnID=8353.

3. Philip L. Gianos, *Politics and Politicians in American Film* (Westport, CT: Praeger, 1995), p. 1.

4. Quoted in *San Jose Mercury News,* November 16, 1986 "Frankenheimer Back in High Gear," Glenn Lovell.

5. Michael Medved, *Hollywood vs. America* (New York: Harper Perennial, 1992), pp. 10, 216.

6. Stephen Holden, *New York Times* Speakers Series, June 10, 2004.

7. Gianos, p. 3.

8. Ibid., p. 8.

9. Louis Giannetti, *Understanding Movies,* 7th ed. (Englewood Cliffs, NJ: Prentice Hall, 1996), p. 293.

10. Ibid., p. 445.

11. Ibid., p. 449.

12. Peter Biskind, *Seeing is Believing: How Hollywood Taught Us to Stop Worrying and Love the Fifties* (New York: Pantheon, 1995), p. 5.

13. Steven Abrahams, "Buying Nashville," *Jump Cut* 9 (1975): p. 7.

14. Giannetti, pp. 83–84.

15. Charles Derry, *The Suspense Thriller: Films in the Shadow of Alfred Hitchcock* (Jefferson, NC: McFarland, 1995).

16. Gianos, p. 38.

17. Leo Braudy, *The World in a Frame: What We See in Films* (Chicago: University of Chicago Press, 2002), pp. 186–187.

18. Giannetti, p. 297.

19. Judd Blaise, review of *Natural Born Killers,* www.allmovie.com.

20. Mark Crispin Miller, "Advertising," in *Seeing Through Movies,* ed. Mark Crispin Miller (New York: Pantheon, 1990).

21. William Goldman, *Adventures in the Screen Trade* (New York: Warner, 1983), pp. 100, 102.

22. James Monaco, *How to Read A Film: The Art, Technology, Language, History and Theory of Film and Media,* 2nd ed. (New York: Oxford University Press, 1981), p. 220.

23. Early film actors themselves did not want to be credited for film work because they also were theater stars, or struggling to be so, and did not want film work to discredit them in the legitimate acting arena, the theater. Fans themselves started inquiring after actors who reappeared in films by certain production companies. Production companies promoted their recurring stars and then fan magazines proliferated, exploiting the stars' images.

24. Monaco, p. 222.

25. Giannetti, p. 516.

26. Gianos, p. 29.

27. Ibid., p. 28.

28. Douglas Gomery, "Conglomerates in the Film Industry," in *The Political Companion to American Film,* ed. Gary Crowdus (Chicago: Lake View Press, 1994), pp. 71–74.

29. Gianos, p. 25.

30. Michael Wood, *America in the Movies* (New York: Basic Books, 1975), p. 22.

31. Siegfried Kracauer, *From Caligari to Hitler* (Princeton, NJ: Princeton University Press, 1974), p. 5.

32. Randall M. Miller, *The Kaleidoscope Lens* (Englewood, NJ: Ozer, 1980), p. 13.

33. F. Scott Fitzgerald, *The Last Tycoon: An Unfinished Novel* (New York: Scribner's Sons, 1969), p. 125.

34. Costa-Gavras, Guardian Lecture, National Film Theatre, London, March 16, 1984.

34. *San Jose Mercury News,* August 17, 1986.

36. James E. Combs, *American Political Movies: An Annotated Filmography of Feature Films* (New York: Garland, 1990), p. ix.

Notes to Chapter 3

1. Larry May, *The Big Tomorrow: Hollywood and the Politics of the American Way* (Chicago: University of Chicago Press, 2000), p. 279.

2. The Moore quote is what I would regard to be public domain, but it can be found (among many other sources) at www.countercurrents.org/iraq-moore10403.htm.

3. Victor Navasky, *Naming Names* (New York: Penguin, 1983), p. 78.

4. Sidney Lumet, "Not a pretty picture. . . . Neither their makers nor their audiences are finding films fun," Glenn Lovell, *San Jose Mercury News,* August 17, 1985.

5. Navasky, p. 146.

6. Ibid., pp. 79–80.

7. Dorothy Jones, "Communism in the Movies," in *Report on Blacklisting 1: The Movies,* ed. John Cogley (New York: Fund for the Republic, 1956).

8. M. Keith Booker, *Film and the American Left: A Research Guide* (Westport, CT: Greenwood Press, 1999).

9. Jones, p. 216.

10. Navasky, p. 300–301.

11. See, for example, Paul Buhle and Dave Wagner, *Radical Hollywood: The Untold Story Behind America's Favorite Movies* (New York: Free Press, 2002).

12. Robert Sklar, *Movie-Made America* (New York: Random House, 1975), pp. 123–124.

13. Jack Valenti, "How It All Began, www.mpaa.org/movieratings/about/content.htm.

14. Chris Roth, "Three Decades of Film Censorship . . . Right Before Your Eyes," *The Humanist,* 2000, January, http://articles.findarticles.com/p/articles/mi_m1374/is_1_60/ai_59021329.

15. Ibid.

16. "Lieberman Attacks Hollywood," news.bbc.co.uk/2/hi/world/Americas/879681.stm.

17. Gary Wills, *John Wayne's America* (New York: Simon & Schuster, 1997).

18. Michael Nelson, "Ol' Red, White, and Blue Eyes: Frank Sinatra and the American Presidency," *Popular Music and Society* (Winter 2000): 1.

19. Movie Production: Long-term Contribution Trends, www.opensecrets.org/industries/indus.asp?Ind=C2400.

20. Eric Alterman, "The Hollywood Campaign," *Atlantic,* August 2004, p. 76. However, also note that every other major industry favors the Republican party; see, for example, www.alternet.org/story/9862/.

21. Nelson, p. 1.

22. Allen Metcalf, quoted at www.csmonitor.com/2003/0718/p02s02-usfp.html.

23. Newt Gingrich, quoted by Garry Wills at www.pbs.org/newshour/gergen/march97/wills_3-20.html.

24. Michael Paul Rogin, *Ronald Reagan: The Movie* (Los Angeles: University of California Press, 1987), pp. 1–8.

25. James Combs and Sara Combs, *Film Propaganda and American Politics: An Analysis and Filmography* (New York: Garland, 1994), p. 4.

26. Ian Scott, *American Politics in Hollywood Film* (Chicago: Fitzroy-Dearborn Press, 2000), p. 156.

27. Connie Bruck, "Supermoderate," *New Yorker,* June 28, 2004, p. 87.

28. Combs and Combs, p. 6.

29. Ibid., p. 8.

30. Ibid., p. 34 (emphasis added).

31. Ibid.

32. Ibid., p. 69.

33. Ibid., p. 90.

34. Oliver Stone, quoted by David Robb at www.amctv.com/article?CID=1284=1=0=15-EST.

35. Major David Georgi, quoted ibid.

36. David L. Robb, *Operation Hollywood: How the Pentagon Shapes and Censors the Movies* (Amherst, NY: Prometheus Books, 2004).

37. Peter Bart, 2001, www.pbs.org/wgbh/pages/frontline/shows/hollywood/picture/corptown.html.

38. Ibid.

39. Ibid.

40. Ray Green, *Hollywood Migraine: The Inside Story of a Decade in Film* (Dublin, Ireland: Merlin Publishing, 2000), p. 280.

41. Jon Alon Walz, "The Dealmaker of Denver," www.boxoff.com/issues/apr01/anschutz.html.

42. Emanuel Levy, *Cinema of Outsiders: The Rise of American Independent Film* (New York: New York University Press, 2001), p. 504.

43. Leonard Klady, January 29, 2003, www.moviecitynews.com/columnists/klady/2003/gb_030129.html.

Notes to Chapter 4

1. I.C. Jarvie, *Movies as Social Criticism* (London: Scarecrow, 1978).

2. Kevin Brownlow, *The Parade's Gone By* (Berkeley: University of California Press, 1968), p. 26.

3. Arthur Knight, *The Liveliest Art* (New York: Signet, 1979), p. 23, and many others. Phil Hall, however, asserts that the quote is only an "urban legend," and that "Wilson was never quoted by any journalist on the subject of the film." Phil Hall, "The 10 Best Urban Legends in Film History," www.filmthreat.com

4. *New York Times,* March 4, 1915.

5. Larry May, *Screening Out the Past* (Chicago: University of Chicago Press, 1980), p. 86.

6. Kenneth W. Munden, *American Film Institute Subject Index to Films of the 1920s* (New York: Bowker, 1971).

7. *New York Times,* December 5, 1924.

8. *New York Times,* January 10, 1926.

Notes to Chapter 5

1. Ray McDonald, SUFG Bulletin, Second Term, 1957.

2. Mark Roth, "Some Warners Musicals and the Spirit of the New Deal," *Velvet Light Trap* 17, (Winter 1977): 3.

3. Andrew Bergman, *We're in the Money* (New York: New York University Press, 1971), p. 102. See also Nick Roddick, *A New Deal in Entertainment* (London: British Film Institute, 1983).

4. Robert L. McConnell, "The Genesis and Ideology of *Gabriel over the White House,*" in *Cinema Examined,* ed. Richard Dyer MacCann and Jack C. Ellis (New York: Dutton, 1982), p. 209.

5. *Photoplay,* June 1933.

6. Bergman, pp. 78–79.

7. *New York Times,* March 25, 1934.

8. Bergman, p. 4.

9. Frank Capra, *The Name Above the Title* (New York: Macmillan, 1971), pp. 287, 292.

Notes to Chapter 6

1. *New York Times,* April 26, 1939.

2. Colin Shindler, *Hollywood Goes to War* (London: Routledge and Kegan Paul, 1979), p. 31.

3. *McCall's,* June 1941.

4. *Monthly Film Herald,* April 12, 1941.

5. *New York Times,* May 2, 1941.

6. Charles J. Maland, *American Visions* (New York: Arno Press, 1977), p. 307.

7. Rudy Behlmer, ed., *Inside Warner Bros., 1935–1951* (New York: Viking, 1985), p. 290.

8. Cited in Colin Shindler, *Hollywood Goes to War* (London: Routledge and Kegan Paul, 1979), pp. 58–59.

9. *New York Times,* April 30, 1944.

10. Cited in *Monthly Film Bulletin,* May 5, 1944.

11. David Culbert, ed., *Mission to Moscow* (Madison: University of Wisconsin Press, 1975), p. 16.

12. Ron Harris, *The Thousand Eyes Magazine* 2, No. 3 (1976), p. 16.

13. *New York Times,* August 2, 1944.

14. Thomas J. Knock, "History in Lightning: The Forgotten Film, *Wilson,"* in *Hollywood as Historian,* ed. Peter C. Rollins (Lexington: University of Kentucky, 1983), p. 95.

15. Leonard Quart and Albert Auster, *American Film and Society Since 1945* (New York: Praeger, 1984).

16. *New York Times,* November 9, 1949.

Notes to Chapter 7

1. Joan Mellen, *Big Bad Wolves* (New York: Pantheon, 1977), p. 189.

2. Michael Wood, *America in the Movies* (New York: Basic Books, 1975), p. 184.

3. Dorothy Jones, "Communism in the Movies," in *Report on Blacklisting I: The Movies,* ed. John Cogley (New York: Fund for the Republic, 1956), pp. 300–301.

4. *Time,* October 17, 1949.

5. Colin Shindler, *Hollywood at War* (London: Routledge and Kegan Paul, 1979), p. 121.

6. Cited in John Cogley, ed., *Report on Blacklisting I: The Movies* (New York: Fund for the Republic, 1956), p. 11.

7. *New Yorker,* July 16, 1949; *New York Times,* July 9, 1949.

8. *New York Times*, April 9, 1952.

9. Quoted in *Variety,* March 26, 1952.

10. Quoted in Peter Biskind, *Seeing Is Believing* (London: Pluto Press, 1984), p. 49.

11. Victor Navasky, *Naming Names* (New York: Penguin, 1983), p. 210.

12. Andrew Dowdy, *The Films of the 1950s* (New York: Morrow, 1973), p. 35.

13. *Variety,* March 17, 1954.

14. *Time,* March 29, 1954.

15. Dowdy, p. 184.

16. Biskind, p. 59.

17. Ibid., p. 159.

18. Ibid., p. 102.

Notes to Chapter 8

1. Kenneth W. Munden, *Subject Index to Films of the 1960s* (New York: Bowker, 1971).

2. *Time,* December 28, 1959.

3. *New York Times,* June 7, 1962.

4. Pauline Kael, *5001 Nights at the Movies* (New York: Holt, Rinehart and Winston, 1982), p. 6.

5. *Time,* March 30, 1962.

6. Ibid., April 10, 1964; *Saturday Review,* April 4, 1964.

7. Quoted in *Variety,* September 15, 1964.

8. Richard Maltby, *Harmless Entertainment: Hollywood and the Ideology of Consensus* (London: Scarecrow, 1983), p. 306.

9. Joan Mellen, *Big Bad Wolves* (New York: Pantheon, 1977), pp. 249, 251.

10. *Saturday Review,* February 14, 1964.

11. Quoted in *Variety,* May 13, 1964.

12. *New York Times,* September 16, 1964.

13. Lawrence Suid, "The Pentagon and Hollywood," in *American History/American Film,* ed. John E. O'Connor and Martin A. Jackson (New York: Frederick Unger, 1979), p. 368.

14. Pauline Kael, *Kiss Kiss, Bang Bang* (New York: Bantam, 1969), p. 79.

15. Quoted in Mason Wiley and Damien Bona, *Inside Oscar* (New York: Ballantine Books, 1986), p. 368.

16. *New York Times,* August 31, 1968; *The New Yorker,* September 13, 1969.

Chapter to Chapter 9

1. Tom Wolfe, "The Me Decade and the Third Great Awakening," *Mauve Gloves & Madmen, Clutter & Vine* (New York: Bantam [reprint], 1999).

2. Dan Ruby, *Star Wars,* *Jump Cut,* August 1978.

3. James Monaco, *American Film Now* (New York: Oxford University Press, 1979), p. 356.

4. Andrew Sarris, *Politics and Cinema* (New York: Columbia University Press, 1978), p. 20.

5. *New York Times,* June 30, 1972.

6. *New Yorker,* August 20, 1979.

7. Alan Pakula, Guardian Lecture, National Film Theatre, London, February 25, 1986.

8. Ibid.

9. *New York Times,* August 3, 1976.

10. William Goldman, *Adventures in the Screen Trade* (London: Futura, 1985), p. 147.

11. Doug Zwick, "The Genre Syndome," and Michael Gallantz, "Meltdown in Hollywood," both in *Jump Cut,* May 1980.

12. Norman Markowitz, "*The Front:* Comic Revenge," *Jump Cut,* July 1977.

13. Pauline Kael, *Reeling* (Boston: Little, Brown, 1976), p. 170.

14. *Film Review,* November 1975, p. 8.

15. *American Film,* March 1979.

16. Ibid.

17. See Peter Biskind, *Seeing Is Believing* (London: Pluto Press, 1983).

18. Michael Cimino, Guardian Lecture, National Film Theatre, London, August 11, 1983.

19. Gilbert Adair, *Hollywood's Vietnam* (London: Proteus, 1981), p. 106.

20. Ibid., p. 165.

21. See Peter Stead, *Film and the Working Class* (London: Routledge, 1989).

Notes to Chapter 10

1. *Stills,* October 13, 1984, p. 15.

2. Ibid.

3. *The Guardian,* July 20, 1985.

4. *Time Out,* April 23–29, 1986.

5. *California,* July 1986.

6. Quoted in *People,* December 16, 1985.

7. "The Chicanery of Silkwood," *New York Times,* December 25, 1983, and *Village Voice,* February 21, 1984.

8. *New York Times,* August 20, 1984.

9. *Chicago Sun-Times,* December 11, 1987.

10. *New York Times,* August 20, 1984.

11. *Film Quarterly,* 35 (Spring 1982): 43–47.

12. Morris Dickstein, "Time Bandits," *American Film,* October 1982, p. 42.

13. *New York Times,* December 4, 1981.

14. *Village Voice,* December 14, 1981.

15. Warren Beatty accepting the Academy Award for Best Director, March 31, 1981.

16. Lecture, London Film Festival, December 3, 1983.

17. *Village Voice,* September 6, 1983.

18. *Guardian,* July 19, 1984.

19. *American Film,* March 1982, p. 79.

20. *New York Times,* cited in *Sunday Times London Magazine,* January 22, 1984.

21. John Powers, "Saints and Savages," *American Film,* January–February 1984, p. 38.

22. *Village Voice,* December 2, 1986.

23. *New York Times,* December 2, 1984.

24. *New Yorker,* October 31, 1983.

25. *Village Voice,* March 11, 1986.

26. *California,* June 1986.

27. *Washington Post,* October 6, 1989.

28. *Nightline,* ABC-TV, December 19, 1986.

29. *Guardian,* February 14, 1987.

Notes to Chapter 11

1. Jon Clark, "Primary Color: Green: Why the Studios Won't Make Political Movies (Bottom Line Continues to Be Financial, Not Political)," *Nation,* April 5, 1999.

2. *Chicago Sun-Times,* August 26, 1994.

3. www.indiewire.com/people/int_Sayles_John_020618.html.

4. Janet Maslin, "Deciding the World's Fate From the Ocean's Bottom," *New York Times,* May 12, 1995.

5. Jack Sheehan, *Reel Bad Arabs: How Hollywood Vilifies a People* (Northampton, MA: Interlink Publishing Group, 2001).

6. Susan M. Akram, "The Aftermath of September 11, 2001: The Targeting of

Arabs and Muslims in America," *Arab Studies Quarterly* 24 (Spring–Summer 2002): 66–86.

7. Ed Zwick, interviewed at www.thescreamonline.com/commentary/comment2–1/index.html.

8. Hal Hinson, *Washington Post,* January 5, 1990.

9. Edward Guthmann, *San Francisco Chronicle,* April 28, 1995.

10. Andrew Gumbel, "Back to the Future: In 1999, *Three Kings*—a Film on the Gulf War—Made Little Impact. Today, It Seems Chillingly Prescient," *Independent* (London, England), May 28, 2004.

11. Rita Kempley, *Washington Post,* May 7, 1993.

12. *Chicago Sun-Times,* December 20, 1991.

13. Roger Rosenstone, "Film Historian Says *Nixon* Follows a Tradition of Mixing Truth and Fiction," *Orange County Register,* December 29, 1995.

14. William D. Romanowski, "Oliver Stone's *JFK*: Commercial Filmmaking, Cultural History, and Conflict. *Journal of Popular Film and Television* 21, no. 2 (Summer 1993): 63–71.

15. J. Hoberman, *Village Voice,* August 4, 1999.

16. Bruce Fretts, "After Surviving One Clash with Tom Clancy, Harrison Ford and the *Patriot Games* Team Head Back into the Danger Zone." *Entertainment Weekly,* August 19, 1994.

17. Charles Taylor, review of *Absolute Power, Salon,* February 14, 1997, www.salon.com/feb97/absolute970214.html.

18. *Chicago Sun-Times,* January 8, 1999.

19. The movie's Web site, http://video.movies.go.com/insider/index_flash.html, provides additional details of the real-life controversy.

20. Philip Hensher, "*The Matrix Reloaded* Should Worry America's Leaders, *Independent,* May 19, 2003, http://argument.independent.co.uk/regular_columnists/philip_hensher/story.jsp?story=410417.

21. Barry Koltnow, "Director Was Not Afraid to Make Political Statement in Disaster Movie," *Orange County Register,* May 27, 2004.

22. Box office analyst Paul Dergarabedian, quoted in Cary Darling, "In Theaters Near You: Lights, Action, Issues," *Dallas Star-Telegram,* July 21, 2004.

Notes to Chapter 12

1. www.allmovie.com/cg/avg.dll?p=avg&sql=1:21924.

2. James Combs and Sara Combs, *Film Propaganda and American Politics: An Analysis and Filmography* (New York: Garland, 1994).

3. www.gallup.com/poll/content/login.aspx?ci=12379, www.cnn.com/2004/SHOWBIZ/Movies/07/22/moore.film.politics.ap/index.html.

4. *Toronto Star,* June 25, 2004.

Notes to Chapter 13

1. James Earl Young, *The Life and Work of Oscar Micheaux* (San Francisco: KMT Publications, 2003).

2. Dan Leab, in "Blacks in American Cinema," in *The Political Companion to American Film,* ed. Gary Crowdus (Chicago: Lakeview Press, 1994), p. 46.

3. *Chicago Sun-Times,* December 9, 1988.

4. *Washington Post,* June 30, 1989.

5. *New York Times,* May 19, 1989.

6. Review of *The Human Stain, Augusta Chronicle,* November 7, 2003, http://mpelembe.mappibiz.com/archives_04/Human_Stain.html.

7. Peter M. Bracke, review of *Amistad,* April 25, 1999, www.dvdfile.com/software/review/dvd-video/amistad.htm.

8. Stephen Holden, review of *Bamboozled, New York Times,* October 6, 2000.

9. *Chicago Sun-Times,* November 20, 1998.

10. http://pro.imdb.com/title/tt0108041/funfacts.

11. *New York Times,* April 8, 1994.

Notes to Chapter 14

1. Jane Gaines, quoted in "Duke Dialogue," www.dukenews.duke.edu/news/dialogue_newsrelease5d56.html?p=all&id=1964&catid=46.

2. Ally Acker, www.reelwomen.com/blachebio.html.

3. www.loc.gov/rr/print/list/126_rosi.html#posters.

4. Jeanine Basinger, *American Cinema: One Hundred Years of Filmmaking* (New York: Rizzoli, 1994), p. 150.

5. Peter Lehman and William Luhr, *Thinking About Movies*, 2nd ed. (Oxford, UK: Blackwell 2003), p. 13.

6. www.rlc.dcccd.edu/annex/comm/english/mah8420/Seduction.htm.

7. www.bbc.co.uk/films/2001/04/12/baby_boom_1987_review.shtml.

8. www.rottentomatoes.com/m/ms_45/.

9. *Washington Post,* May 24, 1991.

10. *Chicago Sun-Times,* December 9, 1994.

Notes to Chapter 15

1. James Linton, "But It's Only a Movie," *Jump Cut* 17 (April 1978): 18.

2. I.C. Jarvie, *Movies as Social Criticism* (London: Scarecrow, 1978), p. 153.

3. Costa-Gavras, Guardian Lecture, National Film Theatre, London, March 16, 1984.

4. Walter Lippman, *The Public Philosophy* (New York: New American Library, 1955), p. 93.

5. Costa-Gavras.

Notes Appendix 1

1. William H. Phillips, *Analyzing Films: A Practical Guide* (New York: Holt, Reinhart, Winston, 1985), p. 8.

2. Ibid., p. 110.

3. Timothy Corrigan, *A Short Guide to Writing About Film* (New York: HarperCollins, 1989), p. 76.

4. Ibid., p. 69.

Subject Index

347

Kazan, Elia, 44, 104–5, 115, 119, 123–24, 129
Kazdan, Lawrence, 190
Keaton, Diane, 38, 185, 266
Keaton, Michael, 267
Keitel, Harvey, 161, 271
Kelly, Gene, 104
Kennedy, John F., 50, 124, 126, 131–34, 146, 151, 210, 213–14, 216, 284
Kennedy, Robert (Bobby), 30, 141
Khouri, Callie, 269
Kibbee, Guy, 84
Kinetoscope, 252
King, Henry, 102
King, Martin Luther, 30, 126, 131, 141, 242
King, Rodney, 233, 247
Klein, Joe, 215
Kline, Kevin, 210
Knox, Alexander, 102
Koch, Howard, 98, 100
Koppel, Barbara, 230
Korea, 110
  Korean War. See war
Kosinski, Jerzy, 169
Kovic, Ron, 207
K-Mart Corporation, 232
Kramer, Stanley, 111, 115, 127–29, 139, 239, 285
Kristofferson, Kris, 170
Ku Klux Klan, 67, 81–82, 84, 87, 180, 241, 281
Kubrick, Stanley, 111, 127, 135–36, 197
Kuwait, 172

labor movement, 204
Lahti, Christine, 189
Lancaster, Burt, 135, 162–63
Lane, Mark, 151
Lange, Jessica, 179
Lansbury, Angela, 106, 134
Larner, Jeremy, 146, 148
Last Tycoon, The, 39
Latin America, 93, 191–96
Laughton, Charles, 130
Laurents, Arthur, 157

Law, John Phillip, 138
Lawson, John Howard, 44, 120
League of Nations, 102
Learned, Michael, 185
Lebanon, 172
Le Carré, John, 205
Lee, Spike, 25–26, 242–45, 247
left, political, 126, 185–89, 210, 281
leftist film, 117, 120
leftists, 112, 178
legal system, 181–82, 218–19, 269–71
Leigh, Janet, 261
Leigh, Vivian, 84
Leighton, Margaret, 131
Lemmon, Jack, 39, 155–56, 192, 212
Lenin, 43
LeRoy, Mervyn, 76
Levinson, Barry, 197, 201
Lewinsky, Monica, 201, 210
  Monicagate, 274
Lewis, Juliette, 203
liberalism, 118, 124, 129, 145, 180, 202, 213
liberals, 114–16, 120, 122, 128, 200
libertarianism, 112–13
Libya, 172
Liddle, George, 221
Lieberman, Joseph, 48–49
Liebman, Ron, 169
lighting and color, 30, 83, 152–53, 254, 296–97
Lincoln, Abraham, 12, 14, 65–67, 77, 80, 87, 279–80
Long, Huey, 107
Los Angeles Times, 81
Losey, Joseph, 118
love story film. See genre
Lowe, Rob, 22
Lubitsch, Ernst, 99
Lucas, George, 144, 145
Lukas, Paul, 99
Lumet, Sidney, 23, 40, 122, 127, 135, 161, 181, 184–85, 188–89
Lund, John, 106
Lyne, Adrian, 263
Lyons, Gene, 236

Film Index

359

About the Authors

Terry Christensen is a specialist on state and local politics and a professor at San Jose State University. He has written seven books, the latest being *Recall! California's Political Earthquake* (2004) and *California Government and Politics* (eighth edition, 2005); both books are coauthored by Larry N. Gerston. Christensen is currently working on a new edition of *Local Politics: Governing at the Grassroots,* a text reflecting his years of teaching and participation in local politics (forthcoming from M.E. Sharpe in 2006). He wrote an earlier version of this book (then titled *Reel Politics*) in 1987 after teaching courses on political movies for several years. Christensen holds a BA from Stanford and a PhD from the University of North Carolina at Chapel Hill. He chaired the SJSU Department of Political Science from 1993 to 2002. In 1998, he was named SJSU's Outstanding Professor. In addition to his scholarship, teaching, and university service, Christensen is active in San Jose politics, advising on many political campaigns and serving on numerous boards and commissions. He is also a longtime shareholder in a locally owned, multiscreen cinema.

Peter J. Haas is a professor in the Department of Political Science at San Jose State University and also serves as the education director for the Mineta Transportation Institute there. He is the author of many journal articles, research monographs, and other publications in a variety of subfields, including a coauthored textbook on program evaluation and policy analysis: *Applied Policy Research: Concepts and Cases.* He received a Fulbright Foundation Senior Specialist grant in 2003 to teach and study in Latvia. He earned his BA in political science at Valparaiso University, his MA in political science at Kent State University, and his PhD in political science at the University of North Carolina at Chapel Hill. He lives next door to a twelve-screen multiplex.